Rethinking Faculty Work

JB JOSSEY-BASS

RETHINKING FACULTY WORK

Higher Education's Strategic Imperative

Judith M. Gappa, Ann E. Austin,
Andrea G. Trice

John Wiley & Sons, Inc.

Published by Jossey-Bass
A Wiley Imprint
989 Market Street, San Francisco, CA 94103-1741   www.josseybass.com

Jossey-Bass books and products are available through most bookstores. To contact Jossey-Bass directly
call our Customer Care Department within the U.S. at 800-956-7739, outside the U.S. at 317-572-3986,
or fax 317-572-4002.

Jossey-Bass also publishes its books in a variety of electronic formats. Some content that appears in
print may not be available in electronic books.

Library of Congress Cataloging-in-Publication Data

Gappa, Judith M.
  Rethinking faculty work and workplaces: higher education's strategic imperative / Judith M. Gappa,
Ann E. Austin, Andrea G. Trice. —1st ed.
      p. cm.
  Includes bibliographical references and index.
  ISBN-13: 978-0-7879-6613-3 (cloth)
  ISBN-10: 0-7879-6613-4 (cloth)
  1. College teachers—United States. 2. Universities and colleges—United States—Faculty.
3. Employee retention—United States. I. Austin, Ann E. II. Trice, Andrea G., 1966– III. Title.
  LB2331.72.G375   2007
  378.1'2—dc22

                                                              2006030500

Printed in the United States of America
FIRST EDITION
HB Printing   10 9 8 7 6 5 4 3 2 1

CONTENTS

Preface   xi

About the Authors   xxi

PART ONE: HIGHER EDUCATION'S CHANGING CONTEXT   1

1. The Changing Context for Faculty Work
   and Workplaces   3
2. Trends in the National Workplace   24
3. Faculty Appointments and Faculty Members:
   Diversification, Growth, and Diversity   49
4. The Academic Profession Today: Diverse
   Appointments to Meet Diverse Needs   66
5. Attracting and Retaining Excellent Faculty   102

PART TWO: THE FRAMEWORK   125

6. The Framework of Essential Elements   127
7. Respect: The Foundation for the
   Essential Elements   145
8. Shared Responsibility and Joint Leadership   157

PART THREE: THE ESSENTIAL ELEMENTS   191

9. Equity in Academic Appointments   193
10. Academic Freedom   226
11. Ensuring Flexibility in Academic Appointments   239
12. Professional Growth   280
13. Collegiality   305

14.   Why Rethink Faculty Work and Workplaces?
          A Call to Action   321

          References   333

          Name Index   355

          Subject Index   361

The Jossey-Bass Higher
and Adult Education Series

To current and future faculty in the hopes that your academic workplaces enable you to fully use your talents and skills throughout your entire careers.

PREFACE

A quick perusal of the *Chronicle of Higher Education* reveals some of the topics considered newsworthy with respect to faculty and their work. The following examples illustrate the interests and issues on faculty members' minds today:

- A headline in the *Chronicle Review* asserts, "We Must Make the Academic Workplace More Humane and Equitable." The article was written by a department chair and prominent scholar (Kerber, 2005).
- An article titled "Working Half Time on the Tenure Track" highlights the fact that some tenure-track faculty want to work part-time but notes that the number of faculty members who actually are able to make such arrangements is small (Wilson, 2002).
- A reflection essay, written by a faculty member who has been a part-time instructor and a visiting assistant full-time faculty member is titled "Adjuncts Should Not Just Be Visitors in the Academic Promised Land" (Murphy, 2002)
- In a recent article, a midcareer faculty member observed, "I'm about to turn fifty, an awkward age for an academic. Tenured and a full professor . . . And so this point in my career has an unsettling quality: I've made it, but still have a long way to go" (Nesteruk, 2005, p. B5)

The faculty in American colleges and universities have always been the heart of the institutions where they work, the intellectual capital that ensures those institutions' excellence. The quality of the faculty relates directly to the effectiveness of a college or a university in facilitating students' learning, creating new knowledge, and linking research and practice in ways that benefit society. But changes are occurring that affect faculty work and workplaces. In the current context of significant change, this book addresses key questions that should be on the minds of all university and college leaders:

What enhances the ability of academic institutions to recruit and retain highly capable faculty members?

What are the essential elements of academic work and workplaces that will help ensure faculty to find their work satisfying and meaningful?

How can colleges and universities fully recognize and build on the intellectual capital that faculty represent, and on the talents and abilities of each member of the faculty?

One may wonder why these questions are important today. After all, American colleges and universities have been attracting bright and committed faculty for years. In fact, for several decades the common concern among graduate students has been the over-supply of faculty and the relatively few faculty positions available. The kind of work that faculty do—touching the future by affecting the lives of learners; discovering new ideas and creating artistic and literary works that inform, explore, and express the human experience; addressing critical problems in society through the application of knowledge—is stimulating, rewarding, and exciting. Being a faculty member has been—and still is, for many people—a very attractive arena for meaningful work.

Nevertheless, the changes that have been occurring in academe are similar to those occurring in other sectors of the economy. As the demands on institutions of higher education become more diverse, what faculty members are being asked to do is growing. The demographic characteristics of faculty are changing as well. Some prospective as well as current faculty—men as well as women—seek greater flexibility in their personal and professional responsibilities and deeper collegial relationships. Academic appointments are changing, too. Renewable contracts and fixed-term positions now comprise the majority of new faculty appointments. Although these non-tenure-track appointments produce considerable debate and concern, the likelihood is strong that such appointments will continue to increase. Finally, given the changing norms in society regarding the place of work in individuals' lives, there are also changes in how faculty members, especially prospective and early-career faculty, prioritize professional and personal responsibilities.

These significant shifts require a rethinking of faculty work and workplaces. The dramatic changes in academe and in the wider society led us to conclude, about four years ago, that colleges and universities, faced with the need to fulfill their institutional missions, are also confronting a strategic imperative: they must ensure that the academic workplace is organized in ways that continue to attract, retain, and support excellent faculty. Specifically, we felt the time was right to rethink the nature of academic work and workplaces in ways that honor historical traditions and values but also take today's realities into account. The overall issue we have been grappling with is this: How can colleges and universities make academic work and workplaces attractive to diverse faculty in diverse appointments and ensure that all faculty are supported in their efforts to work effectively?

Purposes and Organization

The purpose of this book is to provide a vision of academic work and workplaces as expressed in institutional policies and practices that, if adopted, will attract superb faculty who are committed to fulfilling the missions of the colleges and universities where they work. Specifically, here is what the book offers:

- An analysis of the changing context of faculty work in the United States, with attention to the impact of factors affecting institutions of higher education, to shifts in American workplaces across the broader society, to changes in the characteristics of the faculty, and to the emergence of various types of academic appointments
- An overall framework that outlines the fundamental elements of the work experience of all faculty members, regardless of the nature of their appointments
- A discussion of the meaning of each of five essential elements of academic work—equity, academic freedom and autonomy, flexibility, professional growth, and collegiality—and recommendations for how institutions can enhance each element for the benefit of its faculty.

The organization of the book follows the purposes just listed: analysis of the context affecting faculty work and workplaces is followed by the presentation of a general framework for understanding academic work and workplaces, which in turn is followed by analysis of the framework's five essential elements as well as by practical strategies for strengthening each element.

Part I depicts the current situation that colleges and universities and their faculty members confront. Chapter One discusses the contextual factors affecting institutions of higher education—fiscal constraints and increased competition, calls for accountability, growing enrollments, increasing diversity of students, and the rise of the Information Age along with the availability of new technologies—and the implications of those factors for faculty members. Chapter Two discusses changes and trends in workplaces at the national level, providing a backdrop against which to interpret some of the expectations that faculty bring to the academic workplace. Chapter Three describes today's faculty, with attention to their demographic characteristics and to overall growth in the number of faculty members. Chapter Four examines the nature of faculty appointments, shifts in appointment patterns, and the strengths and drawbacks of the three major types of faculty appointments: tenure-track, contract-renewable, and fixed-term appointments. In Chapter Five we examine sources of faculty satisfaction as well as concerns that faculty express about the academic workplace.

Part II begins with Chapter Six, which presents our framework for conceptualizing faculty work and workplaces. The chapter highlights the five elements that, as research shows, are essential to the work experience of all faculty members, whether they work in traditional tenure-track positions or in contract-renewable or fixed-term appointments. The framework acknowledges that the faculty work experience is affected by the characteristics and background that each individual faculty member brings to his or her work as well as by the mission, history, culture, and organizational structure of each institution of higher education. The framework also highlights the kinds of positive outcomes for faculty members and their institutions that, we believe, can result when academic workplaces address what we have called the five essential elements of faculty work. In Chapter Seven, we explore how a workplace that addresses the five essential elements of faculty work is necessarily grounded in a culture of respect that permeates the lives and relationships of all members of the academic community. We follow this discussion with our argument, in Chapter Eight, that the quality and characteristics of the academic workplace are a shared responsibility. Administrators and faculty members both have important roles in creating and implementing policies and practices and in carrying out the daily work of the institution in ways that ensure a dynamic, supportive, and productive environment for everyone.

The first five chapters in Part III offer recommendations for how colleges and universities can use our framework and the five essential elements to rethink the academic workplace. In these chapters we discuss each of the essential elements in turn, and we present ways of incorporating each element into faculty work and workplaces. Our recommendations are accompanied by examples that illustrate different ways institutions with their unique cultures and circumstances can strengthen the various essential elements. Chapter Nine addresses equity issues in academic workplaces. Chapter Ten discusses academic freedom and autonomy. Chapter Eleven focuses on flexibility in faculty work and workplaces, Chapter Twelve addresses professional growth, and Chapter Thirteen examines collegiality. Finally, in Chapter Fourteen, we reiterate our thesis that changes in faculty demographics, in types of faculty appointments, and in the larger societal context require renewed attention to the academic workplace. Colleges and universities, we argue, make wise strategic choices when their leaders recognize that attention to the quality of the academic workplace lays the groundwork for excellence, productivity, and success in fulfilling institutional missions.

Busy readers, after skimming the analyses presented in Chapters Two through Five, may choose to go directly to the framework presented in Chapter Six, which is crucial to an understanding of the recommendations in Part III. After reading Chapter Six, those interested in a particular element may find it useful to turn directly to the chapter where it is discussed.

AUDIENCE

The message of this book, and the specific recommendations it offers, should be of interest to several audiences. First, those concerned with policy issues in higher education—that is, policy makers at the national, state, and system levels as well as leaders of professional associations and collective bargaining organizations—will find that the book establishes a context for rethinking faculty work and workplaces and that it highlights good practice for institutions of higher education. The book should help policy leaders articulate reasons why attention to faculty work and workplaces merits a central place on the agenda of national discussions about higher education policy.

Second, institutional leaders—a group including trustees, university and college presidents, provosts, deans, department chairs, and faculty members serving in governance bodies—set the tone and provide impetus for cultural change in academic workplaces. They will find the framework provides a systematic way to examine their institutions as workplaces, and the recommendations will give them specific strategies to consider in the context of their own institutions.

Third, current as well as future faculty members, are of course also included in the intended audience for this book. Current faculty are key players in creating the quality of the academic workplace through their day-to-day relationships with their colleagues and their involvement in determining institutional policies, recruiting new faculty, and making decisions related to tenure and promotion. We hope that today's faculty will find good ideas for strengthening their academic workplaces and enriching their own work experiences. We hope as well that those who are considering academic work will discover, in reading this book, a vision that attracts them to an academic career.

Fourth, researchers and others with interests in professional employment trends should find this book of interest. As we discuss patterns and changes in academic work and workplaces, we situate our analyses in the larger context of changes in other employment sectors. This analysis of the wider context, as well as the framework of essential elements, may be useful to those considering important characteristics of workplaces outside the academic setting.

RESEARCH METHODS AND SOURCES

The research conducted in the writing of this book took several paths. To begin with, we convened four different advisory groups to guide us in the formulation of our framework, the essential elements, and the rest of the contents of this book. Two of these groups were composed of scholars working actively on research concerning higher education. The other two were composed primarily of administrators, a group that included department chairs, deans, provosts, and presidents, who came from various types of colleges and universities, as well as leaders from a number of national associations. Our meetings with these advisory groups offered us diverse and invaluable perspectives on the changes occurring in the academic workplace and among faculty. They also expanded our understanding of the issues and challenges facing institutions of higher education and their administrative leaders.

We also conducted an extensive literature review to identify sources of information about trends and factors in workplaces both outside and inside academe, and in the demographics and appointments of today's faculty. The literature review uncovered examples of specific policies and practices under the general rubric of faculty employment across various appointment types. In the first two years of work on this book, teams of graduate students compiled annotated bibliographies on specific topics that we had identified as having to do with faculty work and workplaces. These teams also located detailed descriptions of current employment policies and practices in higher education.

Another path of our research led us to analyze the information found in various national databases concerning faculty and institutions of higher education. These sources included the National Survey of Postsecondary Faculty (NSOPF, both faculty and institutional surveys), the Higher Education Research Institute (HERI) Faculty Survey, and the Survey of Earned Doctorates done by the National Opinion Research Center (NORC) in addition to data gathered by the National Center for Education Statistics (NCES).

Along yet another path of our work we searched for examples of innovative practices within a wide array of colleges and universities that address changes in faculty and academic workplaces and that support institutions' and faculty's interests and needs. Several talented doctoral students conducted thorough searches of institutional Web sites and of the literature on higher education to find not only these examples but also data on the impact of innovative policies and practices in the academic world at large and at individual institutions.

Finally, over the past four years, as we met our other responsibilities as faculty members, which included interacting with colleagues and attending conferences and meetings, we took note of strategies and efforts that we encountered, or that we heard were being developed, tested, and implemented at colleges and universities and by foundations. Over time, we accumulated an extensive list of institutional strategies and practices designed to strengthen the academic workplace.

This combination of advisory groups, literature review, data analysis, and searches of publications and the Web provided an extensive information base for our work. But the book that resulted has also been enriched by our individual life experiences. As a team of three, we represent three different stages of academic life. One of us is completing her career, having served at several universities as a senior-level administrator and a professor of higher education. Another is a tenured full professor in midcareer at a large research university, whose early career included five years in a non-tenure-track position. The other is an early-career academic who worked for several years as an administrator and then as a faculty member on the tenure track; more recently, having decided to take more time for family responsibilities, she has chosen to step off the tenure track and create a career as an independent consultant on higher education issues. Simultaneously, each of us is a mother and our children span all ages. Each of us has focused her research over the years on issues concerning faculty work and workplaces. Each of us is also deeply committed to the future of higher education and to the well-being of the faculty. Together, we have done our best over the past four years to bring what we have learned from the various research sources we have highlighted, as well as from our own lives, observations, and experiences, into a book that will encourage administrators and faculty members to strengthen the academic workplace and more fully support all faculty members in their work.

ACKNOWLEDGMENTS

Our project would not have reached fruition without the work and support of a number of people. We are very grateful to Dr. Kathleen Christensen, program director of the Workplace, Workforce and

Working Families Program at the Alfred P. Sloan Foundation, who generously provided grant support for this project. We deeply appreciate her interest in our work and the extensive overall leadership she is providing to encourage higher education institutions to recognize the importance of work/family issues in the workplace.

We also are grateful to Rebecca Stankowski, Owen Cooks, and Sara Stein Koch, all doctoral students at Purdue University, who helped at various stages in the research and writing of this book. As already described, they conducted extensive literature reviews that provided the foundation for the information in Part I of this book and some source material for our recommendations. Justin McHorse, a master's-degree student in higher education administration at Purdue, created an excellent working bibliography and compiled resources for us. Karen Giorgetti and Sue Wilder, doctoral students at Purdue, were very helpful in identifying and exploring useful Web sites, conducting initial data analysis, and organizing the advisory meetings we conducted with faculty, administrators, and professional association leaders. Melissa McDaniels, a doctoral student at Michigan State University, stepped in during the final writing of the book; her work with database analysis and general editing was extremely helpful. We feel very fortunate to have worked with such capable, conscientious, and insightful graduate students, and we extend our heartfelt thanks.

The colleagues and friends who accepted our invitation to meet in the advisory groups expended considerable time to give us their views of current issues and problems facing higher education and faculty members, and shared important ideas and concepts that informed the development of our framework. We appreciate their willingness to listen to our ideas, challenge our thinking, offer their observations and analyses concerning faculty work and workplaces, and suggest effective institutional strategies and policies. In 2003, at the Association for the Study of Higher Education, in Portland, Oregon, we met with Roger Baldwin, Larry Braskamp, Carol Colbeck, Martin Finkelstein, David Leslie, Jack Schuster, Kelly Ward, and Lisa Wolf-Wendel. We convened another advisory group that met at Purdue in January 2004: Nancy Chism, Blair Dowden, Alice Marie Jacobs, Charles Jones, Linda Katehi, Christine Ladisch, Shelley MacDermid, Sally Frost Mason, Suzanne Nielsen, and William Plater. In June of that year, in Chicago, we convened a group of higher education researchers: Roger Baldwin and Larry Braskamp once again, along with John Curtis, Yvonna Lincoln, Gary Rhoades, and Cathy Trower. Then, in October in Washington D.C., we gathered administrators and national association leaders for a fourth advisory group: Carol Cartwright, Russell Garth, Clara Lovett, Ronald Mahurin, R. Eugene Rice, Claire Van Ummersen, Joan Williams, and Jennifer Wimbisch.

We also express our appreciation to David Brightman, higher education editor at Jossey-Bass, for his interest in this project. He was enthusiastic from the start and offered useful suggestions at several important points in our work. Several colleagues, including Roger Baldwin, David Leslie, and Cathy Trower, read drafts of the book and provided insightful feedback. We are immensely grateful for the time and thought these colleagues offered us.

A project like this always affects the people close to home. We thank our support staff for their assistance with many details: Leslie Sigg, in the Department of Educational Leadership and Cultural Foundations at Purdue, and Irene Unkefer, in the Department of Educational Administration at Michigan State University. Most importantly, we thank our families—especially Joe, John, and Rod, our husbands—for their patience, interest, and perseverance as we worked on this book.

Judith M. Gappa
Purdue University

Ann E. Austin
Michigan State University

Andrea G. Trice
Trice and Associates

ABOUT THE AUTHORS

Judith M. Gappa is currently professor of higher education administration at Purdue University. Her recent research has been about faculty and faculty careers. From 1991 to 1998 she was vice president for human relations at Purdue University, where she was responsible for policies and programs to improve the quality of life for students, staff, and faculty. From 1980 to 1991 she was associate provost for faculty affairs at San Francisco State University, with responsibility for faculty appointments, promotion, tenure, and all other personnel actions, and for representing the administration in the implementation of a collective bargaining contract. She was director of affirmative action/equal opportunity programs at Utah State University from 1973 to 1980 and, while on leave from Utah State (1977–1978), senior staff associate at the National Center for Higher Education Management Systems. She has been a faculty member at Utah State and San Francisco State as well as a principal investigator on various research projects. She is coauthor (with David Leslie) of *The Invisible Faculty: Improving the Status of Part-Timers in Higher Education* and author of a number of monographs, reports, articles, and book chapters about higher education and equity issues. She holds degrees from George Washington University (B.A., M.A. in music) and Utah State University (Ed.D. in education administration).

Ann E. Austin is the Mildred B. Erickson distinguished professor of higher, adult, and lifelong education at Michigan State University. Her research and teaching have focused on faculty careers, roles, and professional development; reform in graduate education; improvement of teaching and learning; and organizational change and transformation in higher education. She is coeditor (with Donald Wulff) of *Paths to the Professoriate: Strategies for Enriching the Preparation of Future Faculty* and coauthor (with Mary Deane Sorcinelli,

Pamela Eddy, and Andrea Beach) of *Creating the Future of Faculty Development: Learning from the Past, Understanding the Present.* Currently, she is co–principal investigator for the Center for the Integration of Research, Teaching, and Learning, a five-year National Science Foundation–funded project aimed at improving the preparation of future faculty in science, technology, engineering, and mathematics. In 1998 she was a Fulbright Fellow in South Africa. In 2000–2001 she served as president of the Association for the Study of Higher Education. She holds degrees from Bates College (B.A. in history), Syracuse University (M.S. in higher/postsecondary education), and the University of Michigan (M.A. in American culture, Ph.D. in higher education).

Andrea G. Trice is an independent consultant to colleges and universities. From 2001 to 2005 she was a member of the faculty at Purdue University, where her research focused on faculty roles, foreign-born faculty, and international students. Before her faculty appointment there, she worked for ten years as an administrator at Purdue as well as at Northwestern University and the University of Texas at Arlington. Her administrative positions have spanned the areas of institutional research, international education, and student affairs. Since 1998 she has also worked as a consultant to universities and governmental agencies, primarily on faculty-related projects. She is the coauthor of an earlier book and the author of several articles related to faculty and international students. She holds degrees from Baylor University (B.A. in foreign service and Spanish), Hardin-Simmons University (M.Ed. in counseling and human development), and the University of Michigan (Ph.D. in higher education).

Rethinking Faculty Work

HIGHER EDUCATION'S CHANGING CONTEXT

The characteristics of academic institutions and faculty work are changing in significant ways in the United States. Part I uses a descriptive and analytical approach to examine these important changes.

Chapter One identifies four major forces affecting higher education institutions and their faculty members: (1) fiscal constraints and increased competition, (2) calls for accountability, (3) growing enrollment and increasing diversity of students, and (4) the rise of the Information Age, with its continuous expansion of new technologies. Chapter Two discusses shifts in employment perceptions and practices in American society generally. These shifting employment practices beyond academe are creating new expectations among current and potential faculty members. Chapters Three, Four, and Five examine the current status of faculty members. Chapter Three looks at the growth of the faculty over time and the demographic characteristics of today's faculty. Chapter Four examines the changing nature of faculty appointments in American higher education institutions, including the rising number of appointments off the tenure track. Chapter Five discusses current and potential faculty members' satisfaction with and concerns about the academic workplace. As a whole, the first five chapters set the stage for the central thesis of the book: given significant changes affecting higher education institutions, and given changes in faculty demographics and appointments, faculty are not engaged in business as usual. It is time to rethink faculty work and workplaces.

CHAPTER ONE

THE CHANGING CONTEXT FOR FACULTY WORK AND WORKPLACES

For almost four hundred years, higher education institutions have played a critically important role in American society. Colleges and universities prepare educated citizens, advance knowledge, and engage in service in ways that benefit individuals, communities, states, the nation, and the broader world. Ideas incubated within academe enrich our culture and help solve societal problems.

Today's institutional leaders, however, are faced with myriad challenges that only seem to grow more difficult with each passing year: for example, maintaining technological infrastructures that address both user needs and budgetary constraints; recruiting and retaining students well-matched to their institutional missions; creating environments that value student diversity; finding new sources of revenue as traditional sources of support decline; responding effectively to increasing accountability requirements; and continually enhancing the prestige and prominence of the institution. In recent years, these and other forces have been affecting American higher education institutions, challenging their traditional missions, and shifting the contours of organizational structures. The pace and extent of changes currently affecting higher education far surpass "business as usual." James Duderstadt, former president of the University of Michigan, observed that "we are entering a period in which the capacity to nourish and manage change will be one of the most important abilities of all" (2000, p. 35).

To a significant extent, it is the faculty that enables higher education institutions to meet these numerous demands and fulfill their missions. The teaching, research, creative endeavors, community involvement, professional service, and academic decision making—the work of the university or college—is carried out each day by committed faculty members. Certainly administrators provide much of the vision, leadership, and support essential to institutional success. Their work should never be undervalued. Nevertheless, it is the work of the faculty that is essential to achieving the excellence that colleges and universities envision.

Indeed, the faculty's intellectual capital, taken collectively, is the institution's foremost asset. It is also the institution's only appreciable asset (Ulrich, 1998). Other institutional assets—buildings, laboratories, classrooms, residence halls, power plants, and technology infrastructures—begin to depreciate the day they are acquired. But colleges and universities depend on their faculty members' competence and commitment to increase steadily over time to meet the institution's ever changing circumstances and goals.

Although faculty members are the primary resource for meeting today's escalating demands upon colleges and universities, these same demands are simultaneously altering the context within which they work. Today's challenges place new expectations and require new skills and abilities of faculty members. Nevertheless, many institutions have not seriously considered how support for faculty must evolve to better enable them to accomplish their work. Adding to the complexity of today's changing educational landscape, faculty members are also more diverse than ever before, as are the appointments they hold. Further, many early career faculty members seek to make their personal lives a higher priority than their senior colleagues have often done.

Taken together, these changes mean that traditional academic appointments, employment policies and practices, and supports for faculty work are no longer fully appropriate for today's faculty members and the work they undertake. For example, if faculty members working in nontenure track appointments are to be in a position to do their best work, leaders must provide equitable working conditions and ensure these faculty members' inclusion in the campus community. If today's diverse faculty members are to satisfactorily balance their personal and professional lives, current expectations for academic careers will have to become more flexible. Likewise, as faculty members are challenged to increase their use of technology in the classroom, help generate more resources for the university, and create an academic environment that values students' diversity, many will need easy and continuous access to professional development opportunities that help them obtain the appropriate skills.

In this changing environment, developing and supporting the intellectual capital that each faculty member represents is fundamental to the ability of higher education institutions to manage change and move with strength and effectiveness into the future. For administrative leaders facing constant challenges, an energetic, diverse, and engaged faculty is their most important resource. Investment in the faculty and in the quality of the academic workplace becomes a college's or university's most critical strategic choice.

The stakes are high for institutions that choose not to make this investment. As this and later chapters point out, faculty work and workplaces have not always changed for the better, and some faculty, like their counterparts in other occupations, will leave for better circumstances. People today are not as wedded to their employers or their careers as in previous decades (Downey, March, Berkman, and Steinauer, 2001; Judy and D'Amico, 1997; Cintrón, 1999). For example, in a study focused on corporate management, Ulrich (1998) found that 50 percent of high potential managers at a global company did not think they would stay with that company long enough to retire and 90 percent personally knew someone who had voluntarily left in the past six months.

Similarly, successful faculty members make choices about where and for whom they will work. One third of respondents to the Higher Education Research Institute (HERI) survey indicated that they had considered leaving academe for another job and 28 percent had received at least one firm offer (Lindholm, Szelenyi, Hurtado, and Korn, 2005). Data regarding potential faculty members at the beginning of the academic pipeline also warrant institutional leaders' attention. Sixty-two percent of faculty in a national survey observed that their graduate students pursue academic research careers less often than in the past (Wimsatt and Trice, 2006).

How then can higher education institutions most effectively support faculty in their work and encourage commitment to the college or university? They must rethink the nature of today's academic workplace in recognition of the many and complex demands facing faculty, the shifts in faculty appointment patterns, the diversity of faculty characteristics, and the changes in societal perspectives on work. Moreover, they must also reassess and modify their current policies and practices regarding faculty work in light of the changes that have occurred. The following questions are the focus of this book:

- What changes in faculty work, faculty characteristics, and faculty appointments, as well as in the broader societal context, require fresh perspectives on the academic workplace?
- What are the essential elements of academic work and workplaces that should be part of all faculty work, regardless of the type of appointment?
- What specific institutional policies and practices contribute to academic workplaces that support all faculty members in carrying out excellent work in service to institutional missions?

Attention to the well-being of the faculty and to the quality of the academic workplace strengthens the institution's capacity to achieve its mission and maintain its excellence, effectiveness, and health. This kind of attention enhances the quality of key outcomes, such as recruitment and retention of a diverse and highly talented faculty, increased faculty satisfaction with their work, and a higher level of faculty commitment to the organization. In sum, this kind of attention is a strategic investment in the intellectual capital of the institution.

MAJOR CHANGES AFFECTING HIGHER EDUCATION INSTITUTIONS

Contextual changes affecting higher education institutions today require the best from faculty members even as they simultaneously change the playing field, necessitating new skills and abilities in addition to the traditional talents and competencies expected of professors. Certainly, the specific impact of these forces on a particular institution is mediated by the institution's history, mission, geographical location, size, resources, and a host of other factors. Yet overall, they are having major impacts across the higher education sector and will be familiar to all institutional leaders. Of particular importance for this book is how these forces are affecting faculty and creating an environment within which focused attention on the nature of the academic workplace becomes strategically essential.

This chapter highlights four of the most significant forces creating challenges for higher education institutions:

1. Fiscal constraints and increased competition
2. Calls for accountability and shifts in control
3. Growing enrollments and the increasing diversity of students
4. The rise of the Information Age along with expanded use of new technologies to facilitate learning

The chapter then examines the specific impacts of these four forces on faculty work and workplaces.

FISCAL CONSTRAINTS AND INCREASED COMPETITION

Fiscal constraints and shifts in financial support for higher education form one of the most powerful pressures affecting universities and colleges today. In addition to meeting the ever-increasing costs of operating expenses and compensation packages, universities and colleges are also pressed to increase their instructional technology and overall technology infrastructure, to provide additional student services to meet the needs of more diverse student bodies, to address deferred maintenance, and to handle rising energy costs. Many higher education institutions have enriched their physical plants in recent years, as one strategy to stay competitive in response to growing student expectations for a range of amenities or expanded research endeavors. Some colleges and universities are using tuition discounting as a way to enhance their attractiveness; this strategy, however, is another pull on institutional budgets.

Although rising costs and fiscal pressures are a major challenge for private as well as public institutions, the latter are also dealing with considerable volatility in state budgets. Not only are budget allocations for higher education constrained, allocations are also unpredictable and unstable. In general, there is little expectation that state support for higher education will improve significantly if at all over the coming years, in view of the constantly rising costs of such mandated state programs as Medicare and elementary and secondary education. In a recent article, Don Boyd of the Nelson A. Rockefeller Institute of Government noted that "even if state and local governments close their current budget gaps with regular sources of revenue, instead of relying on gimmicks that provide only temporary relief, the sad conclusion is that most states will face continuing problems in financing current services and will not have sufficient resources to support real increases in spending" (Boyd, 2005, p. 1).

Federal funding, which primarily takes the form of student financial aid as well as research grants and contracts in areas deemed national priorities, also has been stagnant since the late 1970s (Breneman, Finney, and Roherty, 1997). Moreover, as public perception has shifted toward viewing individuals rather than the general society as the primary beneficiaries of higher education, financial aid has shifted from grants to loans.

These factors together contribute to a general scramble for resources by colleges and universities. As Newman, Couturier, and Scurry assert (2004, p. 4), "the search for truth" in higher education institutions "is rivaled by a search for revenues." The need for resources is fueling greater orientation toward entrepreneurialism in colleges and universities as well as increased competition and market orientation among higher education institutions. These circumstances have led some observers to assert that higher education is increasingly functioning as a commodity in a marketplace that values the knowledge and expertise that institutions compete to provide (Eckel, Couturier, and Luu, 2005; Newman, Couturier, and Scurry, 2004; Slaughter and Leslie, 1999; Slaughter and Rhoades, 2004).

Colleges and universities are responding to these fiscal pressures by using budget reductions and cost-containment strategies, striving to build their endowments, seeking to attract foundation support and private gifts, and privatizing some institutional functions, such as food services, bookstores, and remedial support for students. Under these circumstances, some institutions are urging academic departments to develop revenue-producing continuing education programs, or to seek collaborations with industry for technology development and transfer. Faculty members especially are under pressure to engage more aggressively in grant seeking.

As many institutions become more corporate in their outlook by their increasing dependence on the bottom line, the culture is changing on many campuses. Entrepreneurialism, quantifiable productivity, and efficiency are high on the list of expectations that faculty must meet. Leaders need to consider these and other potential outcomes of these shifts:

- How might a culture of increasing entrepreneurialism affect faculty members' commitment to their institutions and thus retention?
- To what extent are financial pressures creating a competitive environment that challenges a spirit of collegiality on the campus?
- Are pressures for faculty to produce revenue creating environments where those who bring in less revenue feel less respected and less equitably treated by their institutions?

Calls for Accountability and Shifts in Control

At the same time that higher education institutions are struggling with financial constraints and increased competition for scarce resources, they also face heightened calls for accountability and responsiveness to societal needs and expectations. The public wants to see wider access; high-quality research; engagement with their surrounding communities and social and national problems; and contributions to economic development (Duderstadt, 2000; Newman, Couturier, and Scurry, 2004). Overall, however, the public appears to have less confidence and trust in higher education institutions as pillars of society than was the case a few decades ago. Criticisms are not hard to find. Employers have expressed reservations about higher education, worrying about the quality of new college graduates' preparation for the workplace. Newspaper articles and television coverage publicize high tuition, scientific misconduct, and student misbehavior. In some states, legislators have felt enough uncertainty about what is happening in public colleges and universities to deliberate over regulating faculty workloads, to institute faculty post-tenure review, to link funding directly to measurable outcomes, and to mandate periodic program reviews. As one recent example of legislative interest in regulating higher education, lawmakers in Virginia, in a broadly supported move, unanimously passed a bill requiring faculty to consider costs when selecting books for their courses (Schmidt, 2006).

The federal government is also seeking to influence the financial decisions of higher education institutions through regulatory policies pertaining to federal student financial aid and research funding. Institutions are being encouraged to refrain from tuition increases, and there are some hints that eligibility for participation in federal student aid programs could be linked to institutional decisions about tuition levels (Zusman, 2005).

Thus institutions need to pay more attention to external pressures for greater accountability and tighter control, and this need has impacted colleges and universities in several ways. At some institutions, presidential authority has increased in response to accountability and budget pressures. Simultaneously, however, decentralization has been the institutional response as some colleges and universities have chosen to push accountability down to the unit level. Strategies such as responsibility-centered budgeting provide departments and units with more autonomy, coupled with greater responsibility to engage in entrepreneurial plans to increase revenue (Zusman, 2005).

Demands for increased accountability are also changing the context in which faculty work. The following questions are worth consideration by institutional leaders:

- Do faculty members feel diminished respect for their work as tighter controls and an increased number of checks and balances become part of their daily reality?
- To what extent have faculty members experienced a loss of autonomy as, for example, requirements for quantifiable outcomes from teaching and institutional review board demands and controls have increased dramatically?

Growing Enrollments and Increasing Diversity of Students

Over the past twenty-five years, total student enrollments have increased almost 50 percent, to around 17 million. Demand is expected to expand even more: the National Center for Education Statistics predicts that, by 2014, enrollments will increase another 15 percent from 2003 levels (Hussar, 2005).

In addition to general growth in the numbers of students on campus, the student body is increasingly diverse in terms of age, background, race and ethnicity, and educational expectations (Keller, 2001; Syverson, 1996). Of particular interest is the considerable growth in the number of students over the age of twenty-five; students in this cohort expect their educational experiences to be characterized by quality, convenience, low cost, relevance, and institutional responsiveness to their needs (Levine, 2000). According to the most current statistics, students twenty-five and older account for about 40 percent of undergraduate enrollments. Further, since 1980 the percentage of the student body that is composed of ethnic and racial minorities has increased, from 16 percent to more than 25 percent (Snyder and Tan, 2005).

Students and their families often view a college education as the ticket to economic success and a middle-class lifestyle. Students are looking for educational experiences that are relevant to their employment prospects, convenient to their personal commitments and life circumstances, and reasonable in cost. Nondegree programs are in demand, as are certificate programs that respond to shifts in the labor environment. Older learners with multiple responsibilities benefit from educational providers who offer extended office hours for educational services, or who provide options (for example, child care) that make pursuing education more possible. The increase in first-generation college and university students makes the availability of academic support services especially important.

Higher education institutions must have the necessary infrastructure to provide a welcoming and supportive environment and to meet the needs of this diverse student body. They must be able to create multicultural environments in which each member is valued and respected. Colleges and universities are also striving to help students enhance their international awareness and knowledge and gain facility in speaking and understanding other languages. These skills help learners prepare for work in a global economy and for participation as responsible and tolerant citizens.

As faculty members are faced with the significant challenges this diverse student body poses, institutions should consider questions such as these:

- Do faculty members across appointment types have the necessary skills to address the learning needs of first-generation students and students from diverse backgrounds?
- As students become increasingly consumer-oriented, is this adversely affecting the nature of student-faculty relationships?

THE RISE OF THE INFORMATION AGE AND THE AVAILABILITY OF NEW TECHNOLOGIES

The rapid expansion of knowledge and the pervasiveness of new technologies are two additional challenges confronting colleges and universities and their leaders. This expansion of knowledge is leading to the emergence of new areas of specialization that challenge the structure of the traditional disciplines. Simultaneously, however, the boundaries between disciplines are blurring, and new interdisciplinary fields of study are emerging. Some institutions have established cross-disciplinary units to support new developments in knowledge and the application of knowledge to societal problems. Faculty members are increasingly working in interdisciplinary contexts and participating in collaborative teams to teach or conduct research. Duderstadt (2000, p. 3) has captured the challenge and the promise confronting faculty members engaging in interdisciplinary ventures for the first time:

> It has become increasingly clear that those within the academy will need to learn to tolerate more ambiguity, to take more risks. This may mean we will be less comfortable in our scholarly neighborhoods; we may have to relax the relatively stable professional selves that we have preserved for so long. Yet most will find working

together much more fulfilling than working apart. Ultimately this will release incredible creativity.

Closely connected to the emergence of the Information Age is the explosion of new technologies that facilitate teaching and learning. Gumport and Chun (2005, p. 402) have suggested that advancements in technology are affecting higher education in three ways: "(1) the nature of knowledge, (2) the process of teaching and learning, and (3) the social organization of teaching and learning in higher education."

Technological developments contribute to the knowledge industry, in which faculty members become, in the words of Gumport and Chun (2005, p. 403), "knowledge consumers and knowledge producers functioning within market forces." One result is the emergence of people and policies to manage intellectual property issues that arise for faculty and for the institutions in which they work. In short, in a society that values knowledge, issues of "ownership and management of academic knowledge" (Gumport and Chun, 2005, p. 403) can affect faculty autonomy as well as academic freedom. Technological developments have also produced new research strategies that expand disciplinary inquiries while contributing to the blurring of boundaries between fields, and offer scholars new ways to interact, unbounded by time and distance.

Technological advances also affect the processes of teaching and learning. At one level, the use of technology in class and in facilitating communication simply builds on typical teacher-learner roles and relationships to make the learning process more efficient. At another level, technological innovation has had a much greater impact, bringing major changes to how learning and teaching occur. Thus, for many years, the typical learning environment involved teachers and students engaging in face-to-face classroom interactions, using books and blackboards to aid the processes of teaching and learning. But the explosion of available technologies over the past two decades has led to new ways of finding information, communicating, learning, and applying knowledge (Twigg, 2002), and even to the formation of new types of higher education institutions that specialize in online learning at any time and in any place.

These technological advances have caused faculty members to find themselves in new roles as they interact with learners and assess students' learning. Students are engaging in more individualized learning experiences, and the issues of time and location for learning are becoming more flexible (Gumport and Chun, 2005), thus requiring faculty to adjust their roles as teachers. They must learn to design and organize learning materials that can be provided via the Web. They must cultivate meaningful relationships with a diverse array of students even in virtual, computer-mediated environments, and they must be able to manage their time now that students can seek faculty interactions via computer any time of the day or night, seven days a week.

The possibilities offered by the Information Age, with its array of new technologies, seem unlimited and exciting—but the challenges, especially for faculty who use these technologies, can also be significant. The following questions are therefore worth consideration:

- To what extent does technology isolate faculty from each other even as it aids communication?
- How is technology affecting faculty members' ability to establish boundaries between their professional and personal lives?
- How can faculty members most effectively and efficiently stay current with technologies that enhance their work?

EFFECTS OF THESE MAJOR CHANGES ON FACULTY

The various factors that cause challenges for higher education institutions are also leading to significant changes in faculty careers and academic workplaces. Specific effects on faculty include:

- Changing patterns in faculty appointments
- Declines in faculty autonomy and control
- An escalating pace of work and expanding workloads
- Increasingly entrepreneurial and high-pressure environments that hinder community and institutional commitment
- A need for continuous, career-long professional development

CHANGING PATTERNS IN FACULTY APPOINTMENTS

Major changes in the nature of faculty appointments constitute one of the most significant responses by universities and colleges to the challenges posed by fiscal constraints, and by the need to stay competitive in a rapidly changing environment where flexibility, responsiveness, accountability, and cost-efficiency are key.

Changes in faculty work are situated within a general restructuring of work throughout the global economy. Handy (1994), an astute observer of societal change, has compared the emerging workplace in the global economy to the three leaves of a shamrock. One leaf contains the professional core, which is becoming a smaller proportion of the workforce. The second leaf includes freelance professionals and technicians who are self-employed and hired by organizations on an ad hoc, per-project basis. The third leaf is made up of the ever-increasing group of contingent workers who are available by the hour. In many employment sectors, the core workforce is becoming smaller as the number of contingent employees increases.

In the United States, changes in higher education have brought about a noteworthy resemblance between Handy's shamrock and the academic workplace, as Rice (2004) and Finkelstein and Schuster (2003) have highlighted. The major structural changes in faculty appointments have resulted in a tripartite system of appointments: tenure track, renewable contracts, and fixed-term or temporary. In this restructuring of academic appointments, full-time tenure-track faculty members typically follow the traditional path of the "prototypical American scholar" (Boyer, 1990) or "complete scholar" (Rice, 1996b) engaged in research, teaching, and service. Faculty with contract-renewable appointments often specialize in either teaching or research and provide flexibility to the employing institution. More and more faculty members, those who constitute the third leaf in terms of Handy's metaphor, are hired temporarily to teach specific courses.

By changing the types of faculty appointments into which talented individuals are hired, colleges and universities usually hope to gain some immediate flexibility or cost savings. But some institutions have shifted the pattern of appointment types without carefully considering the long-term impact on faculty members and the academic workplace. The shifts in faculty appointment types have created a bifurcated faculty, where those with full-time tenure-track appointments enjoy the traditional benefits of professorial work— respect, autonomy, collegiality, and opportunities for professional growth—while those who are not on the tenure track do not necessarily receive those benefits, at least not to the same extent. Furthermore, these different types of appointments cause inequities, which can undermine the sense of commitment that faculty should bring to their work. Institutions need to look carefully at the support and benefits that are in place across the various appointment types now in use. Otherwise, the intellectual capital of many faculty members may be underutilized, if they do not feel supported, respected, and thus committed to the work of the institution.

DECLINING AUTONOMY AND CONTROL FOR FACULTY

Fiscal constraints, calls for accountability, and the availability of new technologies have important implications for the nature and extent of the autonomy and control that faculty traditionally have experienced in their work. In regard to fiscal pressures, Slaughter (1993, p. 276) concludes that retrenchment in the face of budget constraints has "generally undermined faculty participation in governance and faculty authority over the direction of the curriculum." Moreover, as colleges and universities take on more entrepreneurial activities, often to attract more revenue, faculty members' autonomy and control over their work may diminish and shift toward the administrators who manage these revenue-producing activities and make important decisions about them. Furthermore, the efforts of state legislatures to hold public higher education institutions to higher levels of accountability have implications for faculty autonomy. In the context of these trends, Rhoades (1998) has suggested that faculty are losing autonomy and becoming "managed professionals" who are increasingly accountable to administrators, state legislators, governing boards, and funding agencies.

The new technologies are another major factor in faculty autonomy and control. Market forces demanding that higher education institutions be more efficient and cost-effective have caused "unbundling," or differentiation, in faculty work. The development of technology-mediated learning experiences requires an array of different skills. Traditionally, a faculty member envisions, prepares, delivers, and evaluates a course that he or she teaches. In this age of technology, however, these processes of production, distribution, and evaluation are being separated. Curriculum designers may prepare a course; technology specialists may develop the appropriate software to facilitate teaching the course online or in another technology-mediated environment; public relations specialists may market the course; a teacher may work with the students; and an evaluator may determine the effectiveness of the course, of the related technology, and of the instructor. The faculty member is still involved in helping students learn, but the course itself has become a commodity. Faculty members have traditionally believed that they "owned" their courses, but the differentiation of these aspects of teaching has diminished faculty control and ownership.

Academic freedom and autonomy have long been cherished aspects of academic work, yet the current pressures affecting higher education institutions are chipping away at faculty autonomy in subtle ways. Faculty members, regardless of their appointment types, need a sense of control and autonomy over their work, whether they have the traditional full array of teaching, research, and service responsibilities or more focused responsibility for particular parts of the academic enterprise. The creativity and energy of faculty members are enhanced when the autonomy to do their work as they think best is integral to their assignments.

Escalating Pace and Expanding Workload

What is often called "ratcheting" is another outcome of the major factors affecting higher education institutions. External calls for greater accountability and demonstrable outcomes, institutional pressure for faculty to generate revenue, and the necessity of keeping up with the never-ending expansion of new knowledge all conspire to create seemingly endless demands and expectations of faculty members. In fact, ironically, even as the public sometimes expresses skepticism about the amount and quality of work that faculty members are perceived as doing, many faculty members themselves report that they face constant pressure to turn their attention in too many different directions, and that they find the pace of work hectic and relentless (Rice, Sorcinelli, and Austin, 2000). There does not seem to be any limit to or boundary on the amount of work for faculty to do.

Fiscal constraints lead to greater faculty workloads when support staff are reduced or course loads are increased. The prevalence of computer use adds to a sense of "information overload" and to a growing expectation among students, and often among colleagues as well, that faculty members should be available every day, around the clock. With the wide use of e-mail by both students and faculty, asking questions and sending messages at any hour is easy to do and often seems to imply an expectation for rapid response (Young, 2005). These changes in faculty workload are evident in the frequent stories published by the *Chronicle of Higher Education* about faculty members who are grappling with the pressures of work and family responsibilities, or who report that the work involved in gaining or awarding tenure in their departments continues to escalate, or who express doubt about whether the long hours of work are sufficiently balanced by intrinsic rewards to make an academic career desirable.

Many new faculty members, and graduate students aspiring to be faculty members, are expressing concern about what they perceive to be increasing expectations for higher levels of productivity. They often report feeling pulled in many directions simultaneously and wonder whether they can find workable ways to manage their personal and professional responsibilities. Finding enough time to do their work was one of the most frequently mentioned sources of stress among early-career faculty in a range of institutional types (Rice, Sorcinelli, and Austin, 2000). Some graduate students and new faculty, as they observe the stress and long hours that characterize the work lives of their senior colleagues, express uncertainty about wanting to continue pursuing their academic careers. One faculty member echoed the comments of many other respondents: "The main issue on everyone's mind is maintaining equilibrium" (Rice, Sorcinelli, and Austin, 2000, p. 17).

Finally, public calls for accountability and state oversight have led to numerous reporting requirements that involve faculty as well as administrators. Faculty members must account for how they spend their time and must justify their teaching, research, and community engagements with documented evidence of outcomes.

They must prepare annual public reports enumerating the products of their work, often for distribution to a public audience. They must be able to document students' achievement and learning outcomes or explain their research in language that is accessible and interesting to the general public. Such accountability requirements take valuable faculty time.

As colleges and universities seek to recruit and retain excellent and diverse faculty members, provisions for flexibility in how faculty construct academic career paths and organize their personal and professional commitments are likely to be key ingredients of an attractive workplace. In the face of demanding workloads, faculty members—men and women alike—can work most effectively when they have the flexibility to organize their work in ways that enable them also to manage the responsibilities of their personal lives.

POTENTIAL LOSS OF THE SENSE OF AN ACADEMIC COMMUNITY

Taken together, the array of factors affecting higher education institutions—fiscal constraints, calls for greater accountability, the increasing prevalence of new technologies to facilitate teaching and research, and a diverse student body and faculty—seem, to many, to be changing the nature of the academic community. More specifically, the ratcheting of the workload experienced by many faculty members diminishes time available for casual and serendipitous collegial interaction. The commitment of many faculty members, both male and female, to handle significant personal as well as professional responsibilities means that time is at a premium for virtually everyone. The unbundling of aspects of faculty work separates faculty into specific groups by function so that fewer people see the whole picture in regard to the institution's overall mission. Some faculty members are segregated from others by institutions' failure to fully welcome and integrate non-tenure-track faculty into the intellectual life of their departments or their academic institutions. Today's faculty members' diverse backgrounds can also make the formation of strong relationships more challenging. A vibrant sense of academic community requires opportunities and occasions for faculty members to interact—and time to do so. All these trends undermine those necessary conditions.

Early-career faculty, like doctoral students planning to pursue academic careers (Austin, 2002), are especially concerned about the nature of the academic community. When early-career faculty discuss what they value and look forward to experiencing in their careers, they often mention the hope of participating in a "culture of collegiality" (Austin, 2003; Boice, 1992; Finkelstein, 1984; Rice, Sorcinelli, and Austin, 2000; Sorcinelli, 1988; Tierney and Bensimon, 1996; Whitt, 1991). Yet early-career faculty, as they begin to experience their careers, often express surprise and disappointment that their experiences do not match their hopes and expectations (Rice, Sorcinelli, and Austin, 2000).

A strong academic community that values and includes all faculty members contributes to the intellectual vibrancy of a college or university, supports the bonds of commitment that link faculty members to the institution, and creates a climate that enhances students' learning. When institutional leaders recognize the value of nurturing a community that includes all faculty members, regardless of their appointments, they enhance institutional health and success.

THE NEED FOR CONTINUOUS PROFESSIONAL DEVELOPMENT

In order to work creatively and effectively in a rapidly changing context, faculty must engage in continuous learning so as to constantly expand their repertoires of talents and skills. Support for faculty to engage in professional development directly strengthens the quality of their teaching, research, and outreach.

Understanding Students

A faculty member must understand the characteristics of diverse learners and have command of a repertoire of teaching skills in order to address different learning needs. A major challenge facing higher education is how to teach a greater number of people, who are diverse in their needs and goals, in a more efficient and less costly way. Faculty members must be able not only to meet the needs of many different students but to do so in ways that are efficient—for example, knowing a variety of strategies for teaching large classes effectively or interacting with students via the Internet.

Using Technology

New technologies present exciting opportunities for responding to students' needs, enhancing learning environments, and enriching research activities. But new technologies also require faculty to learn to think and work in new ways and to stay current with new technological developments. The World Wide Web has transformed the ways in which people interact with information, requiring adeptness at navigating myriad paths to pursue information, at developing judgments about the relative value of information, and at formulating syntheses of meaning even while knowledge changes and expands (Brown, 2002). Online teaching also involves skills additional to and different from those used in face-to-face teaching. In distance learning, for example, faculty members may teach groups of students whom they never meet in person. Through the use of computers, they have the option to incorporate real-time conversations with experts on relevant topics into their class sessions. Many faculty find it useful to know how to use instructional platforms such as Blackboard or WebCT to facilitate student-faculty interaction, ensure that students have ready access to learning materials, and monitor students' progress.

Engaging in Entrepreneurial Activity

Many universities and colleges are urging their faculty to pursue entrepreneurial opportunities—for example, expanded extension services, continuing education, patents, new programs and certificates, or new options for distance learning—that attract new revenues and constituents. But raising funds and engaging the public in new ways are activities that require skills and knowledge that not all faculty members possess. Faculty need to learn how to write successful grant proposals to obtain support for new programs, how to interact with funding agencies, and how to present their ideas in ways that convince a public outside higher education.

Increased Collaboration and Interdisciplinarity

The rapid expansion of knowledge is resulting in greater knowledge specialization and, simultaneously, in an increase in interdisciplinary work. New units are appearing on many campuses to facilitate cross-disciplinary work addressing complex problems.

Such cross-disciplinary work often involves new collaborations among scholars as well as new theoretical developments and research strategies.

Although the expansion of knowledge has created greater specialization and more fragmentation of knowledge (Rice, 2004), it also, somewhat paradoxically, requires faculty members to join interdisciplinary conversations, teams, or units, to learn to think in new ways, to make new connections, and to develop new skills.

Faculty members accustomed to individual autonomy and disciplinary specialization find that they must engage in decision making with others who often, at least metaphorically, speak a different language. Such collaborations raise many questions for faculty members. For example, what are the rules of ownership of intellectual work? How does decision making occur when a number of people are involved? These questions require faculty members to sort through the values and practices that most appropriately guide academic work under new collaborative conditions.

CONCLUDING THOUGHTS

This chapter has highlighted four major external factors that create opportunities and challenges for higher education institutions: fiscal constraints and increased competition, calls for accountability, the increasing diversity of students, and the rise of the Information Age along with its new technologies. These external factors challenge today's faculty members and the traditions of academic work and life. They have led to

- Proliferation of faculty appointments off the tenure track
- Shifts in faculty members' control over and autonomy in their work
- Continuously expanding workloads
- Increasing fragmentation of faculty work, which undermines a sense of academic community
- Continuous need for faculty to engage in professional growth

Because faculty represent the institution's greatest asset, institutional leaders must pay attention to faculty work and to the quality of academic workplaces, placing these concerns among the highest institutional priorities. As we pointed out at the beginning of this chapter, the intellectual capital and commitment that faculty bring to their colleges and universities are essential to the excellence and health of their institutions. Finding ways to maximize the intellectual capital represented by the faculty—in other words, investing in the faculty—enhances the health and success of a college or university. To thrive, colleges and universities must face this strategic imperative and realign their institutional support of faculty members in ways that more fully address today's institutional missions as well as faculty members' goals and priorities.

CHAPTER TWO

TRENDS IN THE NATIONAL WORKPLACE

The previous chapter addressed challenges that faculty and institutions of higher learning face from the external environments in which colleges and universities function. These challenges are not unique to academia. Nationally, the workforce and the workplace have changed, and professionals in every sector of the economy are experiencing, to some extent, the discomfort associated with a shifting environment.

At the crux of this discomfort is Americans' strong commitment to the long-held vision of the "ideal worker" (Whyte, 1956; Williams, 1999). This chapter begins by discussing both the historical concept of this ideal worker and how that notion was reflected in workplace and workforce dynamics throughout much of the twentieth century. The chapter goes on to explore recent societal changes and the changing characteristics of today's workforce. It examines evidence that the "ideal worker" model no longer fits many of today's workers or the realities of today's workplace, although the concept continues to drive employers' policies and practices.

The chapter then looks at ways in which corporations and professional firms are responding to these changes in the workforce. It is helpful to understand corporations' and firms' responses because these organizations are sometimes ahead of the academy in devising innovative human resources policies, and they are also the academy's competition for talented individuals. Their responses have shortcomings, however. The chapter concludes by comparing organizational responses with what individuals report most wanting employers to provide in helping them do their best work while also fulfilling their personal responsibilities.

THE IDEAL WORKER

The "ideal worker" norm was prevalent across all sectors of the American workplace for much of the past century (Whyte, 1956; Williams, 1999). This vision of workers was formed at a time when most employees entered their professions immediately after completing their education, putting in decades of long hours in order to work their way up their organizations' career ladders. They spent at least forty to fifty hours per week on their jobs but were also available to work additional hours when the need arose. On a daily basis, they could stay late at the office to wrap up a meeting or make a last-minute deadline: the length of ideal workers' days was not determined by the set hours of child care providers or by home repairmen's schedules. Instead, the ideal (usually male) worker had a supportive spouse who did not work outside their home. It was this person who took primary responsibility for managing their home and caring for their children, thus allowing the ideal worker to fulfill the varying demands of work (Bailyn, 1993; Williams, 1999).

In addition, ideal workers did not need to take extended maternity or paternity leave after their children were born or adopted, and they did not tend to "downshift" or take time off to care for young children, aging parents, or other dependents. Instead, their time off consisted only of short annual vacations, often scheduled around slow times at work. Further, they did not try to renegotiate job requirements and work arrangements if they found that their current life situations no longer allowed them to effectively balance their employers' demands with personal responsibilities. Instead, they were stable, predictable, uncomplicated employees, in terms of their fairly uniform needs where employers were concerned. In exchange for their commitment, hard work, and loyalty, their employers offered job security, often in the form of lifelong employment, and took considerable responsibility for their employees' progress up organizational career ladders.

In higher education, a vision of the ideal worker also existed for some time. Ideal academic workers moved from their doctoral programs or postdoctoral fellowships directly into tenure-track faculty positions. Most of them had a supportive spouse who did not seek employment at the hiring institution as part of the hiring negotiations, and who provided the candidate with the flexibility to accept the position being offered even when this entailed moving across the country. Ideal faculty members dedicated themselves fully to their work, particularly during the probationary period. The birth of a child might have caused a worker to cancel one or two class sessions, but otherwise this ideal worker attended to business as usual once the child was home from the hospital. These faculty worked all night in their laboratories when the need arose. Graduate students were free to call them at home late into the evening because these faculty were often working late anyway, and dinner engagements with visiting colleagues did not force ideal workers to juggle child care with spouses who also had evening commitments. Travel to conferences, speaking engagements, and off-site research locations were easily managed because these ideal workers did not have to arrange for extended-hours child care or take nursing infants along on trips.

These descriptions of ideal workers and of these workers' reciprocal relationships with their college, university, or company were apt for the middle-class white men who made up the majority of the workforce from approximately the middle of the nineteenth century to the middle of the twentieth (Gertsel and Clawson, 2000). Nevertheless, although society has changed greatly since those days, these norms remain a deeply ingrained part of the American work culture.

The economic and legal structure of the American workplace also strongly supports the fifty-plus-hour workweek and hinders acceptance of a broader definition of what a highly valuable employee might be.

Since passage of the Fair Labor Standards Act of 1938, business owners and managers have been pushing for longer and longer hours from their "exempt" employees, that is, those to whom certain provisions of the act do not apply. This act, which codified the forty-hour workweek, requires employers to pay overtime wages for additional hours worked. Professional employees, however, who made up 15 percent of the workforce in 1938, were exempt from this provision, and today almost 30 percent of employees are classified as exempt. Employers often expect them to work far more than forty hours a week because there are no marginal costs for "encouraging" this extra time (Hewlett, 2002). In addition, employment benefits, which now constitute a substantial and rising proportion of total compensation, are largely fixed for full-time employees, regardless of the number of hours they work. Again, employers have a strong incentive to develop a culture where employees are full-time and fifty-hour weeks are the norm.

CHARACTERISTICS AND RESPONSIBILITIES OF TODAY'S WORKFORCE

The American legal and economic structures, as well as Americans' long-held perception of what constitutes an ideal worker, all support the status quo: continuous employment from the time of earning one's degree until retirement; long workweeks; and the assumption that dedicated workers must consider work their highest priority. Nevertheless, organizations across the country are employing more women, members of ethnic and racial minorities, partners in dual-career couples, and single parents who are challenging established norms about the ideal worker and work's appropriate role in life.

Consider these statistics: African Americans now comprise 11.3 percent of the U.S. labor force, Hispanic Americans comprise 13.1 percent, and Asian Americans comprise 4.3 percent of the U.S. labor force (U.S. Bureau of Labor Statistics, 2005). These workers bring with them a wide array of perspectives leading to new kinds of demands for flexibility. Cultural and religious backgrounds have grown more diverse, and it has become important for employees to have the flexibility to take time off from work for cultural celebrations or religious holidays. Moreover, because so many cultures are represented in the labor force, views of the appropriate role of work in one's life and of one's work-life balance are becoming more diverse.

Women of all ethnic and racial backgrounds also represent a very significant segment of today's workforce (46 percent), and their participation rates have increased steadily over the past few decades (U.S. Department of Health and Human Services, 2004). In 1970, 43 percent of women participated in the workforce; by 1980, their participation had increased to 52 percent. By 1999, fully

60 percent of women worked outside the home (U.S. Census Bureau, 2000). Among the fastest-growing segments of working women is the group made up of mothers with young children. Over 60 percent of mothers of preschool children are employed (U.S. Department of Health and Human Services, 2004), and approximately 75 percent of mothers with children eight years and younger are employed (Elias, 2004). This change in the workforce means that the majority of couples today include more than one earner. In 1977, 49 percent of married male employees with children had an employed spouse, compared to 78 percent who had an employed spouse twenty-five years later (Bond, Thompson, Galinsky, and Prottas, 2002). In addition, 10.4 percent of all households are headed by a single parent, up from 8.2 percent in 1979 (Bailyn, Drago, and Kochan, 2001).

Women's increased representation in the workforce is not the only change. Women are no longer primarily found in so-called pink-collar roles, such as secretarial or food service positions. Instead, they are entering the professions in record numbers, and with these more demanding positions come the long hours that are typical for doctors, attorneys, and professors.

Although Americans are working more hours, and more women are working outside the home in professional positions, household responsibilities have not lessened. The home repair and home service industries generally have not tried to accommodate full-time workers by extending service hours or providing a range of services in place of the specialized plumbing, lawn care, or painting that remains the typical model. These businesses continue to operate with the assumption that full-time homemakers are available to make arrangements with a number of different service providers and to wait at home for them to arrive (Christensen and Gomory, 1999).

Caring for children also continues to play a very significant role in the lives of many employed people, and men as well as women feel the strain of balancing workplace and household demands. In addition, more than one-third of men and women today provide regular care for a parent or in-law who is over the age of sixty-five (Bond et. al., 2002). Facing these significant responsibilities, 45 percent of workers report that their jobs interfere "some" or "a lot" with their family lives, up from 34 percent in 1977 (Bond et. al.,

2002). More than 70 percent of working mothers and fathers believe that they do not have adequate time to spend with their children (Bond, Galinsky, and Swanberg, 1998), and 63 percent feel that they do not spend enough time with their spouses, up from 50 percent in 1992 (Bond et. al., 2002). Further, almost half feel torn "fairly often" or "very often" between meeting work and family commitments (Bankert and Googins, 1996).

Although men and women alike are expressing concern about their personal lives, women in particular have a difficult time finding a satisfactory balance between home and work. This is largely because most women today maintain the role of primary homemaker, even if they also work full time outside the home (Bailyn, Drago, and Kochan, 2001; Perkins and DeMeis, 1996). As evidence of this claim, a recent national survey of the top 10 percent of women and men, in terms of earnings, found that 50 percent of high-income working women have primary responsibility for meal preparation, compared to 9 percent of men; 51 percent of women in this group take time off from work when a child is sick, compared to 9 percent of men; and 61 percent of these women organize activities such as playdates and summer camp for their children, compared to 3 percent of men (Hewlett, 2002).

Women also shoulder more of the responsibilities related to caring for aging relatives. Overall, they represent 61 percent of these caregivers, and when care requires more than forty hours per week, that proportion rises to 71 percent. Sociologists are now calling this the "daughter track," the later-in-life version of the "mommy track," when women place a lower priority on work in order to provide more care to family members (Gross, 2005). Not only is this care often physically and emotionally demanding, it is also difficult to manage it and work simultaneously. Research shows that when people work while caring for aging relatives, a significant proportion have to leave work early or come in late, take leaves of absence, go from full-time to part-time work, or give up work entirely (Gross, 2005). Indeed, having primary responsibility for the "second shift" of home and family responsibilities causes tremendous stress for many women. (For more about how women in particular are affected by current workplace expectations, see the section titled "Women and the 'Ideal Worker' Norm," later in this chapter.)

Characteristics of Today's Workplace

Changing workforce demographics are not the only reason that the vision of the ideal worker is less appropriate now than it was fifty years ago. In many cases, the nature of the relationship between employees and employers has also changed, as have employers' expectations of their employees. This section describes four major national shifts that are affecting the workforce and workplaces across professions:

1. Less job security
2. Diminished autonomy in doing work
3. Demands for increased access to workers
4. Expectations for workers' increased devotion to their work

Less Security

The large bureaucratic organizations and mass-production facilities that played a dominant role in the early and mid-twentieth century influenced workers' views of work and employers. For many employees, work during these years was routine, fragmented, and unfulfilling. Factory workers faced structural barriers to upward mobility within their organizations, and these circumstances led them to focus more on job security and incremental pay raises. The legacy of the Great Depression also influenced the increased emphasis on job security (Dimitrova, 1994).

In recent years, however, American workers have observed or directly experienced layoffs, downsizing, and so-called "rightsizing" as organizations have attempted to remain competitive in the face of greatly increased needs for flexibility in the global marketplace. The typical employee now spends fewer and fewer years with a single company. In fact, only half of the people who take a position with a new firm will still be there after two years (Downey, March, Berkman, and Steinauer, 2001). In addition to changing jobs far more rapidly than in previous decades, the average American will also change careers several times during his or her working years (Judy and D'Amico, 1997). As a result of working in these dynamic new conditions, many employees feel far less secure in their positions than employees did a few decades ago. Younger workers also express less loyalty to their employers than do those who began working in the 1950s or 1960s: according to a report published by the Radcliffe Public Policy Institute, 82 percent of workers sixty-five and older report being very loyal to their employers, compared to 57 percent of those under forty (Cintrón, 1999).

Diminished Autonomy

In addition to less job security, professionals in fields such as medicine, law, and accounting are in some cases facing nothing less than transformation in the way these professions are practiced and in how individuals view their work. These sectors are facing financial and other environmental pressures that are leading to a restructuring of how work is accomplished.

One of the most significant changes is the corporatization of what used to be private professional practices. In the medical field, between 1983 and 1997, the proportion of physicians who were salaried employees increased from 37 percent to 66 percent (McKinlay and Marceau, 2002). As a result of this shift away from private practice, physicians are losing control of decisions about patient care and are ceding such decisions to organizations offering managed care. They are also increasingly monitored by computer record-keeping systems and reviewed by administrative employees (Borges, 2001; McKinlay and Marceau, 2002). One reflection of these changes in how and where physicians work, and in the erosion of professionalism, is the increased utilization of nonphysician clinicians, such as nurse practitioners and physician assistants, to provide patient care. As for-profit organizations have come to provide more health care in this country, they have sought ways to provide less expensive replacements for physicians. It is expected that by 2010, as much as 34 percent of the care now provided by physicians will be provided by nonphysician clinicians (McKinlay and Marceau, 2002).

Public accounting professionals also face significant workplace changes, given the rise in corporate acquisitions of certified public accounting firms. When CPAs are employed by financial services corporations, they often face pressure to more aggressively generate revenues from tax-preparation services, to cross-sell a firm's other products and services to clients, and, in general, emphasize commercialism and profitability. They must also deal with some loss of control and autonomy as they are increasingly supervised by nonprofessionals (Shafer, Lowe, and Fogarty, 2002).

Nor has the legal field been immune to shifts in autonomy and areas of professional discretion. In this field, software programs allow firm managers to track the amount of time for which attorneys bill. According to one author, associates in a law firm are like pieceworkers in a sweatshop and are often required to work sixty- or seventy-hour weeks to meet billing-hour "minimums" (Fortney, 2000). Lawyers in private practice often feel pressure to attract and retain clients in an environment where practicing law has become "less of a profession and more of a business," and the profession increasingly lacks civility, collegiality, and even strong ethical standards (Schiltz, 1999, p. 5). In fact, according to Fortney (2000), there is evidence that billing pressure often forces the most ethical attorneys out of private law practice altogether.

DEMANDS FOR INCREASED ACCESS TO WORKERS

Professionals in each of the fields just discussed, and in other fields, are facing a loss of control over which clients to serve and which services to provide as well as over fee policies (Shafer, Lowe, and Fogarty, 2002). Adding to this loss of control is the increased accessibility to these professionals that has been brought about by technology. Boundaries between personal time and work time are fading. People are expected to be on call via cell phones, voice mail, beepers, or e-mail virtually around the clock. Almost half of American workers use these devices to conduct work during supposedly nonwork time (Curry, 2003), in part because many employers question employees' commitment if they refuse to be on call while away from work.

An advertising executive described her experience this way:

> I am hooked into a technology that allows work to seep into every cranny of my life. I have a computer and a fax machine in my office and at home, I have voice mail in the office, on my cell phone, and at home, I have e-mail in the office and at home, and my boss has just given me a BlackBerry so I can check my e-mail on the hour every hour wherever I am! . . . The requirement that I be constantly

in touch makes me anxious and preoccupied a great deal of the time [Hewlett, 2002, pp. 104–105].

A systems programmer explained, "You're expected to keep your beeper on and make yourself available on weekends in case there's a problem. . . . Even when you're going on vacation, the boss will say, 'Leave us your number in case something comes up'" (Moore, 2000, p. 144). In fact, fully 83 percent of workers check in with their offices while on vacation (Goodman, 2003).

Expectations for Increased Devotion to Work

Across career fields, employers' demands for workers' time continue to increase, and employees' responses are consistent with the high value that Americans place on work and career success. It is estimated that Americans took 10 percent less time off in 2003 than in 2002 (Goodman, 2003), and in the United States, by contrast with other industrialized countries, we already had fewer vacation days to begin with. European employers, for example, are required by law to provide four or five weeks of paid leave to their employees, and employees in China receive three weeks off. Nevertheless, by contrast, in the United States, the average amount of vacation time is eight days after a year with one company, and ten days after three years (Goodman, 2003). In 2004, to make matters worse, 36 percent of Americans did not expect to use the full vacation time that was available to them through their employers (Galinsky et al., 2005).

On a weekly basis, many employees, particularly women, are giving increasing amounts of their time to their companies. Men worked an average of forty-nine hours per week in 2002, compared to forty-seven hours a week in 1977. Women worked an average of forty-three and a half hours per week in 2002, compared to thirty-nine hours per week in 1977 (Bond et al., 2002). Not surprisingly, the combined workweeks of dual-career couples are also increasing. In 1977, dual-career couples with children worked a combined average of eighty-one hours per week. By 2002, that average had increased to ninety-one hours per week (Bond et. al., 2002). As a result of their lengthening workweeks and relatively short vacations, Americans on average work three hundred fifty more hours per year than their European counterparts, and the gap for professional employees is even wider (Hewlett, 2002; MacDermid, Lee, and Smith, 2001).

Faculty members, too, have come face to face with each of these four trends. Tenure-track positions and the lifelong security they afford are no longer the norm. Faculty members appear to be losing some of their traditional autonomy in decision making and the use of their time, as suggested by the observation that they are becoming "managed professionals" (Rhoades, 1998). Technology is blurring the lines between work and personal time for faculty, as it is for everyone else, and faculty workweeks also continue to grow longer.

ISSUES POSED BY TODAY'S WORKFORCE AND WORKPLACES

WOMEN AND THE "IDEAL WORKER" NORM

The demands for increased access to workers, and for workers' increased devotion to work, affect all employees, but women with significant household responsibilities generally have the most difficult time meeting these expectations. As a result, although approximately 75 percent of mothers with children eight years and younger are employed (Elias, 2004), nearly two-thirds of mothers of childbearing age do not work full time, all year long (Williams, 1999)—and this, "in a society that rigorously marginalizes anything less" (Williams, 1996, p. 754). In addition, many mothers who work full time are marginalized on the "mommy track" because they are not able to put in the long workweeks that advancement to top positions typically requires (Williams, 1999).

Women's opportunities for career advancement are, therefore, severely limited. For example, even after more than twenty-five years of their increased presence in the workforce, women hold just 5 percent of the upper-management positions in corporate America (Conlin, 2000); not surprisingly, many of these executive women fit the "ideal worker" mold. Research has also found that, among men and women who had earned the master's degree in business administration and risen to top jobs in their companies, 27 percent of the women, compared to 14 percent of the men, had not married, and 51 percent of the women but only 26 percent of the men had no children (the average age of the study subjects was forty) (Conlin, 2000). Results from a survey of the top 10 percent of male and female earners across the professions were very similar (Hewlett, 2002).

Women are similarly underrepresented in top positions in the legal field. Large law firms do not seem to favor men over women in hiring young associates (Hull and Nelson, 2000), but associates, once hired, are typically expected to accumulate two thousand billable hours each year. In order to do so, they work sixty to seventy hours per week. According to one young female lawyer, "It's difficult to have a cat, let alone a family" under these circumstances (Rhode, 2002, p. 2208).

Associates who are able to meet senior partners' expectations are invited to become partners in their firms, an offer that comes with substantial perks and security. Given the working conditions, however, a woman's chances of becoming a partner are less than one-third those of a man (Hull and Nelson, 2000). Just ten years after graduating from law school, 30 to 40 percent of female lawyers are neither practicing law nor working in careers that require a law degree (Costello, 1997). Many others decide to work in less lucrative and less prestigious environments—in government, public interest organizations, or educational settings—or to serve as internal counsel because these positions are less demanding, and the hours are more predictable (Hull and Nelson, 2000). In fact, fully 45 percent of women law graduates report that work-life balance was their primary consideration in choosing their current employers (Williams and Calvert, 2002).

Likewise, female accountants face professional demands that many are unwilling or unable to meet once they have children (Alter, 1991). The situation at PricewaterhouseCoopers LLP was described as typical: They "recruit fifty percent women off campus, but as you go up the ladder, the percentage of women drops to thirty and then twenty percent—and by the time you get to the partner level, it's down to thirteen percent" (Stein, DiTullio, Forsman, and Miller, 2002).

In addition to experiencing significant challenges as they try to build fulfilling careers, many women also realize that combining children with a professional career can put substantial strain on a marriage. As the research already cited indicates, many couples find it difficult or impossible to devise an equitable solution to the reality of two people managing the demands of three jobs. As a result, it is the woman who most often places the family above her career in order to establish a better home life. This is not always an easy decision for her. A scholar on work-life policies describes the dilemma as follows:

> One might argue that organizational policies that encourage an all-or-nothing level of commitment generate family stress because they implicitly deny the possibility that the work situation could provide a margin for adjustment. What in fact is a societal issue driven by inflexibility in career structures becomes a private issue between husband and wife in which the only possible solution is for one of them to "sacrifice" [Bailyn, 1993, p. 104].

Data indicate that the same challenges exist for women faculty members. Regarding marriage, tenured women in the sciences are twice as likely as tenured men to be single. Tenured women in the social sciences and humanities are also more likely than tenured men to be single. Across the disciplines, 62 percent of tenured women faculty in the humanities and social sciences, and 50 percent of those in the sciences, do not have children in their households twelve to fourteen years after earning the Ph.D. For tenured men, the statistics are 39 percent and 30 percent, respectively (Mason and Goulden, 2002). In fact, according to these two researchers, only one-third of women respondents who had no children before taking a tenure-track faculty position ever became mothers, and women faculty who did have children were twice as likely as their male colleagues to report having had fewer than they originally wanted (Mason and Goulden, 2004).

PREDICTIONS VERSUS REALITY: EXPECTATIONS REGARDING THE ROLE OF WORK IN AMERICANS' LIVES

The American workplace still largely revolves around the notion of the ideal worker, even though workers' demographics are far more diverse and workplaces have also changed in important ways. As a result, many members of the workforce, particularly individuals in professional positions, are struggling to fulfill multiple life

roles. At this point, many of them would say that they are not succeeding. The human resources consultants Towers Perrin, seeking
to measure American workers' feelings about their jobs, found that
more than half expressed negative emotions; the most important
factors in these responses were their heavy workloads and an accompanying sense that work alone was not satisfying their deeper
needs (Curry, 2003).

The current state of the workforce stands in sharp contrast to
what workers as well as economists expected one hundred years
ago. Throughout the 1800s and the early part of the 1900s, Western industrial workers viewed the Industrial Revolution as something that would increasingly allow them to work fewer hours each
week and to enjoy more leisure time. As productivity and efficiency
increased, it was reasoned, the need for long hours would decrease, thus allowing people more freedom to use their time as
they chose. In fact, working hours did steadily decline through the
nineteenth and early twentieth centuries, and many economists
felt secure in predicting that by the middle of the twentieth century the average worker would be on the job fewer than fourteen
hours per week (Hunnicutt, 1988; Roediger and Foner, 1989).

In the 1920s work grew more scarce, and during the Depression there was widespread agreement that Americans should "share
the work." This meant that people worked fewer hours than they
had in the past, for lower total wages, in order to allow as many
people as possible to have at least some income. As the economy
recovered, however, America was at a crossroads. Was progress to
be defined in terms of shorter and shorter work hours, or was it
to be defined in terms of more production and more consumption? Many business leaders wanted to promote greatly increased
consumption, in order to provide a market for the goods being
made with ever-increasing efficiency. Government supported this
perspective by assuming responsibility for creating jobs for citizens
and replacing jobs that had been lost because of technological advances (Hunnicutt, 1992).

By most accounts, society as a whole firmly embraced the calls
for greater productivity and consumption. Nevertheless, the his-
torian John Gillis offers this comment:

> In reaching the affluent society, we're working longer and harder
> than anyone could have imagined. The work ethic and identifying

ourselves with work and through work is not only alive and well but more present now than at any time in history [cited in Curry, 2003, p. 50].

But in many ways, this work ethic clashes with the reality of current workforce demographics and with what new groups in the workforce need. Across occupations, there are more employees with significant personal responsibilities. The number of dual-career couples, many of whom have children at home, continues to rise, as does the number of single parents in the workforce. The challenges facing higher education that have resulted from changes in workplaces and in the workforce in many ways parallel the changes that are occurring in corporate workplaces.

CORPORATE RESPONSES TO WORKPLACE AND WORKFORCE CHANGES

Many organizations are wrestling with appropriate responses to these workplace and workforce changes. Creating a meaningful and yet organizationally feasible response is a significant challenge because workers' priorities and needs are less uniform and far more complex than they were fifty years ago. This section highlights some of corporate America's most innovative and comprehensive programs and policies aimed at increasing flexibility, although they are by no means typical. Among those described here are some that have brought about intended change as well as some that have not produced the desired outcomes. All of them may prove instructive for leaders in higher education.

CORPORATE POLICIES AND PROGRAMS TO ADDRESS WORKERS' CONCERNS

For today's employees, one of the most significant concerns is finding high-quality child care. According to a nationwide survey conducted by the Society for Human Resource Management, 6 percent of companies offered child care facilities at the work site, 20 percent offered child care resource and referral services, and 9 percent sponsored sick child care (Stein et al., 2002, p. 68). Family-friendly policies such as these are strongly related to firm size; firms with at least one hundred employees are far more likely to provide them (Glass and Estes, 1997).

Family leave policies at some companies have become more generous in recent years. For example, Fannie Mae offers new mothers up to thirty-two weeks of leave, including ten to twelve weeks at full pay (Stein et al., 2002). Nationally, as of 2002, 14 percent of companies offered paid paternity leave (Stein et al., 2002), and for couples who adopted, companies were increasingly willing to help pay adoption expenses and to provide at least a few weeks of paid time off (Stein et al., 2002). Phase-back programs are also growing in popularity, allowing new parents to gradually return to full-time work after the birth or adoption of a child.

Other companies, such as Citigroup, Eddie Bauer, and General Mills, have offered dry cleaning, therapeutic massage, hair salon services, automotive services, and take-out dinners for workers to carry home with them; employer-provided workout facilities and wellness programs have also been becoming more popular (Hammonds, 1996; Stein et al., 2002).

Compressed workweeks are offered by 40 percent of companies nationwide (Armour, 2004), and flextime is gaining in popularity. Under this system, workers, in consultation with managers, can adapt their start and end times. The new hours are typically fixed once the negotiation is complete. Telecommuting is an attractive option for some employees, who are allowed to work from home or from another off-site location, often for a specific amount of time each week. In 2003, 45 percent of employers in one study offered employees this option (Armour, 2004). A limited number of companies are also increasing paid time off for employees. For example, Ernst and Young LLP added two holidays and one personal day for all employees in 2001 (Stein et al., 2002).

Some of the companies that are the most committed to helping workers achieve balance between their work and personal lives offer two additional options: job sharing and part-time professional work (Catalyst, 1998). These employment configurations can include creative arrangements over extended periods of time as employees manage the "ebb and flow [of] work and children" (Rubin, 2002, p. 62). Several years ago, for example, according to Stein et al. (2002, p. 78), ABN AMRO North America, a Chicago-based banking and financial services corporation, offered part-time hours as a standard option at lower levels. Some officers took part in a job-sharing program or worked twenty-hour weeks for prorated salary and full benefits. Vice President Carolyn Stenner, a mother of four, was working twenty-four hours a week and telecommuted at times. She had received two promotions since moving from full-time to part-time work in 1996.

A specific example of the movement in the professions toward more family-friendly policies is found in the practice of law. Attorneys working in private firms now often have multiple career paths from which to choose. In fact, nearly half of the nation's largest law firms offer various types of tiered partnerships instead of the traditional "up or out" system whereby someone not promoted to partner is automatically terminated (Trower, 1998). These alternative paths include attorneys who are designated "of counsel" because they opt to work primarily from home or because they share one full-time position with another person. Firms may also employ "career associates," who are typically technical associates in low-visibility divisions of the practice. Nevertheless, these and other models can create a second class of attorneys and may severely limit advancement opportunities for people in these positions.

At the other end of the spectrum are small legal firms that have made work-life balance a strategic core organizational value. For example, one firm has thirteen attorneys, five of whom work reduced hours and several of whom telecommute. When the firm was founded, one of the partners said, "I could see that there were talented women lawyers out there whom large law firms hadn't figured out how to retain. . . . The large firms were not likely to have part-time policies that really worked" (Williams and Calvert, 2002, p. 40).

For over a decade, the public accounting industry has also been working to redefine its traditional career track so that partnership is not the only meaningful goal available to employees (Trower, 1998). Positions with titles such as "director" or "nonequity partner," which offer significantly diminished annual compensation, can offer far more flexibility and control over work hours than the partner track does. Some firms, such as PricewaterhouseCoopers LLP, are also encouraging their employees to use these firms' flextime programs, which still allow an employee to become a partner (Stein et al., 2002, p. 108; Williams and Calvert, 2002).

Many of the programs just described are also suited to the academic work system, both because of its flexible nature and because of the autonomy normally given to faculty members in scheduling their work.

Two Major Shortcomings of Corporate Policies and Programs

These programs and policies are helpful to many of today's workers, but they also fall short in some areas. For one thing, policies and programs such as care for sick children and flextime assume that all people can and want to fit the "ideal worker" mold as long as they receive some support for their personal responsibilities. However, it is not realistic to assume that all people at every point in their lives can successfully do so. For another, work-life policies may be in place, but leaders and many members of an organization often pay them only lip service, as shown by an organizational culture that does not support utilization of policies that exist in writing. Lack of support can also be communicated when organizational leaders treat work-life policies and programs as benefits that can be quickly removed when there is an economic downturn. Each of these shortcomings is discussed more fully in the passages that follow.

First Major Shortcoming

The first shortcoming is that work-life policies and programs may fail to meet individuals' needs fully. Many of these policies and programs can be grouped into two broad categories (see Table 2.1). One category, consisting of programs designed primarily to ease the demands of household responsibilities, includes care for sick children, dry cleaning services, take-out dinners, and flextime. The focus here is on helping employees strategically manage their personal responsibilities while they continue to work forty or more hours each week. In fact, some of these programs allow employees to spend more hours on the job. Rather than staying home to care for an ill child, for example, an employee can call a special employer-provided child care service. Rather than leaving work before 6:00 P.M. to prepare a family dinner, an employee can use the services of an on-site take-out option and thus stay an extra thirty or forty-five minutes in the evening.

TABLE 2.1. WORK-LIFE POLICIES AND PROGRAMS, ORGANIZED BY PURPOSE

Purpose: *Ease Household Demands*	*Purpose:* *Decrease Professional Workload*
Child care programs (including sick-child care)	Job-sharing policies
Compressed-workweek policies	Part-time work policies
Telecommuting policies	Programs for alternative career paths
On-site support programs (take-out meals, dry cleaning)	Career-break programs

Policies and programs that ease household demands are quite beneficial for individuals who want to work forty or more hours a week and who can, a majority of the time, fit "ideal worker" norms, with minimal flexibility and support from their employers. These programs are a valuable addition to today's workplace. But they are not a good fit for everyone, because they assume the forty-plus-hour workweek as the starting point.

A different category of programs is needed if individuals who are unable or unwilling to fit "ideal worker" norms are also to have successful and challenging careers. This second category of programs, far less common than the first, is aimed at easing employees' workloads, either temporarily or permanently. Under these circumstances, non-normative work configurations, such as part-time career tracks, job sharing, and even career breaks, allow individuals to work less than full time but still engage in meaningful work that contributes in important ways to their organizations. It is this second category of policies and programs that is intended to address more dramatically the substantial changes that have occurred in today's workforce. These are the programs that are beginning to successfully challenge the vision of the "ideal worker" in corporate America.

Likewise, as higher education leaders consider how they will respond to the changing academic workplace and workforce, it is important not simply to create new policies and programs that provide personal support to faculty members so that they can continue to do their work in the same way that it has always been done. The dramatic changes in the workforce and the workplace require more than this. New programs and policies need to be designed so that both the institution and the individual can benefit to the greatest extent possible from each faculty member's work. Providing more support for personal responsibilities is an important and worthwhile investment, but programs that provide real flexibility, such as part-time career tracks, are essential as well.

Second Major Shortcoming

The second shortcoming in some corporations' responses to work-life concerns is these corporations' failure to provide real support for their own formal policies. Many employees fear using the policies that currently exist, because organizational cultures have not kept up with them (Bailyn, Drago, and Kochan, 2001; Glass and Finley, 2002; Kossek, Barber, and Winters, 1999). For example, according to Bankert and Googins (1996, p. 48), "Many of the same companies that have instituted formal policies on flextime or job sharing have a culture in which adhering to the traditional face-time mentality is regarded as one of the strongest criteria for career advancement."

Qualitative evidence indicates that employees will not use family-friendly policies, especially leave, work-reduction, and work-schedule policies, if they feel that doing so will jeopardize their job security, assignments, or opportunities for promotion (Bailyn and Fletcher, 1997; Glass and Estes, 1997). One female attorney's experience of using the part-time schedule appears to be typical: it left her feeling isolated at her firm, and she concluded that her colleagues viewed a part-time schedule as a "special accommodation to the family-challenged" (Williams and Calvert, 2002, p. 7).

Quantitative evidence also supports this view. For example, according to the National Association for Law Placement, provisions for alternative work arrangements do exist in 94 percent of law firms, but almost 50 percent of surveyed attorneys did not believe that they could utilize flexible work arrangements without adverse professional consequences; in fact, only 2.9 percent of these attorneys worked on part-time schedules (Cunningham, 2001). This hesitancy was particularly prevalent among the men, who often felt that their organizational cultures would possibly allow women to scale back their work but would certainly not deal favorably with men who chose to do so (Cooper, 2000; Cunningham, 2001). People who do choose to utilize flexible scheduling and part-time options sometimes realize too late that they are working in organizations whose evaluation procedures and standards hinder the career advancement of anyone who actually uses such alternatives.

Organizational leaders have also communicated lack of support for work-life policies by scaling them back during economically difficult times. In 2003, the Society for Human Resource Management surveyed its members who were personnel executives and found that the percentage of companies offering flextime, telecommuting, job sharing, and compressed workweeks had declined from the previous year; this was the first drop in family-friendly benefits since the 1990s, when they had first been measured in human resource surveys (Geller, 2003). The shift is evidence that organizational leaders see such policies and programs not as entitlements but merely as nice perks for employees when the company can afford them. The reality is that America's work culture, despite new demographics and the changing nature of workplaces, remains largely based on the "ideal worker" norm (Whyte, 1956; Williams, 1999), where work is unquestionably one's first priority and the forty-plus-hour workweek is sacred.

EMPLOYEES' VIEWS OF THEIR WORKPLACE NEEDS

If employers are responding to workforce and workplace changes with policies and programs that many individuals, especially women, do not find particularly helpful or feasible, then what do employees want?

FLEXIBILITY

Most employees want options that can help them find a reasonable balance between their personal and professional lives. Workers want more control over their time, including the option to work fewer hours and to decide when and where they will work (Glass and Finley, 2002). According to a principal at Towers Perrin, "People are very emotional about work, and they're very negative about it. The biggest issue is clearly workload. People are feeling crushed" (Curry, 2003, p. 50).

As evidence of work overload, 94 percent of information technology professionals surveyed for one study indicated that they worked in deadline or crisis mode at least some of the time, and 54 percent brought work home on work nights and weekends "often" or "always" (Moore, 2000). Among young lawyers working in private law firms in Texas, 71 percent agreed with the statement "I must sacrifice fulfillment outside of work in order to attain partnership status" (Fortney, 2000) as they saw themselves as being "asked not to dedicate, but to sacrifice their lives to the firm" (Schiltz, 1999, p. 5). In fact, up to 70 percent of associates in law firms said that they would trade $30,000 to $50,000 of their annual salaries in favor of more personal time (Williams and Calvert, 2002.) In 1997, across the entire labor force, 63 percent of workers reported wanting to work fewer hours, a preference that was equally true for men and women, and a finding that represented a jump of 17 percentage points over the five years between 1992 and 1997 (Bond, Galinsky, and Swanberg, 1998).

One way to help people find balance in their lives is to create more full-time positions that require a commitment closer to the traditional forty hours of work per week. Another is to create part-time career tracks. A survey of high-achieving women, defined as the top 10 percent of female earners in the United States, found that 85 percent were in favor of a part-time career track. This track for high-level jobs would allow for reduced hours and reduced workloads on an ongoing basis but would also include the possibility of promotion (Hewlett, 2002).

Professionals in many fields also desire more flexibility, both with their day-to-day work and with their careers. For women in particular, an appealing option would be an official "career break" whereby a worker could take an extended period of unpaid, job-protected leave (Hewlett, 2002). Professionals are also interested in having a variety of career options that would provide opportunities for them to advance (Jiang and Klein, 1999–2000). Rather than strictly rigid career tracks, such as those that largely exist in the legal and accounting fields and in academe, employees want multiple options. Such options would provide challenging work and opportunities for advancement in positions respected by superiors and colleagues. Another form of flexibility might entail retirement plans allowing employees to take their savings with them if they changed employers, or plans that in other ways did not penalize them for career interruptions (Hewlett, 2002).

SECURITY IN THE FORM OF EMPLOYABILITY

In addition to seeking flexibility from their employers, many of today's workers seek a form of job security that is in line with the reality of today's workplaces. People are coming to view their employers in a new light. Rather than expecting their companies to provide long-term job security in return for strong work performance and loyalty, they now believe it is more realistic to ask their employers for help in maintaining their employability (Hall, 1996; Hall and Moss, 1998; Waterman, Waterman, and Collard, 1994). In this newly evolving work relationship, loyalty would continue to play an important role. While a worker was with an organization, he or she would be committed to its success, and the organization would enable the worker to grow and develop. Both employer and employee would recognize, however, that either party might need to end the relationship at some point, and both would be reasonably prepared when or if that should happen.

As part of this new reciprocal relationship, the individual and the organization would share responsibility for keeping the employee marketable. The organization, for its part, would offer opportunities for the employee to remain current in his or her field and to develop and extend his or her skills. Such opportunities might come in the form of challenging new job assignments, such as appointment to a task force or project team in the employee's area of interest but outside his or her traditional area of expertise. Opportunities might also come through formal training and access to career counseling. Because the organization would provide valuable support and appropriate opportunities for growth, the employee would be committed to it and to its mission and would also be able to produce excellent work as a result of professional development.

In addition, the organization would no longer be expected to have primary responsibility for the employee's career path or long-term success in his or her profession. Instead, the employee would take responsibility for this, keeping abreast of changes in the field and benchmarking his or her skills with industry needs. Developing awareness of his or her interests, values, and skills through self-assessment instruments and work with a career counselor could also play an important role in remaining employable (Hall, 1996; Hall and Moss, 1998; Waterman, Waterman, and Collard, 1994).

Flexibility, and security in the form of employability, are important for many employees today. What employees are not calling for as loudly are many of the policies and programs that employers have created in recent years in their attempts to better address the changing workforce. Employees do find that employer-provided services, such as dry cleaning and take-out dinners, help them manage some personal responsibilities. Nevertheless, research shows that what many individuals want is more time away from work—more time to spend with their families, more time to develop or maintain a personal life outside of work generally, and more time to concentrate on their household responsibilities (Bond, Galinsky, and Swanberg, 1998). Some also want the option of leaving their positions completely for a time while family or other personal responsibilities are at their most demanding (Hewlett, 2002).

Meaningful and Satisfying Work

Yet another priority for many workers today is to have work that is more meaningful and satisfying. As described earlier, professionals in many fields now function in positions that offer less autonomy and more piecemeal work. Such changes can lead to less challenging work, and to fewer opportunities to feel an important sense of ownership of one's work. Workplace changes have also produced a blurring of lines between personal and professional life as employers' demands continue to increase. As a result, time for thoughtful, creative work is becoming more elusive. These characteristics of many positions have caused individuals across career fields to call not just for flexibility, and for security in the form of employability, but also for work that is more meaningful and satisfying (Curry, 2003).

Conclusions

Similar to their counterparts in other professions, the needs of faculty members today include flexibility, security, and work that is satisfying. A top priority for faculty members are policies that provide a real increase in flexibility. Programs aimed primarily at easing personal responsibilities so that faculty members can work more hours will lead only to increased frustration for many. The "ideal worker" is no longer the norm, and employers across economic sectors have not yet fully come to terms with the implications of this change. If academic institutions respond to dramatic changes in the workforce and workplace only with simple programs, such as take-out dinners and after-hours child care, they will continue to find that many women and a growing number of men are unable to establish a satisfactory balance between professional and personal life and are thus unable to produce their best work.

Although many colleges and universities already offer some services designed to address the needs of today's workers, the heart of the problem remains: many workers still find it difficult physically, mentally, and emotionally to manage all their competing responsibilities. Today's workers face multiple, complex demands on their time; addressing this reality through workplace policies and programs will require substantial thought, creativity, and commitment. This is a complex problem, one that is difficult for society, corporations, colleges and universities, and individuals to resolve. How can we successfully combine changing workplace demands and changing demographics?

We address this question in Parts II and III of this book.

CHAPTER THREE

FACULTY APPOINTMENTS AND FACULTY MEMBERS
Diversification, Growth, and Diversity

Faculty members and faculty work are the heart and thus the health of every college and university. Concern for the well-being and productivity of the faculty is a permanent and central issue for higher education institutions striving to meet societal needs and mandates, even as they are confronted with the same rapid changes and shifting expectations that confront other American institutions. But the question of what, exactly, constitutes the faculty has changed greatly over recent decades, a change now requiring us to understand who faculty members are, what kinds of academic appointments they fill, and how their priorities for working environments have changed. Only with this understanding are institutional leaders in a position to reconceptualize whether all faculty members have the support they need to do their best work and whether colleges and universities are benefiting to the greatest extent possible from the intellectual capital that each faculty member possesses.

This chapter specifically describes the growth and increasing diversification of faculty members and faculty appointments in the last half of the twentieth century. Whereas tenure was the coin of the realm in the early twentieth century, now only 27 percent of all new faculty appointments, and 56 percent of new full-time faculty appointments, are in tenure-track positions (U.S. Department of Education, 2004). What was once a predominantly homogeneous and tenured workforce is now a highly diverse workforce in which the majority of faculty members occupy non-tenure-bearing positions.

Chapter Four describes the major challenges within each of the three types of faculty appointments in use today. Chapter Five completes our examination of faculty members and faculty appointments by looking at the current overall attractiveness of an academic career, and the satisfaction and stress levels of these diverse faculty members.

Academic workplaces and employment systems have evolved over time. In the early twentieth century, when tenure was widely adopted as the predominant employment model for the academic career, it was the culmination of a period of growth and development in the American professoriate that had begun in the nineteenth century. Tenure served the needs of colleges and universities at that time. Now, however, tenure as the ideal employment model for academe is increasingly questioned and challenged, and American higher education as a whole is vastly different today from what it was in the early twentieth century. Colleges and universities now face the challenge of ensuring that academic appointments, policies, and practices match the diversity of people and tasks that characterize the profession today. To meet society's priorities and retain global competitiveness, institutions must change in order to successfully recruit and retain the faculty they need.

DIVERSIFICATION IN ACADEMIC APPOINTMENTS

This chapter's discussion of the increasing diversification in academic appointments begins by briefly tracing the development of tenure over the past two centuries as the standard employment model for the academic profession, in order to clarify tenure's continued central role in the American academy today. The focus then turns to the shift, in recent years, from tenure-track appointments to a variety of academic appointments without tenure.

TENURE AS THE MODEL FOR THE ACADEMIC PROFESSION: A BRIEF HISTORICAL OVERVIEW

The American academic profession had its roots in the medieval European universities, where the idea that universities are self-governing collegial communities of scholars was first established.

Young scholars returning from doctoral study at the German research universities brought with them a vision of scholarship as specialized research, a vision that influenced the establishment of American research universities. This European vision of scholarship was augmented by the passage of the Morrill Land Grant Act during the Civil War, which introduced the uniquely American concept of land-grant colleges that provide service to the nation and prepare students for leadership and participation in a democratic society (Geiger, 1999).

With the passage of the Morrill Act, the number of college and university faculty members increased dramatically. Those in land-grant colleges became state government employees who enjoyed employment rights under state law. As state employees, faculty members at land-grant institutions, such as the University of Wisconsin in the 1870s and Cornell University in the 1880s, began to subdivide professorial ranks into assistant, associate, and full, and they codified the procedures for advancement in rank and for the probationary period prior to advancement to tenure (O'Neil and White, 2002).

Discipline-based departments became the foundation of scholarly allegiance and political power, and the focal point for the definition of faculty as professionals (Rice, 1986). The doctoral degree was required for entry into the profession, and publication became the path to promotion for professors. The tendency toward disciplinary specialization also led to

> a culture, even an ethics of fierce independence. . . . While constantly, and even obsessively, judging the work of their fellow specialists, scholars were increasingly insisting on not being judged by anyone else. . . . Faculties everywhere fought for academic freedom and insisted on the institutional corollary of life tenure [Damrosch, 1995, p. 34].

In 1915, the American Association of University Professors (AAUP) was formed. American professors, with their traditional right to freedom of expression, adopted the German concepts of *lernfreiheit* and *lehrfreiheit* (the freedom to study, teach, and advance unpopular ideas publicly), labeled them "academic freedom," and added the concept of continuous employment contracts to safeguard professorial freedom of expression and economic security

(Rudolph, 1990). With the endorsement by college presidents and learned societies of the AAUP's 1940 statement on principles of academic freedom and tenure (American Association of University Professors, 2001b), tenure became the model for employment in the academic profession (O'Neill and White, 2002).

The passage of the GI Bill in 1944, the rise of federal sponsorship of research in American universities to meet national security needs after the war, the mushrooming of student enrollments caused in part by a tidal wave of new community college students, and increasing state support of higher education—together these have produced a transformation of higher education characterized by Jencks and Riesman as the "Academic Revolution" (cited in Geiger, 1999, p. 63). By 1960, research had become a major federal enterprise, with the federal government paying for 70 percent of all university research. Federal funds also provided 20 percent of the operating income of colleges and universities, and 25 percent of the costs of construction on campuses was financed by funds borrowed from Washington. Federal funds also opened the doors of college to new students through federal student aid programs (Rudolph, 1990, p. 490). Between 1945 and 1975, enrollment increased by more than 500 percent, to 11,000,000 students (Cohen, 1998, p. 196).

During this period of expansion, academic professionals enjoyed unprecedented prestige and status. From 1953 to 1962, the occupation of professor rose from seventh to third place in Gallup polls assessing the attractiveness of certain professions, a ranking it held until 1973 (Rice, 1996b). With a shortage of teachers and researchers in almost every field, the academic job market became a seller's market, in which individual professors negotiated premium salaries and the average academic salary improved significantly. Ready employment and rapid career advancement were expected, and mobility among institutions was fairly easy. Institutions awarded early tenure, lowered teaching loads, and increased salaries and fringe benefits to entice new recruits or retain local stars. Professors with significant research funding built their small empires within institutions. It was indeed a golden age for faculty.

At the height of the mid-1960s affluence and expansion in higher education, a consensus emerged regarding what it meant to be a professional academic. Rice (1986) labels this consensus (based on the context of the research university) "the assumptive world of the academic professional":

- Research was the central professional endeavor and focus of academic life.
- Quality in the profession was maintained by peer review and professional autonomy.
- The pursuit of knowledge was understood to be best organized by discipline within departments; professional rewards and mobility accrued to those who persisted in their specializations.
- Reputations were established through national and international associations.

This consensus guided the careers of a new generation of faculty members hired in the 1960s and 1970s. These faculty began retiring during the 1990s, precipitating an unprecedented generational shift (Altbach, 1999). Simultaneously, there was an acceleration in those changes in conditions in higher education that had begun in the late 1970s. With slowing enrollments and worsening financial circumstances, the age of affluence was over, but its assumptions regarding academic professionals and careers continued. Clark (1987) describes the result:

> The greatest paradox of academic work is that most professors teach most of the time, and large proportions of them teach all the time, but teaching is not the activity most rewarded by the academic profession or valued by the system at large. Trustees and administrators in one sector after another praise teaching, but reward research. The paradox indicates that things are broken and should be fixed [pp. 98–99].

By 1975, pressures on colleges and universities to adapt and survive had intensified, and administrators and trustees began to search for new academic personnel policies as part of the solution to a wide range of difficulties (Bowen and Schuster, 1986). The use of part-time faculty accelerated. Faculty salaries reached their peak in 1972–1973 and then tumbled with respect to the salaries of other occupational groups (Bowen and Schuster, 1986). Faculty in Massachusetts and California saw actual salary cuts in the 1970s and the early-1980s recession; in other states, salaries were frozen (Altbach, 1999). The spread of faculty unionism, from 5,200 faculty members in 23 institutions in 1966 to 87,000 in 311 institutions by 1979, led observers to question the need for tenure (Chait and

Ford, 1982). Job security could be guaranteed by union contracts, and state and federal laws now ensured academic freedom. By 1985, unionization had spread to over 700 campuses and over 25 percent of the faculty. Today, 25 percent of all institutions of higher education have some faculty represented by a union, a group encompassing 26 percent of all full-time faculty and 20 percent of all part-time faculty (Berger, Kirshstein, and Rowe, 2001).

GROWTH IN ALTERNATIVE ACADEMIC APPOINTMENTS

Despite these changing conditions, academics value tenure, and tenure remains the prototype of the ideal academic career. Nevertheless, changes in the nature of faculty work, financially lean times, increasing enrollments, and a greater need for a flexible workforce have led institutions to diversify their faculty appointments. Although the number of faculty members has roughly doubled since the end of the period of affluence and growth (around 1975), proportionally fewer faculty members now occupy tenure-track or tenured appointments. Slowly, but inexorably, institutions have migrated from tenure-eligible to non-tenure-eligible appointments that do not have the academic freedom or job security associated with tenure. The academic profession has become a mosaic of different positions and career tracks in highly diverse institutions. On most campuses, however, academic employment policies, rewards, and development opportunities continue to reflect tenure as the normative employment model for the academic profession.

In the early years of the twenty-first century, the total number of faculty members had reached 1,175,000, but only 632,000, or 54 percent, were in full-time faculty positions. Figure 3.1 shows the growth of the faculty over time, for full-time and part-time faculty, from 1960 to 2003.

Accompanying the growth in the numbers of faculty members was the movement away from full-time employment to part-time positions, as seen in Figure 3.2.

The decline in the percentage of full-time faculty has been accompanied by a rise in new types of faculty appointments outside the tenure system (see Figure 3.3).

Figure 3.1. Growth of American Faculty, 1960–2003

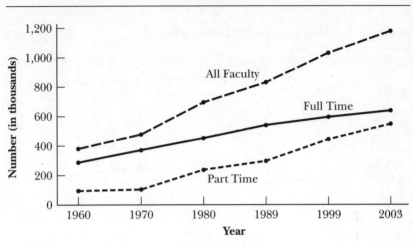

Source: U.S. Department of Education, National Center for Education Statistics, 2004.

Figure 3.2. Full- and Part-Time Status over Time

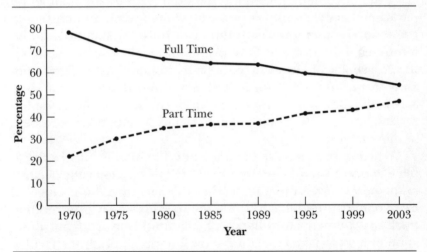

Note: Because of revised survey methods, data are not directly comparable with figures for years before 1987.

Source: U.S. Department of Education, 2004.

FIGURE 3.3. TENURE OVER TIME

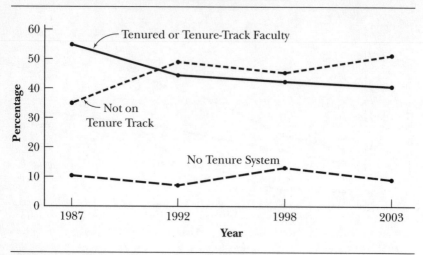

Sources: U.S. Department of Education, National Center for Education Statistics, 1988, 1993, 1999, 2004.

Taken together, these trends toward increasing the number of part-time faculty members (most of whom are not appointed to the tenure track) and the number of full-time faculty in non-tenure-eligible positions have inevitably resulted in a decline in the percentage of faculty in tenure-track appointments. This trend away from full-time tenure-eligible appointments is occurring across all types of institutions and disciplines, as shown in Tables 3.1 and 3.2 (note that only full-time faculty members are included in these tables).

When part-timers are included and the total faculty by discipline is arrayed as full-time-equivalent (FTE) positions, the decline in the percentage of tenure-bearing FTE faculty positions is even more obvious (see Table 3.3). These two shifts—away from tenure-track appointments for full-time faculty, and away from full–time appointments—taken together, show how dramatically the faculty profile has changed.

Faculty members today occupy many different faculty appointments, with different configurations and tasks, a picture that calls to mind the description of the professoriate first offered by Clark

TABLE 3.1. TENURE BY INSTITUTIONAL TYPE OVER TIME,
IN PERCENTAGES, 1987 AND 2003 (FULL-TIME FACULTY ONLY)

	1987		2003	
Type of Institution	Tenured/ Tenure-Track Faculty	Non-Tenure-Track Faculty/ No Tenure System	Tenured/ Tenure-Track Faculty	Non-Tenure-Track Faculty/ No Tenure System
All	79.4	20.6	68.1	31.9
Research	84.9	15.1	67.5	32.5
Doctoral	81.0	19.0	64.8	35.2
Comprehensive	86.5	13.5	78.1	21.9
Private liberal arts	73.8	26.2	66.8	33.2
Public two-year	68.7	31.3	64.2	35.8

Sources: U.S. Department of Education, National Center for Education Statistics, 1988, 2004.

(1987) in his book *The Academic Life: Small Worlds, Different Worlds.* Although tenure remains the commonly defined ideal of academic employment, faculty appointments have clearly diversified, and the faculty members who fill them are more diverse as well.

GROWTH IN NUMBER AND DIVERSITY OF FACULTY MEMBERS

The tremendous growth of the entire American higher education system over time provides a useful context for appreciating the increasing diversity of faculty members themselves (see Table 3.4). As Table 3.4 shows, from the end of the eighteenth century to the beginning of the twenty-first, the higher education enterprise grew from an estimated eleven institutions with 141 faculty members to well over one million faculty members in more than four thousand institutions. The more than sevenfold increase in the number of faculty members just since 1940, when tenure was widely endorsed by the higher education community as the model for faculty employment, is representative of the enormous changes that American higher education and its faculty members have undergone.

TABLE 3.2. TENURE BY DISCIPLINE OVER TIME,
IN PERCENTAGES, 1987 AND 2003 (FULL-TIME FACULTY ONLY)

Discipline	1987		2003	
	Tenured/ Tenure-Track Faculty	Non-Tenure-Track Faculty/ No Tenure System	Tenured/ Tenure-Track Faculty	Non-Tenure-Track Faculty/ No Tenure System
Agriculture and home economics	85.8	14.2	71.3	28.7
Business	78.1	21.9	74.1	25.9
Education	82.4	17.6	60.1	40.0
Engineering	91.2	8.8	79.6	20.4
Fine arts	82.3	17.7	70.3	29.7
Health sciences	72.9	27.1	50.3	49.7
Humanities	84.1	15.9	73.6	26.4
Natural sciences	87.3	12.7	72.9	27.1
Social sciences	89.3	10.7	78.6	21.4
All other fields	80.3	19.7	63.9	36.1
All	79.4	20.6	68.1	31.9

Sources: U.S. Department of Education, National Center for Education Statistics, 1988, 2004.

But growth alone does not necessitate strategic reassessment of the academic workplace and academic work. Today, faculty members as individuals are far more diverse in their demographic characteristics and lifestyles than they were just a few decades ago. This diversity among faculty members affects their employment priorities and needs and, ultimately, their employment decisions. To be more specific, the increasing diversity of faculty members has important implications for their integration into their campuses, for their ability to create an acceptable balance between their work and personal lives, and for their satisfaction with their academic careers.

TABLE 3.3. TENURE BY DISCIPLINE
(ALL FACULTY, FULL TIME AND PART TIME) BY PERCENTAGE FTE

	1987		2003	
	Tenured/ Tenure- Track Faculty	Non-Tenure- Track Faculty/ No Tenure System	Tenured/ Tenure- Track Faculty	Non-Tenure- Track Faculty/ No Tenure System
Agriculture and home economics	77.4	22.6	51.4	48.6
Business	55.3	44.7	37.7	62.3
Education	63.3	36.7	29.5	70.5
Engineering	73.0	26.9	57.8	42.2
Fine arts	47.2	52.8	34.8	65.2
Health sciences	58.5	41.5	33.6	66.4
Humanities	65.3	34.8	41.3	58.8
Natural sciences	69.3	30.7	47.5	52.5
Social sciences	72.2	27.8	50.9	49.1
All other fields	54.9	45.1	34.0	66.0
All	54.7	45.3	40.3	59.7

Sources: U.S. Department of Education, National Center for Education Statistics, 1988, 2004.

FACULTY DIVERSITY BY GENDER

One of the most significant demographic changes for faculty is the increasing presence of women. From 1969 to 2003, the presence of women grew from 20 percent to 44 percent of new faculty members (those in their first six years of full-time employment) and from 15 percent to 34 percent of senior faculty (those with more than seven years of full-time employment) (Finkelstein and Schuster, 2001; U.S. Department of Education, 2004).

This rise in the number of women faculty members is very likely to continue in the foreseeable future because women are

TABLE 3.4. OVERALL GROWTH IN FACULTY MEMBERS, 1790–2003

	1790	1869–1870	1939–1940	1959–1960	1979–1980	2002–2003
U.S. population[a]	3,929,214	38,558,371	131,669,275	179,323,175	226,545,805	288,173,000
Number of students[b]	1,050	52,286	1,494,203	3,639,847	11,569,899	16,611,711
Number of faculty	141	5,553	146,929	380,554	675,000	1,138,734
Number of institutions	11	250	1,708	2,004	3,152	4,168
Number of degrees awarded[c]	240	9,372	203,768	476,704	1,330,244	1,987,982
Funds[d]	—[e]	14,000	715,211	5,785,537	58,519,982	197,973,236[f]

[a] U.S. population based on April census data.

[b] Students based on fall enrollment.

[c] Includes data only on undergraduate and graduate students.

[d] Funds reported in thousands.

[e] No data available.

[f] Funds reflect 1995–1996 data (current fund revenues of degree-granting institutions), the most recent available.

Sources: Cohen, 1998; U.S. Department of Education, 2001, 2002, 2004.

being awarded an increasing share of doctoral degrees. In 2003, for the first time, women earned 51 percent of all doctorates awarded to U.S. citizens and 45 percent of all doctoral degrees awarded. The proportion of doctorates earned by women has grown steadily across all broad fields of study. Women earned 50 percent of the doctorates awarded in the life sciences, 55 percent in the social sciences, 52 percent in the humanities, 66 percent in education, 46 percent in business and other professional fields, and 27 percent and 18 percent, respectively, in the physical sciences and engineering (Hoffer et al., 2005).

Nevertheless, although the percentage of women faculty is increasing, women's status in the profession is not equal to that of their male colleagues. Men are more likely than women to be full professors (36 percent versus 18 percent) and to be tenured (53 percent versus 38 percent). Men also receive higher base salaries ($73,433 versus $57,699) (U.S. Department of Education, 2004) and are less likely than women to be found in non-tenure-track positions (see Figure 3.4).

FIGURE 3.4. GENDER AND TENURE STATUS, 2003

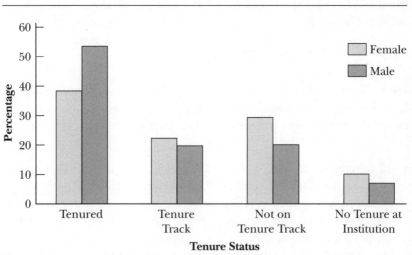

Source: U.S. Department of Education, National Center for Education Statistics, 2004.

Differences between men and women by tenure and rank also vary by discipline because only recently has there been an increase in women Ph.D. recipients in fields such as engineering and the hard sciences. They also reflect the inflexibility of the tenure-track career, which proves difficult for many women because they usually assume primary responsibility for household tasks and child care in addition to their professional responsibilities. Taken together, differences between men and women in types of appointments, rank, and compensation raise questions about gender equity in the profession and about the attractiveness of an academic career for women.

FACULTY DIVERSITY BY RACE AND CITIZENSHIP

The last fifteen years have seen some increase in the number of faculty who are people of color, either native born or citizens who were born outside the United States. (See Table 3.5.) However, the percentage of people of color receiving doctorates has grown substantially in the past twenty years, and an astonishing 64 percent in just the past ten years for U.S. citizens. In 2004, the total number of doctoral-degree recipients who were members of racial or ethnic minority groups constituted 20 percent of U.S. citizens who earned doctorates. African Americans earned the most doctorates (1,869), followed by Asian Americans (1,449) and Hispanic Americans (1,177) (Hoffer et. al., 2005).

Nevertheless, racially and ethnically diverse faculty members are being hired into faculty positions at a rate that is only slowly increasing; they are also being hired predominantly into certain types of colleges and universities. For example:

- 42 percent of all Hispanic and Hispanic American, 40 percent of all Native American, and 37 percent of African American faculty teach at public two-year colleges; only 30 percent of white, non-Hispanic faculty and 15 percent of Asian or Asian American faculty teach at these institutions
- 60 percent of Asian and Asian American faculty teach at research and doctoral universities compared to 25 percent of Native Americans and 25 percent of African Americans (U.S.

TABLE 3.5. TENURE STATUS BY RACE (FULL- AND PART-TIME FACULTY), 1988 AND 2003

	1988			2003		
	Tenured Faculty (%)	*On Tenure Track (%)*	*Not on Tenure Track/ No Tenure System (%)*	*Tenured Faculty (%)*	*On Tenure Track (%)*	*Not on Tenure Track/ No Tenure System (%)*
American Indian or Alaska Native	0.7	0.4	0.9	1.1	1.2	1.6
Asian and/or Pacific Islander	3.3	7.4	3.5	7.6	12.1	5.5
Black/African American (Non-Hispanic)	2.6	4.1	3.4	5.0	7.5	5.9
Hispanic	2.7	2.2	2.2	2.9	4.8	3.4
White (Non-Hispanic)	90.7	85.8	90.1	83.4	74.5	83.7

Sources: U.S. Department of Education, National Center for Education Statistics, 1988, 2004.

Department of Education, National Center for Education
Statistics, 2004)

It is to be hoped that the increase, from 1988 to 2003, in the
number of tenure-track faculty members who are people of color
indicates a trend toward a faculty that is more diverse. To date,
academe has not attracted and does not benefit as much as it could
from the rich diversity of qualified people who are available.

Increases in the number of international students who have
earned doctoral degrees in recent years have also enlarged the diversity of the pool of potential faculty members. This is good news
for the colleges and universities that want to recruit them, but it
also forces consideration of how to make the faculty career attractive to them when compared to other professional occupations.
Only 67 percent of recent doctoral recipients are U.S. citizens
(Hoffer et. al., 2005), and the proportion of doctoral degrees
awarded to international students by U.S. universities rose from 11
percent in 1974 to 29 percent in 2004. In fact, the growing number of doctorates awarded to international students on temporary
visas has accounted for virtually all the growth in doctoral recipients since 1974. This growth in international students who have
earned doctoral degrees in the United States could have profound
implications for the recruitment and retention of new faculty members. This is particularly true for engineering and the physical sciences, which are the most popular fields of study for international
students on temporary visas (Hoffer et. al., 2005).

In sum, entering faculty members are far more diverse today
than they were even twenty years ago. There are also more women,
more members of racial and ethnic minority groups, and more international citizens with doctoral degrees who are available across
all disciplines. As faculty members become less homogeneous, individual priorities and circumstances become more complex, and
collegiality and the sense of a common community of scholars become more difficult to develop and support.

As this chapter has described, American higher education
today is vastly different from what it was in the early twentieth century, when the concepts of academic freedom and tenure, as an
employment system perfectly suited to the academic profession,

flourished. Now, colleges and universities have diverse missions, cultures, organizations, finances, and students. In addition, they are employing increasingly diverse faculty members, many of whom occupy positions that are no longer tenure-eligible. Today's diversity of faculty members and academic appointments raises important questions about the attractiveness of the academic career to prospective and current faculty.

CHAPTER FOUR

THE ACADEMIC
PROFESSION TODAY

Diverse Appointments to
Meet Diverse Needs

A 2005 report from the National Center for Education Statistics captures how much higher education has changed in the last half century. In the fall of 2003, colleges and universities in the United States employed 1,174,000 faculty members, an increase of 60,000 faculty members since 2001. This recent increase, however, has been disproportionately in for-profit institutions, where the number of faculty members grew from 36,000 in 2001 to nearly 52,000 in 2003. And these new faculty members are not being employed in traditional faculty positions. About 630,000, or only 54 percent, were appointed to full-time positions, and 35 percent of all full-time faculty members were not in tenured or tenure-track appointments (Knapp et al., 2005).

This information reflects a restructuring of academic appointments that is well under way. Although the ideal image of the academic profession remains that of the tenured professor, faculty appointments today, as we have seen, tend toward the appointment of fewer faculty members to tenured full-time positions and toward the appointment of more faculty to positions off the tenure track or to part-time teaching positions. In the academic workplace that is emerging as a result of these changes, we see (1) a diminishing core of professionals, (2) a strong component of freelance professionals and technicians hired for specific needs, and (3) an ever-increasing group of contingent workers, a workforce very similar to Handy's shamrock concept described in Chapter One (Rice, 2004).

NEW TERMINOLOGY
FOR FACULTY APPOINTMENTS

This chapter examines the implications for faculty of these trends toward diversification in faculty appointments. It begins with tenure-track appointments—specifically, with faculty experiences and impressions during the probationary period. It then looks at faculty employment in two different types of non-tenure-track appointments.

The first of these two non-tenure-track appointments we have labeled *contract-renewable appointments.* They offer the potential for long-term employment as a faculty member as an alternative to the tenure track. These appointments are commonly associated with the phrases "off the tenure track," "no tenure system at this institution," or simply "full-time non-tenure track" ("FTNTT" in databases, texts, and reports). The second, labeled *fixed-term appointments,* are temporary in nature and are occupied predominantly by part-time faculty members. They are associated with the terms "contingent" and "temporary." Both these labels, contract renewable and fixed term, as used here, augment and replace today's commonly used terminology for non-tenure-track appointments.

The reader will note that these labels for the two different types of non-tenure-track academic appointments eliminate the time base of work as a distinguishing factor. We do not think that the time base of an appointment should be linked to the faculty member's contractual status. For example, an individual in a contract-renewable appointment might work on a 50 percent basis while another faculty member in a fixed-term appointment might begin at a 60 percent time base and then move to full-time status.

This chapter focuses on the current status of these three different appointment types: tenure-track appointments, contract-renewable appointments, and fixed-term appointments. Throughout this and later chapters, we treat the terms just introduced as interchangeable with the terminology in current use. That is, in referring to data or citing other sources, we use the terms used in those sources—therefore, in citing such sources, we refer, as necessary, to contingent or temporary faculty instead of to fixed-term appointments, and to full-time, non-tenure-track faculty (FTNTT) instead of to contract-renewable appointments. In presenting recommendations for change, however, we refer to contract-renewable appointments Stevens and fixed-term appointments because these terms, unlike some of their more conventional counterparts, do not convey negative messages about status or importance. We stress terminology here because a major theme of this book is that attention to the different career tracks in colleges and universities is an important component of what it takes to make an academic career attractive in a variety of institutions with diverse missions, and to a diverse set of potential faculty members.

TENURE-TRACK APPOINTMENTS: THE PROBATIONARY PERIOD

Cooper and Stevens (2002) suggest that the process of finding a home in the academy, settling in, and attaining tenure is much like the process of nest building for birds:

> You look for the resources that will help you at your task: twigs and leaves, people and research projects. You build slowly toward your goal. You read the weather to see what is coming, and if you are very wise, you bank the fires of your body into a small but steady blaze. You pace yourself and try not to be too dazzled by the light of a tenured position in academe. . . . Sometimes you end up on the pavement, stunned by some unexpected event [p. vii].

New faculty members in tenure-track positions are more demographically diverse than their more senior colleagues. These new faculty members are expressing concerns about, and dissatisfaction with, some aspects of the academic career (Armenti, 2004; Austin and Rice, 1998; Olsen and Near, 1994; Rice, Sorcinelli, and Austin, 2000; Tierney and Bensimon, 1996; Ward and Wolf-Wendel, 2004):

- The tenure process, with its lack of comprehensive, clear, and rational guidelines and procedures

- A perceived lack of community
- An inability to manage time, workloads, and personal as well as professional life in the face of escalating pressure to achieve tenure in a limited period of time

We examine each of these sources of dissatisfaction in the passages that follow.

TENURE-TRACK PROCESSES AND TIMELINES

New tenure-track faculty members enter their academic careers because they believe that faculty work involves autonomy, flexibility, freedom to pursue academic interests, and opportunities to serve society through education. Unfortunately, what early-career faculty members hope for does not fully match what they actually experience (Rice, 1996b; Rice, Sorcinelli, and Austin, 2000). Olsen (1993) found that satisfaction with faculty work actually declined over the first several years of a tenure-track appointment, and that this decline was accompanied by an increase in job-related stress attributed to conflicts involving time and work-life balance.

All faculty members, but especially new tenure-track faculty, face multiple demands on their time as well as high expectations for their accomplishment in teaching, research, and service. Their time at work is fragmented among diverse and conflicting priorities: students expect excellent faculty performance in the classroom; senior colleagues seek these new colleagues' participation in departmental, campus, and professional service; and new tenure-track faculty members simultaneously must produce research and scholarly work. Bailyn (1993) describes this situation as follows:

> The academic career therefore is paradoxical. Despite its advantages of independence and flexibility, it is psychologically difficult. The lack of ability to limit work, the tendency to compare oneself primarily to the exceptional giants in one's field, and the high incidence of overload make it particularly difficult for academics to find a satisfactory integration of work with private life. . . . It is the unbounded nature of the academic career that is the heart of the problem. Time is critical for professors, because there is not enough of it to do all the things their job requires: teaching, research, and institutional and professional service. It is therefore

impossible for faculty members to protect other aspects of their lives, and work tends to dominate [p. 51].

Early-career faculty have not expressed a preference for eliminating tenure, but they have reported finding the tenure process and its expectations mystifying (Rice, Sorcinelli, and Austin, 2000; Austin and Rice, 1998). Over and over again, they have made comments like "Everything is so vague, ambiguous, and illusive" or "There is no steady, reliable feedback" or "I cannot get a good read on what it takes to get tenure" (Rice, Sorcinelli, and Austin, 2000, p. 10). One new faculty member referred to the tenure process as "archery in the dark" (Rice, 1996b, p. 31). Insufficient, unfocused, and unclear feedback on performance have only served to exacerbate the lack of clarity about tenure expectations and about new faculty members' progress toward meeting them, and this kind of feedback deficit has added to their stress.

Furthermore, early-career faculty have reported being worried that the senior colleagues responsible for providing feedback and evaluation were raising or changing their expectations, or that their messages were often in conflict. Even when expectations have been clear, participants have perceived the tenure bar as being ratcheted up to a level far above that for the achievements required of the senior colleagues who would decide their fate (Rice, Sorcinelli, and Austin, 2000). Faculty do not learn until the end of the probationary period whether good has indeed been good enough (Chait, 1998, p. 5).

The early-career faculty members studied by Rice and colleagues also reported being concerned about frequently rotating department chairs, turnover in the membership of faculty personnel committees, and closed committee meetings. These structural flaws were seen as contributing to the instability and inconsistency of the tenure process. One participant commented, "The chair has a tremendous impact on the tenure decision. We changed chairs after my hire and I am bitter, upset, and frightened by the way the current chair controls and dominates the process" (Rice, Sorcinelli, and Austin, 2000, p. 11).

For many probationers, the rigidity of the tenure timeline is the most critical aspect of the tenure process (Austin and Rice, 1998). As performance expectations continue to increase, funding opportunities are decreasing, and this gap is causing greater competition for grants to support research in some fields. Academic journals' review processes and schedules often result in long delays before authors are notified about receipt of their work, much less about its acceptance, and there may be even longer delays until an accepted manuscript appears in print. Infrastructure problems can compound these external difficulties. Early-career faculty in the natural and physical sciences and in engineering who were interviewed for the Heeding New Voices project frequently discussed how delays in getting laboratory space and equipment, or funding for graduate or postdoctoral assistants, had delayed their ability to start their research. An inflexible tenure timeline can put a probationary faculty member in a serious bind and may require a peer-review committee to make a tenure decision prematurely (Rice, Sorcinelli, and Austin, 2000; Gappa, 2002).

The end result of the tenure process is that "people stagger to the end of the tenure review" (Tierney and Bensimon, 1996, p. 73). If they attain tenure, they feel relieved rather than elated. One respondent, the first to have gained tenure in his school in ten years, said, "It's been dehumanizing. . . . I'm disheartened by the whole thing"; another commented, "I've got it. I will never give it up, because I would never put my family through that again. Never" (Tierney and Bensimon, 1996, p. 73).

A senior faculty, member writing about ethics in tenure decisions, agrees with probationers' perceptions of the probationary period. He characterizes the process of denying someone tenure as not only taking away someone's job but also taking away his or her self-respect. In making recommendations to senior faculty for evenhandedness and consistency during tenure reviews, he also addresses the importance of ensuring that the quality of probationers' work is evaluated along with its quantity. He recommends that senior faculty

> reject narrow, arbitrary criteria of evaluation, including those that go by the name of "high academic standards"; we should apply our non-arbitrary criteria consistently across candidates and we should apply them to any given candidate consistently from hiring to the final probationary evaluation; we should broadly assume the trustworthiness of the candidate's apparent accomplishments unless we

have positive reason ("probable cause") to doubt them; and we should refuse to cooperate with the cruelty which so easily and so frequently becomes a part of tenure determinations. Significant pieces of evidence in favour of the candidate should be taken to nullify arguments against tenurability. In order to be successful, those who wish to argue against tenurability need to establish their case "beyond a reasonable doubt" [Hogan, 1998, p. 38].

BALANCING WORK-LIFE PRIORITIES

In addition to anticipating more straightforward and manageable tenure processes, new faculty members envision their careers as offering flexible time that they can shape and control, and sufficient time for focused thought and creativity. What they report, however, is an inability to manage their time, along with imbalances between their work and family lives (Rice, Sorcinelli, and Austin, 2000).

The problems of balancing work and family affect many faculty members, but those in the probationary period often feel these problems most keenly. And among probationary faculty members, women continue to be more heavily disadvantaged by their dual roles than men. The simple logistics of the biological clock versus the tenure clock, the physical demands of pregnancy and childbirth, the gendered nature of expectations for family obligations, and the ongoing disparity with which women take on the "second shift" of household responsibilities—all these factors contribute to the stress that women in particular experience as they try to balance work and family (Ward and Wolf-Wendel, 2004).

In general, women believe that having children before obtaining tenure is detrimental to their career prospects. In one study, 59 percent of women assistant professors who did have children reported that the time their children required was a serious threat to tenure. One respondent reported, "My colleagues are quite empathetic and understanding; however, although the chairman may understand my commitment to my family, he is not willing to acknowledge that this may affect my ability to obtain tenure on the designated time schedule" (Finkel and Olswang, 1996, p. 132).

Even with the strict timelines of the probationary period, many women decide to have children during this time, recognizing that often a woman cannot become pregnant exactly when she wants to. Women also fear that if they wait until after the tenure decision, they may exceed the time limits of their biological clocks (Armenti, 2004). Among this group of female faculty members, many feel the need to hide a pregnancy during a job interview, and to strive for a May baby to avoid interfering with teaching and upsetting their colleagues.

When dependents enter the picture, the workweek of men and women alike is affected, but not in the same manner. According to Leslie (2005), analysis of data from the National Study of Postsecondary Faculty indicates that a woman's workweek decreases in length as the number of dependents increases, but a man's workweek actually increases (see Figure 4.1).

As women's responsibilities at home increase, and as they thus become unable to devote as much time to teaching and research in general, the time that they devote specifically to research decreases markedly, whereas the time that men devote to research actually increases with dependents (see Figure 4.2). Leslie (2005, p. 10)

FIGURE 4.1. MEAN TOTAL HOURS WORKED PER WEEK
(ALL FULL-TIME FACULTY, BY NUMBER OF DEPENDENTS AND GENDER)

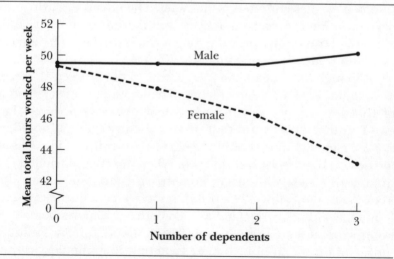

Survey data weighted to estimated population values.
Source: Leslie, 2005.

FIGURE 4.2. MEAN HOURS PER WEEK SPENT ON RESEARCH
(ALL FULL-TIME FACULTY, BY NUMBER OF DEPENDENTS AND GENDER)

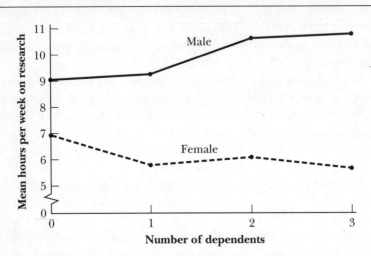

Survey data weighted to estimated population values.

Source: Leslie, 2005.

summed up these findings in this way: "The effects of having children on women's research activity, and therefore on their ability
to succeed career-wise over the long term, is marked. The effect is
clearly to women's competitive disadvantage."

Although the time that women devote to their careers decreases
as the number of their dependents increases, women's overall hours
of work per week are very high when dependents are involved. Tack
and Patitu (1992) found that women faculty who had children
worked eighty or more hours a week, with thirty-five of those hours
focused on housework and children. When the family included children under the age of three, women averaged ninety hours per
week (Tack and Patitu, 1992, p. 43). A more recent qualitative study
found that although men and women both work approximately ten
hours a day at their academic jobs, women work forty-two minutes
more, or almost an hour longer each day, than men do at their
combined work and caregiving responsibilities (Colbeck, Weaver,
and Burkum, 2004).

Given these demanding hours, a very sizable proportion of women faculty members opt to avoid the dual challenge of work and family by deciding not to have children. In fact, as we mentioned in Chapter Two, only one out of three women who accept tenure-track positions before having children ever goes on to become a mother (Mason and Goulden, 2004). Moreover, in order to successfully manage their careers, women choose to have smaller families than they would have liked: in one university system, 38 percent of the tenure-track women who were surveyed indicated that they had fewer children than they had wanted, by comparison with 18 percent of men who gave that response (Mason and Goulden, 2004). As Ward and Wolf-Wendel (2004) have observed, some women faculty also seek to lessen the dual challenge of work and family by working at non-research-intensive institutions, or by securing non-tenure-track positions.

Not only do women choose to have smaller families than they would like in order to manage their faculty careers, they are also less likely than their male counterparts to be married, or to be living in committed relationships. According to data from the U.S. Department of Education, National Center for Education Statistics (2004), 30 percent of women who are tenured, and 32 percent of those who are on the tenure track, are not married, by comparison with 13 percent of tenured men and 21 percent of men in tenure-track appointments.

The traditional academic career leading toward tenure continues to be one that is based on a male model and on men's normative paths. It is based on an assumption of ideal workers for whom the normative career path is free from competing family responsibilities because those are handled by someone else. As a result, of younger women (under the age of forty) on the tenure track who have invested heavily in the success of an academic career, 54 percent report having no dependents, by comparison with only 34 percent of their male counterparts (Leslie and Janson, 2005). On the basis of all these findings, Leslie and Janson (2005) conclude that having dependents disadvantages women and advantages men, and they recommend that institutions look for nondiscriminatory ways (that is, correction of the situation should not cause reverse discrimination) to compensate women for the competitive disadvantages they experience that are associated with marriage and a family. Certainly, the fact that married women with children under the age of six are 50 percent less likely to enter a tenure-track position than are married men with children under six, and, in general, that the women who do are enter a tenure-track position are 20 percent less likely than men to achieve tenure (Wolfinger, Mason, and Goulden, 2004), indicates a discriminatory, disparate impact on women caused by the strict probationary-period timeline.

Given the additional challenges that many women face in the probationary period, it is not surprising that women in full-time faculty positions are less satisfied than men with their workloads, salaries, opportunities for advancement, and job security. They report greater work-related stress, and married tenure-track women are also more than twice as likely as their married male colleagues (8 percent versus 3 percent) to become divorced at some point during the probationary period (Wolfinger, Mason, and Goulden, 2004).

As we have seen, men and women alike can find it very difficult to balance work and family responsibilities during the probationary period, but women tend to struggle more with the combined responsibility of an academic career and a family. This reality has important implications for colleges and universities that are concerned about recruitment and retention of new tenure-track faculty members. Rather than accepting the heavy demands of the probationary period, many women are opting instead for non-tenure-track positions that allow them to devote more time to personal life but that often significantly limit them professionally. Given the increasing number of women now receiving doctoral degrees in all fields, this situation will impede institutions' ability to recruit tenure-track faculty and may lead women advocates to make charges of unfair, discriminatory treatment unless the system is changed. (These issues are explored more fully in the recommendations in Chapters Nine and Eleven.)

TIME CONSTRAINTS FACING ALL PROBATIONARY FACULTY MEMBERS

Women face unique challenges in pursuing an academic career, but men are certainly not insulated from meeting the challenges of the probationary period while also meeting family responsibilities. According to Norrell and Norrell (1996), in the mid-1990s the majority of applicants for faculty positions had partners who had professional careers, and who expected to continue in them, as did 80 percent of people who were already faculty members (Didion, 1996). Nationally, 35 percent of male and 40 percent of female faculty members have partners who are also faculty members (Astin and Milem, 1997). Although women most often have primary responsibility for the home and children, many men also have household and child care responsibilities. The situation is even more complex because men and women alike continue to invest more and more time in their work. And, in dual-career couples where both partners are faculty members and are in commuting relationships, the strain on both partners accelerates.

Nationally, the total hours that full-time faculty members work every week at their institutions have increased. The proportion of faculty members reporting that they work more than fifty-five hours a week has grown by 238 percent since 1972 (from 13 percent in 1972 to 44 percent in 2003), with women and men showing similar increases in hours worked (Schuster and Finkelstein, 2006; U.S. Department of Education, 2004). Although long working hours and imbalance between personal and professional life are problems for many tenured faculty members, probationary faculty in particular feel strongly that their time and attention are spread too thin across too many conflicting duties. In the Heeding New Voices study, very few of the probationers who were making choices about how to spend their time were satisfied with their choices (Rice, Sorcinelli, and Austin, 2000). One probationer, erring on the side of work, commented, "I have two kids, ages 9 and 11. I don't have time to even look at their homework. I'm up at 6 A.M. and gone, back at 11 P.M. All I have time to do is sleep" (Gappa and MacDermid, 1997, p. 8). Other probationary faculty members have expressed concern that finding time for families would jeopardize their careers: "What this means is you are making compromises when not everyone is making them. You are in a horse race with others, and it is very, very costly to start making those compromises" (Wilson, 1995, p. A24). Other faculty have reported working all the time: "I take Friday afternoons off—they're for myself, and I get Sunday mornings for my family. Other than that I work every day" (Tierney and Bensimon, 1996, p. 60).

In sum, faculty members, particularly those with responsibility for families, are experiencing difficulties and stress with the time constraints of the traditional six-year probationary period for tenure. Faculty leaders, institutions, and collective bargaining associations need to rethink these timelines for the probationary period in order to ensure that academic careers remain attractive to new faculty.

Membership in a Collegial Community

One more challenge with respect to the probationary period is the lack of collegiality that some tenure-track faculty now experience. Early-career faculty members want to pursue their careers in a community where collaboration is respected and encouraged, and where interaction and talk about one's ideas, work, and the institution are common. Instead, they sometimes experience isolation, separation, fragmentation, loneliness, competition, and occasionally incivility. Issues of community and collegiality are particularly keen for women and faculty of color:

> I speak to people. I say "Good morning." And some people ignore that. . . . Maybe it's this region of the country. I've even been approaching faculty and making eye contact and they would turn away . . . so I don't know if it's the city, or the college, or my being African American [Tierney and Bensimon, 1996, p. 121].

Other early-career faculty in the Heeding New Voices study mentioned problems and misunderstandings with senior faculty (Rice, Sorcinelli and Austin, 2000). They reported feeling that senior faculty members had limited understanding of the time pressure and obstacles that their younger colleagues faced, and that the senior faculty did not seem able to appreciate the stress involved in the conflicting demands on dual-career couples, because the older faculty had not experienced these demands themselves. Some early-career faculty also questioned whether senior faculty members had enough up-to-date information about the latest developments in their fields to be able to adequately judge their younger colleagues' work, or they worried about molding their own work to the interests of the senior faculty who ultimately would evaluate them for tenure. They also worried about other issues related to departmental life, such as feeling uncomfortable about declining requests from senior colleagues to serve on departmental committees or engaging in other time-consuming activities that would not contribute to their tenure dossiers. Barnes, Agago, and Coombs (1998), in a quantitative study supporting these qualitative findings, discovered that the two most important predictors of a faculty member's intention to leave academia were a sense of frustration over time commitments and lack of any sense of institutional community.

Women often express the most frustration with the organizational climate. Women respondents in the Heeding New Voices study reported difficulty in finding advisors or mentors among senior faculty, and they also reported working in environments where subtle discrimination caused them to struggle to be taken seriously (Rice, Sorcinelli and Austin, 2000). Johnsrud and Des Jarlais (1994) found that women faculty perceived both structural and personal discrimination. Structural discrimination occurred because of institutional failure to support gender- or ethnic-related research, alternative research methodologies, or policies for sick leave and maternity leave. Women also described incidents of personal discrimination, including sexual and racial harassment, stereotyping, and tokenism. Tierney and Bensimon (1996) suggest that the particular experiences of women who are junior professors are shaped not only by the behavior of individuals but also by the gender and power relations within a department or institution that produce behavioral patterns these researchers label "smile work" and "mom work." They define "smile work" as the act of presenting oneself in an always pleasing and agreeable way, and "mom work" as the act of engaging in roles that involve nurturing and caretaking (Tierney and Bensimon, 1996, p. 83).

The probationary faculty member who is also a member of an ethnic and racial minority group is frequently the only one in his or her department or institution. He or she may be one of only a very few in the local community as well. The faculty member in this situation may feel obligated to show good citizenship by serving on campus committees or demonstrating knowledge of and commitment to his or her cultural group. He or she may be sought out by students as an advisor, a role model, or an authority on a particular racial or ethnic group and may be expected to promote an ethic of diversity on campus.

As one African American woman described the situation, "I am asked to speak a lot, to participate in things, and I think it's because they need an African American . . . so that gets a little bit tiring but I have not said 'no' too much," and another woman of color commented, "I was asked to be present at a number of interviews, partly because I was a junior minority woman, and they didn't want those interviews to have only senior white men" (Tierney and Bensimon, 1996, p. 116). Tierney and Bensimon (1996) use the labels "cultural taxation" and "hidden workload" to characterize this kind of required, and substantial, extra effort. Split appointments only compound and aggravate these problems. For example, a Chicana faculty member said, "The major problem, which is Major with a capital M, is that I was hired to teach Ethnic Studies, but Ethnic Studies is not a department, so my appointment is one hundred percent in [an established department], and it is a tug-of-war between how much time I give to each" (Tierney and Bensimon, 1996, p. 113). Nieves-Squires (1992) (cited in Aguirre, 2000, p. 42) attributes the scarcity of Hispanic women in academia to the fact that there are so few of them to begin with, causing them to be

> overburdened by an inordinate amount of student advisees—both those who are formally assigned and those who gravitate toward their doors. . . . The sheer effort of trying to do well by the students while at the same time routing an academic career that encompasses scholarly research, excellent teaching and committee participation ensures that very few Hispanas remain within the academic ranks" [Aguirre, 2000, p. 42].

Minority faculty in predominantly white institutions, confronted with racist remarks in classrooms or graffiti on their office doors, may also find that their colleagues are not necessarily sympathetic or helpful. As Cooper and Stevens (2002, p. 119) point out, "To perceive oneself as an exception, different, unique or extraordinary . . . is to suffer a loss of identity." One woman, alone or with limited peer support, characterized her predominantly white environment with this comment: "I still feel myself a stranger. That is, I am comfortable but not at home" (Cooper and Stevens, 2002,

p. 122). Hughes (2005) describes the phenomenon known among African American scholars in academe as "Racial Battle Fatigue," or "RBF," the physical ailments and mental incapacity spurred by racist attacks and microaggressions endured in classrooms or off campus, in addition to ordinary job-related, day-to-day stress based in racism. These aggressions take a toll and can result in acute stress, similar to that experienced by soldiers in war.

Bonner (2004) lists four problems that sum up the difficulties of being a faculty member of color on the tenure track at a predominantly white institution:

1. Feeling the need to prove one's intellectual competence over and over again
2. Having difficulty making connections and gaining access to established colleagues, mentors, and professional networks
3. Having to switch identities and roles rapidly between two disparate worlds, the white working environment and that of minority students and one's minority community
4. Feeling unwelcome

Given these views, it is perhaps not surprising that Trower and Chait (2002) find the unaccommodating culture of academe to be one of the biggest obstacles in the recruitment and retention of women as well as racial and ethnic minorities:

> Despite earning doctorates in ever-increasing numbers, many women and persons of color are eschewing academic careers altogether or exiting the academy prior to the tenure decision because both groups experience social isolation, a chilly environment, bias, and hostility. Their common concerns include their limited opportunities to participate in departmental and institutional decision making; excessive and "token" committee assignments; infrequent occasions to assume leadership positions or achieve an institutional presence; research that's trivialized and discounted; lack of mentors; and little guidance about the academic workplace or the tenure process. As a result, women doctoral students are less likely than men to want to be faculty members, and persons of color are less likely than whites to desire an academic career. Not surprisingly, both groups are less satisfied in the academic workplace than

white males. More women and minorities than white men leave
the academy in the course of the typically seven-year probationary
period.

Not only are these findings disappointing, they are also a particular cause of concern for those seeking to hire and retain excellent
faculty on the tenure track.

Although individuals must learn how to survive the academy
during their probationary years, the academy itself must be committed to the growth and development of all its participants. Interested and sensitive department chairs can be especially helpful
to new women and faculty of color as they strive to assimilate themselves into the academic culture and career.

To summarize, tenure-track probationary faculty find that their
commitment to an academic career is accompanied by deep concerns about some of its fundamental aspects: an incomprehensi-
ble tenure system, rigid timelines, lack of community, excessive
workloads, and inability to achieve an integrated professional and
personal life. These individuals face mounting expectations within
strict time constraints. As the probationary faculty becomes more
diverse, individual members' priorities and circumstances become
more complex, and community becomes more difficult both to attain and to sustain. These changes are causing the traditional faculty career to become less attractive to some individuals.

CONTRACT-RENEWABLE APPOINTMENTS

The majority of faculty members teaching in American colleges and
universities today are not on the tenure track; either their contracts
explicitly state that tenure is not an option or they teach in institutions that do not grant tenure. This is a dramatic shift in the nature
of the faculty career. In 1975, 58 percent of all faculty members
were in tenure-track positions (Baldwin and Chronister, 2001). Now,
32 percent of all full-time faculty members have contract-renewable
appointments, and 46 percent of all faculty members are part-timers
(U.S. Department of Education, National Center for Education Statistics, 2004). In research and doctoral degree–granting universities, the use of full-time non-tenure-track, commonly known as
FTNTT, appointments increased by 88 percent from 1975 to 1998,

and tenure-track appointments decreased by 9 percent (Bland, Center, Finstad, Risbey, and Staples, 2006). (The terms "contract-renewable" and "non-tenure-eligible" are used interchangeably in this chapter to correctly reflect the source of the data.)

To some extent, issues of cost and flexibility are driving this sea change in academic appointments, and colleges and universities are increasingly using contract-renewable appointments for a variety of reasons. With the end of mandatory retirement, the typical thirty-year career as a tenured faculty member is now expanding. FTNTT faculty appointments represent a more flexible alternative to tenured appointments and are useful in hiring professionals with special expertise who would not necessarily seek or be qualified for tenure-track positions. According to Gappa (1996, p. 1), contract-renewable appointments

> achieve more continuity in academic programs than part-time faculty in temporary appointments, or staff entire areas of the curriculum, teach specialized areas of the curriculum or start experimental programs, or focus on one particular area of faculty responsibility such as teaching, research or clinical practice, or add significant experience and expertise available only outside academe.

In addition, FTNTT appointments can provide faculty members who have been part-timers with opportunities to teach on a full-time basis. In response to concerns about excessive use of part-timers, some colleges and universities have decided to convert part-time positions to continuing full-time, renewable appointments with benefits.

Contract-renewable appointments are most common in research universities and professional schools, where they are seen as alternatives to tenured positions in situations where making a tenure commitment is not considered feasible (Trower, 2000). For example, Saint Louis University's policy for FTNTT appointments states:

> Non-tenure-track faculty members function on a full-time basis in clinical service or supervision, in research positions supported by grants or contracts from organizations outside the university, as aviation specialists, in research, clinical or teaching positions whose

long-term existences are not assured, or under other conditions
that make the attainment of tenure . . . a practical impossibility
[Trower, 2002, p. 117].

Clinical positions are common in the professional schools. For
example, clinical faculty in law schools supervise students who are
handling law cases in practicum experiences (Gappa, 1996). Schools
of education use clinical positions in response to a variety of state
initiatives such as changes in teacher- and administrator-certification
paths or public pressure to solve pressing societal problems in the
nation's schools, for example, violence, slumping test scores, and at-
trition (Hearn and Anderson, 2001). Schools of business hire senior
"professors of practice," that is, people with extensive practical experience in their professions, to augment tenure-track faculty in such
curricular areas as accounting, where knowledge of practice is critical (Gappa, 1996).

The 112 U.S. medical schools have used contract-renewable appointments for years, primarily in clinical positions. In 1981, 68
percent of all clinical faculty occupied tenure-track positions; by
1997, this total had declined to only 46 percent in medical schools
(Jones and Gold, 2001). The rise in contract-renewable positions
has been accompanied by changes in the compensation structure,
both to reward risk and performance and to account for limits to
the tenure guarantee in tenure-track positions. These changes were
essential to medical schools' survival because of the impact of
changes in Medicare funding and other sources of support. By
1998–1999, only 20 percent of revenues in public medical schools,
and 8 percent of revenues in private medical schools, came from
institutional sources, such as tuition, state appropriations, and endowment income combined (Jones and Gold, 2001).

THREE DIFFERENT EMPLOYMENT MODELS

Baldwin and Chronister (2001) looked at institutional policies governing the appointment of FTNTT faculty members and the extent
to which these faculty members were integrated into their academic
communities. They summarize the differences they found among
contract-renewable appointments by conceptualizing three different models that illustrate the continuum of employment policies

and statuses currently used for such appointments. These models are briefly described below to illustrate the different types of appointments used currently for contract-renewable faculty.

The Alternative-Career Model

This model is designed to be a viable alternative to tenure. Faculty members whose appointments fit this model have equivalent credentials and similar employment conditions to those of their tenure-track colleagues. They also have comparable status, respect, and influence. They tend not to be interested in tenure-track positions because they are fully employable in their professions, or they have lifestyle concerns that preclude a tenure-track appointment (Gappa, 1996). One full-time non-tenure-track professor commented:

> I was a tenured professor. . . . I was well situated. My wife was an academic, we had young kids. My wife got an offer. I gave [tenure] up. I came here as a research scientist. . . . I renovated the laboratory and got three NIH grants. Then I got a three-year appointment as a professor without tenure. My wife was tenured. They said "What do we do with him?" They gave me an endowed chair [Gappa, 1996, p. 26].

Faculty members in alternative-career appointments are hired as clinical or research faculty, professors of practice, or distinguished senior lecturers. Typically, they enjoy the perquisites of tenure-track faculty, including full voting rights, and are fully integrated into their departments. As one tenured faculty member commented, "Everyone contributes to the teaching enterprise. We recognize the contribution. It is a team effort. There is no resistance to the clinical faculty, no problem with attitudes with the tenure-track faculty. We need clinical faculty" (Gappa, 1996, p. 25).

These faculty members are initially hired on annual or multiple-year contracts, and, upon completion of a probationary period, are awarded multiple-year contracts ranging from three to ten years. Teaching loads and faculty roles are comparable to those of the tenure-track faculty, as are the clear career-progression systems and available support for professional development. These faculty members are eligible for sabbatical leaves and have salaries that are comparable to or higher than those of tenure-track faculty (Baldwin and Chronister, 2001, pp. 74–75). They function as full-fledged members of the academic community. As one FTNTT professor remarked, "My whole career has been in academe and off the track; it's been an idea-driven career. I've paid no attention to what one needs to succeed, and I've had an extraordinarily rich career" (Gappa, 1996, p. 18).

The Integrated Model

The integrated model for contract-renewable appointments is used to hire individuals with distinctive skills and interests that enhance program offerings and complement the qualifications of tenure-track faculty. The institution's intent is to maintain some long-term staffing flexibility, achieve cost control, and access specialized faculty resources for specific purposes (Baldwin and Chronister, 2001). These individuals are usually employed on annual contracts for a probationary period of three to six years, after which they are eligible for renewable multiyear contracts. Evaluation of their work is structured and consistent. They have sequential ranks and titles, either similar to tenure-track faculty or separate and distinct, such as lecturer to senior lecturer, with potential for promotions. Salaries can be lower than, comparable to, or higher than those of tenure-track faculty, and full fringe benefits are typically provided. These faculty have some voting privileges in their departments or units, primarily on curricular matters, and they are eligible for support for professional development.

In contrast to faculty whose appointments follow the alternative-career model just described, faculty members whose appointments follow the integrated model are viewed by their institutions as clearly different from tenure-eligible faculty. Although they are treated as fully functioning professionals, they typically do not have as broad a range of work assignments. Their teaching loads may be heavier than those of tenure-track faculty and may be accompanied by administrative duties, for example, and their salaries also may be lower than salaries for tenure-track faculty with comparable qualifications (Baldwin and Chronister, 2001, pp. 73–74).

The Marginalized Model

The marginalized model uses contract-renewable appointments strictly to achieve staffing flexibility and cost savings. These faculty members, for the most part, are similar to part timers who make up the majority of faculty in fixed-term appointments. They are hired primarily to teach. Institutional policies make it clear that they serve special functions and are different from their tenure-track colleagues (Baldwin and Chronister, 2001). The formal policy at Lehigh University, as reported by Trower (2000, p. 123), describes their situation clearly:

> Lecturer appointments are intended to replace some appointments as adjuncts, and are not intended to substitute for the integrated role of teaching, scholarship and service provided by regular tenured and tenure-track faculty.

Nevertheless, when institutions consolidate part-time faculty positions into full-time appointments for the purposes of teaching undergraduates or specialized areas of the curriculum, the full-timers usually are treated better than the part-timers they replace, for several reasons. Unlike those in fixed-term appointments

- The full-timers' appointments typically are for one year or longer and are either renewable without limit or of fixed duration with some possibility of renewal.
- Opportunities for promotion are generally available, although the range of titles is generally limited (to instructor and senior instructor, for example, or lecturer).
- Compensation, although lower than for tenure-track faculty, includes some benefits.
- The full-timers receive some support for professional development, although it is limited.

In sum, faculty in these contract-renewable appointments carry heavy teaching loads, with little time for research or other professional tasks. Their participation in governance is limited at best, and job security is a critical issue for some (Gappa, 1996; NEA Higher Education Research Center, 1996).

STATUS DIFFERENTIALS AMONG
FTNTT FACULTY APPOINTMENTS

The three models just described for contract-renewable faculty appointments differ from each other primarily because of the status attributed to faculty in these positions at any given campus. At the high-status end of the continuum, professional schools or research institutions tend to use these positions for clinical or research functions and to see them as fully equivalent to tenure-track appointments. At the lower-status end of the continuum, institutions making FTNTT faculty appointments primarily for teaching tend to clearly distinguish them from the tenure track through the use of very different employment practices and perquisites.

Campus climates, cultures, histories, and current situations underlie the faculty employment systems that colleges and universities use. Baldwin and Chronister (2001), in their research on FTNTT faculty appointments, found that status differentials among types of faculty appointments varied among institutions either because of explicit institutional policies and actions or because of implicit or inferred differences in faculty quality.

Status also varies on the basis of the seniority and credentials of the faculty member in the FTNTT position. Senior faculty members in contract-renewable positions who have credentials equivalent to or better than those of tenured faculty tend to be employed under the alternative-career model and experience few status distinctions from their tenured colleagues. One senior professor of practice commented that for persons like himself, who had established successful careers outside academe and were nearing retirement, status was not an issue, and career development was moot. But he recognized that junior faculty who were developing their careers need assistance with career development and seek inclusion in the campus community. He recommended money, status, and image as important incentives for recruiting junior FTNTT faculty, and he pointed to sabbatical eligibility, voting rights, and a clear system for career progress up the ranks as important tangible indicators of respect and of a proactive attitude toward non-tenure-eligible faculty (Gappa, 1996, p. 33).

Junior contract-renewable faculty who are building their academic careers feel their vulnerability and lack of status more strongly than their more senior counterparts do, even when the junior faculty have had substantial experience in nonacademic settings. One researcher commented as follows (Gappa, 1996, pp. 27–28):

> Basically the research professor is a slave. A university franchise. "We'll give you a lab, space. You bring in the money. If you don't, you're history." . . . People have to have something. What about the person who brings in grants for 20 years? Then he reaches 50 and the grants drop off. What do you do, fire him?"

And a dean of arts and sciences, who was making a concerted effort to remove status differentials, captured the issue with this remark: "The practical reality is that they [tenured faculty] do not view [non-tenure-track faculty as] the same" (Baldwin and Chronister, 2001, p. 129). Status differentials are evident in voting rights as well. Only 7 percent of the 217 institutions surveyed as part of the Project on Faculty Appointments at Harvard University extended voting privileges in governance matters to any FTNTT faculty (Shavers, 2000). Baldwin and Chronister (2001) cite several other examples of status differentials:

> A department in a research university gave all the computer upgrades to its tenured and tenure-track faculty, while the FTNTT faculty were given the hand-me-downs, even though they needed the enhanced computer resources to meet teaching responsibilities.
>
> At another institution, FTNTT faculty were assigned to the end of the faculty line at graduation.
>
> At an all-college retreat, the FTNTT faculty had colored dots on their name tags to make it clear that they were "different from" the tenure-track faculty.

Women faculty, when they are clustered together in a particular program where all faculty are in non-tenure-eligible positions, can feel a sense of disrespect. One commented, "The school has no interest in our development. Another program is in the same position. Both programs are filled with women." One of her colleagues echoed her sentiments: "Our tenured colleagues are white, middle-aged men. They are the ones making the decisions. How many times do I have to break the glass ceiling?" (Gappa, 1996, p. 27).

Comments and actions such as those cited are powerful symbols of a status system that bifurcates faculty into separate classes,
as described by Gappa and Leslie (1993) in their research on part-
timers. Whether the issue is support for professional development,
inability to participate in governance, or lack of a collegial environment, some faculty in FTNTT positions (particularly those in
the marginalized model) feel they are second-class citizens by comparison with their tenure-eligible colleagues.

THE CHALLENGE

FTNTT faculty members in contract-renewable appointments are
generally better off than their part-time colleagues (discussed in
the next section), and some of them are in positions equivalent to
those of tenure-track faculty. Nevertheless, most of them are employed without the benefit of policies and procedures so carefully
developed for the tenure-track faculty. Chronister and Baldwin
(1999, p. 21) found an

> absence of clear-cut policies that regulate their appointments,
> support their performance, and minimize harmful status differ-
> ences among faculty in distinctive categories. . . . We found very
> few well-defined polices to define or regulate the hiring, eval-
> uation, compensation, workload, governance involvement,
> professional development, or career advancement of term-
> appointment faculty. Guidelines for protecting the academic
> freedom of [these] faculty were often notably absent as well.

To counter the absence of clear policy, Baldwin and Chronister (2001) have recommended that institutions address nine areas
for all FTNTT appointments:

1. Defined probationary periods
2. Multiyear appointments after probation
3. Defined dates for contract renewal or termination
4. Equitable salary and benefits systems
5. Career-progression systems
6. Support for professional development
7. Involvement in governance
8. Protection of academic freedom
9. Access to recognition and rewards

Results of a study by Bland et al. (2006) indicate that the effects of these different employment practices *may* influence FTNTT faculty's productivity in research and doctoral degree–granting institutions. Through statistical analysis of available data for measuring productivity in the 1999 National Survey of Post-Secondary Faculty, the researchers found that newly hired tenure-track faculty were more productive than their faculty counterparts in contract-renewable appointments on several measures. They were more productive in research funding received and publications produced, more committed to their positions, and worked about four more hours per week (Bland et al., 2006). However, there were significant differences in the types of work performed and students served. For example, FTNTT faculty members were more likely to teach remedial classes, and they spent more hours per week in actual contact with students. The researchers concluded that their results did not indicate that FTNTT faculty members were less personally committed to their work or less able to be productive than their tenure-track colleagues were; instead, they hypothesized, the non-tenure-track system of employment, as it is currently configured, may be less conducive to commitment and productivity. Given research that demonstrates that the employment system has more influence on productivity than does individual effort, they recommend that institutions examine their current FTNTT appointment practices. The use of alternative academic appointments, they say, should be considered from the perspective of balancing financial flexibility and cost savings with improved faculty productivity and commitment and with the attractiveness of the alternative appointments (Bland et al., 2006).

However, as the alternative-career model described earlier in this section shows, faculty employed in renewable contracts can experience academic employment that is equivalent to tenure in terms of status, responsibilities, and rewards. At a time when institutions and individuals seek diversity in employment practices to meet a wide variety of needs and situations, these positions have considerable potential. The medical schools have made the greatest progress in developing integrated, equitable employment policies for contract-renewable faculty that eliminate status differentials and integrate these faculty fully into academic life (Froom and Bickel, 1996; Gappa, 1996; Jones and Gold, 2001); their employment policies and practices have much to offer other institutions seeking to diversify their academic appointments.

Nevertheless, some institutions use FTNTT positions strictly as an efficient way to employ people in academic positions that are clearly limited by policy, practice, and status. It is this marginalized FTNTT faculty member who most closely resembles the typical part-timer in the academic workforce, and to whom we now turn.

Part-Time Faculty in Fixed-Term Appointments

Most part-time faculty members occupy fixed-term appointments—and here, another word on terminology is in order. In this section, we use the terms "part-time faculty" and "part-timers" as descriptors when those terms match the current terminology used in reporting data about these faculty members who are, generally speaking, employed less than full time. (We note, however, that FTNTT faculty in the marginalized appointments described earlier have similar appointment conditions.) We use the phrases "fixed-term faculty," "fixed-term appointments," and "fixed-term contracts" in connection with part-time faculty employment because these appointments are normally for a semester or a year, without any guarantee of renewal and because the time base can vary from one appointment to the next. We prefer the phrase "fixed-term faculty" to "contingency faculty" because calling part-timers "contingency workers" discounts the contributions that these faculty members make, as well as their occasionally long-term service to their institutions.

Hired primarily to teach, part-time faculty now make up 46 percent of all faculty members (U.S. Department of Education, National Center for Education Statistics, 2004). They range from 67 percent of the head count of faculty in public two-year colleges to 22 percent in public research universities, which frequently use graduate assistants to teach undergraduate courses. Similarly, individual disciplines use part-timers in different proportions. Part-timers make up 53 percent of faculty in the fine arts but only 30 percent of the faculty in agriculture (U.S. Department of Education, National Center for Education Statistics, 2004). The substantial reliance on part-time faculty in professional fields such as business (51 percent), health sciences (38 percent), and law (55 percent) is due to the ready availability and value of practitioners who bring current knowledge of their professions to their teaching. Part-time faculty teaching basic humanities and sciences courses, however, are used to replace full-time faculty teaching introductory courses in core academic subjects (Benjamin, 1998b).

REASONS FOR THE INCREASING USE OF PART-TIME FACULTY: THE INSTITUTIONAL PERSPECTIVE

The expansion of community colleges, declining state support for all public higher education, and the rising number of students attending college are among the most compelling reasons for the expansion in the use of part-timers. From 1970 to 2003, the number of faculty members at two-year institutions grew by 290 percent, compared to a growth rate of only 53 percent at four-year institutions (U.S. Department of Education, 2004), and during the same period the proportion of part-timers in community colleges rose from 50 percent to its current 67 percent (Berger, Kirshstein, Zhang, and Carter, 2002). This increased use of part-time faculty has enabled institutions to handle more students efficiently and effectively, without increased resources. The dean of instruction at one community college cites the role of fluctuating budgets and enrollments to explain why the use of part-time faculty has expanded so greatly:

> My own college was funded last year for just over 1,700 FTE (full-time equivalent) students. Assuming 20 FTE students equal one FT faculty member, full funding would be for 85 full-time faculty members. However, we were funded to an amount equal to about 50 full-time faculty and enough in the part-time pool to teach 700 FTE students. The funding problem was further exacerbated . . . by the fact that we actually teach far more students than we're funded to teach: we taught just under 3,000 FTE students last year. . . . We had just under 50 FT tenure-track faculty and over 150 part-timers and adjuncts [Fulton, 2000, p. 42].

The growth of distance education is another reason that the number of part-time faculty members is increasing. Just as other products and services in the economy have become available on an around-the-clock, seven-day-a-week basis, the demand has increased for high-quality college instruction delivered at any time and to any place. Led by for-profit institutions, many colleges and universities are responding with distance education initiatives that require faculty members to act as facilitators. Unlike many traditional institutions, however, for-profit institutions invest heavily in developing the instructional skills of their part-timers, partly because it is these faculty members who teach the overwhelming majority of their classes. For example, to meet current demand, the University of Phoenix employs 7,000 adjunct instructors to deliver online courses alone. This has enabled it, in five years, to expand tenfold the number of students served (Lyons, 2003, p. 5).

Employment of fixed-term faculty is part of the wider pattern across employment sectors of downsizing, subcontracting, and outsourcing, as discussed in Chapter One. Part-timers are often hired for their expertise in a particular discipline or area; most of these part-timers have positions and careers outside academe, and they teach because they enjoy it or seek supplemental income. Institutions and students value these experts' up-to-date knowledge of their fields, gained from career experience outside higher education (for example, in business, engineering, or the health sciences). These faculty members can add immeasurably to students' learning and career preparation. In addition, part-timers on fixed-term contracts are invaluable in disciplines where full-time expertise is not needed (for example, in the arts).

In addition, increasing enrollment, financial hard times, the loss of control over mandatory retirement, and the need for flexibility have all made institutions more wary about long-term commitments to tenure. Moreover, the preference of some individuals for part-time work, and the lack of evidence that part-timers teach any less effectively than full-time faculty, have contributed to the use of part-timers in traditional institutions (Gappa, 2002). Contrary to popular belief, it appears that higher education's part-time workforce fills a valuable niche in higher education and is here to stay.

Reasons for Using Part-Time Faculty: The Individual Perspective

Faculty members in part-time, fixed-term appointments choose these positions for a variety of reasons. Gappa and Leslie (1993) place them in four different categories:

1. Professionals, specialists, or experts are employed elsewhere in their primary careers and teach because they find intrinsic satisfaction with the work itself and are dedicated to the constituencies they serve. Many have an altruistic desire to help others, particularly those who come from similar backgrounds.
2. Career enders are in life transitions to retirement or are retired.
3. Freelancers work simultaneously in a variety of positions, one of which is part-time teaching.
4. Aspiring academics seek full-time, tenure-track faculty positions. Only 16 percent of all part-timers are aspiring academics.

These categories vary significantly by discipline. For example, in 1998, only 15 percent of part-timers in the health sciences sought full-time academic jobs, in contrast to 65 percent of part-timers in the fine arts and 61 percent in the humanities, who reported that they were teaching on a part-time basis because full-time jobs were not available, either in academe or elsewhere (Leslie, 1998b). Overproduction of doctorates in some disciplines has created an oversupply of candidates with Ph.D. and M.A. degrees, making it impossible for some scholars and teachers to find full-time work at the college level (Nutting, 2003). These aspiring academics generally teach for economic reasons, sometimes at several campuses simultaneously, hoping eventually to gain a tenure-track position. Although some part-timers in some disciplines may be aspiring academics, most part-timers differ from their full-time counterparts in their qualifications for faculty positions. Only 27 percent of part-timers hold a doctoral or equivalent degree (compared to 67 percent of full-time faculty), whereas 54 percent have one or more master's degrees (U.S. Department of Education, 2002).

Employment Policies and Practices for Fixed-term Faculty

According to the 2004 National Survey of Postsecondary Faculty (U.S. Department of Education, National Center for Education Statistics, 2004), 96 percent of part-timers are in non-tenure-eligible appointments. Despite the temporary nature of their employment contracts, these faculty members have occupied their nominally temporary positions for an average of seven years. They spend an average of fourteen hours per week on their paid activities at the institutions where they primarily teach. Their teaching loads vary widely. Although 37 percent of part-time faculty teach only one class each term, 26 percent teach two classes, 14 percent teach three classes, and 16 percent teach more than three classes, indicating the significant role that part-time faculty play in their institutions (Berger et al., 2002).

Although the part-time faculty is largely heterogeneous, made up of people with highly varied life circumstances and motivations for teaching, these faculty members' employment conditions are not heterogeneous. Regardless of their performance, the length of their employment, their qualifications for their positions, or the needs of their institutions, part-time faculty in most colleges and universities are employed under exploitative practices. Fixed-term employment tends to be a casual affair; it is based on informal practices and commitments within academic departments rather than on centrally promulgated and monitored institutional policies that provide fair and consistent treatment. In good circumstances, part-timers become valued and established colleagues despite the informality and insecurity of their employment. In the worst circumstances, part-timers remain marginal and are subject to capricious and arbitrary treatment (Benjamin, 2003; Gappa, 2002; Gappa and Leslie, 1993; Gappa and Leslie, 1997; Rhoades, 1998).

Recruitment and Appointment

In contrast to the rigorous, nationally based recruitment of tenure-track faculty, recruitment of part-timers is usually informal and is handled by department heads because of the need to hire quickly and because of the short-term nature of these appointments. Some vacancies are advertised regionally or locally, but most recruiting is by word of mouth. "Bottom fishing" for the least expensive and most vulnerable (but not necessarily best-qualified) candidates can occur when department chairs are not accountable for their hiring practices (Gappa and Leslie, 1993).

Most contingent faculty (57 percent) are appointed for a single term, and notification of an appointment or its renewal (regardless of the number of semesters previously employed) often comes very late (Berger et al., 2002; Nutting, 2003). As a result, part-timers are left with little time to prepare their classes, and this kind of short notice can have a deleterious effect on the quality of their teaching performance. Failure to be notified in a timely fashion can also have a seriously disrupting effect on the lives of those part-timers who are financially dependent on this kind of employment. Term-by-term appointments, policies limiting the number of possible continuous appointments, and arbitrary limits on the amount of work that part-timers can be assigned all contribute to the insecurity that part-timers feel about their employment. These policies may also disqualify part-timers for benefits. Policies like these are unfortunate responses to institutional desires for flexibility and cost cutting.

Availability of Support Services

Resources for support services, supplies, equipment, and office space are scarce, and part-timers usually receive the lowest priority. Frequently, offices that supply services require part-timers to turn in requests far in advance and are closed evenings and weekends, when many part-timers teach. Unavailability of adequate support services or office space can hamper part-timers' teaching and make advising their students difficult. Funds for professional travel or sabbatical leaves are virtually nonexistent for part-timers, and those professional growth opportunities that do exist are normally limited to on-campus orientation and teaching-development programs (Nutting, 2003; Townsend, 2003; Gappa and Leslie, 1993).

Compensation

Salary policies for part-timers vary greatly according to institutional culture and ability to pay. The vast majority of institutions use a flat rate per course or an established range, defined on the basis of seniority or qualifications. Most part-time faculty receive less than $3,000 per course; even stringing together a number of such appointments does not produce a viable standard of living (Townsend, 2003).

Overall, part-timers earn about 27 percent of their total income through college teaching. Most part-timers (71 percent) have other jobs outside academe, and for 47 percent of part-timers, these are full-time jobs (Berger et al., 2002; Gappa and Leslie, 1997; U.S. Department of Education, National Center for Education Statistics, 2004). Their average total earned income is $51,654 (compared to

$70,764 for full-time faculty members), with $10,346 coming from their institutions (U.S. Department of Education, National Center for Education Statistics, 2004). Mean household income for all part-timers is $92,795, compared to $107,654 for full-time faculty (U.S. Department of Education, National Center for Education Statistics, 2004).

Some institutions are inconsistent in their salary policies, and, in some circumstances, part-timers negotiate their salaries individually with department heads or higher-level administrators, an arrangement that leads to complete erosion of salary policies and equity. Part-timers' views about their salaries also vary. Those employed in full-time jobs elsewhere generally express little concern; those who depend on their salaries as an important source of income want a fair wage and merit increases.

Few institutions provide benefits to part-timers. Lack of benefits was the issue receiving the most "dissatisfied" responses (54 percent) from part-timers in the 1999 NSOPF survey, the most recent data available (Berger, Kirshstein, and Rowe, 2001). Medical insurance (available in some form to 32 percent of part-timers versus 99 percent of full-timers), retirement plans (available to 18 percent of part-timers versus 99 percent of full-timers), and tuition grants or waivers (available to 9 percent of part-timers versus 48 percent of full-timers) are most important to part-timers (Berger, Kirshstein, and Rowe, 2001; Gappa, 2002). And because institutions formulate benefits policies according to the time base of an individual's appointment rather than his or her cumulative years of service, part-time faculty with ten to fifteen years of continuous teaching experience are usually treated the same as part-timers hired to teach for one semester (Gappa, 2002).

Job Security

Many part-timers have enjoyed long and mutually productive associations with their colleges and universities, but these stable employment histories have resulted from institutional goodwill, not from any right that the part-timers had to job security. Part-timers receive no assurance of having classes to teach on a regular basis, or even any guarantees that they will be teaching from term to term. Those fortunate enough to be assigned courses for continuing terms remain at the mercy of enrollment trends: when full-time faculty members' classes fail to meet minimum enrollments and are cancelled, the full-timers often take over the part-timers' classes (Nutting, 2003). Part-timers believe that a system is unfair in which long-term service and distinguished performance do not ensure continuing employment.

PART-TIME FACULTY'S SATISFACTION WITH THEIR ACADEMIC EMPLOYMENT

In interviews at eighteen colleges and universities, many part-time faculty expressed anger and frustration about their second-class status and the lack of appreciation for their efforts (Gappa and Leslie, 1993). Instead of feeling connected to or integrated into campus life, they often felt alienated, powerless, and invisible.

These interviews showed that part-time faculty's sense of membership in their academic communities and their satisfaction with their employment were largely based on the treatment they received in their departments. Many part-timers expressed annoyance about their lack of involvement in departmental decisions affecting them, an annoyance that was exacerbated by the knowledge that protesting could jeopardize their continued employment. Part-time faculty's "invisibility" in some academic departments was often due to the decentralization of policy, practices, and resources to the departmental level, to lack of leadership by department chairs, or to departmental culture. Two department chairs interviewed by Gappa and Leslie (1993, p. 186) expressed two very different views of the role of part-timers, and thus the environment in their departments as well:

> The arts faculty treat . . . adjuncts as full members of the departmental family. They do shows together, eat together, and so forth. Their schedules are arranged to bring them together more frequently. We try to do a lot together and have a department party every semester.

> The part-time faculty haven't been integrated and haven't felt integrated. My predecessor never thought of inviting them to meetings. Now they get invited to meetings but can't vote. It's rare that they come. . . . A lot of our part-time faculty are commuters. . . . It's the attitude of the faculty and the nature of the part-timers themselves. They are not counting on this institution as their primary job.

For the most part, however, colleges and universities benefit from employing part-timers, and the part-time faculty themselves are satisfied with their employment, if not with their treatment in their departments. Of part-time faculty who responded to the 2004 NSOPF survey, 91 percent reported that they were somewhat or very satisfied with their jobs overall (U.S. Department of Education, National Center for Education Statistics, 2004). Nevertheless, although they expressed satisfaction with their teaching assignments, they were less satisfied with various aspects of their employment. For example, according to Berger et al., 2002, part-time faculty members' responses to the 1999 NSOPF survey (the most recent data available) showed that 47 percent were dissatisfied or very dissatisfied with their salaries, 51 percent were dissatisfied or very dissatisfied with opportunities for advancement, and 39 percent were dissatisfied or very dissatisfied with their level of job security.

Benjamin (1998b), also using data from the 1993 NSOPF survey, examined the satisfaction and dissatisfaction of part-timers in four-year institutions by comparing those who taught in vocationally oriented (VOC) disciplines with those who taught in liberal arts–oriented (LAC) disciplines. His analysis indicates that the VOC part-timers expressed substantially more satisfaction than the LAC part-timers did with their jobs overall as well as with benefits, salary, job security, and time to keep current in their fields. Benjamin attributes this finding to the respondents' reasons for teaching on a part-time basis: 60 percent of the LAC faculty, versus 27 percent of the VOC faculty, indicated that they had accepted part-time positions because no full-time positions were available. The LAC faculty members were also more dependent on their part-time employment. Their household income was lower on average than that of the VOC part-timers ($58,858 versus $92,846), and job security and health benefits did not come as frequently from other employers.

Institutions of all types would be wise to pay more attention to their part-time faculty. Policies and practices for fixed-term appointments should be centrally promulgated and monitored to ensure fair and consistent practice across a campus. At the departmental level, part-time faculty need to be better supported in their work, to be more integrated into their units, and to receive rewards and recognition for long-term service and distinguished performance. Individual faculty members as well as their institutions will benefit when policies and practices change.

CONCLUSIONS

This chapter has examined tenure-track, contract-renewable, and fixed-term appointments. From the perspective of faculty members, each appointment type has several significant problems. Men and women on the tenure-track find it difficult to balance their personal and professional lives as the workweek increases and tenure-related expectations rise. Many women find that the lack of flexibility in their careers makes it difficult if not impossible to combine a career with bearing and rearing children. Tenure-track faculty also express dissatisfaction with the structure and operation of the current review process, and faculty of color report feeling isolated and alone. Faculty members outside the tenure system lack opportunities to fully participate in a collegial community or to take advantage of professional development programs and benefits. Part-timers are largely disenfranchised, vulnerable, and invisible.

Faculty members as well as their colleges and universities would benefit from an enhanced work environment, one that could more easily allow institutions to fulfill their missions and faculty members to realize their career and personal goals. Institutions and faculty members seek essentially the same outcomes: a satisfied and stable faculty workforce, utilization of the intellectual capital that faculty bring for the enrichment of the institution, students who become educated citizens, and significant contributions to the public good through research and service.

Academic institutions are no different from other employers in today's market. They must compete successfully for new faculty members. Their success in recruiting and retaining high-quality faculty members directly affects their ability to achieve their missions and goals and satisfy their constituents. Successful competition for faculty members requires rethinking both the academic career and the faculty workplace, the subject of later chapters. We turn now to an in-depth examination of faculty members' satisfaction with their current academic careers and with their workplaces.

CHAPTER FIVE

ATTRACTING AND RETAINING EXCELLENT FACULTY

Chapters Three and Four looked in depth at changes in the size and diversity of the faculty workforce and at the employment policies and practices currently in use for tenure-track, contract-renewable, and fixed-term academic appointments. This chapter continues this exploration of today's faculty by looking at their career satisfaction.

The first section of this chapter examines faculty satisfaction and stress levels, with special attention to the gender and racial differences that exist. The second section provides evidence that demand for faculty is expected to be increasingly strong over the next decade. This fact makes faculty stress and satisfaction levels particularly important issues because they are directly related to a faculty member's intention to leave his or her current position or to leave academia altogether (Barnes, Agago, and Coombs, 1998; Hagedorn, 1996; Rosser, 2004). The chapter concludes by asking a critical question: If faculty members and their academic appointments have changed significantly from the traditional "ideal" models, are there elements of faculty work and workplaces that, regardless of appointment type or demographics, are essential to successful recruiting and retention of greater numbers of faculty members? To answer this question, research on faculty satisfaction and theories of worker satisfaction are reviewed. This literature indicates that faculty as a whole express common needs that, when addressed, help them feel satisfied and produce their best work.

SATISFACTION AND STRESS LEVELS OF TODAY'S FACULTY

How satisfied are faculty with their jobs overall? Analysis of several Carnegie Foundation for the Advancement of Teaching surveys conducted between 1969 and 1997 shows that for decades full-time faculty members have remained generally satisfied with their career choices and their institutions (Gappa, 2002). Very few have indicated that they would change their profession if they had it to do over again. They have retained their positive attitudes about their academic careers even though their workloads have escalated and their salaries have not always kept pace with inflation. And, as described in Chapter Four, part-timers (91 percent) are just as satisfied overall as their full-time counterparts, despite their differential employment conditions (U.S. Department of Education, National Study of Postsecondary Faculty, 2004).

In their responses to the 2004 National Survey of Postsecondary Faculty, faculty members also showed a high degree of satisfaction (87.5 percent) with their jobs overall, regardless of appointment, time base, institutional type, gender, or ethnic background. This level of satisfaction even increased over time in some categories (see Table 5.1).

A caveat is needed here, however. One reason for the high level of satisfaction found in the faculty surveys just cited may be the population from which the samples were drawn; these findings are based on the responses of current faculty members and not on the responses of those individuals who were dissatisfied enough to have left the academy. Indeed, a survey of tenure-track faculty members at six research universities led to less positive results. In this case, 25 percent responded that they were either dissatisfied or very dissatisfied with their college or university as a place to work (Trower and Bleak, 2004a). This population of early-career faculty in highly competitive environments may have included a significant proportion of individuals who were in the process of determining whether they really wanted to continue building their careers in the academy. Researchers as well as colleges and universities would probably gain important insights from systematic collection of the reasons for faculty members' departures.

TABLE 5.1. OVERALL JOB SATISFACTION OF FACULTY MEMBERS BY
INSTITUTIONAL TYPE, GENDER, RACE/ETHNICITY, APPOINTMENT TYPE, AND
TIME BASE, IN PERCENTAGES, 1987, 1998, AND 2003 (ALL FACULTY)

	Year		
	1987	*1998*	*2003*
All Faculty			
Satisfied	85.3	84.7	87.5
Dissatisfied	14.7	15.3	12.5
Institutional Type			
Research	86.0	83.6	86.1
Doctoral	83.4	83.3	85.0
Comprehensive	82.6	83.0	85.8
Private liberal arts	85.4	84.5	89.3
Public two-year/other	88.9	88.6	92.2
Gender			
Female	83.9	83.4	87.9
Male	85.9	85.5	87.2
Race/Ethnicity			
American Indian or Alaska Native	80.7	80.7	89.5
Asian or Pacific Islander	82.1	81.1	83.3
Black/African American, non-Hispanic	85.1	83.9	87.3
Hispanic	85.4	82.5	84.8
White, non-Hispanic	85.4	85.2	88.1
Appointment Type			
Tenured/tenure-track position	85.8	85.0	87.0
Non-tenure-track position	80.1	83.8	88.6
Time Basis			
Full-time appointment	85.3	84.7	87.5
Part-time appointment	87.3	85.2	91.3

Source: U.S. Department of Education, National Center for Education Statistics,
1988, 1999, 2004.

REASONS FOR HIGH LEVELS OF OVERALL SATISFACTION

This caveat not withstanding, why are most faculty members so satisfied with their academic careers? Two decades ago, Bowen and Schuster (1986) ascribed the attractiveness of the career to its essential feature: the pursuit of learning. Potential faculty members attracted to academe find the pursuit of knowledge a worthwhile endeavor. They believe in it. They also seek autonomy in doing their work, and they seek freedom of thought and expression. Many faculty members, especially full-time faculty with tenure, operate with a minimum of supervision from their institutions and outside agencies, structuring their work as they want. They participate in governance of their institutions regarding educational matters, and, in ideal cases, they are surrounded by congenial and sympathetic scholars, similarly employed, with whom they can enjoy friendship and good conversation. Many tenured faculty members would agree with Bowen and Schuster's assessment that they work in a very desirable occupation. They have a sense of vocation, a love of the academic life and community, and the security that tenure provides. They also value teaching and derive intrinsic satisfaction from it. Even faculty members at research universities consider teaching at least as important as research, despite the fact that the reward systems at those institutions favor research and publication (Leslie, 2002).

Faculty members choose an academic career because it offers autonomy, intellectual challenges, and freedom to pursue personal interests. They derive considerable satisfaction from the contributions they make to research, student development, or social change. Full-time, tenure-track faculty members interviewed by Lindholm (2003) commented that they resonated with the college or university atmosphere, that they were "comfortable" in the academic work environment, and that they felt "called" to an academic career. They experienced a sense of place in their institutions that was distinctively their own, where they felt comfortable, respected, and appreciated. Further, they had colleagues who stimulated their creativity, were open to discussion, and helped buffer them from professional stresses. They also had sufficient structural support—physical, organizational, and financial—to achieve their professional goals. In sum, they felt connected to the academic environment and found their careers meaningful. These statements are confirmed by responses to the most recent Higher Education Research Institute (HERI) survey, in which 85 percent of faculty respondents reported being satisfied with the autonomy and independence in their jobs (Lindholm, Szelenyi, Hurtado, and Korn, 2005).

These descriptors are mainly associated with the traditional model of the academic career. As described in Chapter Four, however, qualitative research in particular indicates that the descriptors are lacking for some current participants, particularly women, people who belong to racial or ethnic minority groups, probationers, and those off the tenure track. With regard to tenure-track positions in particular, the stress of the probationary period and increasing workloads can override academic traditions, such as autonomy and collegiality, that are typically associated with the career. Although 78 percent or 88 percent of faculty report that they are satisfied with their jobs overall, depending on the survey results utilized (Lindholm et al., 2005; U.S. Department of Education, National Center for Education Statistics, 2004), concerns about their careers do surface when we examine survey results about satisfaction with specific components of the career by subpopulation.

DIFFERENCES IN SATISFACTION LEVELS ACROSS SUBPOPULATIONS

With an increasingly diverse faculty have come varying levels of satisfaction across subpopulations. Women as well as people who belong to racial and ethnic minority groups express less satisfaction with certain aspects of their work than do Caucasian men. Women in full-time faculty positions are less satisfied than men with their teaching loads (51.7 percent versus 56.8 percent), salaries and benefits (44.3 percent versus 49.4 percent), opportunities for advancement (49.1 percent versus 54.8 percent), and opportunities for scholarly pursuits (46.8 percent versus 57.2 percent) (Lindholm et al., 2005). In a study that surveyed full-time tenure-track faculty at six research universities, Trower and Bleak (2004a) also found that women tenure-track faculty were less satisfied than their male counterparts on a number of different measures. Women rated their institutions as workplaces significantly lower than did men and were significantly less satisfied with their salaries and the balance between their personal and professional lives. They were also significantly less satisfied with the commitment of their department chairs to their success, and with the mentoring and other interactions they had with the senior faculty in their departments.

Trower and Bleak (2004b) did find that junior faculty who were members of ethnic and racial minority groups generally expressed a level of satisfaction with their workplaces that was similar to the level of satisfaction expressed by Caucasians on the tenure track, but the minority faculty were less likely than Caucasian junior faculty to report that tenure decisions were based on performance and were more likely to believe that tenure decisions were based on politics, relationships, or demographics. These faculty were also less satisfied with the influence they felt they had over their research focus. In addition, according to Rosser (2004), the 1999 NSOPF survey results showed that full-time faculty at all career stages who were members of ethnic and racial minority groups were significantly more likely to intend to leave their careers or institutions than were Caucasians.

SOURCES OF DISSATISFACTION: SALARIES AND WORKLOADS

Faculty members as a whole also indicate sources of dissatisfaction and job strain in their current employment. In the 2004 NSOPF, part- and full-time faculty both expressed far less satisfaction with their salaries by comparison with their overall satisfaction: 91 percent of part-timers and 88 percent of full-timers expressed satisfaction overall, but only 66 percent of part-timers and 63 percent of full-timers were satisfied with their salaries. Asked what would be important in a new job, full-time faculty of both genders and all ages responded that salary was one of the most important factors (U.S. Department of Education, National Center for Education Statistics, 2004).

Rising educational costs have made it difficult for colleges and universities to keep up with salaries in competing professions. On average, faculty members in public and private institutions earn less than their nonfaculty counterparts who have earned graduate degrees. Faculty at public colleges and universities earn about 30 percent less than their nonfaculty counterparts, and faculty members in private colleges and universities earn about 22 percent less than their counterparts outside of the academy (NEA Higher Education Research Center, 2004).

Meanwhile, the total hours that full-time tenure-track faculty work weekly at their institutions have increased. The percentage of faculty members reporting that they work more than fifty-five hours a week has grown from 13 percent in 1972 to 47 percent in 2003, with women (44 percent) showing a slightly smaller increase than men (48 percent). The average hours that full-time tenure-track faculty work weekly has increased from fifty-one in 1988 to fifty-six in 2003 in research universities, from forty-six to fifty-three in comprehensive institutions, from forty-eight to fifty-four in private liberal arts colleges, and from forty-one to fifty in all other institutions. These averages vary little by gender (no more than 2 percentage points), nor do they vary appreciably by age (Schuster and Finkelstein, 2006; U.S. Department of Education, National Center for Education Statistics, 1988, 2004).

FACULTY STRESS

This increase in workloads underlies the other factors that full-time faculty cite as sources of stress: managing household responsibilities (73.5 percent report this as a source of stress), institutional procedures and red tape (65.8 percent), lack of personal time (73.8 percent), and the tenure- and promotion-review process (44.4 percent). Faculty members also cite their physical health (51.4 percent), child care (29.5 percent), and care of an elderly parent (32.9 percent) as important sources of stress (Lindholm et al., 2005).

Research also indicates that, just as women and members of ethnic and racial minority groups are less satisfied with specific aspects of their faculty careers than are white males, they experience significantly more stress related to a number of different issues. Ethnic and racial minority faculty are likely to experience higher levels of stress related to academic advancement (the review and promotion process, subtle discrimination, and research or publishing demands) than are Caucasians (Hendel and Horn, 2005).

As detailed in Chapter Two, women, for their part, generally shoulder a larger share of the responsibility for meeting family and household needs. For this reason, it is not surprising that more women than men report stress from home-related issues (managing a household, child care, children's problems, and marital friction) and from issues related to aging (care of an elderly parent and their own physical health). Women also experience significantly more stress from work overload (teaching loads, time pressure, and lack of a personal life), faculty interactions (committee work, faculty meetings, and contact with colleagues), and issues related to academic advancement (the review and promotion process, subtle discrimination, and research or publishing demands) (Hagedorn, 2001; Hendel and Horn, 2005; Hult, Callister, and Sullivan, 2005).

Examples of gender differences as reflected in responses to several specific items from the most recent HERI survey are included in Table 5.2. Although more women than men experience stress from these sources, it is important to note that a significant proportion of men also feel the weight of these responsibilities. In particular, because so many faculty members are partners in dual-career couples, men also experience stress from managing household responsibilities, and many report experiencing stress from the care of an elderly parent.

TABLE 5.2. SOURCES OF STRESS COMPARED BY GENDER

Source of Stress	Males	Females
Committee work	54.7%	61.1%
Teaching load	61.6%	70.8%
Tenure review/promotion process	40.3%	50.8%
Subtle discrimination	17.9%	34.2%
Lack of personal time	68.5%	81.9%
Management of household responsibilities	68.0%	81.8%
Care of elderly parent	30.7%	36.4%

Source: Data from Lindholm et al., 2005.

INCREASING DEMAND FOR FACULTY

The length of the faculty workweek is increasing, faculty stress levels are high (particularly among women), and women as well as members of ethnic and racial minority groups are expressing less satisfaction with various aspects of their employment than are Caucasian men. These factors help to explain why 31 percent of faculty are considering work outside the academy (Lindholm et al., 2005), why many women and members of minority groups in particular are opting for nonacademic careers after graduation (Trower and Chait, 2002), and why married women, both with and without children, leak out of the academic pipeline at a disproportionately high rate at every stage of the academic career (Wolfinger, Mason, and Goulden, 2004).

Institutions must think more strategically about how to address the dramatic changes occurring in academic work and workplaces, in part because they may find it more difficult to meet the demand for excellent faculty in the future. Student enrollments are growing, leading to an increased demand for faculty, retirements are expected to increase, faculty retention continues to be a challenge for many institutions, and young Ph.D. graduates are increasingly interested in nonacademic positions. Each of these issues is explored below.

INCREASING COLLEGE ENROLLMENTS

The demand for faculty is predicted to increase. The Bureau of Labor Statistics projects faculty growth of more than 24 percent over the 2000–2010 decade, which is significantly faster than the 15 percent growth projected for all occupations (Jones, 2002–2003). This projection is based on expected increases in college enrollments, resulting from greater numbers of traditional-age students and from higher attendance rates for both traditional-age and older students who are pursuing higher education.

Increasing demand for faculty is not a new trend for many colleges and universities. From 1993 to 1998, 44 percent of all higher education institutions reported an *increase* in the number of full-time faculty. The percentage increases ranged from 34 percent at private liberal arts colleges to 6 percent at public research universities, with an overall average of 20 percent. As a result, 8 percent of all full-time faculty members were new hires in the fall of 1998 (Berger, Kirshstein, and Rowe, 2001).

INCREASING NUMBER OF RETIREMENTS

Retirements are also expected to increase over the next decade: across institutional types, 37 percent of all full-time faculty members are at least fifty-five years old, compared to 24 percent in 1989 (Lindholm, Astin, Sax, and Korn, 2002; Lindholm et al., 2005). The mean age of tenured full-time faculty members at four-year colleges and universities is in the mid-fifties (Leslie and Janson, 2005). The overall age distribution is shown in Table 5.3.

As Table 5.3 shows, 50.5 percent of tenured faculty members are at least fifty-five years old. Faculty project that they will retire around the age of sixty-five; as they age, however, the individual decision to retire is increasingly based on personal circumstances. Nevertheless, Leslie and Janson (2005) still project that most faculty will retire at the age of sixty-five or sixty-six, with a subpopulation of more "successful" and better-paid faculty remaining until the age of seventy. If these projections are accurate, Table 5.3 would indicate a significant stream of tenured faculty retirements in the next decade.

TABLE 5.3. TENURE STATUS BY AGE
(FULL-TIME FACULTY, FOUR-YEAR INSTITUTIONS ONLY), 2003

Age	Tenured	On Tenure Track	Not on Tenure Track/ No Tenure System
<35 years	0.3	18.3	15.6
35–44 years	13.3	47.0	29.1
45–54 years	35.9	23.9	31.4
55–64 years	39.6	9.6	20.1
65–69 years	7.9	1.1	2.7
70+ years	3.0	0.2	1.2

Source: U.S. Department of Education, National Center for Education Statistics, 2004.

FACULTY RETENTION

In addition to the growth in college enrollments and an increase in retirements, lower retention rates for faculty who are not at retirement age may also result in more demand for faculty. The Bureau of Labor Statistics projects that between 2000 and 2010 a higher than average proportion of faculty will be needed to replace those currently employed who are leaving their positions permanently. Retirement is one key reason why faculty members are leaving their institutions, but turnover is a significant factor as well: 23 percent of full-time faculty respondents to the 1999 NSOPF who said that they were likely to leave their institutions in the next three years, and who did *not* expect to retire, stated that they were likely to accept nonacademic positions. In addition, 41 percent stated that they were likely to accept full-time faculty positions at different institutions (NEA Higher Education Research Center, 2001). One-third of respondents to the most recent HERI survey also indicated that they had considered leaving academe for different jobs, and 28 percent had received at least one firm offer (Lindholm et al., 2005).

As a result of the growing demand for faculty, because of increasing enrollments and the turnover of current faculty, institutions and university systems as a whole are faced with a challenging task:

- Currently, the California State University (CSU) system is searching for approximately 1,200 new faculty members each year, with a success rate of 75 percent. To meet its goal of a 75 percent tenured and tenure-track full-time faculty, in addition to replacing faculty who leave, the CSU system projects that it will need to hire between 1,800 and 2,000 faculty each year. The projected cost for each new faculty member is $88,700 in recruitment, relocation, and salary, whereas the estimated savings from each permanent faculty separation or retirement is $82,700 (California State University, Office of the Chancellor, 2002).
- Similarly, between 2001 and 2010 the University of North Carolina system projects the need to hire 10,000 new faculty members, to replace those who retire and to meet new enrollment

demands. The annual cost is estimated to begin at $32 million per year and increase to $61 million at the end of the decade (Betsy E. Brown, personal communication, March 16, 2005).

Recruiting New Faculty

With the demand for faculty increasing, institutional leaders are wise to consider how they can attract highly qualified individuals into faculty careers. This may be a more difficult task than in the past, however. Competition from industry is strong, and many new recipients of doctoral degrees do not find a faculty career particularly attractive. In fact, 62 percent of faculty in a national survey indicated that their graduate students were pursuing academic careers less often than in the past (Wimsatt and Trice, 2006). An especially high percentage of faculty (65 percent to 72 percent) from the biomedical and life sciences, health sciences, and engineering indicated that this was true.

The decision about whether to pursue an academic career has traditionally varied greatly by discipline because it was largely based on the particular field's dependence on the academic world (Jones, 2002–2003). Indeed, academe can continue to expect a very competitive market for new faculty in the high-demand fields of science and engineering. But a more subtle shift may also be taking place for doctoral-degree recipients in the humanities and social sciences. According to an economist with the Bureau of Labor Statistics, "Although nonacademic employment historically has been concentrated in science and engineering, in recent years nonacademic options for nonscience Ph.D. graduates have begun to gain recognition" (Jones, 2002–2003, p. 33). One indicator of strong competition for all recent Ph.D. graduates is their unemployment rate. Across career fields, only 1 percent are unemployed one to three years after earning a doctorate (Jones, 2002–2003).

All in all, higher education institutions are likely to find themselves competing in a challenging market for the best new Ph.D. graduates. This is particularly true because academia has been slow to adapt the norms of the academic career to the needs and priorities of today's potential new faculty members. And, if past trends continue, new hires into tenure-track positions probably will not be drawn from those currently in non-tenure-track appointments, thus further narrowing the potential market of qualified faculty. A recent study by Finkelstein, Liu, and Schuster (2003) found little movement of part-time faculty members to full-time appointments, or of full-time faculty from non-tenure-track appointments to tenure-track positions.

To summarize, the market for new faculty members will remain competitive, both among institutions of higher education and with other occupations or organizations. Although potential and current faculty members still find an academic career attractive and satisfying, they also cite sources of dissatisfaction and stress and a willingness to change jobs. This is especially true for women and for members of ethnic and racial minority groups, who are steadily increasing their share of doctoral degrees earned, more likely to report significant stress from a number of sources, and less satisfied with many aspects of their careers. As a result of all these factors, they also will be more difficult to recruit.

CONTRIBUTORS TO JOB SATISFACTION FOR FACULTY AND TO JOB SATISFACTION IN GENERAL

This section describes research that has sought to answer the broader question of those factors that contribute to the job satisfaction of faculty members. To impart a fuller understanding of this important question, general theories of worker satisfaction, along with related research, are reviewed in some detail. Because previous chapters describe numerous factors that contribute to faculty stress, such as family responsibilities, workloads, the tenure-review process, and service expectations, research on faculty stress is not specifically reviewed again in this chapter.

Faculty members today are increasingly diverse, and, by comparison with the situation a few decades ago, fewer fit the "ideal worker" mold that was based on traditional male work patterns. In addition, faculty members are increasingly being appointed to positions off the tenure track, positions that have traditionally offered lower status, lower salaries, and a narrower range of opportunities. Given these significant changes in appointments and demographics, how should institutions respond? What is required to attract and retain faculty today? More specifically, what is needed in each appointment type, and by each faculty member, in order for faculty members to be satisfied with their careers and in a position to produce their best work?

To begin this discussion, work-related satisfaction can be defined as "a positive emotional state resulting from the appraisal of one's job or job experiences" (Locke, 1976, p. 1300). It "results from the perception that one's job fulfills or allows the fulfillment of one's important job values, providing and to the degree that those values are congruent with one's needs" (Locke, 1976, p. 1307).

Contributors to Faculty Members' Job Satisfaction

What contributes to faculty job satisfaction? Research shows that positive interactions with and support from the institution's administration is related to satisfaction (Hult, Callister, and Sullivan, 2005; Iiacqua, Schumacher, and Li, 1995). More specifically, support from the chair and "humane treatment by the dean" (Donohue, 1986) are related to higher levels of work satisfaction (Olsen, Maple, and Stage, 1995). The department's overall climate is also important. For example, women's belief that they are treated fairly at their institutions is a predictor of women's satisfaction (Hagedorn, 2001). For all faculty, positive interactions with colleagues and perceived positive relations among faculty generally are predictors of satisfaction (Donohue, 1986; Hult, Callister, and Sullivan, 2005; Olsen, Maple, and Stage, 1995). Conversely, when faculty members do not experience a sense of community at their institutions, they are significantly more likely to indicate that they intend to leave the academy altogether (Barnes, Agago, and Coombs, 1998).

Satisfaction with salary is another important factor related to overall job satisfaction (Black and Holden, 1998; Hult, Callister, and Sullivan, 2005). Further, perceived salary inequities have been found to negatively influence satisfaction (Hagedorn, 1996). In addition to monetary rewards, receiving recognition for one's work predicts satisfaction (Olsen, Maple, and Stage, 1995).

Autonomy and perceived control over one's career are important predictors of satisfaction, as are having a sense of accomplishment with one's work and growing professionally (Iiacqua, Schumacher, and Li, 1995; Olsen, Maple, and Stage, 1995). Growth and autonomy can lose significance, however, when job demands are overwhelming; research indicates that when faculty members experience frustration due to time constraints, they are significantly more likely to report that they intend to leave academia (Barnes, Agago, and Coombs, 1998).

Having both adequate and equitable access to campus resources influences overall satisfaction levels (Hult, Callister, and Sullivan, 2005; Johnsrud and Rosser, 2004; Rosser, 2004). Resources specifically cited in past studies include secretarial and office support, technical support, library services, availability of materials, teaching and graduate assistants, support for professional development, and support for research activities in general.

Surveys that have directly asked faculty about their career priorities reveal some results that overlap with the results of the satisfaction studies. In responding to a question about the most important characteristics of a new job if a faculty member were to leave his or her current institution, tenured and tenure-track faculty replied that tenure was very important (83 percent), followed by job security in general (71 percent), and geographical location (70 percent). These faculty members also placed a high priority on spousal employment (69 percent) and advancement opportunities (69 percent) (U.S. Department of Education, National Center for Education Statistics, 1999).

The 2001–2002 HERI survey asked faculty members what factors were very important in the decision to work at their colleges or universities. Respondents ranked institutional emphasis on teaching (53 percent), geographical location (46 percent), and colleagues (37 percent) as the most important factors (Lindholm et al., 2002).

In addition, Trower's (2002) research on the job choices of new doctoral-degree recipients and new faculty in the first or second year of employment shows that faculty as well as new Ph.D. graduates prefer tenure-track appointments for the economic security and academic status they provide. Respondents also indicated, however, that they would select non-tenure-track appointments for the sake of geographical location, flexibility, and balance between teaching and research.

Five themes run through these findings, and through the literature cited here, that are related to faculty members' job satisfaction and career priorities:

1. Faculty members value equity, and when they perceive in-equitable treatment, their job satisfaction diminishes. Whether the issue is equitable pay, equal access to the resources neces-sary to do their jobs, or equitable treatment of women, faculty members are sensitive to and negatively affected by inequities in the workplace. But the importance of equity is not limited to perceptions of one's own fair treatment. A study outside higher education also found that if workers perceive that mar-ginalized employees are treated unfairly, their satisfaction lev-els decrease (Witt and Nye, 1992).

2. Collegial relationships are important to faculty. Positive rela-tionships with administrators and colleagues directly predict satisfaction, as does the perception that colleagues have posi-tive relationships with each other. In addition, when faculty do not experience a sense of community at their institutions, they are significantly more likely to indicate that they intend to leave academia.

3. Faculty members are most satisfied when they believe they are growing professionally. Their satisfaction is positively influ-enced by access to the resources necessary to do good work, by autonomy in and control over their careers, and by their sense of accomplishment in their work.

4. Faculty members place a high value on security, which is most often found in the form of a tenure-track position. Neverthe-less, security in other forms, such as a five-year continuously rolling contract, may be an acceptable alternative to tenure for potential faculty members if, for example, they are also able to gain flexibility or spousal employment in the process of nego-tiating for a non-tenure-track position.

5. When faculty members feel supported by their department chairs, by their deans, and by institutional administrators, they tend to be more satisfied overall. Moreover, when they receive recognition for their work and believe that their salaries accu-rately reflect the value of their contributions to their institu-tions, they report higher levels of satisfaction.

Several of these themes are particularly relevant to faculty ap-pointments that are off the tenure track. As described in Chapter Four, faculty in these positions often are not integrated well into their departments, they may have fewer opportunities to grow professionally, they may be treated with limited respect by colleagues and administrators, and they may receive inequitable treatment in terms of salary and access to the resources needed to accomplish their work. As the proportion of faculty members in contract-renewable and fixed-term appointments has grown, institutions have too often failed to consider how to create workplaces where every faculty member is treated equitably and supported in ways that allow them to do their best work.

CONTRIBUTORS TO JOB SATISFACTION IN GENERAL

The complex concept of workers' satisfaction in general has been explored and empirically researched by numerous authors outside the context of higher education. Several leading theories of workers' satisfaction align closely with research on faculty specifically, and point to consistent ways in which work can be both understood and supported.

Frederick Taylor undertook some of the earliest research on workers' satisfaction and motivation. In the context of mass production, he proposed that workers first and foremost want high wages from their employers. To motivate them to work efficiently and productively, he suggested paying them the highest possible wages (Dimitrova, 1994; Mullins, 1996). Nevertheless, as workers felt increasingly dehumanized and demotivated in the large bureaucratic organizations and mass-production facilities of the mid-twentieth century, research interests shifted toward the role of interpersonal needs in motivating and satisfying workers. The so-named human relations movement emphasized the key roles that supervisors and work groups play in determining employees' satisfaction (Locke, 1976).

In the ensuing years, a number of theories regarding satisfaction grew out of this increased focus on social organization and the individual worker. These theories are generally classified into two categories: (1) *content* theories, which explain job satisfaction in terms of needs that must be met or values that must be present in work in order for workers to be satisfied, and (2) *process* or *discrepancy* theories, which focus on the actual process of motivation.

These theories explain job satisfaction in terms of the level of similarity between an individual's work values or goals and what the individual receives and experiences in the workplace. The content theorists include Maslow, Alderfer, McClelland, Herzberg, and the team of Hackman and Oldham. Locke is an example of a process theorist.

To look first at content theories, Maslow's needs-hierarchy theory (Maslow, 1970) proposes that people are motivated by a desire to satisfy a variety of needs. These needs can be arranged in a hierarchy of five levels, listed here from lowest to highest:

1. Basic physiological needs (food, water, air, sleep)
2. Safety needs (shelter as well as psychological security)
3. Social needs (belonging, acceptance, and love)
4. Esteem needs (receiving recognition for accomplishments and respect from peers)
5. Self-actualization (reaching one's highest potential and attaining a sense of fulfillment through advancement, autonomy, and opportunities for creativity)

Maslow proposed that lower-order needs must be at least partially satisfied before the individual's attention shifts to higher-order needs. Only unsatisfied needs motivate a person. Maslow theorized that most workers would be unable to satisfy fully the higher-level needs. Therefore, they would remain perpetually motivated. Maslow's theory has been useful in reminding employers to focus on more than simply salary and physical working conditions as they consider what motivates and satisfies individuals.

Alderfer (1972) was one of the first to empirically evaluate some of Maslow's basic hypotheses (Arnolds and Boshoff, 2000). Through this work, he built on Maslow's theory and proposed three levels of human needs:

1. Existence needs, similar to Maslow's basic physiological and safety needs
2. Relatedness needs, like Maslow's social needs, which include the need to belong and the need for respect
3. Growth needs, analogous to self-actualization needs

Alderfer believed that these needs are more like a continuum than a hierarchy and that individuals can simultaneously have more than one need activated. Nevertheless, he still viewed them as lower-level (existence) and higher-level (growth) needs.

Rather than focus on human needs generally, McClelland (1975) dealt specifically with workers' satisfaction. An important contribution was his belief that factors leading to satisfaction differ across individuals as well as across occupations. He proposed that workers find satisfaction by meeting three central needs: achievement, power, and affiliation. All workers have these needs, but a particular need tends to dominate in each person. Those with a high need for achievement, for example, find satisfaction in solving difficult problems on their own, doing outstanding work, and trying to get ahead in their jobs. Power needs, according to McClelland, manifest themselves as individuals seek to influence and control others' activities. Individuals with these needs are status- and prestige-oriented more than performance-oriented. Finally, some people have a high need for affiliation, which causes them to focus naturally on interpersonal relationships in their work and to be more satisfied in cooperative rather than competitive work environments. Research into McClelland's theory of achievement motivation has generally supported his ideas, particularly for managers (Medcof and Hausdorf, 1995; Riggio, 1990).

Herzberg (1966) extended the human relations school of thought by proposing the two-factor theory. Job satisfaction, he argued, is not based on a single continuum ranging from dissatisfaction to satisfaction; instead, he proposed, job satisfaction and dissatisfaction are separate and independent dimensions. If one set of factors is missing, their absence leads to dissatisfaction, but if those factors are present, they do not lead to satisfaction. These factors are related to the external nature of one's job, and Herzberg called them "hygienes." They include salary, supervision, interpersonal relations, and working conditions. He further argued that intrinsic features of work, or "motivators," including achievement, recognition, the work itself, responsibility, and advancement, generate job satisfaction. The hygiene factors approximate Maslow's lower-level needs, and the motivators reflect the higher-level needs.

Subsequent research testing this theory has led to mixed results. Some researchers have questioned the presence of two distinct factors, and others have found that the theory does not take individual differences into account. For example, hygienes and motivators are not consistently divided across individuals; a given factor, such as salary, may cause satisfaction for some people but dissatisfaction for others (Mullins, 1996; Riggio, 1990).

One more content theory that explores the relationship between job characteristics and job satisfaction was presented by Hackman and Oldham (1976). According to their job-characteristics model, satisfaction requires three important psychological states: workers must feel that their work is meaningful, they must feel a sense of responsibility in their jobs, and they must have knowledge of the results of their work. In addition, five job characteristics contribute to meaningfulness, responsibility, and knowledge of results:

1. *Skill variety,* a worker's ability to use a number of abilities and skills in his or her work
2. *Task identity,* a worker's involvement with an entire job or function
3. *Task significance,* a worker's perception of the extent to which his or her work has a significant impact on people in or outside the organization
4. *Autonomy,* a worker's ability to choose how to schedule and perform job assignments
5. *Feedback,* a worker's ability to receive direct and clear evaluation of his or her performance

According to Hackman and Oldham, these five characteristics do not play equally important roles in determining whether a job will be satisfying. Specifically, the authors argue that autonomy and feedback are essential, and that at least one of the other three factors must be present as well. In addition, one's need for personal growth and development serves as a moderator. If a worker does not desire to grow, improving the five core job characteristics will probably not lead to increased satisfaction. Researchers have tested this model extensively, and the results have generally supported its hypotheses (Fried and Ferris, 1987).

As already stated, process or discrepancy theories emphasize the degree of similarity between what an individual worker values or desires and what the workplace provides. Locke (1976) in particular emphasized the important role that an individual's values, goals, and perceptions of the work environment play in determining satisfaction. The level of satisfaction is a combination of "the *discrepancy* . . . between what the individual wants . . . and what he perceives himself as getting, and the *importance* of what is wanted . . . to the individual" (Locke, 1976, p. 1304).

The theories just cited vary significantly: some focus on satisfaction through work itself (Herzberg, 1966; Hackman and Oldham, 1976), and others focus on general human needs that work can in part fulfill (Maslow, 1970; Alderfer, 1972; McClelland, 1975). Some theories are more appropriate for white-collar workers (Herzberg, 1966; McClelland, 1975), but others apply more easily across occupations (Maslow, 1970; Alderfer, 1972; Locke, 1976). Further, some of these theories consider how workers vary in their needs and priorities (McClelland, 1975; Hackman and Oldham, 1976; Locke, 1976), whereas others assume that all workers have traits in common (Maslow, 1970; Herzberg, 1966; Alderfer, 1972).

What several of the theories have in common is that workers have the following needs:

- To form meaningful relationships with coworkers; to belong to and participate in the organization (Alderfer, 1972; Herzberg, 1966; Maslow, 1970; McClelland, 1975)
- To have challenging work, with opportunities for creativity, that leads to personal growth (Alderfer, 1972; Hackman and Oldham, 1976; Herzberg, 1966; Maslow, 1970; McClelland, 1975)
- To be treated with respect (Alderfer, 1972; Maslow, 1970)
- To have ownership or a sense of responsibility for one's work (Hackman and Oldham, 1976; Herzberg, 1966)
- To have autonomy in one's work (Hackman and Oldham, 1976; Maslow, 1970)
- To receive recognition for one's work and have the opportunity for advancement (Herzberg, 1966; Maslow, 1970)
- To receive feedback about one's work (Hackman and Oldham, 1976; Locke, 1976)

To summarize this research, individuals value satisfying work. There are many components of this kind of work, and not all people define the concept in the same way. Nevertheless, experiencing a sense of belonging, growing professionally, feeling respected, and having autonomy in one's work are key concepts that run through the literature on workers' satisfaction.

CONCLUSIONS

Higher education leaders, taking these lessons from empirical research to heart, need to recognize the importance of constructing work environments where every faculty member has the opportunity to create meaningful and satisfying work for himself or herself. Academic work has traditionally been seen as a profession that provided abundant opportunities for self-actualization. In addition, important job characteristics—such as opportunities for recognition, for engaging in new and challenging work, and for promotion—have been typical of tenure-track positions. The challenge today is to provide an environment where, regardless of appointment type or individual demographics, all faculty members have the opportunity to maximize their intellectual talents, to grow professionally, to have their work respected, and to be members of the academic community. Simultaneously optimizing these qualities in faculty work should not only help institutions improve faculty recruitment and retention but also help every faculty member be in a position to do his or her best work.

The chapters in Part II present a framework for re-envisioning faculty work. This framework reflects changes in the American workplace broadly, and in faculty work and the academic workplace as specifically described in Chapters One through Five. The framework is designed to help institutional leaders create faculty work configurations that will better meet institutional as well as individual needs. Grounded in empirical research, and based upon a foundation of respect, it highlights the importance of key elements of faculty work: equity, academic freedom and autonomy, flexibility, professional growth, and collegiality in every appointment type. These key elements are drawn from the literature on faculty satisfaction (Barnes, Agago, and Coombs, 1998; Black and Holden, 1998; Donohue, 1986; Hagedorn, 1996; Hult, Callister, and Sullivan, 2005; Johnsrud and Rosser, 2004; Olsen, Maple, and Stage, 1995; Rosser, 2004) and from the more general literature on satisfying and meaningful work that has been reviewed in this chapter (Alderfer, 1972; Hackman and Oldham, 1976; Herzberg, 1966; Maslow, 1970; McClelland, 1975). By using this framework, institutional leaders can examine the strengths and weaknesses of their workplaces and the extent to which they are strategically utilizing and supporting the talents and abilities of all faculty members across different appointment types.

The academy has the opportunity to be a leader in providing solutions to the challenges of a changing workplace and workforce because the academic career is suited to new configurations that can serve as models for other professions. In this way, academia can make a valuable contribution to American society. It can stay ahead of the competition, too. To recruit and retain excellent faculty, higher education institutions need to offer a wider array of attractive work options. Universities and colleges cannot offer the highest salaries, at least in some fields (NEA Higher Education Research Center, 2004). Therefore, it is wise to offer work environments that take into account and address the needs, interests, and motivations of today's workers.

PART TWO

THE FRAMEWORK

Given the changes that are affecting faculty work and workplaces, it is time to rethink how to create academic environments that attract and retain excellent faculty, because the work faculty do is critical to the ability of higher education institutions to fulfill their missions.

Chapter Six presents a framework for conceptualizing faculty work. The framework features five essential elements that are important in the work experience of all faculty members, regardless of the types of academic appointments they hold. The framework also accounts for the characteristics and backgrounds that faculty members bring to their work as well as for each institution's unique history, mission, culture, and organizational structure. Furthermore, the framework suggests the kinds of outcomes likely to occur when its essential elements are incorporated into faculty work.

A culture of respect and a commitment to shared responsibility from faculty members and administrators alike are both critical to fostering an environment where the essential elements are part of faculty work and the academic workplace. Chapter Seven discusses the qualities of a culture of respect and how it can be nurtured. Chapter Eight delineates the shared responsibilities for the quality of the academic workplace and the important leadership roles played by academic administrators and faculty members.

CHAPTER SIX

THE FRAMEWORK OF ESSENTIAL ELEMENTS

Making the academic career attractive to talented people is fundamental if U.S. higher education is to continue both its worldwide preeminence and its contributions to American society. But this is a challenging task, as earlier chapters have shown. Colleges and universities are struggling today to meet escalating demands for greater productivity and accountability across numerous and conflicting priorities, and within increasing fiscal constraints. They are doing so with a more diverse faculty in a variety of academic appointments.

Given the growth in the sheer numbers and diversity of backgrounds and lifestyles of faculty members, the normative notion of what constitutes an academic career needs to be expanded. Furthermore, as the chapters in Part I have shown, colleges and universities, trying to meet increasing and conflicting external demands, have hired faculty members into an array of appointments. This proliferation of various types of faculty appointments, with their differences in compensation and support structures, raises important questions about whether all faculty members are treated equitably and with respect by their institutions, and about whether their talents are being fully utilized. Hallmarks of the traditional academic profession, such as opportunities to participate in shared governance, enjoy the rights associated with academic freedom, and participate in collegial scholarly communities, are not necessarily included in all academic appointments, nor are all faculty members eligible for participation in various programs and activities aimed at professional growth. As a result, many faculty

members today do not necessarily experience the traditional autonomy of the academic profession; instead, they work as "managed professionals" (Rhoades, 1998). When any member of the
academic community is not respected or valued, or when his or
her talents are not fully utilized, both the faculty member and his
or her college or university loses. Higher education leaders are
faced with the dilemma of meeting all these challenges at a time
when resources are scarce and societal expectations for higher education are expanding.

To meet these challenges, faculty and administrators need to
give thoughtful attention to rethinking academic work and workplaces in order to meet institutional goals and priorities, recruit
and retain excellent faculty, and maximize the intellectual capital
represented by all faculty. A piecemeal approach to dealing with
the various elements comprising the dramatic changes in academic
workplaces, faculty, and society, as discussed in Part I, will not provide long-term solutions to the issues now facing higher education.
To remain competitive and accomplish its many societal mandates,
the higher education community must rethink the academic career, the organization of faculty work, and how universities and colleges utilize and support all faculty members in their varied roles.

In this chapter, we propose a framework of essential elements
for rethinking the academic career to meet the needs of the twenty-
first century. Our framework retains the essential principles and values of the academic profession but expands on them to answer this
strategic question: How can academic work be organized in ways
that more fully achieve institutional and faculty goals and priorities?
This general question can be stated more specifically:

- What are the essential elements of faculty work and the academic workplace that, when in place, enhance institutional
  efforts to recruit and retain highly capable faculty?
- What specific institutional policies and practices contribute to
  an academic workplace that supports all faculty members in
  carrying out excellent work in service to institutional missions?

The framework that we present applies and expands essential
features of the traditional academic profession to the diverse faculty members, academic appointments, and colleges and universi-

ties that characterize higher education today. The framework is intended to be a resource for faculty and administrators in individual institutions who seek to build essential and valued components of the academic profession into the variety of academic appointments and career paths that exist today, and who want to recognize more fully and maximize the contributions of all faculty members (young and old, tenured and not) in the achievement of institutional goals. The chapters in Part II explain the framework and its major components. The chapters in Part III explore each of the essential elements of this framework in turn and offer specific recommendations for incorporating them into academic work and workplaces in individual colleges and universities.

THE TRADITIONAL FOUNDATIONS OF THE ACADEMIC CAREER

The traditional relationship between faculty members and their institutions was codified by the American Association of University Professors in 1940, in a statement that was subsequently affirmed by many leaders in higher education associations and institutions (American Association of University Professors, 2001c). The AAUP statement, by codifying key values and elements of the academic profession, has worked well. Its provisions are just as timely now as they were nearly seventy years ago. But what is needed now is a reformulation of those principles, based on today's higher education institutions and faculty members.

The AAUP's 1940 statement defined tenure as the ideal employment system for protecting the academic freedom of faculty. According to the statement, the way to ensure academic freedom was through an employment contract that guaranteed permanent or continuous employment and due process in the event of termination for cause. During the twentieth century, tenure was seen as playing a major role in the excellence of American higher education.

Tenure defined a mutually beneficial, reciprocal relationship between colleges and universities and their faculty members. Tenured faculty members were guaranteed job security, autonomy in the exercise of their responsibilities, and academic freedom at their institutions. In exchange, faculty members made long-term commitments to their institutions, used their intellectual capital for the benefit of their academic communities and society, and assumed responsibility for academic decision making in an environment of shared governance.

In sum, the tenure contract constituted an ideal and sufficient employment relationship between faculty and their institutions when the higher education enterprise was much smaller and more collegial, and when faculty members were predominantly "ideal workers" or men whose spouses assumed household responsibilities. Today, colleges and universities have enormously complex and varied missions, cultures, and resources. Faculty members are diverse men and women of varying lifestyles and backgrounds; many seek a balance between their academic careers and their increasingly complex lives. And the majority of faculty members today occupy non-tenure-track positions.

In this current context, it is important to find ways to retain the substance of the key traditions of tenure, academic freedom and sufficient job security, and simultaneously to ensure that all faculty members, regardless of their appointment types, are supported in their work and valued by their institutions. The framework described in this chapter aims to retain the essence of these academic traditions but apply them to all types of faculty appointments.

Discussion of this framework begins with an examination of the nature of today's reciprocal relationship between faculty and their institutions and of their shared responsibility for the well-being of the faculty as well as of the colleges or universities that employ them. Although reciprocity and mutual dependence have always characterized the relationship between faculty members and their institutions, the academic employment system is now multifaceted. Alongside their tenured colleagues, faculty members without tenure also do valuable work. They have, however, a different kind of reciprocal relationship with their colleges and universities. Faculty employed outside the tenure system maintain job security through their multiple-year contracts and employability, or marketability (Waterman, Waterman, and Collard, 1994). These two phenomena, multiyear contracts and employability, form the basis of a new kind of reciprocal relationship. This new relationship emphasizes faculty's commitment to their institutions' success during their time of employment and faculty's use of their intellectual capital for their institutions' benefit. In return, colleges and universities enhance individual faculty members' employability by providing a new form of job security that comes from continuous professional growth and multiyear contracts. With their portfolios guaranteeing their ability to relocate as necessary, faculty members today, in keeping with the professional workforce outside academe, are less concerned about a contractual guarantee of continuous employment over their entire careers.

The reciprocal relationship between the individual faculty member and the institution is the essential foundation for tenured and non-tenured faculty alike. On the one hand, all faculty members need to be supported in their work, to be treated with respect and fairness, and to have some measure of security in their appointments. On the other hand, faculty members owe their institutions good work and participation in institutional governance. In sum, faculty members as well as administrators are responsible for the well-being of the college or university. An updated concept of the traditional academic reciprocal relationship retains the AAUP's belief that "the variety and complexity of the tasks performed by institutions of higher education produce an inescapable interdependence among governing boards, administration[s], [and] faculty" (American Association of University Professors, 2001b, p. 218). The framework presented here yields its maximum value when faculty members and their institutions share responsibility and work together to define and develop strategies for improving their current working environments and for ensuring that all faculty members participate in the benefits derived from these improvements.

Framework for Rethinking Faculty Work and Workplaces

Today all faculty appointments, regardless of whether they are to tenured, contract-renewable, or fixed-term appointments, should embrace a set of essential elements of faculty work. These essential elements are the glue that holds the individual faculty member and the college or university in a mutually rewarding reciprocal relationship. They need to be incorporated into every faculty member's appointment, regardless of whether it is to a tenure-track position or not. When the essential elements are in place, academic institutions and their faculty members benefit from a work environment that places a high priority on achieving excellence by making faculty work meaningful and manageable. In addition, ensuring that all faculty members benefit from the essential elements improves recruitment and retention and enhances the intellectual capital that each faculty member brings to his or her institution. These outcomes are fundamental to institutional success because the intellectual capital of the faculty is the most valuable resource that institutions have for achieving their goals. Every faculty member, regardless of his or her appointment type, contributes to the intellectual mosaic created in a college or university. Therefore, colleges and universities will improve their overall excellence by creating environments in which the intellectual contributions of all faculty members can be fully realized.

The framework presented here is intended to be a resource for colleges and universities and their faculty members. It is a comprehensive and strategic tool for each institution to use in examining its current academic employment policies and practices and deciding where, what, and how it wants to change. Institutions that are just beginning to look at potential changes in the academic work environment will find the framework a useful guide. Institutions that are in the midst of changing appointments and policies to meet emerging needs will find a wealth of ideas from other campuses. Colleges and universities that have already made considerable changes in their academic work environments can use the framework offered here to evaluate their efforts.

At the heart of the framework are the five key elements that all faculty members, regardless of their appointment types, should experience in their work:

- Employment equity
- Academic freedom and autonomy
- Flexibility
- Professional growth
- Collegiality

These essential elements are built upon and surround a foundation or core requirement of respect. Because respect is a fundamental requirement of the framework, it is discussed in some depth in Chapter Seven. The presence of these essential elements enhances faculty work and contributes to the strategic priorities of colleges and universities.

These elements have always been important to faculty members, but how they are addressed in academic institutions must be revisited so as to take account of the significant changes in faculty members and faculty appointments in recent years. When individual faculty members benefit from the availability of policies, programs, and services associated with each of these essential elements, higher education institutions are likely to realize certain important outcomes as well. The entire framework is shown in Figure 6.1.

FACULTY AND INSTITUTIONAL CHARACTERISTICS

The work environment for faculty at any given college or university is a composite of faculty and institutional characteristics. The left side of Figure 6.1 highlights the unique characteristics of the faculty as a whole and of the institution itself at any given college or university. Within a college or university, these faculty and institutional characteristics need to be understood before the framework can be fully utilized.

Faculty Characteristics

Each faculty member enters a college or university with his or her individual set of sociodemographic characteristics and work experiences. The "Faculty Characteristics" area of Figure 6.1 includes the composite sociodemographic variables of an institution's faculty, such as age, race or ethnicity, and gender; personal attitudes and values; and prior education and work experiences. All these variables shape the individual faculty member's understanding of and expectations for faculty work (Blackburn and Lawrence, 1995). When these variables are aggregated, a composite picture of the sociodemographic characteristics of the faculty as a whole emerges. The "Faculty Characteristics" area also includes all the characteristics of the different types of academic appointments held by faculty members. Each college or university has its unique mix of tenure-track, renewable-contract, and fixed-term appointments. These various appointment types influence the work experiences of faculty members and their perceptions of the academic career.

FIGURE 6.1. FRAMEWORK OF ESSENTIAL ELEMENTS

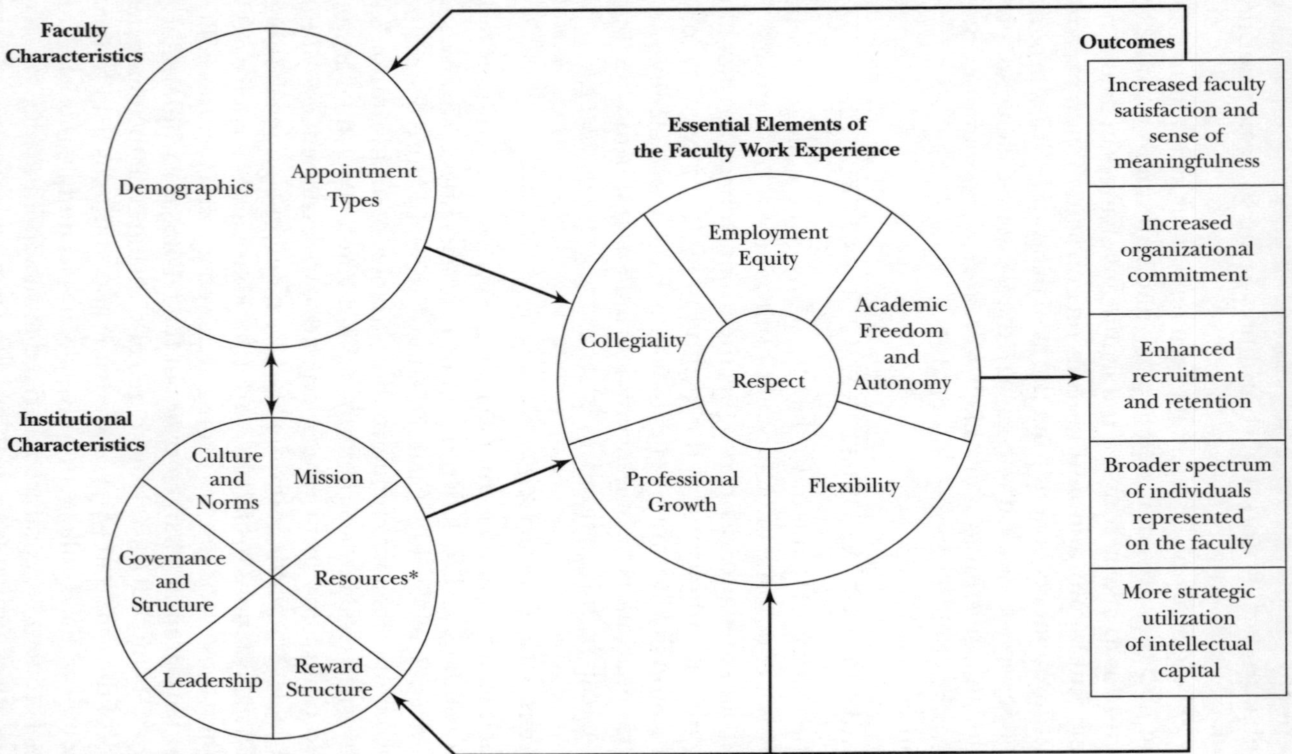

Faculty Characteristics

- Demographics
- Appointment Types

Institutional Characteristics

- Mission
- Culture and Norms
- Governance and Structure
- Resources*
- Leadership
- Reward Structure

Essential Elements of the Faculty Work Experience

- Respect
- Employment Equity
- Academic Freedom and Autonomy
- Collegiality
- Flexibility
- Professional Growth

Outcomes

- Increased faculty satisfaction and sense of meaningfulness
- Increased organizational commitment
- Enhanced recruitment and retention
- Broader spectrum of individuals represented on the faculty
- More strategic utilization of intellectual capital

* Fiscal, Human, Physical Resources

Understanding the characteristics of the faculty as a whole allows administrators and faculty members at a particular college or university to focus on those elements of the framework that would best meet the needs of the institution's unique faculty currently. For example, to ensure that all new faculty members understand the nature of faculty work and academic communities, institutions recruiting large numbers of early-career faculty may want to place greater emphasis on their orientation programs. Graduate preparation for the professoriate typically does not prepare students fully and systematically for future faculty careers (Austin, 2002; Wulff, Austin, Nyquist, and Sprague, 2004). Thus, aspiring and early-career faculty members often have a very limited understanding of the career itself, of what will be expected of them, of differences among institutions, and of higher education's history and cultures. Institutional orientations would help new faculty understand their various roles, their performance expectations, and the policies, practices, and perquisites governing the different types of academic appointments they occupy. As another example, an institution may study faculty characteristics, and realize that it has a large proportion of faculty who are approaching retirement. This institution may find it desirable to develop phased-retirement options, both so that faculty members can plan their transitions and so that the institution can better support them at this stage.

Institutional Characteristics

The academic workplace is also defined by various institutional characteristics, as is the way it is experienced by faculty members. Each college or university, and each of its subunits, has a distinctive culture, mission, and organizational history as well as distinct priorities and values (Austin, 1991, 1992a, 1994; Becher, 1984, 1987; Clark, 1987). For example, institutions are either public or private; and are variously structured as research universities, comprehensive universities, liberal arts colleges, or community colleges, with distinctive resources and academic offerings. Furthermore, although institutions generally have shared governance systems, there is great variance in how these systems are structured, how they function, and how faculty members can and do participate in them. Therefore, although academic workplaces have certain common features that make them distinct from corporations and from nonacademic not-for-profit entities, such as hospitals, each institution has its unique attributes in the higher education community. How each institution addresses and supports faculty work will vary according to particular institutional characteristics. Thus, each institution using this framework must take into account its unique characteristics.

Each institution is also uniquely organized into various academic units and subunits. These units, in turn, differ in their organizational structures and cultures, on the basis of size, complexity, mission, history, and resources. Thus institutional characteristics, as experienced by individual faculty members, can vary considerably from one unit to another within the same college or university. In addition, although employment policies may be centrally promulgated, employment practices as well as structures for evaluation and rewards can vary greatly among departments within the same institution. Communication patterns also vary by department or unit. An institution using this framework needs to consider these department- or unit-based differences.

SHARED RESPONSIBILITY FOR FACULTY WORK ENVIRONMENTS

To gain maximum value from the framework, administrators and faculty members must make a joint commitment to rethinking academic workplaces and sharing responsibility for change. Faculty members and administrators must work together to assess current institutional support for the key elements of faculty work, and to identify and prioritize specific ways to improve the institutional environment to enhance both the workplace and the faculty's contribution to the institution. The reciprocal relationship between faculty members and their institutions is depicted in Figure 6.2 in the arrows between the circles labeled "Faculty" and "Administrators." The shared responsibility of faculty and administrators is symbolized in the arrows that go from the circles labeled "Faculty" and "Administrators" to the essential elements.

Shared governance has been a hallmark of the academic career. Because shared responsibility is fundamental to using the framework, Chapter Eight discusses this topic in depth; here, it is simply incorporated into the framework to capture the fact that

FIGURE 6.2. IMPACT OF FACULTY AND
INSTITUTIONAL CHARACTERISTICS ON THE ESSENTIAL ELEMENTS

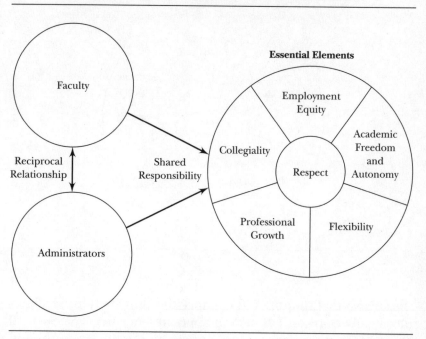

faculty and administrators must take joint responsibility and work together to ensure that academic workplaces function to enhance faculty work and faculty members' contributions to the institution.

RESPECT AND THE ESSENTIAL ELEMENTS OF THE FACULTY WORK EXPERIENCE

The central circle of the framework contains the five essential elements of faculty work and workplaces that apply to all types of faculty appointments, surrounding the core requirement of respect (see Figure 6.3). These essential elements are drawn from the literature on faculty satisfaction and from the more general literature on satisfying and meaningful work (see Chapter Five). They constitute the centerpiece of the framework and are critically important in enabling colleges and universities to achieve faculty

Figure 6.3. Five Essential Elements

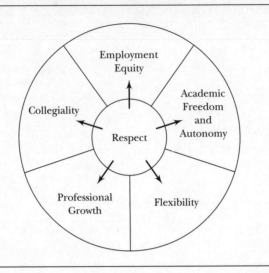

workplaces that support and enhance the contributions of all faculty members, regardless of their appointment types. The essential elements serve as benchmarks for examining the strengths and weaknesses of faculty workplaces in institutions and for gauging the extent to which institutions are strategically utilizing and supporting the talents and abilities of all faculty members.

These essential elements should pervade each faculty member's work, but how they may be manifested at different institutions will vary according to the needs of faculty members, types of appointment used, and institutional cultures and resources. For example, professional development programs and activities for faculty would differ among institutions according to institutional missions and goals. How the elements apply to individual faculty members at a particular institution would also vary according to their particular situations or appointment types. For instance, where the element of employment equity is concerned, peer review of faculty members' performance would occur for all faculty members at an institution, but the format and timing of those reviews would vary according to the type of appointment. Or again, professional development opportunities would be available to every faculty member, but various types of programs and services would be aimed at the needs of faculty members at different times in their careers, or at faculty members in particular assignments.

THE CORE OF RESPECT

By placing respect at the very center of the circle, we make respect a foundational requirement for each element. The definition of respect varies by context, but the term as used here means the basic human valuing of every faculty member. Respect is a fundamental entitlement for every faculty member (indeed, for every employee) and is at the core of any reciprocal relationship between faculty members and their institutions. Only in an environment of respect for every faculty member can institutions and faculty members fully benefit from the five essential elements that surround the core of respect.

Our placement of respect at the framework's center, as its core requirement, is based on theories related to motivation and work satisfaction (Herzberg, 1966; Maslow, 1970; Alderfer, 1972) that emphasize the importance of intrinsic factors (including respect) and on research from the corporate sector that shows respect to be a fundamental or basic need of most employees (Campbell and Koblenz, 1997). Respect underlies all institutional efforts to provide an academic work environment that stimulates personal and institutional growth and success. The five essential elements of faculty work cannot be effective without their core of respect, because, unless and until all faculty members (in fact, all employees) feel that they are respected, they are less likely to place much importance on the other elements or to benefit from them.

THE FIVE ESSENTIAL ELEMENTS DEFINED

Each of the five essential elements is related to a unique dimension of faculty work. Each element stands as a separate and unique attribute of faculty work and workplaces that individually makes its contribution to the quality of every faculty member's work experience. But the elements are also interdependent and nonhierarchical. They interact with each other. The benefits derived from practices developed to enhance one element can and do impact and enhance other elements at the same time. For example, equity in faculty employment cannot be achieved without flexibility during the probationary period for tenure-track faculty.

Taken together, the essential elements provide a road map that leads to strategic actions that administrators and faculty members can take to improve their academic working environments, enhance meaningfulness and satisfaction for faculty members, and strengthen institutional excellence. In this section each of the five essential elements is defined and illustrated. These definitions are, of necessity, very general. Faculty members and administrators in each college or university will need to define the operational parameters for each element in light of their own circumstances and resources. The intent, however, is to ensure that each element is available to all faculty members, regardless of their appointment types, so that each faculty member can do his or her best work and find satisfaction and meaning in so doing.

Employment Equity

This element is defined here as the right of every faculty member (regardless of appointment type or time base) to be treated fairly in regard to all aspects of his or her employment by the institution and its departments, to have access to the tools necessary to do his or her job, and to have status as a fully fledged, albeit necessarily different, member of the faculty. Here are two examples of equity in action:

- For each type of academic appointment, employment policies (such as defined probationary periods, explicit evaluation criteria and processes, time frames for peer reviews for decisions regarding contract renewals, and equitable compensation plans, including benefits) are developed in accordance with institutionwide guidelines and carried out consistently across the institution.
- All faculty members, regardless of their appointment types, are provided with sufficient office space, equipment, tools, and support services to successfully accomplish their work.

Academic Freedom and Autonomy

This element is defined here as the right of all faculty members to freely express their views in research and in the publication of results, in the classroom in discussing their subjects, and as citizens without institutional censorship, when such views are appropriately and responsibly expressed (American Association of University Professors, 2001c), and the right of all faculty members to make decisions autonomously about how to perform their assignments. Here are three examples of academic freedom and autonomy in action:

- Academic freedom rights are clearly defined and extended to all faculty members, regardless of their appointment types, for the duration of their terms of employment.
- Procedures for grieving alleged violations of academic freedom rights for different types of faculty appointments provide due process and are specified in faculty manuals.
- All faculty members have autonomy with regard to how they teach the courses they are assigned.

Flexibility

This element is defined here as the ability of faculty members to construct work arrangements to maximize their contributions to their institution as well as the meaningfulness of their work and personal lives. Here are two examples of flexibility in action:

- Policies and practices allow tenure-track faculty members to take leaves or change their full-time commitments during the probationary period in order to meet their personal as well as their professional responsibilities.
- Assistance is given to individuals in managing their personal responsibilities through provision of referrals to services for elder care.

Professional Growth

This element is defined here as opportunities that enable faculty members to broaden their knowledge, abilities, and skills, to address challenges, concerns, and needs, and to find deeper satisfaction in their work. Here are two examples of professional growth in action:

- Orientation programs provide information about college or university policies, services, programs, and resources to all new faculty members, regardless of their appointment types.
- Opportunities are offered to faculty in departments to plan their workloads as a unit so that every continuing faculty

member has occasional reductions in his or her teaching workload and can engage in experiences aimed at professional growth.

Collegiality

This element is defined here as opportunities for faculty members to feel that they belong to a mutually respectful community of colleagues who value their unique contributions to their institutions and who are concerned about their overall well-being. Here are two examples of collegiality in action:

- Opportunities are available to participate in decision making at the departmental, college, or institutional level as appropriate.
- There is respectful and comfortable communication among faculty members, regardless of their appointment types.

Combined, these elements form a comprehensive whole, and they work together to achieve their maximum effectiveness. For example, fair treatment that does not include either collegiality or the opportunity to grow professionally is of little value. Likewise, individuals who have too little flexibility in their positions find that they may not have the time or occasion to enjoy opportunities for professional growth, significant participation in governance, or collegial relationships.

Responsibility for enhancing these essential elements of the faculty work experience must be shared between faculty and administrators on each campus. Members of both groups need to participate in making strategic decisions about which elements most need attention and which specific approaches best fit the campus's culture and needs. Creating working environments that enhance intellectual capital and nourish the minds and spirits of faculty members cannot be accomplished by administrators or faculty alone; participation and commitment from both is vital for success.

Outcomes

The right side of the framework shown in Figure 6.1 lists outcomes obtained from increased attention to the essential elements. When the essential elements are incorporated into faculty work and workplaces, individual as well as institutional benefits accrue. When all faculty members are treated respectfully and equitably, have access to appropriate opportunities for professional development, participate in decision making about their work as members of a community of scholars, and can arrange for flexibility in their academic careers so as to meet their personal responsibilities, they are more likely to find satisfaction in their work and have greater commitment to their institutions. In turn, colleges and universities with working environments that are characterized by the presence of the essential elements should expect greater success in their efforts to recruit and retain excellent and diverse faculty members.

Both sets of outcomes—increased faculty satisfaction and institutional success—feed back into and enhance overall faculty and institutional characteristics. We believe, for example, that when faculty have the opportunity to develop cutting-edge teaching skills, balance their personal and work lives, and participate in decisions about curriculum design, they will be better able to provide an enriched learning environment and to contribute in significant ways to their colleges or universities. At the bottom line, positive outcomes for faculty lead to enhanced institutional outcomes, such as the enrichment of the learning environment for students, increased scholarly and research productivity, and greater contributions to the college or university community and to the public good.

CONCLUSIONS

The framework introduced in this chapter is an organized and comprehensive format for rethinking the academic work experience. It suggests the elements that every college or university needs to have in place in order to create an attractive and supportive academic work environment for all faculty members, regardless of their appointment types. The framework can be a useful tool for campuses seeking to assess and strengthen their faculty work environments. Each institution will prioritize different issues according to its own circumstances, and individual departments or units within institutions may emphasize different areas. We also invite readers to use the framework as a basis for further research and to test the relationships between the essential elements and the various individual and institutional outcomes.

Some readers will immediately link the essential elements to institutional resources and tough financial times by wondering how much it will all cost. Others will question how the essential elements, with their emphasis on equity for all faculty members, are to be reconciled with union contracts, which may stipulate, for example, hierarchical approaches to reductions-in-force, with senior tenured faculty at the very end of the line. Still other readers will claim that competitive environments emphasizing status and prestige, not equity, are what foster faculty productivity and hard work. All these questions and assumptions miss the rationale for our having developed the framework and its essential elements. Research argues that these essential elements are critical to employees' well-being and productivity. The essential elements are intended to be used to assess various components of individual campuses' faculty workplaces so that institutions can take action to enhance the intellectual contribution that each faculty member makes. The essential elements, taken together and working synergistically, are powerful tools for recruitment and retention of excellent faculty members. Although each campus will use these elements in different ways, those campuses that realign their faculty workplaces to reflect the presence of the essential elements are likely to experience increased faculty satisfaction and organizational commitment to the achievement of institutional goals and missions.

CHAPTER SEVEN

RESPECT: THE FOUNDATION FOR THE ESSENTIAL ELEMENTS

Respect is the basic human valuing of people for who they are and for what they uniquely contribute to their organizations. Respect is a fundamental entitlement of every faculty member, and it must be at the center of institutional efforts to provide academic work environments that stimulate personal and institutional growth and success.

In Chapter Six, we proposed a framework for rethinking academic work and workplaces. We believe that when the framework's five essential elements are in place, faculty performance is enhanced, faculty members experience greater satisfaction in their work, and institutional excellence is strengthened. But only in an environment where each faculty member is respected can institutions and faculty members fully benefit from the five essential elements. Likewise, unless all faculty members believe that they are respected, they are unlikely to value or benefit from the essential elements. This chapter explores more fully the importance of respect and then suggests strategies for ensuring that respect permeates the campus culture.

THE IMPORTANCE OF RESPECT

Our concept of respect as the foundation for an attractive work environment is based on theories that emphasize the importance of intrinsic factors in achieving and maintaining motivation and work satisfaction (Herzberg, 1966; Maslow, 1970; Alderfer, 1972). In particular, work by Herzberg (1966) and others differentiates those things that motivate and satisfy and those that simply alleviate dissatisfaction. Herzberg's work identifies such intrinsic factors as achievement and recognition, which serve as motivators as compared to extrinsic factors, such as interpersonal relations and security, which at best only diminish dissatisfaction.

Also of interest is a study by Campbell and Koblenz (1997) for the Baxter Healthcare Corporation that shows the importance workers placed on respect in their work environment. The study concerned dissatisfaction in the corporate sector, but the responses of the employees who participated have relevance to our framework. In that survey, employees viewed some aspects of the work experience as "entitlements" and some as "benefits." Specifically, they reported that feeling respected was an entitlement and was essential to satisfaction. Second in importance was being able to achieve a reasonable balance between work and personal life, and for most workers this was also perceived as an entitlement. Flexibility in how and when their work was accomplished was third in importance to these employees, followed by work-life programs. Flexibility and work-life programs were both perceived to be benefits rather than entitlements.

Of course, what is perceived to be an entitlement rather than a benefit varies from workplace to workplace and is embedded in organizational culture. But, as in Maslow's hierarchy of needs (Maslow, 1970), the results of this study show that those components of work that were perceived as entitlements did not, when addressed, provide a positive return to the organization because employees believed they were owed them and thus were not grateful for them. When the perceived entitlements were *not* addressed, however, employees reported turnover, apathy, low productivity, and unwillingness to go the proverbial extra mile. They also indicated that unless respect and balance were provided, the benefits that the organization offered in the form of flexible policies and programs (such as child care) to support their work were not valued. In other words, there are costs associated with failure to provide the entitlements, and without them, the benefits are not perceived to be benefits. The results of the Campbell and Koblenz (1997) study clearly show that employees regarded respect as the foundational entitlement.

Despite the importance of respect, not all members of an organization experience it. Whether respect is perceived as part of one's experience is in the eye of the beholder: it is an intangible, felt sensation. Nevertheless, although the presence or absence of respect is difficult to measure and describe, faculty members certainly sense whether they are valued by their colleagues, as excerpts from interviews with part-time faculty reveal (Gappa and Leslie, 1993):

> Part-time faculty mail slots in the humanities department were set up as a separate class, positioned below those for the full-time faculty. After we protested, they are now alphabetically integrated. It is the little things like this . . . that make us aware of status inferiority [p. 191].

> In my department they have a reception for new teachers. I'm teaching for the first time and I was invited. But as a part-timer I was not mentioned. No one thought of introducing me as a new person. I'm a nonperson. I'm teaching the course better than it's ever been taught, but I'm a nonperson [p. 192].

CULTIVATING A CULTURE OF RESPECT

Even though a culture of respect may be intangible, it is the core foundation from which to nurture other elements that enhance academic work and workplaces. Creating a culture of respect is not easy, however, and no single person can accomplish this. Instead, each member of the community must play a role. Proactive leadership at all levels is essential, as is faculty commitment to ensuring that respect is integral to all activities and interactions. Chapter Eight explores more extensively the shared responsibility of faculty and administrators to address and support each essential element. Here, we emphasize several specific strategies that enhance a culture of respect.

Periodic "pulse taking" to assess the extent to which a culture of respect characterizes the academic workplace is a good starting place. Once a cultural audit is complete, it is important to consider how to create and support organizational values and how to actively include all members in the academic community. Each of these topics is addressed in turn in the sections that follow.

Auditing the Culture

Creating and nurturing a culture of respect requires periodic assessment of the college's or university's culture, academic workplace, and faculty satisfaction in order to see what is actually happening and set priorities for the future. Knowledge gained must then be shared with the campus community so that constituents are fully informed. Institutional research offices are key to accomplishing this periodic monitoring and assessment, but the leadership must come from presidents.

The cultural audit process that occurred at Kent State University provides a useful case study. The president initiated the process in 1997 by hiring external consultants to conduct an extensive cultural self-study of the institution in preparation for its next round of strategic planning. After receiving the consultant's report, the president appointed a cultural self-study advisory committee that was charged with analyzing the implications of the study and recommending ways for the university to address them.

The committee held several open forums to answer questions and gather suggestions about the process of developing recommended action steps. The committee then developed eight overriding themes that helped in organizing the recommendations in the report. First among these themes was the issue of respect. Exhibit 7.1 emphasizes its importance.

The committee ultimately determined that the most useful action would be to offer a limited number of recommendations, some requiring urgent attention and some acknowledging the need for more gradual change. Once the committee had developed a draft of its recommendations, the members circulated highlights to all university personnel and asked for feedback. On the basis of this feedback, a full report was issued in 1999, two years after the cultural self-study began. Exhibit 7.2 indicates the impact of the cultural audit on the campus community.

Another way to audit an institution's or department's culture, and to assess the extent to which it includes respect, is to use an organizational framework developed by Bolman and Deal (1997).

EXHIBIT 7.1. CULTURAL SELF-STUDY REPORT, KENT STATE UNIVERSITY

A. RESPECTING EACH PERSON'S ROLE

The bedrock of a successful culture is respect—true, deep, pervasive re-spect for each person's contribution. This is the cultural foundation upon which all of the other foundations are built. Without this base to build on, the other foundations will never last, and the organization is doomed to mediocrity, or worse. Trust in working relationships is per-haps the most valuable expression of respect.

Respect is one of the most powerful forces in human life. Data from previous projects has shown that when people's contribution to an organization is not respected, the result is almost always a dramati-cally less effective, less producing organization. This is equally true if their contribution is respected but they are unaware that this is the case. Barriers of distrust are inevitable without a strong culture of re-spect. People stop caring about their work. They lose all sense of com-mitment and loyalty. No one is willing to step forward and show leadership. Innovation withers.

Source: http://dept.kent.edu/ksucultural_survey/#executiveSummary (retrieved June 20, 2006).

Examination of a culture through Bolman and Deal's four lenses—structural, political, human resources, and symbolic—can help leaders pose important questions and provide a better under-standing of the culture's strengths and weaknesses.

The structural perspective is especially interested in policies and procedures in addition to the structures in place at an insti-tution. Consideration of this frame might lead to questions about how the organization of the institution, and of specific depart-ments, supports and respects all faculty members. Are support ser-vices available to faculty members who are not on campus during regular business hours? Do policies restrict the use of a number of programs on campus to tenure-track faculty members? Are ad-vising, teaching, and committee work assigned equitably across ap-pointment types and take into account varied workloads?

The political lens is concerned with how power is distributed among the members of an organization as well as with how scarce

EXHIBIT 7.2. COMMITTEE RECOMMENDATIONS, KENT STATE UNIVERSITY

The *encouragement of respect* for each person's role across the campus community stands out as one of the primary areas of need. Put simply, we recommend that when we appreciate what someone has done, we should let that person know. Leaders can be role models for this recognition. We further recommend concerted action to develop a community that values and reflects diversity. Finally, because staff feel particularly undervalued, we recommend special steps to make their voice heard and to use their talents.

Because quality communication is the lifeblood of an organization, we recommend *strong commitment at all levels to clear, concise, civil, honest, and open communication* without fear of reprisal. We also address the need for widespread awareness of University processes and issues and better communication across unit boundaries.

To *encourage innovation and input at all levels,* we recommend several strategies for the reduction of bureaucracy and encouragement of innovative ideas at all levels.

In order to *push constantly for improvement at all levels,* we urge for improvement of relationships among departments. . . .We also suggest development of a performance evaluation system for administrators and exploration of financial incentives for classified civil service staff. . . . We urge wide dissemination of this committee report and frequent updates about the implementation of its recommendations. We also recommend continuing recourse to the original Self-Study Report in coming years as we develop ways to further improve the organizational culture of Kent State University.

Source: http://dept.kent.edu/ksucultural_survey/#executiveSummary (retrieved June 20, 2006).

resources are allocated. It also focuses on how coalitions as well as individuals influence the formation of goals and decisions. Working from this perspective, leaders might consider the extent to which faculty members experience respect by feeling enfranchised. Are faculty members with renewable contracts included in the faculty senate? Do probationary faculty members have a voice on important campuswide committees? Do fixed-term faculty participate in curriculum decisions in their departments? Leaders might also consider how resources for administrative support services are distributed across appointment types.

The human resources frame stresses the relationship between people and organizations. From this perspective, faculty members' skills, attitudes, and commitment are essential resources whose presence can make an institution flourish and whose absence can cause it to flounder. Here, the questions might include the extent to which faculty with renewable contracts or fixed-term appointments feel committed to the institution because they experience a reasonable level of job security through their contracts. At the unit level, the questions might include the extent to which faculty with renewable or fixed term contracts feel that the chair is accessible to them. A final question might be whether faculty members in all appointment types are benefiting from professional development opportunities.

In looking through the symbolic lens, emphasis is placed on what events mean more than on what actually takes place, and on the importance of rituals and ceremonies, stories, and myths. Using this framework, leaders can ask how symbols convey respect or lack of respect for faculty members. Are faculty with renewable contracts and fixed-term faculty assigned office space alongside tenure-track faculty members, or are their offices in a less desirable location, or even in a separate building? Does a departmental directory list the names of lecturers and fixed-term faculty below the names of tenure-track faculty rather than integrating them into one list? Using this frame, leaders might also explore the extent to which diverse faculty members are included in the ceremonies that are highly valued at the institution.

CREATING AND SUPPORTING ORGANIZATIONAL VALUES

After leaders have evaluated the extent to which respect permeates the institution's culture, they must take concrete steps to promote respect across the campus. One important step is for institutional leaders to articulate respect as a core value to all institutional constituencies. The president of Richland College, in the Dallas County Community College District, guided the development of Richland's "ThunderValues" as part of the college's mission and goals (see Exhibit 7.3). These "ThunderValues" clearly and forcefully communicate an environment of respect and community.

Increased attention to the five essential elements in our framework can also enhance the level of respect felt by all faculty members. For example, offering professional development opportunities designed specifically for mid-career faculty can convey a powerful message about the value of their work to the institution. Likewise, restructuring the probationary period to make it more flexible sends an important message of respect for the work of faculty members who have significant personal responsibilities. Formally extending academic freedom to faculty with renewable and fixed-term contracts may have symbolic as well as functional importance as they are assigned a right of "real" faculty members. Establishing equitable compensation packages for faculty with renewable and fixed-term contracts may be one of the most significant ways an institution can demonstrate respect for these faculty members' contributions.

Administrators can articulate institutional values and set policies, but faculty members are the heart of the university or college. It is they who have the opportunity, through daily interactions, to set the tone for campus life and ensure that all faculty members are respected. For example, faculty members are the ones who largely control the extent of collegiality on a campus or in a department. They determine whom to include in a lunch group or in a peer mentoring group. They also decide whether they will seek out faculty who are different from them for informal conversations that convey respect for their opinions.

In addition to their important role in supporting the essential elements, faculty members have responsibility for ensuring that the behavior of individual faculty members is not detrimental to the well-being of the whole faculty or to the respect with which each member of the faculty should be treated. Faculty, especially senior faculty, must monitor faculty behavior and seek corrective action in the rare instances when their colleagues fail to meet institutional standards of conduct. Chapter Eight discusses faculty responsibility for faculty conduct in more detail; here, we simply point out that faculty, individually and collectively, play a key role in ensuring a campus culture of respect, in their classrooms and through their interactions with colleagues, students, and staff.

Exhibit 7.3. ThunderValues

Richland College is a community of *learners*. . . . We strive to provide the highest quality *learning* and work environment. Richland College affirms these values for our learning and work together.

- *Mutual Trust:* We value students and employees as whole persons—sharing perspectives, valuing and accommodating both differences and commonalities, assuming motives are trustworthy.

- *Wholeness:* We believe authentic people best learn, teach, serve, lead, and build community. Thus, our programs, services, and facilities nurture integral mind-spirit-body and the emotional and intellectual intelligence inherent in meaningful lives.

- *Honesty:* We speak and act truthfully, . . . saying when we make mistakes or do not know, keeping commitments, avoiding silence when it may mislead, identifying and working with each other to . . . solve problems.

- *Fairness:* We treat students and employees justly and expect the same in return—applying rules with equity, giving all the benefit of the doubt, and providing opportunities for individual success.

- *Considerate, Open Communications:* We share information, ideas, and feelings—listening carefully, speaking forthrightly, respecting diverse views, participating productively in dialogue and conversations.

- *Mindfulness:* We respect silence, using it for reflection and deeper understanding. . . . We rush not to judgment but turn to wonder what was intended or being felt. . . .

- *Cooperation:* We work with students and employees to achieve common goals—looking beyond self-interests. . . . (We strive to) build consensus toward positive results, and help one another in shaping meaningful lives.

- *Diversity:* We value and encourage diversity, intercultural competence, originality, innovation, and vision—freeing students and employees. . . .

- *Responsible Risk-Taking:* We respond well to challenges—considering carefully, . . . and moving forward in spite of possible criticism.

- *Joy:* We value laughter, play, love, kindness, celebration, and joy in our learning and work.

Source: http://www.rlc.dcccd.edu/mission/rlc.htm (retrieved June 20, 2006).

INCLUDING ALL MEMBERS IN THE ACADEMIC COMMUNITY

Feelings of respect come from the ways in which faculty members are treated, individually and collectively, by the college or university, their departments, and their peers. It comes from how messages are communicated. Lack of respect is evident in the following policies and practices:

- Titles for faculty appointments emphasizing that some faculty are an alternative to "regular" faculty (for example, part-time, adjunct, or non-tenure-track faculty)
- Recognition of the accomplishments of tenure-track faculty members only in departmental newsletters and college or university publications
- The assigning of little merit or worth to a fixed-term faculty member's comments or suggestions in a committee meeting
- The exclusion from governance activities and professional development opportunities of faculty members in certain types of academic appointments

All these policies and practices, whether formal or implicit, communicate a lack of respect that may be hard to define but that is individually perceived. Thus respectful communication requires constant attention and sensitivity on the part of all members of the academic community. We highlight ways to convey respect in the following recommendation, the first of 37 that we offer in this book:

Recommendation 1

Convey respect through verbal messages and through institutional and individual actions, such as those that follow:

- Welcome all new faculty members to the institution and the department through orientation programs and through their inclusion in departmental faculty meetings, social events, and informal hallway conversations.

- Review all titles for faculty appointments to determine whether they convey the respect that the institution intends. Titles for non-tenure-bearing appointments should positively reflect appointment status rather than label

the faculty in these appointments as "other than tenured," with tenure
viewed as "ideal."

- Ensure that each faculty member is provided with the essential resources
  to support his or her work, such as departmental office space, equipment,
  and support services, beginning with the first day of employment.

- Periodically examine the language used in all publications and pronouncements to ensure that it refers respectfully to all faculty members.

- Include all faculty members, regardless of their appointment types, in positive publicity about the institution and in ceremonies where recognition
  and rewards are conferred.

- In periodically surveying faculty members on their satisfaction with their
  employment, ask questions about faculty members' perceptions of whether
  they are treated respectfully and included in departmental and campus
  meetings and events.

Issues of respect are felt most keenly by faculty members who are
not on the tenure track. The American Association of University Professors, in its 2003 policy statement *Contingent Appointments and the
Academic Profession* (http://www.aaup.org/statements/SpchState/
Statements/contingent.htm, retrieved July 4, 2006), argues that to
support the essential mission of higher education, faculty in all types
of appointments, including "contingent appointments" (defined by
the AAUP as non-tenure-track positions), should participate at least
to some extent in the full range of faculty responsibilities and be incorporated into all aspects of university life. They should be actively
engaged with their academic disciplines and with the teaching and
mentoring of students. They should participate in academic decision making and in service to the campus and the surrounding
community. Thus, for example, if faculty who are part-timers in
fixed-term appointments were envisioned as major contributors to
and full participants in the academic profession and their institutions, their concerns about whether they are respected would diminish significantly.

In summary, respect for every faculty member must be at the
core of all institutional efforts to provide an academic work environment that stimulates personal and institutional growth and

success. When faculty members do not feel valued, they are likely to feel disenfranchised from the work of their institutions and to feel a low level of motivation for and satisfaction from their work. As a result, achievement of institutional goals is hindered because not all faculty members are contributing in as full a way as possible. For this reason, our framework makes respect the basic requirement, without which the five essential elements of faculty work will not be as effective.

Chapter Eight

SHARED RESPONSIBILITY AND JOINT LEADERSHIP

Challenging times require everyone's efforts, the mutual commitment of all stakeholders to the well-being of their college or university. All members of the academic community must accept responsibility and work together to ensure high-quality, supportive academic workplaces where each member is respected and valued for his or her contributions. One group by itself cannot accomplish the significant changes envisioned by our framework of essential elements. Everyone has a role: faculty members individually and collectively, department chairs, deans, provosts, presidents, and various governance bodies all play a part.

This chapter describes the varied roles and responsibilities for ensuring attractive academic workplaces that emphasize recruitment and retention of excellent faculty. For example, faculty members individually and collectively make important decisions; changes do not happen without their participation. Individually, through their advice and recommendations, they contribute to departmental decisions about peer review, curricula, student graduation criteria, research priorities, and more. As individuals, faculty members also have responsibility for active participation in collective decision making. Working collectively through departmental, school, or campuswide committees and task forces, they establish cultures of collegiality, engage in rigorous peer review, revise student admission criteria or academic programs and curricula, insist on equitable treatment, and ensure academic excellence.

Department chairs, deans, provosts, and presidents allocate and manage resources. Their decisions and actions create academic environments that either do or do not foster what we have called the essential elements and support faculty in their work. Administrators ensure wise use of faculty time and effort, develop and define reward structures that encourage faculty excellence, and foster collaboration among different units. Institutionwide decision-making and governance bodies, such as boards of trustees, presidential advisory committees, faculty senates, and unions, make decisions in their areas of responsibility that also contribute significantly to campus cultures and to the realization of the essential elements.

This chapter explores these shared responsibilities for realizing the essential elements in faculty work and workplaces. It begins by reviewing the strong tradition of shared responsibility and decision making in academe. It then examines the roles of the various stakeholders. We turn first to faculty responsibilities, looking at faculty roles in academic departments, and at faculty as members of campuswide committees and governance bodies or as union members. The section concludes with a discussion of faculty accountability. The pivotal roles of department chairs and deans in the management of academic units and in the well-being of the faculty are considered next. Then provosts' and presidents' responsibilities for campuswide leadership are discussed. The final part of the chapter discusses two major issues within shared responsibility for effective leadership: rethinking academic organizational structures, and strategic planning and assessment.

TRADITIONS OF SHARED GOVERNANCE AND DECISION MAKING

Participants in advisory groups for this book described faculty and administrators as members of separate cultures, lacking understanding and appreciation of each other's different roles. But they also recognized that mutual respect and understanding are a two-way street. Too often, faculty members do not understand or appreciate the legal and fiduciary responsibilities of the president or trustees. At the same time, harried administrators do not always take time to acknowledge and thank faculty members for especially noteworthy accomplishments or generous use of their time on behalf of the college or university. Nevertheless, the academic profession has traditionally emphasized shared responsibility for the health and well-being of a college or university and its faculty members, and this tradition is as important today as it has been in the past.

The long-standing tradition of shared responsibility for decision making was codified by the American Council on Education, the Association for Governing Boards, and the American Association of University Professors in their joint "Statement on Government of Colleges and Universities" issued in 1966, prior to the AAUP's decision to engage in collective bargaining. It states, "The variety and complexity of tasks performed by institutions of higher education produce an inescapable interdependence among governing boards, administration, [and] faculty" (American Association of University Professors, 2001a, p. 218).

In the joint statement just cited, the governing board's authority was made clear: "The governing board of an institution of higher education in the United States operates, with few exceptions, as the final institutional authority" (American Association of University Professors, 2001a, p. 220). Thus the board of trustees, or the president upon delegation of authority, makes final decisions that are then implemented at each administrative level within an institution. But faculty members also play an important role in decisions related to educational policy: "The faculty has primary responsibility for such fundamental areas as curriculum, subject matter and methods of instruction, research, faculty status and those aspects of student life which relate to the educational process" (American Association of University Professors, 2001a, p. 221).

These two decision-making entities operate simultaneously, yielding a governance structure that is both hierarchical and horizontal. The hierarchical structure of governance shows the steps or levels in decision making: from academic departments to schools, divisions, or colleges, and then to central institutional-level administrators, and finally to boards of trustees. This hierarchical structure of administrative decision making is balanced and enriched by the horizontal decision-making structure, which consists of faculty input into decisions at each level of the aforementioned hierarchy. Faculty input occurs within each academic department; through division, college, or school councils that advise deans; within institutionwide governance bodies such as faculty senates; or through leadership positions, as when faculty serve as union representatives.

At the top of the hierarchy, for example, some boards of trustees include faculty as fully fledged members, whereas others invite their input. Presidents and provosts are routinely advised by faculty senates that represent the faculty and by faculty representatives on key campuswide task forces. The president of Cedar Valley Community College, in Texas, goes a step further: to ensure faculty participation, she includes faculty representatives as members and full participants in her cabinet (Jennifer Wimbish, personal communication, October 24, 2004). These faculty representatives have an active role in institutional decision making, and they facilitate improved communication between faculty and administrators throughout the campus. Deans typically have their own faculty advisory bodies or councils of department chairs. Within departments, faculty make decisions about: faculty members individually through peer review, faculty hiring, workloads, student admission and graduation, courses and curriculum, and many other matters. Although some observers would find this simultaneous horizontal and hierarchical decision-making structure unwieldy, unresponsive, and slow, most observers would attribute much of the excellence of American higher education today to the strong traditions of shared governance and faculty commitment to institutional well-being.

The more recent unionization of faculty members at campuses has modified some dimensions of shared governance. In 1973, the AAUP formally endorsed collective bargaining "as a major additional way of realizing the Association's goals in higher education" (American Association of University Professors, 2001a; Statement on Collective Bargaining, pp. 249–252). Certainly, unionization in and of itself does not prevent healthy shared governance on the part of faculty and administrators, but it does, by the very nature of the contractual relationship and the presence of union representatives, change the campus environment in which shared governance is practiced. As unions point out, however, collective bargaining sets the rules that make both union representation and shared governance possible (American Federation of Teachers and the National Education Association, 2005). And unions, where they are present, have been helpful in drawing more attention to faculty in part-time and non-tenure-track positions and in endorsing their roles in decision making about matters important to them, such as the curriculum and the courses they teach.

Faculty Roles and Responsibilities

Faculty members today face vexing issues and changes in their work and workplaces. As we pointed out in earlier chapters, faculty members are highly diverse themselves, and they occupy different types of appointments. They are confronted with rapidly changing environments where students are more demanding and often less prepared, technology improvements are sources of both increased efficiency and frustration, academic cultures are increasingly entrepreneurial and managerial, and workloads continuously expand while support for faculty's efforts decrease. Yet many faculty members were initially drawn to the academic career because of its academic freedom and autonomy, collegial scholarly communities, opportunities for professional growth, and shared decision-making traditions. Faculty members have primary responsibility, individually and collectively, for protecting and extending these values and practices of the academy that drew them to the academic profession in the first place, both for their own personal benefit and for the benefit of future generations of faculty members. And they must exercise this responsibility in their institutions, where key decisions are made that affect overall faculty welfare and well-being, as well as in their departments, where today's challenges impact them the most. In sum, faculty members individually and collectively must be proactive and take responsibility for ensuring that the essential elements are incorporated into the academic workplace.

Faculty Participation in Shared Governance

At all levels of decision making in a college or university, shared governance can be only as good as faculty and administrators make it. Faculty members have responsibility for participating effectively. It is through shared governance that all faculty members, junior and senior, tenured or not, can be leaders and advocates for the kinds of institutional changes that will reflect today's new academic work and workplaces, that will embody the essential elements, and that will benefit all faculty members. Participation in shared governance is key to achieving changes in policies and practices that, for example, open up flexibility in the academic career, ensure fair treatment for fixed-term faculty, or change professional development programs to better match faculty needs and interests today.

To be effective, faculty members must choose when and how to participate, carefully keeping in mind their other commitments. They also need to understand and be willing to accommodate the managerial necessity for decisions to be made within unavoidable time constraints and serious fiscal limitations. At the same time, when administrators ask faculty members to participate, they need to remember that frequently this service is in addition to all other faculty work, so they need to provide appropriate support or release time to accommodate the added responsibility. Institutional rewards are also critical to ensuring significant faculty participation in and benefit from governance, and this point touches on our second recommendation:

Recommendation 2

Faculty accomplishments with regard to shared governance activities should be recognized in the faculty rewards system. To appropriately recognize these contributions, standards depicting the quality and significance of governance accomplishments should be developed as part of the criteria for contract renewal, tenure, and promotion.

At times, faculty participation in decision making can be notoriously detailed, deliberate, and slow. Faculty are experts in their disciplines but are not necessarily efficient as committee members. They can spend hours on details, thus limiting the time available to discuss other important agenda items. But colleges and universities need to act flexibly and rapidly in response to today's challenges. Meyer and Kaloyeros (2005, p. B16) recommend enhancing faculty participation in institutional decision making by selecting committee members on the basis of their expertise rather than their memberships in particular units or organizations, thus making a committee's work more productive, and by involving faculty members in both decision making and implementation so that they have a sense of ownership of and responsibility for new policies.

Ideally, faculty representatives on finance or campus planning committees, for example, would be well versed and interested in these areas. As experts, they will be more able to make valuable

contributions and may be able to link their participation in institutional decision making to their teaching or scholarly responsibilities. But administrators and faculty members need to carefully
consider when and where faculty participation is necessary or desirable. Faculty members have diverse and occasionally overwhelming workloads. Extra committee assignments can be a burden.
Appropriate administrative support of committees would enable
faculty members to focus their participation in ways that use their
expertise but do not waste their time.

Moreover, not every institutional decision requires or benefits
from faculty participation. Faculty input is essential only in decisions that affect their specific interests—for example, decisions
about the academic mission or employee benefits. For other types
of decisions (such as those involving parking fees or allocation of
parking spaces), faculty can be consulted through their representative governing structures.

Committee assignments should be allocated to junior faculty
members judiciously. The participation of junior faculty members
is essential to making changes and to helping junior faculty become accustomed to their roles and responsibilities in decision
making. But their participation should not be overly burdensome
to them. Junior faculty also must manage their time and focus their
efforts on those areas of responsibility that are critical to their even-
tual tenure or contract renewal.

Senior Faculty Responsibilities in Their Departments

Department heads and senior faculty members establish the working environment where most faculty spend their time. When senior faculty care about junior faculty members, regardless of
appointment types, and work collegially with them, all faculty in
the department benefit. Senior faculty are responsible for ensuring that each junior faculty member or newcomer is welcomed,
treated with respect, mentored, and introduced to new colleagues
with similar interests. Senior faculty ensure that all faculty members are invited to participate in decisions that affect their work,
such as decisions about new curricula or the courses they will
teach. When every faculty member, regardless of appointment type,

is included in decision making, as appropriate, departments become more inclusive communities of scholars. Senior faculty also ensure that important academic traditions, such as academic freedom and autonomy, are transmitted to new generations of faculty members.

The senior faculty's predominant role in faculty hiring and peer review is critical to the overall quality of an institution's faculty. Senior faculty must hold each other accountable for conscientious and fair decision making regarding initial hiring, tenure, and contract renewal. While the president and the board make final decisions on promotion and tenure, faculty peer review occurs at every administrative level in a college or university, in keeping with faculty responsibilities for shared governance. The importance of this peer review to the quality of decision making regarding faculty is emphasized in New York University's policy (see Exhibit 8.1), which succinctly describes the extent of faculty responsibility for these reviews and how this responsibility is exercised at each administrative level. In recognition of the importance of the final decision to the individual faculty member and the institution, it also provides for extension of the process when more information is needed. No wise administrator or board would depart from faculty recommendations made during such an extensive peer-review process without solid evidence of serious extenuating circumstances.

FACULTY RESPONSIBILITY FOR FACULTY CONDUCT

Faculty individually and collectively are also responsible for holding every faculty member responsible for his or her behavior toward students, staff, and colleagues, and in all academic settings, including, for example, classrooms and research laboratories. A hallmark of the academic profession is faculty members' autonomy in the conduct of their responsibilities. But autonomy carries with it individuals' responsibility for their actions with regard to the well-being of their students, departmental colleagues, the faculty as a whole, and the respect with which they and their colleagues are viewed within and beyond the institution.

These faculty responsibilities for ensuring professional conduct were recognized by the AAUP in its original *Statement on Professional Ethics,* first adopted in 1966, and revised and endorsed

EXHIBIT 8.1. GUIDE TO ADMINISTRATIVE PLANNING,
POLICY, AND PROCEDURES, NEW YORK UNIVERSITY

Promotion and Tenure

The Dean of the Faculty of Arts and Science makes recommendations
to the President of the University regarding promotions and the con-
ferring of tenure. The recommendation of the Dean is expected to
be informed by the faculty at large, the department, and experts in
the candidate's field. In the Faculty of Arts and Sciences, tradition
and faculty approved policy hold that this occurs through a multilevel
process involving detailed evaluation within the department, review
by the FAS Promotion and Tenure Committee consisting of elected
and appointed members from the three divisions of FAS, independent
external evaluations at both the department and FAS Promotion and
Tenure Committee levels, and such other information as deemed appropriate by the Dean.

While there is often a remarkable degree of unanimity in the recommendations made at the various levels of review, it is not unusual
for there to be divergent opinions.

Disagreement may occur because of differences in perspective,
differences in the weighing of strengths and weaknesses in the case, additional information not evident in preceding stages of the evaluation
and so on. In case of seriously divergent recommendations, the Dean
may choose to extend the process and seek additional information, but
has no obligation to do so.

Source: http://www.nyu.edu/fas/GAP/FAS/AppointRecord2.html (retrieved
June 22, 2006).

again in 1987 after its decision to engage in collective bargaining
(American Association of University Professors, 2001d). The statement outlines specific responsibilities for advancing knowledge,
protecting academic freedom, and upholding scholarly and ethical standards in teaching and student relationships. Similarly,
the AAUP's 1940 "Statement on Principles of Academic Freedom
and Tenure" provides for termination for cause after due process (American Association of University Professors, 2001c, pp. 4,
133–134).

Senior faculty have primary responsibility for ensuring that the
behavior of individual faculty members is not detrimental to the

well-being of the whole faculty, the academic profession, and the respect with which the faculty is viewed. This requires faculty, especially senior faculty, to monitor faculty behavior and seek corrective action when their colleagues fail to meet departmental and institutional standards of conduct. Therefore, we offer the following recommendation:

Recommendation 3

Review and revise institutional policy statements on faculty responsibilities, standards of conduct, and discipline and grievance procedures as necessary to ensure that they cover every faculty appointment type and provide appropriate and sufficient due process rights as well as sanctions. These policies should specify the behaviors that constitute actionable cause and how they will be handled.

The first step is for faculty members to define appropriate standards of faculty conduct so that a violation of the standards is readily apparent. The University of Rochester distinguishes between personal and academic conduct in its general statement of standards of conduct in its Faculty Handbook.

Cause shall be restricted to physical or mental incompetence or moral conduct unbefitting the position. Academic cause shall be defined as the failure by a member of the faculty to discharge responsibly his or her fundamental obligations as a teacher, colleague, and member of the wider community of scholars. [http://www.rochester.edu/provost/FacultyHandbook/FacultyPolicies/Revocation.html (retrieved June 22, 2006)].

Other institutions have adopted explicit statements of what constitutes unprofessional conduct. Utah State University, for example, has described faculty responsibilities in detail in its "Faculty Standards of Conduct" (see Exhibit 8.2). The complete policy includes separate sections for academic freedom, professional obligations and responsibilities, responsibilities to students, and responsibilities to the institution. Excerpts from the standards for responsibilities to students are shown in Exhibit 8.2 as an example of the specificity and concrete guidance to faculty members about

EXHIBIT 8.2. FACULTY STANDARDS OF CONDUCT,
UTAH STATE UNIVERSITY

Responsibilities to Students

1. Faculty members should engage in reasonable and substantial preparation for the teaching of their courses, appropriate to the educational objectives to be achieved.

2. Faculty members should meet scheduled classes. Schedules are altered or canceled only for valid reasons (beyond the control of the faculty member) and only after adequate notice is given to students and the department head. . . .

3. Faculty members should inform students of the general content, requirements, and evaluation criteria at the beginning of any course they teach. Faculty members should evaluate student course work promptly, conscientiously, without prejudice or favoritism. . . .

4. Faculty members with teaching responsibilities should maintain regular office hours for consultation with students, or should otherwise assure accessibility to students.

5. Faculty members should not plagiarize the work of students. . . .

6. Faculty members should not use their positions and authority to obtain uncompensated labor or to solicit gifts or favors from students. . . .

7. Faculty members should not reveal matters told to them in confidence by students except as required by law, and then only to persons entitled to such information. . . .

8. Faculty members should create and maintain environments in which students are provided the opportunity to do original thinking, research, and writing.

9. Faculty members should avoid the misuse of the classroom by preempting substantial portions of class time for presentation of views on topics unrelated to the subject matter of the course. Faculty members should not reward agreement or penalize disagreement with his or her views on controversial topics.

10. Faculty members do not engage in the sexual harassment of students.

Source: http://www.usu.edu/policies/PDF/Faculty-Standards/pdf (retrieved July 24, 2006).

what their responsibilities are and what will be considered unprofessional conduct. Taken together, the standards are unusually thorough, and they provide specific guidance for every faculty member at Utah State regarding what constitutes acceptable conduct and what does not.

Grievance procedures for hearing cases of faculty misconduct must protect individual rights to due process. But these procedures should also be conducive to use when they are needed. Too frequently, academic grievance procedures are so lengthy and unwieldy that they discourage use and are avoided.

FACULTY RESPONSIBILITY IN A COLLECTIVE BARGAINING ENVIRONMENT

Collective bargaining is commonly perceived as an adversarial process. Traditionally, collective bargaining negotiations involved positional bargaining whereby each party would bring its proposals to the other party, which would reject them and present its own proposals regarding the issues. The parties then would bargain, often adversarially and publicly, from these separate opening positions to agree on one position, for example, the level of salary increases for the coming year or so. Fisher and Ury (1981) argued that positional bargaining is inefficient and does not result in good agreements. In keeping with movements toward alternative dispute resolution at the time their book was published, they endorsed interest-based negotiation and win-win bargaining (Barrett, 2004). Interest-based bargaining begins with an analysis of the situation or problem by both parties working together. Each party defines its interests, and this process is followed by joint discussion and a search for solutions that will satisfy both parties. The ultimate objective is to produce an agreement that is better than the results that could be obtained without negotiating.

Interest-based bargaining is built on the concept of respect and preserves the collegial environment. In addition to the bargaining process, smooth working relationships between responsible administrators and faculty union representatives during contract negotiations can lead to quiet and thoughtful resolution of complaints and grievances and better contract implementation during the life of the bargaining agreement. Contract negotiations can be conducted, and contracts can be administered, in ways that foster the essential elements of faculty work. The important things are goodwill, excellent communication, and openness between the parties.

MANAGING ACADEMIC UNITS: DEPARTMENT CHAIRS AND DEANS

Department chairs and deans occupy key decision-making roles within the overall organizational structure of colleges and universities. They are the pivotal midpoints of an administrative and communications system that is both hierarchical and horizontal, where information and instructions flow up and down and to and from individual faculty members, faculty governance bodies, provosts, presidents, and governing boards. They have the challenging task of representing faculty viewpoints to the administration, and the reverse.

CHALLENGES IN DEPARTMENT CHAIR'S ROLES AND RESPONSIBILITIES

Department chairs are simultaneously respected peers in the senior faculty, serving as primary spokespersons for their departments, and front-line administrators responsible for carrying out campus policies and missions as members of the administrative team. When the administrative function is emphasized, the term frequently used is "department head." When the focus is primarily on representing the department, the term "chair" is normally used. Here, the term "chair" is used throughout for simplicity.

Chairs are where the action is because departments are where faculty spend their time and effort. The chair is critical to the daily lives of all faculty members in the academic department, and to the realization of the essential elements. Chairs set the tone for departmental cultures; they foster environments of collegiality and respect. They are the knowledge base and arbiters of college or university polices and of how these policies are to be interpreted and promulgated. They are the facilitators of faculty integration into the department, the providers of support services and office space, the ultimate determiners of faculty assignments and work-loads, the overseers of faculty peer reviews, and the career coaches and resources for faculty professional development. Thus chairs are pivotal in the realization of the essential elements.

Historically, department chairs were prestigious scholars, presiding over their departments in an almost ceremonial manner. Today chairs wrestle with budget cuts, declining enrollments, productivity reports, mandated accountability measures, fund-raising, and changing technologies. When chairs fulfill their scholarly as well as their managerial roles, there is good communication between the administration and the faculty; when they do not, there is lack of respect, mistrust, and misunderstanding (Hecht, Higgerson, Gmelch, and Tucker, 1999).

How the position of department chair is defined, and the myriad responsibilities it entails, make it difficult for chairs to focus on their primary job: promotion of academic excellence and the faculty's well-being. For example, Gmelch (1998) asked department chairs participating in workshops to list their most important tasks; a typical list included recruiting and selecting faculty, evaluating faculty performance, reducing faculty conflicts, and providing informal faculty leadership in addition to a host of administrative or managerial functions related to budgets, long-range planning, representing the department to other university or college constituents, and daily administrative activities. In another study, Wergin (2003) queried groups of chairs about the characteristics of high-quality departments. The responses included external recognition, high academic standards, active scholarship, innovation, collegiality, successful students, adequate facilities, strong support staff, and respect for diversity.

Both these descriptions of the challenges chairs face show that faculty in departments expect their chairs to combine the roles of senior colleague and administrator, to emphasize academic excellence, and to ensure students' and the faculty's well-being. But administrative activities fragment department chairs' time and take them away from their most important responsibilities for academic excellence and the faculty's well-being. Therefore, we offer the following recommendation:

Recommendation 4

Ensure that candidates for the position of department chair have a clear and comprehensive understanding of the chair's roles and responsibilities. Select, train, support, and reward department heads in keeping with their complex responsibilities. Allocate a sufficient time base for the chair assignment to accommodate these myriad duties and responsibilities.

Recognizing that the department chair's role is both pivotal and difficult is an important first step in ensuring that department chairs have sufficient time and support for their jobs and are rewarded for their efforts. In response to the realization that the chair's role is stressful at best and requires diverse skills and talents, colleges and universities have developed user-friendly, up-to-date, readily accessible training programs and manuals for department chairs. For example, Carleton College has developed an unusually comprehensive, regularly updated Web-based handbook for department chairs. The handbook contains a description of the chair's role in a friendly message from the dean (see Exhibit 8.3), important dates in the academic calendar, and information about a variety of topics, organized alphabetically, so that chairs can readily access what they need to know about their responsibilities anytime.

The level of detail in the Carleton College handbook is aimed at providing immediate information to department chairs about every facet of their positions. But the Web site's friendly, conversational tone also encourages department chairs to ask questions and seek additional advice from their deans about specific situations or problems in their particular units. Exhibit 8.4 shows an example of this user-friendly tone in a passage about salary recommendations.

Training sessions are another important method of preparing department chairs for their responsibilities. The president's office of the University of Missouri system offers a yearlong training program for department chairs. Called the President's Academic Leadership Institute, the program is aimed at developing leadership skills for department chairs, directors, and assistant and associate deans. The program begins with a four-day session to assess leadership styles and enhance personal leadership skills. Ten additional day-long meetings, scheduled at intervals throughout the academic year, focus on such topics as leadership theory and models;

EXHIBIT 8.3. DEPARTMENT CHAIRS' HANDBOOK (2005–2006), CARLETON COLLEGE

The purpose of this *Handbook* is both to help those with little previous administrative experience learn as quickly as possible how to chair a department and to provide a handy reference for experienced chairs. . . .

So . . . You're the Chair

As department chair, you are in a position crucial to the department and important to the College. There are many specific tasks that chairs must do . . . and at times you may be tempted by various pressures to regard the chair's role as a super-secretary or clerk of the department. But, you are much more than a caretaker or seat-holder; you must be a leader, facilitator, mentor, manager, mediator, and agent of development for the departmental program as a whole and for the individuals in your department. This is not always an easy role to play, but it is a very important one.

By far the most important function of the chair is to see that excellent faculty are recruited, retained, supported, and rewarded in their work. After teaching and scholarly or creative work, the faculty's most important contribution to the institution is to hire and nurture colleagues who will enable Carleton to continue to be . . . true to its mission of providing a first-rate liberal education to undergraduates. This means you must take responsibility for supporting the professional development of individual faculty members in your department. . . .

These responsibilities are also opportunities, of course. Your activities can help shape the department and its program for years to come. It is important for you to protect yourself from the daily demands of the job enough so that you can think now and then about longer-term goals; in other words, don't always let the urgent crowd out the important. . . .

Source: http://apps.carleton.edu/campus/doc/faculty_resources (retrieved July 25, 2006).

benchmarks, assessment, evaluation, and feedback; negotiation; conflict resolution; and dealing with differences. In addition to gaining knowledge, participants build invaluable networks and contacts (see http://www.umsystem.edu/pali, retrieved July 25, 2006). (See Chapter Twelve for more information about professional development for department chairs.)

EXHIBIT 8.4. SALARY RECOMMENDATIONS: FACULTY

The Dean and President rely on information from department chairs when making faculty salary decisions. In February, you will be asked to write a letter about all of your departmental colleagues. The Dean and President already have information from the prior year's biennial reports and department reports. But they want to know your perspective about people's activities and contributions over the past year and will ask for your judgment about who should be distinguished from the majority of faculty doing good solid work, either above or below the norms, and why. Sometimes a colleague has borne an extraordinary burden of work of which the Dean and President are unaware—onerous responsibilities for recruiting, directing "comps", organizing symposia, etc. Make these functions known.

Source: http://apps.carleton.edu/campus/doc/faculty_resources (retrieved July 25, 2006).

   The two approaches to department chair training highlighted here—Carleton College's Web site and the University of Missouri's in-depth leadership training and support-building workshops—illustrate the scope of information and assistance necessary for department chairs to gain the knowledge and skills they need for their important and pivotal assignments. Nevertheless, despite numerous campus efforts to educate and assist department chairs, the chair's role remains paradoxical. Chairs are academic managers responsible for shaping the department's future, meeting the daily needs of faculty and students, and serving as their departments' spokespersons. In today's environment, however, they are increasingly expected to manage significant administrative responsibilities while also responding to pressure from external entities, such as accrediting agencies, state boards of higher education, and granting agencies. These multiple functions can cause conflicts. For example, faculty may be outraged to think of their chair as an agent of the administration, and at the same time the central administration may be irritated with a department chair who argues for the needs of the department in the face of an institutional crisis (Hecht et al., 1999, p. 4). In addition, department chairs are frequently assigned this demanding role on a part-time basis. For these reasons, we offer suggestions for rethinking the role of the department chair later in this chapter.

THE LEADERSHIP ROLE OF DEANS

Deans, as both academic leaders and central administrators, choose courses of action that enhance the faculty's well-being in their schools, colleges, or divisions, within the constraints of institutional missions and available resources. As change agents, deans must think outside the proverbial box and strive to remove impediments to the faculty's work rather than getting in the way. They make thoughtful choices with limited resources, take risks, and find creative approaches to accomplishing their goals. In sum, at their best they are visionary and proactive leaders in strategic positions where their actions can contribute significantly to achieving the essential elements of faculty work and workplaces.

Deans, as academic leaders and administrative executives over large units, develop the academic vision for their schools or colleges, define responsibilities, ensure action, and hold people accountable. In sum, they make things happen. With today's competition for limited resources and today's rapid pace of change, deans must decide which among their many strategic priorities are most important and timely and then figure out how to accomplish them. Deans remove impediments to change and support faculty in their work. To use a metaphor, they enfranchise an informed electorate in a democratic, self-governing republic.

One dean, for example, sensitive to time pressures facing faculty and wanting to enhance a sense of community, decided to open a restaurant in the college's building. Having their own space and facility where the faculty could gather and share meals fostered collegiality and saved time and effort. Another dean, in a predominantly white rural community, met each semester with faculty members in his college who were members of ethnic and racial minority groups. These meetings served several important purposes in his efforts to build a diverse and engaged community of scholars where one had not existed before. During these casual and relaxed evening meetings, faculty members shared with him their impressions and concerns about their experiences in their departments and classrooms, and they got to know each other across departmental lines. These meetings provided the dean with a candid appraisal of the collegiality and respect that these faculty members were or were not experiencing, and they also made him aware of issues that needed attention. They benefited his faculty members of color, too, who were isolated in different departments, by giving them a unique opportunity to get to know each other and share their concerns in a supportive environment.

Sometimes deans' actions are more comprehensive. For example to ensure the well-being of his faculty members the dean of the College of Arts and Sciences at Georgia State University (Rule, 2002) undertook a series of changes in faculty employment. Using a shared-governance system in which department chairs and faculty committees played significant roles, he led the overhaul of faculty salaries to make them more equitable, shifted workloads to achieve balanced effort among faculty, and adapted a positive, formative model for post-tenure review. Subsequently, using the same approach, the dean changed patterns of faculty staffing by shifting resources from part-time and visiting appointments to tenure-track or contract-renewable appointments. In one year, the College of Arts and Sciences went from 189 part-time faculty teaching 36 percent of all courses offered to 65 new full-time, contract renewable faculty with full benefits and better salaries (Honan and Rule, 2002; Wilson, 1999). According to associates, the dean's success was due to his openness, his championing of issues he believed in, and his tireless efforts to find common ground. One associate dean remarked, "Our dean is indefatigable at building bridges. He will sit down with folks until a bridge is found or he will go and build it himself" (Rule, 2002, p. 35).

PRESIDENTS' AND PROVOSTS' ROLES AND RESPONSIBILITIES

College and university leaders establish priorities for entire campuses or systems. The priorities they choose, the decisions they make, and the people they select for key positions are critical to the preservation and enhancement of the institutions' resources, including the intellectual capital of the faculty. And, administrators' regular communication with campus constituencies ensures that information about institutional initiatives, policies, and programs is widely disseminated and available to all faculty members, thus keeping lines of communication among faculty, departments, and central administrative offices open and working well.

In short, the leadership of presidents and provosts is critical to realizing the essential elements. Nevertheless, the success of these efforts is dependent on the communication strategies and infrastructure established by the central administration. The following list of responsibilities and functions of central administrators offers a general overview of their important role in ensuring the well-being of the faculty:

- Recognizing and publicizing exemplary performance by faculty members in all types of appointments
- Designating and publicizing individuals and offices that are responsible for shared governance and the well-being of the faculty
- Codifying and publishing, in faculty handbooks, all policies, procedures, and practices regarding faculty employment; making them readily available to all faculty members; and ensuring that they are routinely updated
- Monitoring and regularly reviewing the effectiveness of institutional policies and practices regarding faculty, and the consistency of their implementation in academic departments and units
- Ensuring that effective grievance procedures are in place for addressing complaints about faculty members' employment, academic freedom, and the exercise of responsibilities; and monitoring their use
- Publishing and disseminating information useful to faculty, such as information about orientation programs, training opportunities, or new programs and services available to assist faculty with managing their academic responsibilities, enriching their academic careers, and balancing their professional and personal lives

As the campus spokesperson, the president makes public pronouncements that are important to the creation of academic workplaces that reflect the essential elements and foster excellence, and to informing publics beyond the campus about the excellent work that the faculty are doing. By recognizing accomplishments from a broad spectrum of faculty, and by endorsing new programs or initiatives, the president acts as a change agent. Presidents and provosts also occupy bully pulpits on campuses; as the instigators of campuswide change, they can be particularly influential in changing established cultures and customs through their speech and actions. For example, we know of one provost, a past professor of English, who changed the culture of his large, politically connected English department by refusing its proposed tenure-track hires. He then reconstituted the membership of the English department's faculty hiring committee to include faculty of color from other departments, changed departmental hiring processes, and carefully monitored that department's faculty hires for five years. He was initially condemned by angry faculty in a public meeting, but the English department's culture began to change. After the five-year period had elapsed, the English department's faculty had hired and retained excellent and diverse faculty members and voted to continue with the hiring committee's new membership and the department's changed hiring process.

So that all faculty members have up-to-date information, proactive leaders ensure that faculty handbooks comprehensively cover the policies, practices, and procedures governing all types of faculty employment, and are made readily available to all faculty members, both in hard copy and over the Internet. Stanford University's handbook, available at http://facultyhandbook.stanford.edu, is exemplary in its readability and its comprehensive coverage of policies governing faculty employment for all types of faculty appointments.

At large institutions, to meet all the responsibilities highlighted here, associate academic vice presidents or similarly designated administrators occupy key positions. Associate academic vice presidents with their in-depth knowledge about every type of faculty personnel action, can educate and advise about new policies, proper procedures, or individual problems. Usually they review all faculty-related personnel recommendations coming from academic departments and deans to the central administration for final action, to ensure that the recommendations have followed institutional policy, procedures, and guidelines. Individuals in these positions, with their bird's-eye view of individual decision making in faculty matters, become institutional sources of knowledge and wisdom about fair and respectful treatment of all faculty members. As experts in these areas, they often serve as confidential sounding boards or ombudspersons for individual faculty members seeking advice or help, and for chairs and deans with problems or questions.

Centralized expertise about faculty matters makes sense today, when institutions are continuously impacted by external events, laws, regulations, and competition for scarce faculty talent. In institutions with faculty collective bargaining, such centralization is essential to ensuring a uniform, campuswide approach to contract administration and to resolution of complaints about contract violations or other grievances.

FACULTY STAFFING PLANS

The allocation of faculty positions to colleges, schools or divisions, and to academic departments is a key function of the provost or academic vice president and constitutes a major institutional decision about resources. Thus it is normally the culmination of a large-scale planning effort that involves all levels of academic decision making.

Faculty staffing plans provide institutions and academic departments with an opportunity to assess the qualifications and competencies thought to be necessary in current and future faculty members so that an institution can achieve its missions and goals. Department chairs and faculty members in each department must decide what kinds of faculty appointments, and in what specialties, are essential to attracting excellent faculty in order to accomplish departmental goals. Deans must prioritize the various departmental requests. Provosts or academic vice presidents need to routinely assess current faculty staffing profiles from the perspectives of how academic work has changed and what kinds of faculty and academic appointments are needed in order to meet institutional goals. Review and revision of plans and budgets for faculty staffing are a critical aspect of annual budget cycles and long-range planning. We offer the following recommendation for faculty staffing:

Recommendation 5

Using institutional guidelines, develop plans for faculty staffing in each academic department or unit on the basis of the kinds of faculty resources that are needed to accomplish the educational goals of that unit. While developing faculty staffing plans, recognize and plan for the budget support and facilities implications of each new hire, regardless of the type of appointment or time base. Routinely review and evaluate plans for faculty staffing to ensure that they continue to meet departmental and institutional objectives.

Faculty staffing plans that are developed in each academic department and approved by deans and provosts illustrate again the hierarchical and horizontal decision-making processes in colleges and universities and should be an integral part of institutional strategic planning. Every newly hired faculty member should be viewed as making a distinct and valued contribution to the overall excellence of his or her academic department and college or university. Making each faculty member a valued resource for the achievement of institutional objectives promotes a culture of respect in addition to ensuring wise use of scarce resources. Developing plans for faculty staffing also helps departments negotiate workloads, accommodate faculty's needs for flexibility, and provide time and resources for professional growth.

EFFECTIVE LEADERSHIP IN ACADEMIC GOVERNANCE

In this chapter, we have been looking at the responsibilities of multiple decision makers in the crowded enterprise of institutional governance and decision making, and we have outlined the responsibilities involved in achieving the essential elements at each level of decision making of a college or university. We turn now to two areas that span the entire organization: first we discuss the potential need to rethink the current academic organization and support structures. Then we discuss the importance of continuous data gathering and monitoring of ongoing decision making to inform campus constituents about progress toward changing faculty work and workplaces. Both areas have become increasingly crucial to colleges and universities as they confront ever-declining external financial support, accompanied by continuous calls for increasing accountability.

RETHINKING CURRENT ACADEMIC ORGANIZATION AND STRUCTURES

As stated earlier, the department chair's role is crucial but difficult. The simultaneous responsibilities of academic leader and front-line departmental manager can conflict with each other, and the acquisition of the skills necessary to carry out these different responsibilities successfully is often incompatible with both the time base allotted the department chair and the custom of regularly rotating the assignment of department chair. As currently configured and supported, the department chair's roles of academic leader and administrator, both on a part-time basis, may be a weak link in ensuring that institutional policies, practices, and programs for faculty work and workplaces are promulgated and supported throughout the organization. Certainly, for many department chairs the allocated time base and rewards are already insufficient for the range of tasks assigned. Continuous decentralization of certain administrative functions (such as processing travel requests, preparing course schedules, and overseeing the regulatory aspects of faculty hiring) to individual academic departments may be unnecessarily time-consuming and an expensive use of the chair's time. We think it is time to rethink the roles of department chairs in academic governance, and we therefore offer the following recommendation:

Recommendation 6

Involve department chairs, deans, and faculty leaders in an examination of the roles and responsibilities of department chairs, in view of the time base and duration of the chair assignment, and consider alternative structures and support systems that can better accommodate the roles and responsibilities of the department chair.

Department chairs currently serve in one of two different roles based on the size or complexity of the department:

1. As his or her department's academic leader, with some release time from faculty responsibilities for a fixed period, after which the chair assignment rotates to other senior faculty in the department (the department chair in this role is seen as a leader of his or her peers)
2. Primarily as an administrator, in a full-time position that may occasionally be nationally advertised and usually has a longer term

Whichever role is chosen, the department chair needs expertise and sufficient administrative support. At some point, moreover, the continuous movement toward spiraling decentralization becomes inefficient. Some currently delegated departmental functions can be more efficiently handled by trained and experienced staff members appointed to larger units (normally a college, division, or school) and working with chairs of multiple departments to cover common administrative tasks. More centrally located support staff and professionals with the requisite skills and knowledge can release significant time for department chairs' roles as academic leaders, and they can perform tasks that are currently handled by overworked and undertrained departmental clerical staff, or by faculty members themselves in the absence of sufficient support staff.

An examination of one common administrative function illustrates the benefits of considering some centralization of services. The process of hiring new faculty members no longer involves only academic decision making. Federal and state laws governing equal opportunity must be adhered to, records of applicants must be kept, and decisions must be justified. There is no academic reason to train each search committee and every department chair in all the administrative responsibilities and tasks that accompany the search for a new faculty hire, nor is there any particular benefit to be gained if every faculty member on a search committee individually screens several hundred separate applications when a trained staff person can more efficiently and impartially complete an initial screening and report the results to the committee. Trained human resources staff can prepare draft position descriptions and recruitment plans that are based on decisions made by faculty members. They can place advertisements, verify the credentials of finalists, conduct preliminary reference checks in confidence, set up interview schedules, and prepare required reports of the hiring process for audit purposes, much more skillfully and efficiently than untrained faculty committee members conducting a search as an add-on to their current workloads. Faculty members in their academic departments would retain responsibility for defining the position to be filled, deciding how it should be advertised, identifying and personally recruiting qualified applicants, screening the applications of those deemed qualified, and interviewing the finalists. Thus their traditional academic decision making would be preserved, but they would not be burdened with the accompanying administrative tasks.

Hiring new faculty is just one example of how benefits could be realized through rethinking the roles of department chairs and the administrative structures of departments. Learning about all the details of administrative requirements for personnel and budget actions may not be the best use of the chair's time. Department chairs' time might be better spent if they served as leaders and spokespersons for faculty and departmental needs and interests. Centralizing some administrative and staff functions in a division head's or dean's office, and making these functions the responsibility of well-trained personnel (such as associate deans, budget managers, human resources professionals, or full-time clerical staff) can be more efficient and less costly than each autonomous academic department performing these functions regardless of its size or resources. Further, department chairs and faculty members might receive more support services from better-trained individuals occupying more permanent positions in a larger structure.

Centralizing some functions and resources at the divisional, school or college, or institutional level would also facilitate consistency in decision making and better coordination among autonomous academic units, internal administrative offices, and external agencies or audiences. For example, associate deans of schools or colleges could simultaneously (1) provide advice and support to departments, (2) monitor decision making regarding faculty hiring, evaluation, promotion, and tenure, (3) ensure that institutional policies and procedures are followed, and (4) manage college or school budgets.

One example of the services that are already typically handled centrally is technology. Technology infrastructure planning, decision making, purchasing, repair, and support services are too expensive and change too rapidly for academic departments to handle individually except, perhaps, in large units. Most technology infrastructure is administered at the college, divisional, or institutional level, especially when it serves administrative functions, as opposed to those associated with specific curriculum or research projects.

In addition, some universities already have centralized support for financial and administrative decision making in academic schools or colleges. For example, Purdue University has a unique stratum of business managers in its academic colleges and large departments (see Exhibit 8.5). These individuals work with academic

---

EXHIBIT 8.5. BUSINESS MANAGERS, PURDUE UNIVERSITY

Business Managers coordinate and supervise all business aspects of the University's academic departments, schools, and administrative units. They are the link between the academic department or unit they represent and other areas of Business Services. More than 65 Business Managers at the West Lafayette Campus support and serve the University's Vice Presidents, Deans, Department Heads, Faculty, and other staff by providing services in these areas:

- Protocol for researching issues and answering questions
- Account management
- Budgeting
- Cash handling
- Human resource services
- Moving expenses
- Payroll
- Procurement
- Signature delegation
- Supervision
- Travel

Source: http://www.purdue.edu/bs-ba (retrieved June 22, 2006).

administrators and faculty as staff members responsible for budget oversight and other administrative tasks.

Smaller institutions might choose to centralize some of these functions in the college dean's or provost's office. Regardless of the institution's size, centralization of some administrative and technical functions currently performed in each academic department (such as scheduling courses, managing financial accounts and record keeping, or hiring, evaluating, and training clerical and professional staff) could result in considerable time and cost savings and enhanced academic decision making.

MONITORING PROGRESS: INFORMATION FOR CAMPUS PLANNING AND ASSESSMENT

Incorporating the essential elements requires collection of information and periodic assessment of a college's or university's culture, academic workplace, and level of faculty satisfaction in order to modify or set new priorities for future action. When responsibility for faculty work and workplaces is shared among many participants, information must routinely be disseminated throughout the campus community so that all decision makers are kept fully informed. This section discusses collecting and reporting information as well as assessment and planning as requirements for incorporating the essential elements of the framework.

Two fundamental principles of the academy are to ground arguments in data and to draw conclusions from systematic analysis. Data are a catalyst for change and can have a profound influence on what happens. Data do matter. What is measured and reported is what is important, but sometimes ignored, in decision making. Jean Keffeler, former regent of the University of Minnesota, commenting on that institution's efforts at tenure reform, and on the resulting controversy, offers the following observation and advice:

> A university should be a community in which inquiry and the
> pursuit of information are encouraged and protected, even when
> controversial, united by civility and high common purpose. . . .
> [But] the faculty and administration stonewalled the production
> of meaningful, timely information about tenure practices and fac-
> ulty profiles. . . . Provide your administration and trustees with

information, not anecdotes . . . hard data, benchmark data, best practices information. Do anything that can be done to get beyond the natural insularity and myopia of the institution you serve, including its familiar social patterns and mythology. In Minnesota, there was too little information, too late. We allowed the process to jump to an emotional debate where no one wins [Trower and Honan, 2002, p. 275].

But storytelling, anecdotes, impressions, and beliefs are also important sources of information for making decisions. Members of the advisory groups for this book endorsed "management by walking around," or gathering data through continuous feedback and real transparency. Both sources of information are important in decisions affecting faculty work and workplaces.

Data for decision making can be viewed with suspicion. As one provost participating in the Project on Faculty Appointments at Harvard University Graduate School of Education remarked: "On our campus, there is an inherent fear of being overmanaged. . . . A fear of the corporatization of higher education . . . a sense that 'you' the administration, want to boil 'us' the faculty down to numbers and make decisions based upon them . . ." (Trower and Honan, 2002, p. 280). Institutional research offices can play a critical role in overcoming such fears by providing essential, accurate, and understandable information routinely and publicly so that campus constituents become familiar with having timely, accurate information and using it for decision making. One faculty member, responding to data generated by the Project on Faculty Appointments, which surveyed employment data at 250 colleges and universities, remarked, "Seeing data like these allows us to look at ourselves, to consider possibilities and explanations. It opens the door for a conversation. It puts these issues into play" (Trower and Honan, 2002, p. 286). Data do make a difference.

Collection and Dissemination of Information

With regard to faculty work and work lives, institutional researchers can examine and provide information to answer questions such as these:

- Are our policies and practices working as those promulgating them intended them to work?

- How are our policies and practices affecting our efforts to re-cruit and retain excellent faculty?
- Are there differences in implementation of policies among departments, and, if so, what is the effect on faculty members?
- How well do faculty members understand and use institutional policies, practices, and programs aimed at orientation to the campus, flexibility, and professional growth?

In the context of these questions, we offer the following recom-mendation:

Recommendation 7

Review existing institutionally collected data and reports about faculty to en-sure that they are

- Accurate and timely

- Sufficient for assessment of the current working environment for faculty and overall faculty well-being

- Useful for continuous monitoring of faculty policies and practices

- Understandable to all campus constituents involved in decision making

Data play important roles in assessment and decision making, both of which require accurate information about all faculty mem-bers and their appointments. Regularly collected and well-analyzed data can help institutions evaluate their policies and practices, monitor progress toward goals over time, and make decisions that are based on information. Some of the necessary information for assessment and decision making with regard to the essential ele-ments is already routinely collected and available in standard in-stitutional reports required by federal or state governments or accrediting agencies. These reports would be useful for internal assessment as well.

Here are some examples of the types of data necessary for as-sessment and planning:

- Trend data regarding the success rates of probationary faculty receiving tenure and promotion, by cohort group and depart-mental locations, can provide important insights into the effectiveness of tenure and promotion policies and consistency of their implementation across academic units.

- Data obtained from confidential exit interviews conducted by impartial people can lead to better understanding of why faculty members leave, whether they received respectful treatment in their departments, and sources of faculty dissatisfaction.
- Data can confirm or refute what is considered common knowledge about faculty workplaces and well-being. Thus data are important in clarifying issues or making a case for internal and external audiences. For example, information about the number and types of grievances filed by faculty with grievance committees, and about their patterns of resolution, can provide important insights into how well the procedures are known and used, the issues that are causing grievances, and how the grievances were resolved. Or data about the use of institutional benefits, programs, and policies that provide flexibility can inform decisions about whether to continue, modify, or replace them with something that would better meet faculty needs and institutional needs.
- Data about the total length of continuous employment of part-time faculty hired in fixed-term appointments could lead to conversion of some of these positions to full-time status or to increased use of multiyear contracts.
- Routine benchmarking with peer or comparison institutions can demonstrate accountability to trustees or external agencies and provide important insights to internal audiences into how a campus compares with its peers on important indicators of faculty satisfaction, employment policies, and benefits.

With these considerations in mind, we offer the following recommendation:

Recommendation 8

Share data reports openly so that all participants in joint decision making have the same information.

As a starting point for decision making, faculty and administrators throughout the campus community need access to information about current policies, programs, and services and how well they are working. Public pronouncements, internal newsletters, Web sites that report on the activities of a faculty senate, the efforts of union leaders in institutions with collective bargaining, and meetings between faculty members and the president, the provost, deans, and department heads are examples of how those participating in decision making can be helped to stay current and well informed.

In addition, participants in shared decision making must have available to them the specific information they need, and they must be able to understand it. In order to ensure that information is understandable and used, institutional research offices need to establish common sets of terminology and standardized reporting formats.

Assessment and Use of Data for Decision Making

There is no one solution to the many issues that confront colleges and universities and their faculties. Each campus is unique. It has its own culture, its own relationships between faculty and administrators, and its own traditions that will guide its choices about using the essential elements. The particular choices that each institution makes regarding policies and practices for faculty work and workplaces result from the institution's assessment of its current situation: its institutional and faculty characteristics; its existing policies, practices, and programs; and its plans for faculty staffing.

At any campus, some faculty and administrators are already enthusiastic proponents of planning and change. Some need a better understanding of why these activities are essential and an opportunity to explain their reservations about the data themselves or about the essential elements. Others simply do not understand the importance of assessment for decision making or do not accept the need for any change. Assessing the current campus culture and the policies and practices pertaining to faculty is an important first step in achieving shared understanding about those changes that would be most beneficial. Therefore, we offer the following recommendation:

Recommendation 9

As a basis for making decisions about changes needed in faculty work and workplaces, and in order to accomplish goals and ensure a culture of respect, periodically collect, review, and report data about faculty characteristics; personnel decisions concerning such matters as hiring, promotion, tenure, and contract renewal; policies, procedures, and practices for faculty employment for all appointment types; participation in governance and decision making; use of professional development programs and opportunities; working conditions; grievances filed; and levels of faculty satisfaction.

Results of assessments of faculty characteristics, performance, and satisfaction will help institutions see how well they are accomplishing their most important strategic goals, including wise use of their most important resource: their faculty members. Strategic questions, such as those that follow, will enable each institution both to decide whether its current mix of faculty, resource allocations, and reward structures supports the accomplishment of its mission and goals and to make appropriate changes:

- How successful are we with regard to recruitment and retention of a high-quality faculty? To what extent are faculty members satisfied with their working environments? How productive are they, and why?
- To what extent does the mix of current faculty characteristics and faculty appointments match the institution's goals and mission?
- To what extent do the current financial resource allocations support the work of different types of faculty?
- To what extent does the current allocation of physical resources (space) support the work of different types of faculty?
- Do current faculty workload allocations reflect activities associated with achievement of the mission? Is faculty effort optimally deployed, or does it need to be redirected?
- To what extent do compensation and reward structures for all faculty members reflect their work and the contributions they make to the institution, across all types of faculty appointments? Do they reward achievement of desired outcomes? Are they administered fairly and monitored for equity?
- To what extent do faculty governance activities reflect faculty's shared responsibility for the institution's well-being and contribute to achieving the institution's mission and goals?

CONCLUSIONS

The activities described in this chapter—sharing responsibility for change, nourishing proactive leadership, and periodically assessing the institution's current situation (including its human, financial, and physical resources) in view of its mission and goals—all lead to enhancing the essential elements in faculty work and workplaces.

One action by a campus, such as developing faculty staffing plans in each department, as discussed earlier, can contribute to the institution's overall effort to rethink its working environment and incorporate the essential elements in a multifaceted way. Not only do plans for faculty staffing lead to decisions about the new faculty positions that will be needed, they also enable departmental faculty members to rethink their current activities and priorities, adjust their workloads, take advantage of professional development opportunities, and move in new directions. Thus, the one action of instituting plans for faculty staffing can contribute to the realization of increased equity, flexibility, and professional development.

The term "rethinking" encapsulates the reasons that shared responsibility is such an important and integral part of building a foundation for change: in a college or university, when decision making is shared among faculty members and administrators at all levels, the campus atmosphere is conducive to thoughtful, deliberate, creative approaches to incorporating the essential elements, and to good working relationships between administrators and faculty. Moreover, successful incorporation of each of the essential elements into faculty work and workplaces requires knowledge of what needs to change, or a periodic assessment of what the campus has achieved and where improvements can be made. These activities provide a solid foundation for our examination of the essential elements in the chapters that follow.

PART THREE

THE ESSENTIAL ELEMENTS

Conceptualizing the essential elements of faculty work and work-places offers a platform from which to move to action. Building on the framework discussed in Part II, the chapters in this section of the book examine how each of the essential elements might be incorporated into policies and practices in universities and colleges. Each chapter describes one of the essential elements in particular and makes recommendations for addressing and embedding that element into faculty work and workplaces. These recommendations are highlighted by specific examples from institutional practice. Chapter Nine addresses equity across all faculty appointment types. Chapter Ten looks at academic freedom and how it can be preserved and sustained when there are multiple appointment types. Chapter Eleven discusses the need for flexibility in academic appointments and careers to meet the needs of a diverse faculty workforce. Chapter Twelve describes ways to ensure that professional growth is part of the work experience of all faculty members. Chapter Thirteen looks at ways to foster collegial academic communities.

Taken as a group, these chapters in Part III are intended to be helpful to faculty and administrative leaders as they engage in new ways of thinking and decision making about faculty work and work-places that incorporate the essential elements of the framework presented here. Chapter Fourteen reminds readers that the work of all faculty members is critically important to the excellence, health, and effectiveness of higher education institutions. Incorporating the essential elements will help universities and colleges attract and retain superb faculty who find their work satisfying and meaningful and who use their intellectual capital for the benefit of their institutions. Rethinking faculty work and workplaces is the wise strategic choice for colleges and universities in the twenty-first century.

CHAPTER NINE

EQUITY IN ACADEMIC APPOINTMENTS

The traditional model for the academic profession has been a tenured professorship. Tenure confers an important status on faculty members, and long-term employment allows individuals the requisite time for the reflective thought and study so essential to scholarly work. In exchange, colleges and universities expect a great deal from their faculty members. As Chait (1995, 2002) and others have remarked, no better model has been found for academic careers. The tenured American professoriate is the most accomplished in the world, and the long-term commitment of tenure gives faculty members some governing authority over academic decisions and serves as a bulwark between the insistent pressures in our society for immediate yield and the more valuable and lasting contributions of a contemplative, independent, and superior mind (Michaelson, 2001).

But the tenure system is no longer the universal model for all academic appointments. In 2004, the proportion of faculty members who had tenure or were on the tenure track had fallen to only 40 percent of the total faculty and 68 percent of the full-time faculty (U.S. Department of Education, National Center for Education Statistics, 2004). Instead, faculty members are increasingly employed in a variety of nontenure positions with varying responsibilities and employment conditions. Faculty members as individuals are as diverse in their lifestyles and backgrounds as their employing colleges and universities are in their missions, functions, and resources.

As a result, the ideal faculty career is no longer perceived by all faculty or administrators to be necessarily based on a tenured appointment. Colleges and universities are defining the types as well as the mix of academic appointments that are most likely to meet institutional needs. Individual faculty members also vary in their views of academic appointments. In other words, the ideal academic career today is institutionally and individually defined, and it includes choices.

Thus higher education is faced with a conundrum. The AAUP's 1940 statement on principles of academic freedom and tenure (American Association of University Professors, 2001c) established the standards or norms for the academic profession, which are still the mainstays of the profession today. The tenure system has worked well for those faculty members who are in it, and for their institutions. For many colleges and universities, tenure is and will remain the primary academic career path. Increasingly, however, institutions and prospective faculty members are seeking alternatives that can provide them with more flexibility to meet their changing needs and responsibilities. While the numbers of faculty appointed to these alternative career tracks have increased, their standards have not been so clearly defined or established in the academic profession. New prototypes for the profession are needed.

This chapter aims to resolve the conundrum by offering recommendations for achieving equity in all appointment types and for retaining the traditional standards and values of academic appointments embodied in the AAUP's 1940 statement on principles of academic freedom and tenure (American Association of University Professors, 2001c).

The chapter begins by defining equity in academic appointments. It then applies that definition to the three major types of faculty appointments in use today so that each of these academic appointments can better meet institutional and individual needs and ensure equity and respect.

- Tenure-track appointments
- Contract-renewable appointments that offer attractive and comparable alternatives to tenure
- Fixed-term appointments, typically but not exclusively used for part-time faculty

EQUITY IN EMPLOYMENT DEFINED

Employment equity begins with respect: respect for every faculty member, regardless of academic appointment type or time base, as an individual who can make substantial contributions to achieving institutional goals for educational excellence. According to the framework that we present in this book, respect should guide each institution's underlying employment philosophy. In turn, this institutional philosophy should guide how employees are treated, permeate the institution's employment policies and practices, and set standards for equitable treatment in each academic appointment type and every academic unit.

Equitable treatment in academic appointments presumes certain conditions (Gappa and Leslie, 1993; Baldwin and Chronister, 2001). First, all faculty should be fully accepted and valued as members of the academic community, regardless of differences in their appointment types, job responsibilities, or personal situations. This implies that the key components of traditional faculty appointments—such as faculty members' ability to participate in governance decisions affecting their employment, their right to the protections of academic freedom, and the opportunities to pursue professional development while performing their duties as faculty members— are retained as integral parts of all academic appointments. But a caveat is needed here. Although all faculty members should be treated according to carefully established college or university policies and procedures, *equitable* treatment does not mean *identical* treatment. Equity is not the same as uniformity. Instead, equitable treatment means ensuring that each faculty member is treated fairly after differences among faculty members are taken into account, and that each of the three types of academic appointment is governed by its own set of institutionally based employment policies and practices. These appointment-specific policies and practices, although different from each other, should address the same general employment areas, such as notification of contract renewal or termination, equitable compensation (including benefits), systems of sequential rank, explicit evaluation criteria and processes, and grievance procedures for addressing complaints of unfair treatment.

Second, all faculty members should receive respectful and consistent treatment according to established and widely circulated institutional policies and practices. Faculty members in each academic unit should receive the same basic treatment that their peers receive in similar appointments in other units. Fairness requires that implementation of institutional policy not be conditioned on the availability of resources in a given department, or on the whims of department chairs or senior faculty members. Without consistency of treatment across academic units, faculty members will not believe that the employment system is fair.

Third, faculty members should have employment options that offer flexibility so that individuals can accommodate their academic careers as well as various life circumstances. Options are essential because equal treatment of faculty members in similar appointments can lead to very unequal consequences when individual differences and external constraints are not taken into account. For example, the American Council on Education (2005), Mason and Goulden (2002, 2004), and Leslie and Janson (2005) have described how women are disadvantaged in the academic profession because their careers progress at a rate different from what is typical of men's careers, with differing probabilities of women's long-term success. Options and flexibility become essential to recruiting and retaining a diverse faculty.

Fourth, equitable treatment means that all faculty members have access to the tools they need to do their jobs well. Fixed-term faculty members need access to computers, office equipment and supplies, and support staff to prepare their courses and classes, just as any other faculty member would, even if fixed-term faculty are teaching on a short-term, part-time basis.

TENURE POLICES THAT RECOGNIZE FACULTY DIVERSITY AND ENSURE FAIR TREATMENT

Traditionally, tenure policies have been based on the AAUP's 1940 statement on principles of academic freedom and tenure (American Association of University Professors, 2001c). Today, however, tenure policies must meet the needs of diverse faculty members with varying lifestyles, and must ensure that tenure processes are well established, consistently administered, and fair.

FLEXIBILITY IN TENURE-TRACK APPOINTMENTS

Flexibility in tenure-track probationary periods is essential to ensuring equity for today's diverse faculty members. Policies and practices that do not provide flexibility may appear neutral in their requirement for full-time service over a limited number of years, but in fact, they create the possibility for discriminatory treatment, particularly of women, who are entering academe in increasing numbers in all disciplines. If colleges and universities want to compete for the very best faculty members, they will have to accommodate the realities of women's (and increasing numbers of men's) lives (see Chapter Three). Therefore, we offer the following recommendation:

Recommendation 10

Provide flexibility during the tenure-track probationary period by taking the following actions:

- Allow variable time bases (for example, half- or two-thirds time) in tenure-track (and tenured) appointments, and adjust the probationary period accordingly.

- Redefine the length of the probationary period to a maximum number of years of full-time service or its equivalent (FTE service), and allow faculty members to work toward tenure at varying time bases and/or with occasional breaks in service over an extended period of total calendar time (for example, nine to twelve years).

Not all potential tenure-track faculty are able or willing to meet the requirements of seven consecutive years of full-time effort. They seek flexibility during probation for a variety of important reasons. Recommendation 10 retains the concept of a certain maximum period of service in which probationary faculty can demonstrate sufficient scholarly proficiency for a tenure decision to be made, but it also provides flexibility for faculty who need it. The recommendation proposes that a college or university could decide to keep the traditional maximum of seven years of full-time service for the probationary period as an FTE requirement but could also allow individual faculty members to extend the available

FTE time across a larger number of actual calendar years by using varying time bases, occasional leaves of absence, or a combination of the two. Regardless of the variation among individuals in their time bases or leaves of absence during their probationary periods, the same standards for academic tenure would apply to all probationary faculty members. And although the total elapsed calendar years of service may vary among probationary faculty members, the total FTE service and the criteria for the award of tenure would remain the same for everyone. Various members of a cohort of new probationary faculty hired in a given year would come up for tenure review at different points in calendar time, but everyone would be evaluated by the same criteria.

This recommendation is aimed at providing extended calendar time for early-career faculty seeking to fulfill personal as well as professional responsibilities. It is not intended to allow *everyone* additional time for meeting probationary performance criteria. Colleges and universities should specify appropriate reasons for deviations from full-time continuous service in their policies that allow for flexibility during the probationary period in order to accommodate particular circumstances. Personal health; the health of a spouse, partner, or other dependent; childbirth or adoption; infant care; elder care; unusual professional opportunities requiring a leave of absence; unexpected disasters involving significant loss of professional time—these are all bona fide reasons for extending the probationary period. Some institutions have made tenure-track clock extensions available automatically for specified situations such as those listed above, but they often require a faculty member using such a policy to sign a statement specifying the hours spent in caregiving or emergency situations. Such requirements help preserve the intention behind adding flexibility to the defined probationary period. (See Chapter Eleven for an extended discussion of policies and practices for incorporating flexibility into tenure-track appointments.)

Some college and university faculty members and administrators will object that flexibility during the probationary period will tie up a tenure-bearing position for too long, or that such flexibility could adversely impact traditionally stringent standards for accountability and quality of work. They may worry that lengthening the probationary time frame could result in de facto tenure. These objections must be taken into account, and changes in tenure policies must be carefully drafted and reviewed by legal counsel. But flexibility during the probationary period for individuals with concomitant personal responsibilities or unique situations will be essential to attracting and retaining high-quality faculty in the future.

To encourage faculty members to use policies providing flexibility, institutions will need to give assurances that faculty are not putting their careers in jeopardy. Therefore, flexibility during the probationary period must be a matter of institutional policy rather than a departmental prerogative. Moreover, to protect individual faculty members as well as their institutions, any changes in the typical full-time probationary period for a tenure decision should be put in writing and, to the extent possible, agreed to at all levels of tenure review before the changes take effect. Further, an individual faculty member will be more likely to pursue a change to part-time status or to take a leave in the following circumstances:

- When the procedures for doing so are specified and understood by administrators and senior faculty
- When the faculty member has the option of retaining his or her benefits
- When there is a clear understanding regarding the appropriate reduction in responsibilities

Departments will be more amenable to flexibility in probationary appointments if institutional policy requires that the salary savings resulting from a leave of absence or a reduced time base are returned to departments to cover the costs of replacing the absent faculty member (Drago and Williams, 2000).

TENURE-REVIEW PROCESSES, CRITERIA, AND EXPECTATIONS

Tenure-review processes must be clearly communicated and consistently administered to ensure that all probationary faculty members are treated with respect. For that reason, we offer the following recommendation:

Recommendation 11

Ensure clarity, respect, and fairness in tenure-review processes throughout the probationary period.

Faculty members in probationary status have expressed concerns about the way the tenure-review process works (see Chapter Four). Colleges and universities have the responsibility of ensuring that probationary faculty members campuswide have timely information about tenure-review processes; understand what is expected of them as well as when and how the reviews will be conducted; and perceive the reviews to be fair, clear, and consistent.

Orientation

Orientation sessions are an ideal setting for all new tenure-track faculty members to gain important information about the campus and become familiar with its expectations and processes for tenure. Campuswide orientation sessions for new tenure-track faculty provide an important introduction to academic life and key administrators, and are a good place to introduce new faculty members to useful sources of information about tenure policies. Subsequent training sessions are also needed to communicate tenure expectations, outline tenure-review processes, and discuss the do's and don'ts of probation.

Each academic department or unit can build on this common campuswide orientation with its own meetings about tenure standards and review processes, where questions can be answered. (Because orientation is the first essential component of what must be a continuous investment in the professional growth and development of all faculty members, it is dealt with more extensively in Chapter Twelve.) Probationary faculty often find it useful to attend sessions on tenure and promotion more than once. In the first year of probation, they need an overview of the tenure-review process; with several years of experience, they can focus more attention on the details of the tenure-review process and on strategies for building a portfolio for the tenure decision.

Information distributed at these sessions must be augmented by easy access to institutional tenure policies and procedures posted on Web sites and printed in faculty manuals. San Francisco State University's comprehensive Web site (http://www.sfsu.edu/faculty.htm, retrieved June 28, 2006) exemplifies up-to-date information for new as well as continuing faculty members. The Web site contains University guidelines for tenure and promotion, the collective bargaining agreement, and key resources for assistance during the tenure process. The Web site's easy-to-understand language and friendly tone is characteristic of the campus's communication. Exhibit 9.1 shows the extensive table of contents covering preparation for tenure and promotion.

Criteria and Expectations

Tenure criteria and expectations for each faculty member are normally stated in the initial letter of appointment to the faculty member that is sent by a dean or provost. But departments usually have their own specifications for tenure, and these, although they must be consistent with general universitywide standards, also correspond to the norms of the departments' particular disciplines. To ensure consistency between institutional and departmental policies and practices, Duke University requires central review of all departmental statements of policy and procedures (see Exhibit 9.2).

At the departmental level, department chairs and tenure-review committee members meet with new faculty to focus on processes and time frames of the tenure review and on senior faculty's expectations of junior faculty. Such meetings should include a discussion with each new faculty member about the qualitative and quantitative expectations for tenure. Communicating what is expected is critical to relieving probationers' anxiety about escalating or changing expectations or ratcheting requirements, and this type of information helps probationary faculty members sort out the numerous requests for their time and involvement in tangential activities so they can stay focused on the tenure expectations.

Emphasizing the quality variables that are important, and stating that they will be judged independently of quantity, will add clarity and precision to the criteria. Michigan State University, in its policy and instructions to all probationary faculty, emphasizes the importance of demonstrating the quality of faculty activities and accomplishments (see Exhibit 9.3).

Exhibit 9.1. Preparing for Tenure and Promotion

Introduction

As a probationary faculty member at San Francisco State University, you will want to know about the ways best to prepare for tenure and/or promotion review. One is to read the relevant language in three sources: The San Francisco State University Academic Senate Polices on Retention, Tenure and Promotion; the San Francisco State University Faculty Manual; and the Collective Bargaining Agreement. Reviews for tenure and promotion of probationary faculty normally take place during the same cycle. The more you know about the retention, tenure, and promotion processes, the timelines, the criteria, and standards, and the ways that you can most effectively document your accomplishments, the greater the chances of your success will be.

Information available to you

Frequently asked questions concerning retention, tenure and promotions

Normal time periods for probationary faculty

Annual review for probationary faculty

Criteria for retention/tenure

Eligibility for promotion

How candidates learn about the university's level of expectations for promotion

Criteria and rating for promotion

Expectations of faculty teaching performance

Departments' obligations in evaluating teaching performance

How to demonstrate professional achievement and growth

Categories and criteria for professional achievement and growth

Criteria for contributions to campus and community

Preparation of the working personnel action file (wpaf) for retention, tenure and promotion

Retention/tenure flow chart

Promotion flow chart

Source: http://www.sfsu.edu/faculty.htm (retrieved June 28, 2006).

EXHIBIT 9.2. FACULTY HANDBOOK, DUKE UNIVERSITY

Responsibilities of the Department, Program, or School

All Trustee-authorized faculty-hiring units (e.g., departments, programs, schools) must have a set of formal procedures to govern their internal evaluation processes. The deans, directors, and department chairs are responsible for submitting these procedures to the provost. The provost will review the procedures and assure that they are generally acceptable and consistent with the policies described herein. The deans, directors, and department chairs will be responsible for distribution of these procedures, once endorsed, to all members of the department, program, or school and to new members of the faculty at the time of their appointment.

Source: http://www.provost.duke.edu/pdfs/fhb/FHB_Chap_3.pdf, retrieved June 28, 2006.

To further ensure consistency and fairness, the initial tenure expectations should remain in effect for the duration of the probationary period. Whenever tenure criteria are changed in midstream, the changes should be stipulated in writing, and probationary faculty members should be given the requisite time to meet any new standards. Time frames for completing the tenure requirements for research and publication are already short, especially in disciplines where the competition for funding and publication is great. Where criteria and standards are unclear or changing, probationary faculty members are understandably apprehensive and stressed.

Stable membership of peer-review committees is critical to ensuring consistency and fairness during the probationary period. Regular rotation of committee members according to widely accepted and understood departmental practices increases the likelihood that probationary faculty will receive consistent feedback and guidance throughout, and it helps ensure that the committee members responsible for tenure recommendations have in-depth knowledge of each candidate's performance over time.

Probationary faculty members also need regular, timely, and useful feedback on their progress toward tenure. Committee members and/or the department head need to meet annually with each

EXHIBIT 9.3. FORM D INSTRUCTIONS,
PROVOST'S OFFICE, MICHIGAN STATE UNIVERSITY

All faculty activities and accomplishments must be judged upon their quality, which requires both continuing improvement and continuous engagement. A specific framework for evaluating scholarly activities and contributions includes (but is not restricted to) the following dimensions: scholarship, significance, impact, and attention to context. . . . These dimensions are embedded as possible criteria for assessment in the summary evaluation by chairpersons and directors for each functional area.

- Scholarship—To what extent is the effort consistent with the methods and goals of the field and shaped by knowledge and insight that is current or appropriate to the topic? To what extent does the effort generate, apply, and utilize knowledge?
- Significance—To what extent does the effort address issues that are important to the scholarly community, specific constituents, or the public?
- Impact—To what extent does the effort benefit or affect fields of scholarly inquiry, external issues, communities, or individuals? To what extent does the effort inform and foster further activity in instruction research and creative activities or service?
- Attention to Context—To what extent is the effort consistent with the University Mission Statement, issues within the scholarly community, the constituents, needs, and available resources?

Source: http://www.hr.msu.edu/HRsite/forms/FacultyForms/FormInfoRrpt Pages.htm (retrieved June 28, 2006).

probationary faculty member to discuss his or her progress, review the expectations for tenure for that faculty member, and, as necessary, provide assistance and advice. Most tenure-review processes are responsibly handled, but explicitly stating the process and the criteria that are used, and describing the responsibilities of the senior faculty and department chair, can go a long way toward reassuring probationary faculty. In sum, every effort should be made by the senior faculty and administrators responsible for tenure review to provide each probationary faculty member with opportunities for success.

The faculty handbook at the University of Virginia's School of Medicine outlines how one institution defines the responsibility of the department chair for the success of junior faculty members (see Exhibit 9.4).

When denial of tenure is unavoidable, it is best handled through quiet counseling and assistance with career transition before the final tenure decision. If a college or university reserves the right to base the award of tenure on institutional circumstances beyond the control of the probationary faculty member, such as shifting student interests or declining resources, this stipulation should be stated in the tenure policy. For example, the Arizona Board of Regents has adopted an explicit statement that provides for denial of tenure because of a need for different specializations or new emphases, or for the position or resources to be shifted to another area (Hustoles, 2000). Nevertheless, in order to retain faculty's confidence in the integrity of the tenure system, this option, when available, should be used infrequently, and only with the advice of counsel, and such decisions should not normally wait until the end of the probationary period.

Monitoring the Tenure-Review Process and Results

One way to know how well the tenure-review process is working is to monitor it regularly. The central administration's routine monitoring of each cohort of new probationary faculty, by tracking each faculty member's progress through the probationary period, can provide important insights into the success or failure of the decision-making procedures in every academic department. Deans, department chairs, and faculty leaders need to be informed and take corrective action when there are unusual patterns of tenure award or denial, when procedural problems with tenure reviews occur, or when there are unusual numbers of complaints and grievances. In addition, routine exit interviews conducted by impartial persons in offices far removed from the academic department can help institutions understand the reasons underlying each faculty members' decision to leave prior to the tenure decision.

In sum, clearly established, fully communicated, and consistently implemented tenure-review policies and procedures are

EXHIBIT 9.4. FACULTY HANDBOOK, UNIVERSITY OF VIRGINIA SCHOOL OF MEDICINE

Responsibilities of Department Chairs in the School of Medicine (Excerpt)

(2) *Faculty.* The chair is responsible for recruitment, management, compensation and retention of faculty. . . . The chair nominates all faculty for initial appointment, additional term appointments, and promotion and tenure within the department. The chair will manage faculty personnel in a manner consistent with the strategic plans of the UVA Health System and School of Medicine. . . .

   It is the responsibility of the faculty member and the department chair to develop a clear understanding of the faculty member's goals, supported by plans for developing and documenting the academic dimensions of his or her career. . . . The academic portfolio becomes the framework for academic development and should be periodically reviewed and updated; each faculty member should do this in consultation with her or his department chair.

   An annual conference must be conducted between each chair . . . and each of his/her faculty members eligible for promotion and/or tenure. The conference should include . . . the original . . . letter of offer (job description) for consistency with actual activities, the faculty member's performance and accomplishments of the prior year, and his/her plan for the forthcoming year. The occurrence of this conference must be documented . . . , signed by both parties, and kept on file in the department.

   Maintenance of relatively small academic School of Medicine departments does place tremendous responsibility on the dean and the chair, since all assistant professors potentially will wish to advance academically. The appropriate department chair must assess the assistant professor's ability, encourage his/her continuing education and training, document his/her professional growth, and aid him/her in setting goals. The chair must then assume the responsibility for providing the assistant professor appropriate support so that he/she may have a reasonable opportunity to achieve his/her goals.

Source: http://www.healthsystem.virginia.edu/internet/som-fhbook/ (retrieved July 26, 2006).

essential to building new faculty members' confidence in the system, helping relieve the stress that many probationary faculty members experience, ensuring that junior faculty members' careers progress, and protecting the institution's interests and those of the publics it serves.

CHANGING THE PROBATIONARY TENURE-REVIEW SYSTEM

Other, more fundamental changes in tenure reviews are being discussed or have been adopted. For example, Chait (1998) has suggested "tenure by objectives" (TBO) as an alternative to the fixed time period of most current reviews. Chait's proposal has several elements similar to those of doctoral-degree programs, where, for example, there are no set time limits, and where specific requirements for the degree are delineated at the outset and signed off on when completed. Under a TBO system, candidates would be encouraged to submit portfolios of work samples and other documentation of their accomplishments to substantiate their competence and goal attainment throughout the probationary period. The departmental review committee and the chair, upon determining that the evidence is persuasive, would establish and certify the candidate's competence in a particular area, and the candidate would be able to refocus his or her efforts on another goal or area of competence. Further milestones, when reached, would be similarly certified. A TBO system would allow each probationary faculty member to proceed at an individual pace, influenced primarily by his or her own research agenda and responsibilities. Faculty members in a probationary cohort would complete the tenure-review process at different points in time, but still within some specified period, such as ten years.

Other suggestions for changing tenure have dealt with redefining the locus of the tenure commitment (Trower, 2000) and thus providing either more security of employment (tenure at the campus or system level) or less (tenure at the departmental or disciplinary level), or with changing the concept of what constitutes base salary, thus linking salaries more closely to annual performance or market competition (a practice common in medical schools, for example).

Another variation on the usual tenure-review system is the current practice at some institutions of awarding tenure only at the rank of professor. For instance, the Harvard University Graduate School of Education awards tenure only at the rank of full professor, and after a national search. Nevertheless, although alternative concepts of tenure may work well at certain institutions, the traditional path of peer review during a probationary period remains the customary process for achieving tenure. We think that many of the concerns that today's probationary faculty have about the probationary period can be addressed by following the recommendations we have offered, thus making tenure-track appointments more attractive. We now turn to alternative appointments outside the tenure system.

Equity for Contract-Renewable Appointments

Increasingly, and for a variety of reasons, current and prospective faculty members and their institutions are finding attractive alternatives to tenure-bearing appointments. Alternative appointments, when carefully planned and articulated, can offer colleges and universities and new or potential faculty members employment that is comparable to the tenure track but better suited to some institutions' or individuals' needs. The key to making these new faculty appointments attractive is to make them structurally equivalent: to eliminate status differentials between tenure-track and non-tenure-track appointments, and to differentiate work assignments, performance criteria, and reward structures while simultaneously emphasizing career development, participation in academic governance, and membership in the academic community across all appointment types (Leslie, 2002; Gappa, 1996). Therefore, we offer the following recommendation:

Recommendation 12

Create contract-renewable appointments that are comparable to tenured appointments in terms of status, career tracks, and rewards. Contract-renewable appointments would have these features:

- Defined probationary periods, with explicit evaluation criteria and processes

- Renewable multiyear contracts after successful completion of the probationary period, with defined dates for notification of contract renewal

- Appropriate professorial titles and promotion through sequential ranks

- Equitable salary and benefit programs that compensate contract renewable faculty with higher salaries or enhanced benefits in exchange for the job security that is forgone (see Breneman, 1997)

- Job security through guarantees of sufficient time to successfully relocate after notification of contract nonrenewal

- Support for professional development, opportunities to participate in governance, and recognition and rewards for contributions to the academic department or institution

- Protection of contractual rights, including the right to academic freedom (see Baldwin and Chronister, 2001)

MODELS FROM THE PROFESSIONAL SCHOOLS

The professional schools have been leaders in designing faculty appointments off the tenure track because of their need for a variety of skills and backgrounds in their faculty members. Successful models from the professional schools incorporate the key components in Recommendation 12, and offer ideas to more traditional academic institutions and disciplines for ways to broaden academic career tracks. These models have been successful partly because the credentials of the faculty in these alternative appointments are equivalent to or better than those of the tenure-track faculty. Research professors, professors of practice, and clinical faculty members do typically have credentials similar to those of their tenure-track colleagues, but they choose different career emphases.

The medical schools have been among the leaders in the development of faculty positions that are comparable to positions on the tenure track but that do not offer contracts guaranteeing continuous employment, for reasons associated with clinical practice. The University of Virginia School of Medicine, for example, has five different career options, with tenure possible in three (a fourth option is not shown in Figure 9.1). The track that is most appropriate for each new hire is decided at the time of the initial appointment and is specified in the letter of appointment. Similarly, the faculty handbook for the University of Virginia Health Sciences Center contains detailed descriptions of the expectations for appointment,

FIGURE 9.1. UNIVERSITY OF VIRGINIA SCHOOL OF MEDICINE MISSION

Faculty Structure: In considering the policies for promotions, the award of appointments without term (tenure), and the structure of the faculty of the School of Medicine, we specifically include as members of the faculty to be governed by these rules those appointed in the basic science departments of the School of Medicine and (those appointed) in the clinical departments. This inclusion shall apply, subject to the appropriate rules, whether the appointment is to the tenure-eligible track or to the tenure-ineligible track.

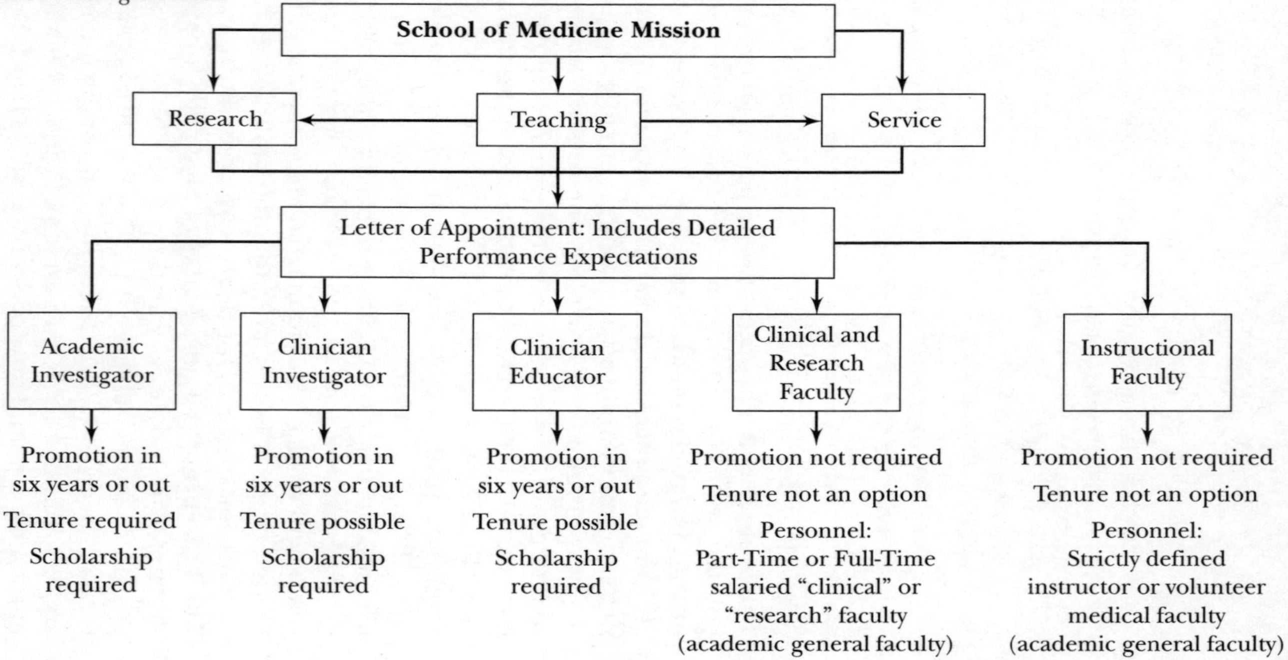

School of Medicine Mission

Research — Teaching — Service

Letter of Appointment: Includes Detailed Performance Expectations

Academic Investigator	Clinician Investigator	Clinician Educator	Clinical and Research Faculty	Instructional Faculty
Promotion in six years or out Tenure required Scholarship required	Promotion in six years or out Tenure possible Scholarship required	Promotion in six years or out Tenure possible Scholarship required	Promotion not required Tenure not an option Personnel: Part-Time or Full-Time salaried "clinical" or "research" faculty (academic general faculty)	Promotion not required Tenure not an option Personnel: Strictly defined instructor or volunteer medical faculty (academic general faculty)

Source: http:www.healthsystem.virginia.edu/internet/som-fhbook/ch.3.cfm (retrieved July 27, 2006).

promotion, and tenure, where applicable, in each of three required areas (scholarship, teaching, and service) for each academic rank in each of the five tracks (see Exhibit 9.5). Although the criteria differ among the appointment types, the requirements and procedures are the same for reviews of all faculty members in every track and are specified in detail in the faculty handbook.

The University of Virginia School of Medicine is highlighted here because it has eliminated the separate status and perquisites that normally accompany a contract renewable appointment. The faculty handbook for the Health Sciences Center discusses both tracks simultaneously, treating them as equally important but different in function. Appointment to a given track is a *choice* made by the university and the individual, in view of the function to be performed. This kind of choice may be more feasible in a medical school, where clinical faculty members enjoy relatively high incomes from their practices, and where status in the profession accrues from success as a doctor, but the concept of comparable and parallel academic career tracks, with equivalent status but different employment arrangements, would provide alternative career paths in academe that could benefit institutions as well as faculty members seeking such alternatives.

Stanford University also uses contract renewable appointments without tenure, which provide employment security and opportunities for promotion in the academic ranks. Stanford includes its non-tenure-track faculty members in its Academic Council, giving them full rights to participate in governance (see http://faculty handbook.stanford.edu/ch1.html#theacademiccouncil, retrieved June 28, 2006). Stanford also uses academic-rank designations for professorial titles, regardless of tenure status. It separates titles in the two comparable tracks by applying a descriptor, such as "research" or "teaching" and, in the medical school, the appropriate medical specialty, such as "surgery," after the academic rank (see http://facultyhandbook.stanford.edu/ch2.html, retrieved June 28, 2006).

Similarly, Harvard University's Graduate School of Education uses the term "professor" for tenure-track and non-tenured appointments. When "professor" is used for a non-tenure-bearing appointment, it is followed by appropriate designations such as "of practice." A professor of practice is hired after a national search

EXHIBIT 9.5. FACULTY STRUCTURE,
UNIVERSITY OF VIRGINIA HEALTH SCIENCES CENTER

Faculty Structure

In considering the policies for promotions, the award of appointments without term (tenure), and the structure of the faculty of the School of Medicine, we specifically include as members of the faculty to be governed by these rules those appointed in the basic science departments of the School of Medicine. . . . This inclusion shall apply, subject to the appropriate rules, whether the appointment is to the tenure-eligible track or to the tenure-ineligible track.

Tenure-Eligible Faculty

The four tenure-eligible faculty appointment designations are academic investigator (AI), clinician-investigator (CI), clinician-educator (CE), and academic-educator (AE). . . . These four tenure-eligible appointments reflect the diverse responsibilities of faculty at the University of Virginia Health System. Appointment to one of the four tenure-eligible designations is made according to the major focus of faculty effort as specified in the initial or modified letter of appointment. The criteria for assistant, associate, and full professor appointments to the three tenure-eligible designations are described in the "Tenure-Eligible Faculty" section of this document.

Tenure-Ineligible Faculty

The School of Medicine has established, within the academic general faculty, the designations clinical faculty (CF), research faculty (RF), and instructional faculty (IF). . . . [T]he . . . protection of tenure will not apply to such faculty members. Accordingly, although they may be deserving of protection by contract, . . . such faculty [will] be considered outside the scope of the 1940 [AAUP] "Statement of Principles."

Appointment to one of the tenure-ineligible designations is made according to the major focus of faculty effort as specified in the initial or modified letter of appointment. The criteria for assistant, associate, and full professor appointments to the three tenure-ineligible designations are described in the "Tenure-Ineligible Faculty" section of this document.

Source: http://www.healthsystem.virgina.edu/internet/som-fhbook/ch.3.cfm (retrieved July 27, 2006).

and has a distinguished, nationally recognized record of service in his or her field. Similarly, senior lectureships are reserved for persons of unusual distinction who have demonstrated excellence in professional work. These appointments are for five years and are renewable, thus providing significant job security. Non-tenurable senior lecturers and professors (term) are considered members of the senior faculty, negotiate their employment arrangements individually, and frequently have long-term careers at Harvard. They participate fully in the governance of the Harvard Graduate School of Education, and their participation includes serving on peer-review committees and making decisions about the future appointment and promotion of faculty members (Gappa, 1996).

At the lower ranks in the Harvard Graduate School of Education, junior lecturers serve as educational practitioners. They have annual appointments, renewable without limit, for the primary purpose of teaching and advising. They work on various projects, building their portfolios by moving laterally among different assignments or external positions (thus exemplifying the concept of employability, as discussed in earlier chapters). As one junior lecturer commented, "Our security is in our portfolios" (Gappa, 1996, p. 19).

In sum, the professional schools provide many examples of alternative academic appointments that have status, perquisites, privileges, and requirements comparable to those of the tenure track but different contractual provisions regarding continuous employment. By making the positions equivalent and retaining academic titles, they eliminate the status distinctions and treatment differentials commonly associated with non-tenure-bearing academic positions. Thus the professional schools offer potential models for other faculty members. Artists and musicians, for example, who typically pursue their artistic work both on and off campus, might appreciate the flexibility that some of these alternative appointments offer.

ENHANCED REWARDS AND INCENTIVES

To maintain comparability between contract-renewable appointments and tenure-track appointments, Breneman (1997) and others argue, salaries of non-tenure-track faculty should reflect an appropriate premium, to adjust for the risk of nonreappointment that the faculty member assumes. Breneman suggests that a premium of about 5 percent above the salary levels for tenure-track faculty would be sufficient.

Chait (1994) suggests an alternative model to be used in exchange for the non-tenure-track faculty member forsaking the financial security of tenure. In each year of a five-year contract, the administration would place 20 percent of a faculty member's salary in an escrow account along with the appropriate pension contribution. If the institution, at the end of the fourth year, decides not to renew the appointment, the faculty member has the right, at the end of the fifth year, to receive either a year's paid leave, with office and title, or a lump-sum payment equal to one year's salary and pension payments. If the college decides to offer another five-year contract, the faculty member has the option of taking either a year's paid leave or the lump-sum payment from the escrowed funds before the onset of the second contract. In Chait's view (1994, p. 29), this arrangement correlates risk with reward. And even though some would say that this is an expensive option, Chait points out that enriched-term contracts, with their additional up-front costs, compete very favorably with the expense entailed in the loss of flexibility that is associated with the lifetime commitment of tenure. Boston University's School of Management has adopted some of Chait's ideas. Faculty who forgo or relinquish tenure receive ten-year renewable contracts, with a salary premium of 8 to 10 percent. They retain all rights to participate in governance, and academic freedom is guaranteed (Clotfelter, 2002, p. 230).

Faculty compensation plans in medical schools, in contrast to Chait's and Breneman's concepts of added reward for added risk, are designed for the schools' largely tenure-ineligible clinical faculty members. The first component of this kind of compensation is a base salary that is linked to a standard measure, such as average salary by rank of basic-sciences faculty, average national salaries of medical school faculty, or average salary of university faculty campuswide (Jones and Gold, 2001). The fixed base recognizes the equal values of the teaching, research, and institutional service that are provided by all faculty members. The second component, a variable level of supplemental compensation, provides flexibility in total compensation because of market differences between basic scientists and clinicians, or among different clinical specialties. The third component is a bonus or incentive, which rewards exceptional performance during the previous year. Thus total salary is viewed as a composite of factors, and this arrangement lowers institutional commitment to the base salary, however defined. Although these salary concepts were developed in medical schools to address their unique circumstances, they offer interesting models that can be adapted to differential reward structures for other faculty, and to ideas for enhancing the compensation of contract-renewable faculty members who forgo the security of tenure.

INSTITUTIONS WITH "HYBRID" SYSTEMS OR WITHOUT TENURE

Some institutions have forgone tenure completely and offer their faculty members only renewable contracts. For example, Florida Gulf Coast University opened in the late 1990s with a mandate from the board of regents that it would not grant tenure. It uses multiyear appointments, which are rolling three-year contracts, or renewable multiyear appointments (see http://www.fgcu.edu/FacultyStaff.asp, retrieved June 28, 2006). Chait and Trower (1998) found that Florida Gulf Coast University, without offering tenure, was still able to attract outstanding faculty members because applicants were excited by the opportunity to launch a new university with a mission focused on undergraduate education, and because they were attracted to an environment that did not have a traditional tenure system.

Webster University, in a system featuring incentives similar to those recommended by both Chait and Breneman, hires all new full-time faculty members on probationary status, with annual contracts for five to seven years. By the third year, each faculty member must declare a preliminary choice to be either on the tenure track or on the faculty development leave (FDL) track. The criteria and standards for the two tracks are identical. After six years of probation and positive performance reviews, successful candidates are granted "continuing" status, either as tenured or FDL faculty. The FDL option at Webster offers a significant incentive to forgo tenure (see Exhibit 9.6).

Similarly, at Greensboro College, non-tenure-track faculty, after an appropriate probationary period, are either awarded

EXHIBIT 9.6. FACULTY DEVELOPMENT LEAVE POLICY, WEBSTER UNIVERSITY

A Viable Alternative to Tenure

Any institution that seeks to eliminate tenure must ask itself some difficult questions. One of the most important is: What is the alternative? How does an institution without tenure sustain a commitment to quality education for its students?

The FDL option was initiated by the Webster faculty in the early 1970s. Here is how it works. Faculty members who choose the FDL option can apply for a sabbatical after every third year. After three years on faculty, professors can apply for a summer at full salary or a semester at half salary. After four years, professors can take a semester at full pay. After five years, they are eligible for a year at half pay or a semester at full salary with major financial support for a summer. Under the traditional tenure system, professors must wait six years before applying for sabbatical. Webster faculty who choose the FDL alternative to tenure are reviewed at least every five years for continuing status. At that time, they may receive a one-year terminal contract or be granted renewal of their continuing FDL status.

Although FDL may seem to offer faculty less security, most feel confident enough in their ability and contribution to the University to take the option. At Webster University approximately 13 percent of the full-time faculty are tenured.

The value of the FDL for Webster lies in the new experience, excitement, and energy that faculty bring back to campus—and to students. Our faculty have more opportunities to become immersed in scholarship, which increases their long-term value to the institution. FDL allows for continual renewal. It is a sound investment.

Source: Neil George, executive vice president and vice president for academic affairs, personal communication, August 1, 2005.

---

continuing-contract status or terminated. If they are terminated, they are guaranteed one year's severance pay. If they are continued, they receive a summer faculty development grant and an annual salary supplement equivalent to 10 percent of the average faculty member's salary at this rank (see Exhibit 9.7). In contrast, Curry College, in Massachusetts, uses job security as an incentive. After receiving a positive evaluation for his or her initial appointment, a faculty member who is eligible receives a rolling contract

Exhibit 9.7. Continuing-Contract Salary Supplements, Greensboro College

Continuing-Contract Salary Supplements

As provided for in the section of this Handbook concerning continuing-contract status, each full-time faculty member with continuing-contract status shall receive an annual salary supplement. The annual salary supplement shall be based on the average base salary at the Assistant Professor, Associate Professor, and Professor ranks. The annual salary supplement shall be a minimum of 10 percent of the average salary for full-time faculty at the rank held by the faculty member on continuing-contract status. Continuing-contract supplements will take effect on January 1 following the granting of continuing-contract status by the Board of Trustees. Adjustments to the amounts of the supplements will take effect annually on January 1.

Source: http://faculty.gborocollege.edu/02handbook (retrieved June 28, 2006).

that provides continuous three-year terms. Rolling three-year contracts offer a significant degree of employment security (see www.curry.edu/faculty+staff/Faculty+Employment, retrieved June 28, 2006).

Thus there are advantages to forgoing tenure completely, but there are disadvantages as well. A comprehensive review process can generate a burdensome workload for the faculty members being reviewed, for faculty reviewers, and for administrators when all faculty members, rather than just probationary faculty, are up for review on an annual basis. It can also lead to "toothless performance reviews," because peer reviewers sooner or later are themselves reviewed; as one faculty member commented, "One consequence of everyone voting on everyone is logrolling. We . . . flatter one another's teaching" (Chait and Trower, 1997, p. 22).

Summary

There is considerable employment security in three-, five-, or ten-year contracts with guaranteed notice of nonrenewal of several years, or in rolling contracts. For some faculty and institutions, contract-renewable appointments can become comparable to tenure when salary enhancements or incentives are added. When the perquisites that characterize tenure are present in alternative appointments—for example, sabbaticals; full membership and voting rights in the academic community; equivalent office space, research space, and support services; the ability to pursue grants as a principal investigator; and access to professional development programs—these contract-renewable appointments represent an attractive alternative to tenure, for institutions and for potential faculty members (Baldwin and Chronister, 2001).

The use of contract-renewable appointments as an alternative to tenure-bearing appointments is also attractive to a wide variety of colleges and universities, from major research universities and large professional schools to comprehensive institutions such as Webster University and small institutions such as Greensboro College and Curry College. New ideas and incentives to complement tenure, or to encourage faculty to forgo tenure, are coming from across the spectrum of higher education institutions because the market for faculty members is pushing innovation. Examples such as those mentioned in this chapter provide ideas for other institutions, regardless of size, mission, or finances, and encourage other institutions to think creatively about how to realign their academic appointments to better meet their own and potential faculty members' needs.

EMPLOYMENT EQUITY FOR FACULTY IN FIXED-TERM APPOINTMENTS

Much has been written about the inequitable and haphazard treatment of part-time and temporary faculty members who are hired for a fixed term—typically for one semester or one year—with no guarantee of continuing employment. But part-timers now represent a significant proportion of the total faculty. Regardless of the typically part-time and contingent nature of these fixed-term appointments, all faculty members contribute to the academic mission of their institutions. In view of this reality, we offer the following recommendation:

Recommendation 13

Develop institutionwide policies and practices that provide equitable and respectful treatment for faculty in fixed-term (that is, part-time or temporary) appointments.

All faculty members, regardless of the type or duration of their appointments, require an equitable and respectful academic environment in order to do excellent work. As a first step in ensuring respect, their titles should not reflect the negative images conveyed by such terms as "contingent," "temporary," or "part-time." Thus, in this book, we have used the neutral phrase "fixed-term appointment" in connection with these faculty members, to accurately convey the nature of their contracts, but without a negative connotation.

The following criteria, which are appropriate for short-term employment, characterize a system that ensures equitable treatment in fixed-term appointments. They are based on earlier research (Gappa and Leslie, 1993; Baldwin and Chronister, 2001), and they incorporate standards recommended by the American Association of University Professors in its 1993 "Statement on the Status of Non Tenure-Track Faculty" (American Association of University Professors, 2003). These criteria are as follows:

- All term appointments should be for a fixed duration, with specified dates for notice of contract renewal or termination, and with clear descriptions of the specific duties to be performed.
- Every fixed-term faculty member should be evaluated regularly and, on the basis of the position's specified duties, provided with feedback regarding his or her performance. Decisions regarding reappointment, compensation, and promotion should be based on these regular evaluations.
- Timely notice of reappointment, and advance notice of course assignments, should be given to all fixed-term faculty members so that they can adequately prepare to continue in their positions or find alternative employment.
- After a certain number of fixed-term appointments, faculty members should be considered for reappointment with annual contracts or, when possible, with multiyear-term contracts (perhaps for two, three, or five years).
- Compensation for faculty in fixed-term appointments should be based on an institutionwide salary system and a defined package of fringe benefits appropriate for that appointment type. Every faculty member except those in the most temporary positions (for example, positions with a total duration of

one semester) should have access to basic benefits including some medical insurance and some option for a retirement plan.

- Faculty members in fixed-term appointments should have opportunities to participate in orientation and professional development programs. Every new faculty member needs basic information about his or her institution and some assistance in getting started.
- Fixed-term faculty members should be eligible for recognition and rewards for exemplary performance. Their noteworthy contributions to the campus should be publicized.
- All faculty members, including those in fixed-term appointments, should have access to procedures for addressing and reporting complaints and grievances regarding unfair treatment.
- Sufficient office space, equipment, and support services should be provided to all fixed-term faculty in order for them to successfully accomplish their jobs.
- The treatment, across the college or university, of faculty members in fixed-term appointments should be monitored regularly to ensure that all faculty members in these appointments receive equitable and respectful treatment; have access to support services, office space, and opportunities for professional growth opportunities; participate in decisions concerning their work; and are recognized for their contributions and achievements.

Ensuring that fixed-term faculty employment meets these criteria requires review of the policies and practices currently in place before any action is taken. In 2001, for example, the University of North Carolina's board of governors undertook an unusually extensive self-study of the university's use of fixed-term appointments, in which the board examined most of the criteria just outlined as a precursor to making changes. The board appointed a systemwide committee on non-tenure-track faculty to examine the current employment of fixed-term faculty at the University of North Carolina "from numerous perspectives, including the needs of the institutions as well as the conditions of employment for this group of faculty," and to "make a series of recommendations that [met] both the needs of faculty [the university employed] and the institutions in need of their services" (see http://www.northcarolina.edu/content/

php/aa/reports/ntt_faculty/BOG.NTT.faculty.report.PDF, retrieved
July 27, 2006).

This systemwide committee of academic administrators and
faculty members made a series of recommendations for change.
The recommendations called for each institution in the system to
develop its own staffing plans that would (1) define the desired
mix of various types of faculty appointments, (2) provide clear descriptions of positions and appropriate titles for full- and part-time
non-tenure-track positions, (3) contain guidelines for proper compensation, and (4) institute central, campuswide oversight of non-
tenure-track employment. The committee also included additional
recommendations aimed at improving equity and fostering a
climate of respect. The Board's acceptance of the committee's recommendations led campuses in the system to rewrite their non-
tenure-track policies, to convert part-time adjunct positions to
full-time lectureships with benefits and multiyear contracts, and,
in some cases, to develop faculty staffing plans (Betsy E. Brown,
personal communication, July 27, 2005).

A starting point for fixed-term faculty to become integrated
into campus life is publication of a handbook that is aimed especially at their needs and filled with information useful to them.
Baruch College of the City University of New York publishes an adjunct handbook on its Web site for the purpose of giving newcomers a good source of information to get started and a handy
reference throughout their appointments. The handbook opens
with a warm, welcoming message and links to the faculty handbook
(see Exhibit 9.8). Each of the deans of the various schools at
Baruch posts a welcoming message to new adjunct faculty (see Exhibit 9.9). These messages stress the importance of adjuncts to the
quality of instruction at the college. The handbook also highlights
activities and opportunities available to adjunct faculty; among
them are opportunities to enhance their teaching skills (see Exhibit 9.10).

Baruch College operates under a collective bargaining contract
for adjunct faculty employment. The handbook has references and
links to the bargaining agent and the contract, and to other sources
of information, such as details about employee benefits. Thus the
handbook's purpose, for which its format and tone are ideally
suited, is to emphasize the adjunct faculty's roles and participation
in a collegial community and to orient new faculty to the campus.

EXHIBIT 9.8. ADJUNCT FACULTY HANDBOOK, BARUCH COLLEGE

This handbook has been created to acknowledge and support the significant role of Baruch's adjunct faculty in our classrooms and on our campus. Owing to the limited amount of time adjuncts spend on campus and the fact that many adjuncts arrive after full-time staff is gone and offices are closed, navigating through the systems can be challenging.

The handbook has been arranged to take you through your time at Baruch chronologically, from the time you're hired through the submission of your grades at the end of the semester. Using the Table of Contents, you'll become familiar with campus buildings, locations, and services; learn how to order texts, get listed in the Directory, and have classroom repairs fixed. You'll also come to know about the many resources available to enhance your own teaching and professional experience at Baruch.

An alphabetical index of all sections has also been included for quick reference. You'll also find sections for Checklist for Adjuncts, Questions for the Associate Provost, and Letters from the Frontline.

Throughout this handbook there are links to sections of the Faculty Handbook (vs. the Adjunct Faculty Handbook) or the Baruch Web site.

Source: http://www.baruch.cuny.edu/facultyhandbook/adjunct/index.htm (retrieved July 27, 2006).

EXHIBIT 9.9. WELCOME MESSAGES FROM DEANS, BARUCH COLLEGE

Stan Altman, Dean of the School of Public Affairs:

The faculty and staff of Baruch College's School of Public Affairs warmly welcome its new adjunct faculty members. SPA's programs are interdisciplinary in character, and our student body diverse and enthusiastic. Whether you are introducing recent high school graduates to the basics of public administration or helping seasoned managers refine their skills in budgeting or policy analysis in one of our executive programs, we think you will find Baruch's School of Public Affairs a very intellectually stimulating environment. Our students on both the graduate and undergraduate level see their studies as opening doors to careers in government, non-profit administration, education (both K–12 and higher education). Our part-time faculty adds scope and depth to the educational opportunities we offer through the practical experience they bring to the classroom. We place tremendous value on your contributions to our mission.

Source: http://www.baruch.cuny.edu/facultyhandbook/adjunct/index.htm (retrieved July 27, 2006).

EXHIBIT 9.10. FACULTY DEVELOPMENT SEMINARS, BARUCH COLLEGE

Like the carpenter who keeps his tools sharp, clean, and oiled—ready for the next job—and who adds new tools as they prove worthwhile, we adjuncts should be seeking to improve our capacity to deliver value to the students. Faculty Development Seminars are very useful in this regard. The schedule for faculty development seminars can be found in the Faculty Development Seminars section of the Faculty Handbook.

Source: http://www.baruch.cuny.edu/facultyhandbook/adjunct/index.htm (retrieved July 27, 2006).

Examples abound of institutional good practice with regard to fixed-term faculty appointments. The three examples that follow were chosen to highlight three aspects of respectful, equitable treatment in institutions' policies or practices. The first example shows how one institution has avoided the common phenomenon of continuous reappointment of individuals in fixed-term appointments without appropriate notification of contract renewal. The second example shows one institution's response to concerns about salary equity. The third example stresses the need to ensure fixed-term faculty feel that they are respected and that they belong to a community of scholars:

- Smith College's faculty manual specifies that all lecturers are normally appointed for one to three years. The reappointment decision is based in part on a formal review of the candidate's teaching. Faculty on one-year contracts must be notified by January 15 regarding reappointment; faculty in multiyear appointments must be notified by December 15 of the final year. Lecturers who have served more than five years must be given a year's notice of nonreappointment (see www.smith.edu/deanoffaculty/policy, retrieved June 28, 2006).
- At Vancouver Community College, instructors who teach on a half-time basis are paid half of the full-time salary. Part-timers also earn vacation leave at the same rate as full-timers, and they receive health benefits and sick leave (Smallwood, 2003).
- Arcadia University emphasizes support for the essentials and perquisites that are so frequently missing at other institutions, such as desks, e-mail accounts, listings in campus directories,

faculty parking, free campus theater tickets, tuition remission, and health benefits for part-time faculty who have taught at least nine courses over three years. Part-timers at Arcadia are also occasionally selected to participate in an important faculty perquisite: taking a free trip to London with the freshmen (Smallwood, 2003).

AN INNOVATIVE APPROACH
TO FACULTY APPOINTMENTS

This chapter has explored the three major types of academic appointments in use today: tenure-track appointments, contract-renewable appointments, and fixed-term appointments. This exploration has been conducted from the perspective of ensuring that each appointment type is characterized by equity, fairness, and respect and that it represents an attractive choice for prospective faculty members. The chapter has analyzed current policies and practices for each type of appointment, made recommendations for achieving equity in the different types of appointments, and illustrated these recommendations with examples of good practice in a wide array of colleges and universities. The recommendations, for the most part, have been for thoughtful changes to existing policies, programs, and benefits rather than for costly interventions. The goals have been to present examples of how the recommendations in the chapter might be implemented in different colleges and universities, and to help faculty members and administrators think creatively about ways of ensuring respect and equity in the various types of faculty appointments used at their institutions.

A primary objective in rethinking current faculty appointments is to recognize and value the different types of academic appointments in use today and ensure that they are attractive to prospective faculty members. That has been the purpose of this chapter. But we conclude with one more example, one that illustrates how colleges, thinking creatively and working together, can develop new prototypes for faculty appointments that combine features of various appointment types in new formats that simultaneously are attractive to prospective faculty members and benefit their institutions. The example offered here is the result of extensive collaboration among institutions that were brought together by their need to solve a mutual problem.

A consortium of five colleges in New England has gone beyond campus boundaries in creatively rethinking what part-time faculty employment can be. The Five College Consortium consists of the University of Massachusetts and Amherst, Hampshire, Mount Holyoke, and Smith Colleges, all within ten miles of each other. With tight budgets for appointing new faculty members, these institutions pooled their resources to hire a group of professors whom they share. They have been sharing professors over the years, but now they are jointly hiring new full-time faculty, some of whom are in tenure-track appointments. Others have three-year contracts with the possibility of conversion to tenure-track status. Each shared professor has a home department and college, where he or she teaches one course on a part-time basis, holds office hours, and is evaluated for tenure or contract renewal. But each shared professor also teaches an additional course each semester at another campus, where he or she borrows an office from a faculty member on leave. The shared professors have access to all the campus facilities at both institutions. The program is viewed as beneficial, both by the faculty members who are shared and by the institutions, which are able to offer academic programs, such as Asian/Pacific American studies, that would not be feasible at only one of the small campuses (Wilson, 2004b). The shared faculty members in the Five College Consortium exemplify the message of this chapter: "Think outside the proverbial box."

In sum, achieving equity in a respectful environment for all faculty, regardless of their appointment types, requires commitment, innovative thinking, thoughtful consideration of alternatives, and willingness to experiment with new ideas. Fortunately, these are the traditional hallmarks of the academic profession. Administrators and faculty members working together will find new and innovative solutions that preserve important academic traditions and are suited to particular environments. The ideas and examples expressed in this chapter are intended to be starting points for thoughtful analysis, discussion, and decision making on individual campuses.

CHAPTER TEN

ACADEMIC FREEDOM

Academic freedom encompasses the norms and values that protect each faculty member's freedom of intellectual expression and inquiry. Thus academic freedom lies at the heart of the academic profession; it is an essential component of faculty members' core responsibility to educate students and develop knowledge. The need to protect faculty members' academic freedom was the fundamental rationale underlying the concept of tenure when it was promulgated by the American Association of University Professors in its 1940 Statement (American Association of University Professors, 2001c) and subsequently endorsed by more than 180 scholarly and professional organizations. Since that endorsement, the concept of academic freedom has been buttressed through case law from three different legal sources of rights:

- The First Amendment to the Constitution, which applies to public employers such as state colleges and universities
- Contractual rights, such as statements in letters of appointment, faculty handbooks, institutional rules and regulations, and collective bargaining agreements (see, for example, *Greene* v. *Howard University,* cited in Euben, 2002)
- Academic custom or common law (see, for example, *Perry* v. *Sindermann* and other cases cited in Euben, 2002)

Professors' right to academic freedom has been defined to include professors' freedom in the classroom to discuss their subjects, freedom to conduct research and publish its results, and freedom to speak and write as citizens. But the right to academic freedom also encompasses a more elusive but closely related concept of autonomy, or the ability to manage one's work. To professors, autonomy means the right to decide how to do one's work within one's particular assignment. For example, faculty members have the autonomy to plan their courses, select the materials they will use, and decide the best methods by which to teach the material to students. Similarly, in research, faculty members decide the best methods to use to examine their topics, and they exercise considerable discretion in seeking funding to engage in research and disseminate the results. The autonomy of the academic profession, or the right to define and structure one's work within a particular assignment, gives faculty satisfaction. Thus it is a major hallmark of faculty work. In this chapter, we include the concept of autonomy as an integral part of the overall concept of academic freedom.

The AAUP statement links academic freedom directly to the awarding of tenure. The tenure contract provides that, after rigorous peer review, a college or university makes the commitment to employ a faculty member continuously until his or her retirement and guarantees due process prior to dismissal for cause (American Association of University Professors, 2001c). But all faculty members, regardless of their appointment types, require freedom to express the truth as they see it. Faculty members in contract-renewable or fixed-term appointments need the same basic right to academic freedom as their tenured colleagues, in order to function as full-fledged academics and fulfill their professional obligations without reservation. As Baldwin and Chronister (2001, p. 185) note, if the basic right to academic freedom is compromised for some members of the faculty, the faculty as a whole is compromised, and thus the institution's integrity and academic programs are diminished. The question thus becomes how to extend academic freedom, an essential component of the academic profession, to faculty appointments that do not have a guarantee of continuous employment.

This chapter explores this question by way of a three-pronged approach. First, it examines several policy statements on academic freedom to see how they include faculty members who are in fixed-term and contract-renewable positions and how they guarantee those faculty members' rights. Second, the chapter makes recommendations for educating the campus community about academic freedom and its importance to the academy. The last section of the chapter discusses ways to extend the right to academic freedom to all faculty members through procedures for addressing complaints when policies concerning academic freedom appear to have been violated.

Because the right to academic freedom, when it was originally defined, was inextricably linked to tenure, extending academic freedom to those who do not have tenure poses difficult issues. Therefore, a caveat is in order here. The ideas expressed here have not been vetted for their legality and do not constitute legal advice. Any institution seeking to revise its policies regarding faculty members' rights to academic freedom and due process will need to involve its own legal counsel. That said, we offer the following recommendation:

Recommendation 14

Clearly define what constitutes academic freedom, and include the definition in the contracts for contract-renewable and fixed-term academic appointments. Extend the protections of academic freedom to all faculty members through policy statements and faculty handbooks. When developing grievance procedures for reporting alleged violations of academic freedom, ensure that such procedures address the various types of academic appointments. Provide information about policies related to academic freedom through orientation programs or campus convocations.

Inclusion of All Faculty Members in Policy Statements

Inclusive institutional policy statements are the beginning point for ensuring that all faculty members have academic freedom. Here, we highlight two institutional policy statements that, taken together, encompass the basic elements of ensuring that all faculty members are covered by policies on academic freedom. The University of Mississippi's policy statement (Exhibit 10.1) emphasizes the importance of academic freedom in the campus environment and describes what it covers. Nevertheless, although the University of Mississippi's statement explains what academic freedom is and highlights the university's commitment to it, it does not mention how faculty members' academic freedom is protected, nor does it

EXHIBIT 10.1. STATEMENT CONCERNING ACADEMIC FREEDOM,
UNIVERSITY OF MISSISSIPPI

The University of Mississippi is a community of teachers and students bound together by a common love for learning and by their cooperative efforts to preserve and increase their intellectual heritage. Good learning increases, minds are creative, and knowledge is turned to useful purposes when men and women are free to question and seek for answers, free to learn, and free to teach.

The teacher, therefore, is entitled to freedom in research and in the publication of his/her results, subject to the adequate performance of his/her other academic duties. The teacher is entitled to freedom in the classroom in discussing his/her subject, but he/she should be careful not to introduce into his/her teaching controversial matter that has no relation to his/her subject. All members of the faculty, whether tenured or nontenured, enjoy this same academic freedom, with the rights and responsibilities that the term implies. . . .

The University of Mississippi endorses the 1940 Statement on Principles of Academic Freedom and Tenure of the American Association of University Professors, as revised and refined since 1940, and also the Statement on Professional Ethics of the same organization, insofar as these are not limited by state law or the policies of the Mississippi Board of Trustees of State Institutions of Higher Learning.

Source: https://secure.olemiss.edu/umpolicyopen/ (retrieved July 28, 2006).

refer to any grievance procedures that can be invoked in claims that academic freedom has been violated. The University of New Mexico statement (Exhibit 10.2) is more specific in defining faculty members' right to academic freedom; it describes procedures by which non-tenure-track faculty can address alleged violations of academic freedom, and it provides due process in the event of non-renewal or termination of a faculty member's contract.

EDUCATING FACULTY MEMBERS ABOUT ACADEMIC FREEDOM

Endorsing academic freedom in campus policy statements and specifying that academic freedom policies include nontenured

EXHIBIT 10.2. FACULTY HANDBOOK, UNIVERSITY OF NEW MEXICO

Article I. The University Faculty

Sec. 1(a) Membership: The University Faculty shall consist of the Professors, Associate Professors, Assistant Professors, Lecturers, and Instructors, including part-time and temporary appointees. . . .

  1.1. General Principles on Academic Freedom

   (a) All members of the faculty tenured and non-tenured, full-time and part-time, on main campus and branch campuses are entitled to academic freedom. . . .

  5.4. University-Initiated Termination of Contract of a Non-Tenured Faculty Member

   (a) The University has the discretion whether or not to renew the annual contract of probationary or non-tenure-track faculty members. . . .

   (b) Under the extraordinary circumstances and with proof of adequate cause as outlined in Sec. 5.3.2, a non-tenured faculty member's annual contract may be terminated before its expiration. . . . A decision to terminate the contract of a non-tenured faculty member . . . shall be made by the Provost/VPHS after recommendations by the chair and the dean. At each administrative level, the faculty member shall be fully informed in writing of the reasons proposed for such termination and shall be given an adequate opportunity to respond in writing and/or orally . . . prior to the final decision. The faculty member shall have the right to appeal a termination decision by the Provost/VPHS to the Academic Freedom and Tenure Committee on grounds within the Committee's jurisdiction (Sec. 6.2. . . .

  6.22. Dismissal or Non-Renewal of a Non-Tenured Faculty Member
   If the annual contract of a probationary faculty member is not renewed . . . or a probationary or other non-tenured faculty member is dismissed during the term of his or her contract, and if the faculty member believes that violation of academic freedom, improper considerations, or prejudicial violations of the procedures specified in this Policy occurred, the faculty member may appeal the action to the [Academic Freedom and Tenure] Committee.

Source: http://www.handbook.unm.edu/~handbook (retrieved July 28, 2006).

faculty members are important first steps, but they are not enough. Faculty members also need a clear understanding of what constitutes academic freedom, of which activities are protected and which are not. Olswang (2003) recommends that what constitutes academic freedom be clearly delineated in policy statements and differentiated from what does not constitute academic freedom. Bryne (1997, p. 6) offers the following clarification:

> Academic freedom includes the following rights and duties:
>
> 1. Faculty members have the right to pursue chosen research topics and to present their professional views without the imposition or threat of institutional penalty for the political, religious, or ideological tendencies of their scholarship, but subject to fair professional evaluation by peers and appropriate institutional officers.
> 2. Faculty members have the right to teach without the imposition or threat of institutional penalty for the political, religious or ideological tendencies of their work, subject to their duties to satisfy reasonable educational objectives and to respect the dignity of their students.
> 3. Faculty members may exercise the rights of citizens to speak on matters of public concern and to organize with others for political ends without the imposition or threat of institutional penalty, subject to their academic duty to clarify the distinction between advocacy and scholarship.
> 4. Faculty members have the right to express views on the educational policies and institutional priorities of their schools without the imposition or threat of institutional penalty, subject to duties to respect colleagues and protect the school from external misunderstandings.

New faculty members need clear and understandable definitions, such as Bryne's, and an introduction to the concept of academic freedom because it is not commonly found outside academe or stressed in graduate schools. All faculty members need continuous updating of information about what is covered by policies concerning academic freedom because the concept is evolving. Therefore, we offer the following recommendations:

Recommendation 15

The institution's policy, specific provisions, and protections regarding academic freedom should be included in orientations for all new faculty members so that they learn about what academic freedom means, and about their rights and responsibilities with respect to academic freedom.

Recommendation 16

Policies concerning academic freedom should be updated as necessary to reflect new developments, should be communicated regularly to all faculty members, and should be addressed periodically in campus convocations or other, similar events.

Academic freedom is, after all, an important element of academic culture and faculty roles. All faculty, but especially new faculty, need to understand what academic freedom is and is not, and where to go for guidance if they have questions. All faculty members must also be continuously prepared to address the differences in viewpoints and the clashes of competing ideas that take place on campuses, especially in the classroom.

New and continuing faculty members alike also need to be informed about changes in or constraints on academic freedom that arise from federal regulations, advances in technology, or societal views. For example, academic freedom has been impacted by various federal regulatory requirements dealing with controls on exports, such as the International Traffic in Arms Regulations administered by the Department of State and the Export Administration Regulations administered by the Department of Commerce (Euben, 2004). And in the Internet era, with the proliferation of e-mail, Web pages, and bloggers, faculty members are increasingly embroiled in controversies over academic freedom. Euben (2004) recommends that faculty and administrators work together to protect academic freedom from governmental constraints and to develop policies with regard to acceptance of classified research grants or contracts, access to personal computer files, and sharing of information with external agencies.

An example of action that a professional organization can take to educate its members about new developments regarding academic freedom is the January 6, 2006, Board of Directors' statement from the Association of American Colleges and Universities (AAC&U), *Academic Freedom and Educational Responsibility* (http://www.aacu.org/about/statements/academic_freedom.cfm, retrieved July 4, 2006). It addresses new challenges to academic freedom involving viewpoint discrimination and is aimed at all faculty members who have responsibility for teaching and curriculum development. Pointing out the inevitable tension between faculty members' freedom to teach and students' freedom to form independent judgments, the statement, in a thoughtful discussion of three major points, clarifies what is *not* required in the name of intellectual diversity:

1. In an educational community, freedom of speech, or the narrower concept of academic freedom, does not mean the freedom to say anything one wants (for example, the freedom to participate in speech that includes the threat of physical danger or a hostile environment).
2. Students do not have the right to remain free from encountering unwelcome or "inconvenient" questions, whereas they do have the right to hear and examine diverse opinions that have been determined by scholars to be reliable and accurate.
3. All competing ideas on a subject do not deserve to be included in a course or program.

For seasoned as well as new faculty, the AAC&U's carefully reasoned guidelines are useful and timely in rethinking classroom behavior and course content and in opening up conversations on campus about what does and does not constitute academic freedom and appropriate student behavior. As the AAC&U's statement points out, faculty need to continuously rethink academic freedom and how it applies to their work, and the campus is an ideal forum for that purpose.

To meet this continuing need for education about academic freedom for all faculty members, a college or university might consider appointing senior faculty or recent retirees as educators and ombudspersons, working under the auspices of the faculty senate or within the provost's office. These senior faculty would receive training and could be available to discuss potential abuses of academic freedom, or to answer questions and provide guidance to individual faculty members on a confidential basis. They could also be responsible for continuous education of the campus community about new developments with regard to academic freedom. For example, trained faculty experts could provide groups of faculty with updates on or interpretations of policies and practices concerning academic freedom through departmental meetings, campuswide training sessions, various publications, and Web sites. Occasionally making academic freedom the focus of a campuswide convocation would stimulate ongoing discussion and reaffirmation of its importance and would also attract broader audiences.

Academic freedom is the lifeblood of faculty work. Therefore, discussions of what it means and how it operates need to be ongoing and to be an ever-present element of campus life. Ideally, faculty governance bodies will ensure that their colleagues and the campus community stay well informed. As Euben (2004) points out, to do this well requires leadership and good working relationships among faculty, administrators, and legal counsel.

Procedures for the Protection of Academic Freedom for Nontenured Faculty

Extending academic freedom to nontenured faculty raises significant questions of both substance and process (Bryne, 2001). As Bryne points out, the protection of academic freedom has been embedded in specific institutional arrangements, such as tenure and peer review, which have not been traditionally available to non-tenure-track faculty, especially adjuncts. The right to academic freedom is for the protection of faculty members' speech that is professional in nature (speech in classrooms, in conference presentations, and in written articles or papers). But faculty members' professional speech is regularly evaluated as one aspect of peer review, thus making peer review the traditional bulwark of academic freedom. In this construct, the difference is readily apparent between, on the one hand, the protection of academic speech through the right to academic freedom and, on the other, the protection of lay speech from official penalty through the protections inherent in the First Amendment (Bryne, 2001, p. 585).

But fixed-term faculty members often lack meaningful peer review of their teaching or other professional activities. They are on short-term contracts with perfunctory performance reviews, at best. The tenuousness of the fixed-term faculty member's contract presents a persistent risk of violations of academic freedom. Yet, as earlier chapters have shown, fixed-term and contract-renewable faculty members are now the majority of all faculty members. It is no longer reasonable not to offer them some protection of academic freedom. As Bryne (2001, p. 587) has aptly said, "Most full-time faculty understand that a threat to academic freedom of any professor in a university is a threat to all."

As this chapter has outlined, the beginning points for protecting the academic freedom of all faculty are (1) the promise on the part of the college or university, in its policy statement, that it will not violate the right to academic freedom and (2) the institution's operational definition of what academic freedom means on that particular campus. But before meaningful procedures for hearing complaints regarding violations of academic freedom can be developed, the following principles and structures need to be in place (Bryne, 1997, 2001; Michaelson, 2001):

- The policy statement must clearly state that policies and procedures concerning academic freedom apply to all faculty members, and that violations of academic freedom can be remedied through open and impartial grievance procedures.
- Similarly, the policy should state the institution's promise that it will not violate the academic freedom of faculty members through discipline, dismissal, or nonrenewal of contracts.

As Bryne (1997) points out, the institution, having promised faculty members academic freedom and defined the scope of that protection in its policy, has given faculty members a legal right to action if the promise is violated; that is, breach of contract can be claimed. But before a faculty member can go to court for a violation of his or her right to academic freedom, he or she must utilize internal procedures and give the college or university an opportunity to correct any mistakes that may have occurred. Therefore, the institution should have procedures in place for addressing complaints that its policy on academic freedom has been violated.

The following suggestions provide commonsense, nonlegal advice for policies and procedures concerning the right of nontenured faculty to protection of their academic freedom, with the caveat that any complaint-related procedures that are ultimately developed will need thorough review by legal counsel:

- Any faculty member should be able to receive an official explanation for an adverse personnel action (see the American Association of University Professors' 1989 *Statement on Procedural Standards in the Renewal or Nonrenewal of Faculty Appointments*, http://www.aaup.org/statements/Redbook/Rbrenew.htm, retrieved July 4, 2006).
- The decision not to renew a contract for a *contract-renewable* faculty member should be based on written peer evaluations of his or her performance, using professional criteria, and on a finding that the faculty member should not be retained. Such a judgment from a peer-review committee should be confirmed by the academic supervisor.
- The decision to renew an appointment for a *fixed-term* faculty member should be based on a need for his or her continuing services, and, if that need exists, on peer review of his or her performance.
- Every faculty member protected by the policy on academic freedom should be entitled to have his or her complaint reviewed by an impartial body in order to determine whether a nonreappointment represents a violation of the institution's policy on academic freedom.
- The grievance procedure should make use of familiar legal devices common to discrimination complaints, such as a prima facie case and shifting burdens of proof (Bryne, 1997, p. 8). In other words, a complaining faculty member should bear the initial burden of proof and should be able to show that his or her exercise of academic freedom led to an adverse employment decision. Once the faculty member has done so, the burden of proof shifts to the institution to show that no violation of its policy on academic freedom occurred, or that its actions regarding the complainant's protected academic freedom did not play a substantial role in the adverse personnel decision.

- Faculty members serving on an institution's investigative or grievance committee who are responsible for reviewing and, where necessary, resolving complaints that the policy on academic freedom has been violated need to be protected themselves from possible retaliation by the institution. In other words, they should be tenured professors or should hold long-term contracts so that they will have adequate independence.

CONCLUSIONS

This chapter has focused on the essential element of academic freedom. With the proliferation of fixed-term and contract-renewable appointments, academic freedom policies and procedures for hearing complaints regarding alleged violations need to be expanded to include all faculty members, regardless of their appointment types. As this chapter has emphasized, this is not easy to do, because academic freedom has traditionally been inextricably linked to tenure. The suggestions made here for policies and procedures are intended to motivate campus leaders, professional associations, and others to discuss ways of incorporating traditional principles of academic freedom into the diverse academic appointments that now exist. Forums such as the Annual Conference on Law and Higher Education, held by Stetson University College of Law, or the annual meeting of the National Association for College and University Attorneys are ideal settings for rethinking procedures involved in protecting the right to academic freedom.

This chapter began by discussing the fostering of a campus culture that values and protects the right to academic freedom of faculty members. Responsibility for fostering this culture belongs to the senior faculty, whose roles in this effort are primarily educational. One of our recommendations calls for ombudspersons or senior faculty to be appointed as educators and as counselors who can listen informally to potential faculty complaints regarding academic freedom and help resolve them informally, when possible. Another possibility would be to expand the role of ombudspersons who are already available for informal complaint resolution and use them to help resolve complaints about violations of academic freedom, with the stipulation that they would also be well versed

in policies concerning academic freedom and faculty rights. Whatever mechanisms are chosen, the emphasis should be on continuous education of the academic community about their rights and
responsibilities pertinent to academic freedom, and on early and
informal attempts to resolve complaints related to academic freedom. Both are key to achieving a campus community where academic freedom flourishes.

CHAPTER ELEVEN

ENSURING FLEXIBILITY IN ACADEMIC APPOINTMENTS

The American workforce today no longer matches the workforce of the early twentieth century that was based on the traditional family formation of one member working in the labor force full time while the other handled household responsibilities. Nevertheless, workplace dynamics have been slow to change to reflect the present reality of dual-career and single parent households, where most full-time employees have significant household responsibilities and no one stays home to manage them. Accordingly, in academe, most faculty members do not have a spouse or partner who manages their home. As a result, many find that there are periods of time when personal responsibilities demand a more prominent role in their lives. A baby is born, a troubled teenager needs special attention, a spouse or partner is in a serious car accident, or an aging parent is diagnosed with a serious illness. During these seasons, some faculty members need institutional support, such as elder care services, to help them manage their personal responsibilities while continuing in their usual professional roles. Other faculty members would prefer to decrease the number of hours that they commit to their work or to disengage from work altogether for a time to better address family needs.

This chapter focuses on our framework's essential element of flexibility in the academic workplace by describing ways that institutions can address these needs. The following pages provide strategies for developing policies, programs, and services that will better allow individuals to manage successfully both their personal and professional responsibilities. Most of the suggestions are established policy at only a minority of institutions (Hollenshead et al., 2005), and this within the past several years. At many institutions, only a few of the strategies are available, and strictly on a case-by-case basis. For the sake of equity, we argue that they should be codified in policy and implemented consistently across a campus.

This chapter begins with an overview of what flexibility is and why it is needed today. Then two approaches to flexibility are discussed. (1) Strategies for providing flexibility in how faculty members allocate their time between personal and professional responsibilities, such as personal leaves and flexible time bases, are presented in two major sections. The first discusses flexibility in leaves; the second discusses flexibility in time base. (2) The chapter then moves to a description of resources, programs, and services, such as on-site child care, that institutions can provide to assist faculty members in effectively managing multiple demands on their time. (Providing options that allow faculty members to continue developing professionally, thus avoiding stagnation, is also an important component of career flexibility. This is addressed in Chapter Twelve.) The chapter concludes with recommendations for the implementation of new policies and procedures for flexibility.

WHY THE CONCERN ABOUT FLEXIBILITY?

Flexibility is a way of defining how, when, and what work is accomplished, and how careers are organized (Healy, n.d.). Many faculty members already enjoy significant autonomy in their day-to-day routines, determining much of what they accomplish on a given day, where they will work, and how they will go about fulfilling their responsibilities. Nevertheless, the concept of flexibility goes beyond the autonomy inherent in faculty work to recognize individuals' other responsibilities beyond the workplace. Flexibility, as it is understood here, means adjusting work schedules, such as shifting to part-time work or taking a leave at any time during one's academic career. Flexibility also encompasses providing career-path options, such as multiple points for entry, exit, and re-entry into a faculty position, and the ability to shift between tenure-track and contract-renewable appointments. According to one scholar of work-life policy, "True flexibility of time flows from a basic belief in the legitimacy of a balance of commitments between the private and public spheres" (Bailyn, 1993, pp. 95–96). When this kind of work-life flexibility is integrated into the culture and policies of an institution, faculty members are able to negotiate work arrangements that reflect the current level of their personal responsibilities. As the following section describes, research has also shown that flexibility puts faculty members in a position to produce their best work.

The Rationale for Flexibility

Why is flexibility an essential element of faculty work? First and foremost, flexibility in the academic workplace provides equitable treatment to faculty members who have significant personal responsibilities that make it impossible for them to operate as if they were ideal workers. Men as well as women increasingly need workplace flexibility to successfully meet their personal and professional responsibilities. One study found that 80 percent of faculty members have spouses or partners who are working professionals, meaning that they do not have someone who manages their homes on a full-time basis (Didion, 1996).

Although the life circumstances of men and women today necessitate increased workplace flexibility, it continues to be women who shoulder most of the family responsibilities and thus are hurt most in the absence of flexible policies. Women still have 70 to 80 percent of child care responsibilities (Williams, 2000) and, largely for this reason, only 8 percent of mothers between the ages of twenty-five and forty-four work fifty or more hours per week on a year-round basis (Williams, 2002). Nevertheless, the average work week for full-time faculty members at most types of institutions is at least fifty hours per week (U.S. Department of Education, National Center for Education Statistics, 2004). As described more fully in Chapter Four, when women faculty members have children, the time they devote to research decreases. Men, however, are actually able to increase their time on research after they have children (Leslie, 2005), probably because a greater proportion have spouses or partners caring full time for the children and the home. A separate study found that married women with a child under six years of age are 50 percent less likely even to enter a tenure-track position than are married men with a child under the age of six, and, in general, the women who do are 20 percent less likely to achieve tenure than are the men (Wolfinger, Mason, and Goulden, 2004). Thus this disparate impact on males and females of having children becomes a significant equity issue in the workplace.

If those with significant caregiving and household responsibilities are to have the opportunity to succeed in a faculty position, they need policies and programs that can support them as they fulfill their personal responsibilities. They also need sufficient flexibility to be able to decrease their work responsibilities for a time or to take a career break to focus fully on their personal responsibilities when they are most demanding. Only when an increasing number of today's faculty members are allowed to function outside the "ideal worker" norms that are based on traditional male work patterns will they be able to establish and maintain successful academic careers. Thus institutional policies and practices that provide flexibility are an important component of strategic efforts to recruit and retain excellent faculty members.

Beyond the crucial issue of ensuring equity, flexibility also makes good business sense, according to research from the corporate sector (Bond, Galinsky, and Hill, 2004). First, it helps to create a more attractive workplace for recruiting and retaining employees. In 1998, half of 614 companies surveyed ranked flexibility as their most effective retention tool, more important than above-market salaries, stock options, or training (Friedman, n.d.). Second, flexible work policies and other resources that support employees with significant household responsibilities can also help individuals accomplish more at work. For example, a study by the MetLife Mature Market Institute and National Alliance for Caregiving (2006) estimated that it costs American businesses almost $34 billion, or $2,110 per employee per year, when employees cannot get the support they need for their adult family member. These costs are primarily due to absenteeism, crisis in care, unpaid leaves, and hiring replacement workers.

Third, offering flexibility to help individuals meet their personal and professional responsibilities can enhance employees' well-being and productivity (Bond, Galinsky, and Hill, 2004). Full-time faculty report that they experience a number of different stressors: managing household responsibilities, time pressure, lack of personal time, child care, and care of an elderly parent. In each case, a greater proportion of women than men indicated that these were sources of stress for them (Lindholm, Astin, Sax, and Korn, 2002). When individuals experience significant stress in their lives, they often have less commitment and focus in their work. By contrast, a study at DuPont found that employees who used the company's work-life and flexibility programs were more committed and less burned out than those who did not use any of the programs (Friedman, n.d.). Thus, for several reasons, flexibility is an essential and strategic element of today's academic workplace.

CHANGING WORKPLACE NORMS REGARDING FLEXIBILITY

The preceding discussion has focused on the need to provide flexibility for those individuals who have significant familial responsibilities. At the heart of the argument for these policies is the legitimacy of caring for young or weak family members while also maintaining a successful career. Another important argument being put forward today calls for a more dramatic shift in how employers conceptualize employees' time and their commitment to the organization. As described in the following paragraphs, this second argument suggests a new paradigm for assigning value to an employee's professional contributions.

Today's norms dictate that for professionals to evidence strong commitment to their work, they must do more than perform at a high level. They must also demonstrate that their commitment to work supersedes other commitments. By emphasizing "face time" at their work sites and spending minimal time on personal responsibilities and interests, they show that work is their priority. Managing ever-increasing amounts of work is another means of demonstrating commitment to one's career. Thus today's workplace norms establish the time base as a key determinant of a person's commitment to work. Periods in one's career in which one does not work full time, or in which one takes a leave from work, are seen as clear indicators that work is not a high priority (Bailyn, 1993).

Bailyn (1993) argues for a new relationship between employers and employees, in which the focus shifts from time on task to value of output. The fact of one's working full time rather than part time would determine neither the quality and value of the output nor one's commitment to a career or to an employer. Likewise, a high number of hours dedicated to work each week might indicate a highly productive employee, or it might be just as likely to indicate an inefficient worker.

With Bailyn's new paradigm, an employee's responsibilities would shift to an agreement to meet specified goals within a certain time. During some periods of their careers, employees might be responsible for achieving demanding goals that required heavy travel and sixty-plus-hour workweeks. Remuneration would reflect this workload. During other periods, they would be able to work less than full time in order to focus more on their personal responsibilities and interests. During still other periods, they might remove themselves from work for a time and have no goals for which they were responsible. Again, the focus would be on employees' ability to accomplish clear goals for their organizations, but the magnitude and the number of goals for which they would be responsible would change during various phases of their careers, as would their compensation. Eventually, Bailyn (1993) predicts, this paradigm shift will occur across occupations, for all the reasons outlined in the previous section of this chapter. Nevertheless, her ideas represent a significant shift in employers' thinking about time and personal responsibility.

In higher education, national associations making recommendations about flexibility in the workplace (for example, the American Council on Education, 2005) and scholars writing about this topic such as Friedman, n.d.; Bond, Galinksy, and Hill, 2004; and Williams, 2005 have taken a more conservative approach than Bailyn's. They have examined flexibility from the perspective of meeting colleges' and universities' more immediate goal of addressing today's faculty members' personal needs. Certainly, many work-life policies being put in place today could be used for a variety of reasons that are unrelated to family responsibilities. Nevertheless, the rationale for extending policy use beyond family-related issues would require acceptance of Bailyn's paradigm shift to a scenario in which commitment and productivity would be measured by new methods, with that paradigm shift extended to all employees.

In the end, each institution must determine the extent to which it is ready to shift its thinking about time and professional commitment. Institutions ready for significant reshaping of their organizational norms may choose to include under the umbrella of their flexibility policies the right for any employee to take a personal leave or to work at a reduced time base for any reason, including personal interests (for example, training for a marathon, or volunteer work with an overseas nonprofit organization). We endorse the expansion of flexibility policies to include these options. Nevertheless, the focus of this chapter is on the more immediate need for colleges and universities to help faculty members manage their personal responsibilities so that the institutions can recruit and retain excellent faculty and provide them with an equitable work environment. Although most of the examples in this chapter focus specifically on faculty with young children or elder care concerns, they are also applicable to individuals needing flexibility to meet personal or "family," as broadly defined, concerns.

Flexibility Through Leaves

The ideal worker in the early twentieth century rarely had personal responsibilities that superseded work commitments. The reality today, however, is that many faculty members, men and women alike, have infants, children, spouses, partners, or aging parents who require intensive care for a time, or faculty members' own health may interfere with their ability to meet their work commitments. Institutions can recognize these situations and develop policies and programs that allow faculty members to increase the time that they must occasionally devote to personal concerns.

Some faculty will be best able to meet their personal responsibilities through a leave that lasts from several weeks to several months. Others will prefer to cut back on their work responsibilities for a time but will remain engaged on a less than full-time basis while they spend more time caring for a family member. Still others who are parents of young children will prefer to take a leave of several years, or to delay entry into a faculty position until after their children are of school age. Each of these situations requires flexibility in a faculty career path that traditionally has stipulated rigid timelines for tenure-track positions and given lower status to positions off the tenure track.

The following sections describe different approaches that institutions can take to increase workplace flexibility, especially for tenure-track faculty members, through policies for maternity, parental, and family leaves, including policies related to extension of the tenure clock during the probationary period. Next, recommendations are made for changing the time base of appointments for a period and for job sharing. Then career breaks and reentry opportunities are discussed; these are intended to support those who want to or must leave the workplace entirely for an extended period. Here, we offer the following recommendation:

Recommendation 17

Provide work-life leave policies that support faculty members during specific periods of personal and family-related need.

PERSONAL LEAVES

Faculty members with significant personal or familial responsibilities need ways to substantially lessen or completely leave their work responsibilities for relatively short periods of time, and to do so without penalty. Personal leaves from work include three types: maternity leave, for women after they give birth to a child; parental leave, for the care of a newborn baby or a newly adopted child; and family leave, for the care of a family member who is seriously ill or has special needs.

Maternity Leave

The Pregnancy Discrimination Act of 1978 provides the framework for maternity-leave requirements. As employers, colleges and universities must offer the same disability benefits for pregnancy and childbirth as they do for all other physical disabilities. They cannot legally place arbitrary six- or eight-week limits on a maternity leave, require more stringent notification periods, or offer less pay or less teaching relief than they do for other temporarily disabling conditions (Williams, 2005).

A study of 255 institutions' faculty work-family policies found that they use a variety of methods for providing paid childbirth-related time off (Hollenshead et al., 2005). The most common method is sick leave (69 percent), followed by disability leave (43 percent), vacation leave (36 percent), and maternity leave (25 percent), as distinct from other kinds of leave. (The percentages do not add up because institutions may use more than one policy to cover childbirth.) The study's authors caution institutions regarding potential problems associated with the use of policies specific to both sick and disability leave for maternity leave. Sick-leave policies may not lead to adequate coverage of teaching responsibilities while a faculty member is on maternity leave. If arrangements are handled informally and only part of a term's classes are covered for the faculty member, she may be required or pressured to return to the classroom before the end of the six- to eight-week leave after childbirth that is considered to be good medical practice. In addition, using sick-leave policies for faculty members on maternity leave may cover those on twelve-month appointments but exclude faculty members who are on six- or nine-month appointments (Hollenshead et al., 2005). An institution's use of disability leave for childbirth may also be problematic. Some colleges' disability benefits begin only after a faculty member has been disabled for six or more weeks, an arrangement that makes most women ineligible for paid leave immediately before and after the birth of a child (Hollenshead et al., 2005). The study's authors therefore recommend that institutions determine whether their leave policies for pregnancy and childbirth actually allow women to take adequate time off.

Parental and Family Leave

Employers with fifty or more employees are required under the 1993 Family and Medical Leave Act (FMLA) to provide unpaid leave to those giving birth; to those caring for newborns, for newly adopted children, or for new foster children; and to those caring for children, spouses, or parents with serious health conditions. The FMLA also requires that a person be able to take a medical leave for his or her own serious health condition. Employees can take up to twelve weeks of FMLA leave within a twelve-month period; this is the baseline on which the rest of our suggestions regarding parental and family leave are made.

In general, an institution that combines, under the same umbrella, parental leave and leave to care for a seriously ill family member will find that faculty who do not have children are less likely to resent policies for family leave because these policies include family members other than newborn or newly adopted children (Williams, 2005). The University of Rhode Island, for example, has a very clear, detailed policy that encompasses parental and family leave as well as maternity leave (see Exhibit 11.1). There is no payment beyond accrued sick leave for a maternity leave, and so it is likely that many faculty members will be unable to afford an extended leave in the event of childbirth or adoption. Nevertheless, the policies do expressly provide details about health care coverage, the maximum length of a leave, and the circumstances under which a leave can be taken. This specificity promotes equitable treatment across the institution and is also helpful to faculty members who may hesitate even to inquire about a leave for fear of appearing uncommitted to their work. The fact that the University of Rhode Island is a unionized institution is not coincidental. Research indicates that unionized master's degree–granting and research universities are more likely than their nonunionized peers to offer leaves whose terms are more generous than those stipulated by FMLA policies (Hollenshead et al., 2005). Moreover, unionized institutions often have the most explicit work-life policies overall (Sullivan, Hollenshead, and Smith, 2004).

Specific Suggestions Regarding Parental Leave or Modified Duties

This section focuses on specific suggestions for parental leave or modification of duties for new parents. Joan Williams, a legal expert on work-family issues, has written extensively on work-life policy and cites Harvard Law School's policy as an excellent model for parental leave (Williams, 2005). Harvard Law School grants paid leave from teaching responsibilities to any faculty member who is the sole caretaker of a newborn baby or a newly adopted child during at least half of regular business hours. This policy is noteworthy for its flexibility regarding faculty members who have different work preferences and different needs related to the birth or adoption of a child. It also is equitable in that teaching relief is provided to the primary caregiver regardless of whether that person is the father or the mother (see Exhibit 11.2). Harvard Law School's policy, by explicitly defining the primary caregiver, avoids a problem that some institutional leaders have encountered when this type of equitable policy has been in place for a few years. In practice, some

Exhibit 11.1. Family Leave Policies, University of Rhode Island

20.12 Leave Without Pay

    a. Upon written application, a staff member may be granted a leave without pay normally not to exceed six (6) months for reasons of personal illness, disability or other purpose deemed proper and approved by the President or his/her designee. Staff members on leave without pay due to personal illness, disability, parental leave or family leave are eligible for one (1) year of State paid health benefits and when applicable must pay the employee's share of the optional health plans. . . .

    b. *Parental Leave* is leave by reason of the birth of a child of an employee or the placement of a child 16 years of age or less in connection with adoption of such child by the employee.

    c. *Family Leave* is for a family member defined as a parent, spouse, child, mother-in-law, father-in-law or other immediate family member. For the purpose of this article, other immediate family members shall include domestic partners of the same or opposite sex who have lived in the same household for at least six months and have made a commitment to continue to live as a family. Family leave is granted for reasons of serious illness of a family member. Serious illness is defined as disabling physical or mental illness, injury, impairment, or a condition that involves in-patient care in a hospital, nursing home, hospice or out-patient care requiring continuing treatment or supervision by a health care provider. The staff member shall provide the University with written certification from the physician caring for the person who is the reason for the employee's leave and such certification shall state the probable duration of the employee's requested leave.

Source: http://www.uri.edu/psa/psa_contract.html (retrieved June 29, 2006).

men and women have utilized a policy for parental leave without actually serving as primary caregivers but instead have concentrated on their research. When this kind of abuse occurs, colleagues who are not on leave are disadvantaged because they are ultimately expected to perform at the same level in order to secure tenure, promotions, or merit-pay increases (Williams, 2005). For this reason, some institutions now require that a faculty member

EXHIBIT 11.2. PARENTAL TEACHING-RELIEF POLICY, HARVARD LAW SCHOOL

1. *Purpose.* The purpose of the School's parental teaching relief policy is to provide assistance in the form of relief from teaching obligations to faculty members who are the primary caregivers to their newborn or newly adopted children.

2. *Definition.* For purposes of the School's parental teaching relief policy, "primary caregiver" means a faculty member who is the sole caretaker of his or her newborn or newly adopted child at least 20 hours per week, from Monday through Friday, between the hours of 9:00 A.M. and 5:00 P.M.

3. *Policy.* A faculty member who is the primary caregiver for his or her newborn or newly adopted child is entitled to paid relief from teaching duties, for up to 5 classroom credits. The 5-credit reduction from the normal annual 10-credit load must be taken within one year before or after the birth or adoption. Subject to the limitation set forth in paragraph 5 of this subsection, the 5-credit reduction may be taken in a single semester, or spread across two consecutive semesters, as determined by the Dean in consultation with the faculty member and the School's curriculum planners.

EXAMPLE: A faculty member expects to give birth in September and become [the child's] primary caregiver. With the consent of the Dean, the faculty member will teach 0 credits in the Fall semester. She resumes her full-time teaching in January. She receives her full pay throughout the year.

EXAMPLE: A faculty member expects his spouse to give birth on July 1, and he will become the child's primary caregiver. With the consent of the Dean, the faculty member will teach 2 credits in the Fall semester and 3 credits in the following Spring semester. He receives his full pay throughout the year.

Source: www.law.harvard.edu/faculty/faculty_leave_policy.pdf (retrieved June 29, 2006).

on parental leave sign a document explicitly stating the number of hours per week that he or she serves as primary caregiver.

Grinnell College, in Iowa, provides another good example of flexible leave options for new parents. At this institution, the leave can encompass more than just relief from teaching duties. Specifically, parents can decide whether to take a leave from all responsibilities for a semester or to take a course reduction spread over two semesters. If both parents are employed at Grinnell, one parent can utilize the semester leave, or they may choose to share the two-course reduction between them (see Exhibit 11.3).

Institutions cannot be expected to pay full salary or even to extend full benefits when someone is on a leave that extends six months or longer. Even if only partial salaries and benefits are offered, the implementation of leave policies can be quite expensive for an institution. At the very least, however, it is essential to offer access to benefits if a faculty member is to be truly in a position to take an extended leave.

EXHIBIT 11.3. POLICY FOR PARENTAL LEAVE, GRINNELL COLLEGE

Parental leave following the birth of a child or following placement of a child for adoption or foster care:

Upon request by the parent, the College will grant either a one-semester paid leave or a total of two course reductions in teaching over two consecutive semesters. This leave must be completed within one year of birth or placement of the child; only one such leave will be granted in any twelve-month period. If requested, the College will grant a one-year delay in the evaluation for promotion and tenure.

If appropriate, the College will provide staff for course replacements; if the courses are replaced, the College, not the parent, is responsible for finding a faculty member to teach these courses.

If both parents, as Grinnell faculty members, are eligible for a family leave on account of the birth or placement of a child, the College will grant a one-semester paid leave to only one of the two parents. If the parents select the two-course reduction option, this reduction may be divided between the two parents. Normally, only one parent may receive a one-year delay in the evaluation for promotion and tenure.

If both parents, one as a Grinnell faculty member and the other as a member of the Grinnell staff or administration, are each eligible for a family leave on account of the birth or placement of a child and both wish to have paid leaves, the College will grant a one-course reduction to the faculty member and up to a six-week paid leave to the staff member.

Source: http://www.grinnell.edu/offices/dean/handbook (retrieved June 29, 2006).

Whatever the approach that an institution chooses to take, allocating the financial burden to academic departments will lead to differential treatment of individual faculty members, whose ability to take leave is then determined in part by the financial situation in their departments. The poorest academic departments are often those with the highest percentage of women, and thus the highest percentage of employees on parental leave. Therefore, to ensure equity in the use of leaves, wise administrators will ensure funding from the central administration for family leave that provides for any level of salary or benefits beyond what is required by law. This approach helps departments to be flexible, and it makes faculty members feel more comfortable in utilizing leaves. Therefore, we offer the following recommendation:

Recommendation 18

Fund work-life leave at the level of the central administration to ensure that access to leave is uniformly available to all faculty members, regardless of their departmental affiliations.

AUTOMATIC EXTENSION OF THE TENURE CLOCK WITH A PERSONAL LEAVE

Policies that allow leaves for new parents, or for faculty with family members who are seriously ill, provide the flexibility necessary to an accurate reflection of the demographics and personal responsibilities of today's faculty. In addition to policies on parental leave, automatic extensions of the tenure clock contribute significantly to the ability of tenure-track faculty members to take the time needed to address family concerns. Recommendation 10 (see Chapter Nine) urges a far-reaching adjustment of the tenure clock, one that is not in common use today. We refine that recommendation more specifically here, recognizing that a faculty member may need multiple extensions:

Recommendation 19

Automatically extend the tenure clock for a tenure-track faculty member who takes a family-related leave.

In recognition of the time lost from work, institutions should automatically extend the tenure clock by one year when an individual on the tenure track takes six months or more of family-related leave. More than one extension should be possible during the probationary period if a faculty member takes leaves, or moves from full-time to less than full-time work, for a period of time to care for family members. However, a more conservative approach to adjusting the tenure clock is in place at 43 percent of the institutions that responded to a national survey (Hollenshead et al., 2005). This conservative approach puts limits on the amount of leave or on the number of time extensions for the probationary period. But, it is still an important first step. We cite this more conservative type of policy here, despite its limitations, because of the scope of its coverage and for other reasons. Nevertheless, we continue to endorse the concept of more flexible probationary periods.

Making an extension of the tenure clock automatic with a leave is very important, given most colleges' and universities' cultural norms regarding family responsibilities. Research has shown that even when an institution has family-friendly policies, such as extension of the tenure clock, faculty members often do not use them if they are not automatic because they fear career repercussions. In a study of 5,087 faculty members, for example, almost a third of the men and women surveyed had not requested parental leave because they feared it could have damaged their careers. Approximately 20 percent of the respondents had not asked to stop the tenure clock, even though they believed that would have helped them manage their workloads after the birth of a child (Drago and Colbeck, 2003). These results highlight the need for institutions to make flexible work arrangements a culturally acceptable component of the workplace. Attractive policies can exist in writing, but the policies have no value if faculty members believe their career progress will be jeopardized by using them.

Along with offering an extension of the tenure clock, the institution needs to make clear what expectations, if any, there are for a faculty member's productivity while he or she is on leave. A faculty member should be truly able to focus on family responsibilities while on leave without also being expected to keep up with the majority of his or her work. If research or service expectations remain, and only teaching responsibilities are eliminated, the individual is not fully free to address family concerns during a period of high need. We do recognize, however, that leaving work altogether, for any period of time, is unlikely for many people who have laboratories and funded research, regardless of any policies that are in place.

Vanderbilt University has a comprehensive policy that addresses many facets of parental leave. One semester of paid leave is automatic when a full-time tenured or tenure-track faculty member gives birth or adopts a child. Although not included in the policy excerpt that follows, a one-year extension of the tenure clock is also automatic when a tenure-track faculty member utilizes the leave. The policy specifies that the faculty member will be relieved of teaching, research, scholarship, and faculty service responsibilities during the leave. Again, this detail is quite valuable because the institution has truly removed productivity expectations while the faculty member is on leave (see Exhibit 11.4). It was very helpful at Vanderbilt that a specific unit—the Women's Center—was able to play an instrumental role in developing and implementing the policy.

FLEXIBILITY IN THE TIME BASES OF APPOINTMENTS

In addition to the option of personal leave, faculty members need flexibility to scale back their time commitment to work, either permanently or for lengthy periods of time, in order to devote a greater proportion of time and attention to personal responsibilities. Like the leave policies already described, these strategies can prove valuable for faculty at every career stage. They are particularly important, however, for faculty on the tenure track who desire to have both an academic career and a family.

Flexible time bases and job-sharing policies can also benefit institutions and save costs. Research indicates that there is not a linear relationship between time and productivity (Kelly and McGrath, 1980). Instead, as Parkinson's Law has it, work expands to fill the time available. When time is seen as constrained, people tend to be more efficient (Bluedorn and Dernhardt, 1988); when time is

Exhibit 11.4. Parental Leave Policy, Vanderbilt University

Availability of Parental Leave

When a full-time faculty member who is tenured or [on the] tenure-track, or that faculty member's spouse or declared domestic partner, becomes the parent of a child, either by childbirth or adoption of a pre-school-aged child, the faculty member shall, upon written request to his or her Department Chair or Dean, be entitled to a parental leave of one semester at full pay for purposes of serving as the child's primary caregiver. If a faculty member and his or her spouse or domestic partner would otherwise both be eligible for parental leave under this policy, either one, but not both, may take this parental leave. . . .

Salary, Benefits, and Responsibilities during Leave

A faculty member who takes parental leave under this policy shall receive the same salary and benefits that he or she would have received that semester if not on leave, and shall be relieved of his or her normal duties and responsibilities during the period of leave as follows.

A. Teaching

The faculty member shall be relieved of the obligation to teach during the semester in which the leave is taken. If the semester during which leave is taken is one in which the faculty member would otherwise have taught more than half of his or her normal annual teaching load, the faculty member may be required to teach one additional course in another semester to be agreed upon by the faculty member and his or her Department Chair or Dean.

B. Research and Scholarship

The faculty member shall be relieved of research and scholarship expectations for one semester.

C. Service

The faculty member shall be relieved of all faculty service responsibilities, including committee work and student advising, for one semester.

Source: www.vanderbilt.edu/facman/FacultyManualPartVI.pdf (retrieved June 29, 2006).

seen as unconstrained or infinite, workers defer to the accepted time needed to be a "dedicated employee" (Bailyn, 1993). Part-time work and job sharing actually increase productivity per hour worked (Cohen and Gadon, 1978; Ronen, 1984) because of the benefits of constrained time and also because fatigue and a limited attention span affect productivity (Bailyn, 1993). Therefore, we offer the following recommendation:

Recommendation 20

To the extent possible, given the reality of institutional constraints, support individual preferences regarding the time base of work, and adjust the probationary period accordingly for faculty members on the tenure track.

Full-time faculty work, on average, translates into at least fifty hours per week (U.S. Department of Education, National Center for Education Statistics, 2004). This amount of time at work can lead to an untenable work-life balance, particularly for junior faculty members who have young children. For this reason, some faculty members, both on and off the tenure track, who have full-time appointments seek the opportunity to work on less than a full-time basis. Some of these individuals may want to retain the option of returning to full-time work within a specified time period. Such flexibility would allow them to retain a permanent full-time position, despite a short-term need to devote less time to work. Others seek a more permanent adjustment in their time commitment to work. To accommodate these needs for less than full-time work, two options are available: a program offering a flexible time base for those seeking temporary adjustments, and job sharing for those desiring a long-term part-time commitment.

A program offering a flexible time base allows a faculty member to work on less than a full-time basis while maintaining a proportion of his or her regular full-time responsibilities. One way to describe these positions is with the adjective "pro rata," rather than "part time," to avoid the negative connotations that can be associated with part-time positions (Williams, 1999). Use of the term "pro rata" may also encourage a more flexible approach to negotiations when the optimal arrangement for the institution as well as the individual would not be an appointment at strictly 50 percent or 100 percent time.

Teaching responsibilities for a pro rata position are usually formally agreed upon, but department chairs should also clarify the research and service expectations for tenure-track faculty serving less than full time. Moreover, the tenure-track timetable should be adjusted to reflect these faculty's less than full-time status. Nevertheless, academic and other standards required for granting tenure should remain the same as for those faculty members working full time. (Again, see Chapter Nine for a more detailed explanation of these suggestions.) Finally, the faculty member moving for a time to a pro rata position should be encouraged to continue his or her involvement in institutional governance and other campus activities so that he or she can continue to be perceived as a regular faculty member.

Recommendation 20 includes the reality that offering pro rata appointments may conflict with institutional needs. For example, a college in a rural area may be unable to find a qualified person to teach courses previously offered by a person wanting to decrease his or her time base. Because of constraints such as these, faculty members and administrators need to work together to find solutions that meet the needs of all parties. Usually when there is a collegial environment and mutual goodwill, such a solution can be found.

Policies in effect at three private undergraduate colleges illustrate a variety of options for tenure-track appointments at less than full-time; these three offer interesting comparisons and contrasts. First, Calvin College, in Michigan, has a "reduced load" policy that maintains fluidity between part-time and full-time appointments (see Exhibit 11.5). An individual may choose to stay in a reduced-load appointment indefinitely, but he or she is also able to move back to a full-time position after working in a reduced-load position for a period of time. Note that Calvin College's policy retains the faculty member's prerogative to participate in governance, an arrangement that gives him or her an important voice as a full-fledged faculty member. Second, Amherst College, in Massachusetts, has a clearly established policy regarding tenure and benefits for part-time positions (see Exhibit 11.6). Third, Carleton College, in Minnesota, conveys respect for part-time faculty members by specifically stating that tenure, research grants, and sabbaticals are not the exclusive domain of full-time faculty (see Exhibit 11.7). By requiring both the department head's and the dean's formal

Exhibit 11.5. Policy for Reduced-Load Appointments, Calvin College

3.3.4 Reduced-Load Appointments

A reduced-load appointment is a regular or term appointment which involves teaching on a less than full-time basis but not less than 50 percent of a full load. Such an appointment differs from a part-time appointment in that it is an appointment to the teaching faculty and it carries other faculty responsibilities beyond teaching. Conditions that apply to such appointments are the following.

3.3.4.1 Other Responsibilities

Reduced-load appointees shall participate in the non-teaching responsibilities of the faculty in proportion (roughly) to their teaching load.

3.3.4.2 Franchise

Reduced-load appointees shall have the franchise in both the department and the faculty. Their vote shall not be pro-rated.

3.3.4.3 Appointment

The procedures for new appointments with reduced-load status are the same as those for full-time appointments. Moreover, the credentials and qualifications for reduced-load appointees shall be the same as those for full-time appointees.

3.3.4.4 Change in Status from Full-Time to Reduced-Load

Persons on full-time appointments may request reduced-load appointments either for a designated period of time or indefinitely. Before granting or denying the request, the president and Board of Trustees shall seek the advice of the appropriate department and its chairperson, the academic deans and provost, and the Professional Status Committee. If a request for a reduced-load appointment for a designated period of time is granted, and if the employment of the person making the request is continued beyond that period (as in the case of tenure or successful, regular reappointments), full-time employment will resume at the end of the period. If a request for indefinite reduced-load status is granted, reappointments or, in the case of tenure, continuous employment will involve a teaching-load of not less than 50 percent of a full load.

Source: http://www.calvin.edu/admin/provost/fac_hb/chap_3/3_3.htm (retrieved June 29, 2006).

Exhibit 11.6. Policy for Part-Time Appointments, Amherst College

---

Tenure for Regular Part-Time Members of the Faculty

Members of the Faculty who teach part-time, but not less than half-time, on a regular basis at Amherst College are eligible for tenure under the same qualitative standards as full-time members of the Faculty. It is intended that a person holding a regular part-time appointment from Amherst College regard that appointment as his or her primary professional obligation.

The appointment procedure for a regular part-time member of the Faculty usually requires three three-year appointments, with a review during the third and sixth years, and with the tenure decision occurring no later than the eighth year of part-time teaching. This schedule applies irrespective of the actual number of courses taught during the aggregate period. In the case of a faculty member who begins part-time teaching at Amherst after a number of years of full-time teaching at Amherst or at another college or university, or after regular part-time teaching at another college or university, appropriate adjustments in the timing of appointments may be made at the time of the initial appointment. . . .

Should a full-time tenured member of the Faculty wish to negotiate a part-time arrangement on a temporary basis without change to permanent part-time status, he or she may proceed with these negotiations with the department or departments concerned. Final determination of the matter requires the consent of the Dean of the Faculty and the President. . . .

Regular part-time members of the Faculty qualify for most benefits and perquisites of full-time faculty members on a prorated basis. These include eligibility for housing, and, on a prorated basis, disability and life insurance, pension plans, health insurance, and death benefit. Regular part-time members of the Faculty qualify for leaves according to the same schedule as full-time Faculty, although their compensation during leaves is on a prorated basis.

Source: http://www.amherst.edu/~deanfac/handbook/tenureparttime.html (retrieved July 20, 2006).

EXHIBIT 11.7. POLICY FOR PART-TIME APPOINTMENTS, CARLETON COLLEGE

1. A regular part-time faculty member at Carleton is one who meets the following conditions:

    1. A regular part-time faculty member normally carries at least a half-time teaching load for the school year (half of the normal teaching load in the particular department) and teaches during at least two terms.

    2. A regular part-time faculty member is expected to take part in non-teaching service to the College. He or she is expected to serve on committees and act as an academic advisor. However, for regular part-time faculty members such responsibilities should be roughly proportionate to teaching load.

    3. Regular part-time faculty members share with the regular full-time faculty a commitment to long-range professional aims and improvement.

2. All regular faculty, part-time as well as full-time, may enjoy the privileges of tenure, leaves with pay, and grants in support of scholarship. Except when they are officially on leave, regular part-time faculty have the same voting privileges as full-time faculty members. Tenure criteria and procedures for regular part-time faculty are the same as those for regular full-time faculty, but the tenure decision is made at a later time than is usual for full-time faculty. . . .

    Faculty on regular part-time appointments are eligible to participate in the College's sabbatical leave program. . . .

3. If requested to do so by a member of the faculty, the dean of the college and the chair of the relevant department(s) will attempt to negotiate with that faculty member a change from full-time to part-time status. . . . A position converted to regular part-time status has only such rights of return to full-time status as are agreed upon in writing by the dean, the department chair, and the faculty member at the time of the initial conversion. . . .

Source: http://apps.carleton.edu/campus/doc/faculty_resources/faculty_ handbook/fh_regular_part_time_faculty (retrieved June 30, 2006).

approval, this policy protects both the faculty member's and the institution's interests.

A Model Half-Time Tenure Policy

Drago and Williams (2000) have developed a model half-time tenure-track policy that addresses the need for time-base flexibility to accommodate caregiving responsibilities while protecting institutional interests (see Exhibit 11.8). It is included here because

---

Exhibit 11.8. Model Half-Time Tenure Policy

- Following a request for a leave from a probationary faculty member which documents family commitments or personal circumstances requiring reduced time, the leave shall be granted on a nondiscretionary basis using the same procedures and criteria employed to provide coverage for a faculty member during a sabbatical year or other leaves of absence commonly granted to faculty.

- Faculty members who work half-time in a given year shall be paid one-half their annual salary. The other half shall be returned to the affected department to cover resulting teaching needs.

- During the half-time workload, the university will contribute one-half of the amount it would have contributed for retirement, health and other benefits the faculty member would receive on full-time status.

- Half-time employment causes the tenure clock to run half as fast. Half-time employment for a year automatically moves the tenure clock back a year. Half-time employment for 11 or 12 years would be associated with a mandatory tenure decision in the twelfth year of employment.

- Other than the change in years of service required for a tenure decision, the academic and other standards required for granting tenure shall not differ from those applicable to faculty members who are full-time. Calculations of faculty productivity will be based upon FTE years rather than calendar years in service.

The faculty member must represent that the requested leave is for substantial caregiving commitments. The half-time tenure policy is not to be used to gain additional time on the tenure clock.

Source: Drago and Williams, 2000, p. 51.

it is comprehensive in its coverage of the multiple issues that affect simultaneously working less than full time and being in a tenure-track position, and because it takes into account both the individual's and the institution's needs and responsibilities.

Job Sharing

Another option for providing time-base flexibility is to allow two individuals to share one position. Calvin College is used again as an example because its policy clearly provides important protections to those who share a position (see Exhibit 11.9). At Calvin, the department chair is responsible for ensuring that teaching and non-teaching assignments are in proportion to the work arrangement.

Such an arrangement can benefit an institution in its efforts to retain junior faculty, or to attract faculty with different areas of expertise who are needed only on a part-time basis. But, an institution may realize added costs as a result of a shared appointment, as when each of two individuals has his or her own office space, receives full benefits, or requires his or her own set of equipment. Costs associated with increased access to support facilities can also be greater. These can be very real institutional constraints. Calvin College's policy addresses the second of these cost issues by stating that access to support facilities will be commensurate with the appointment. Whatever policies an institution creates, the most important step is to establish, on an institutionwide basis, the basic structures and characteristics of shared positions (Wolf-Wendel, Twombly, and Rice, 2003).

Career Breaks and Delayed Career-Entry Options

Some individuals will choose to address significant family responsibilities, not by cutting back their time commitments to their professorial responsibilities, but by leaving the workplace altogether for a period of time to focus solely on their personal responsibilities.

Career breaks are an option that fit the realities of some of today's faculty members. The average age for women to earn the doctorate is thirty-four (Hoffer et al., 2005). Fertility for women

EXHIBIT 11.9. POLICY FOR SHARED APPOINTMENTS, CALVIN COLLEGE

3.3.5 Shared Appointments

Two persons may be appointed to share a single position. For most purposes (salary, benefits, evaluation, etc.), each person is considered to have a reduced-load appointment and the conditions of Section 3.3.4 apply to each. However, the following special conditions apply:

1. It is not required that each of two persons have at least a 50 percent teaching load if they share at least a full teaching load.

2. Faculty sharing a single faculty position will be provided with the facilities and technical support necessary to carry out their teaching, research, and advising as effectively as possible, within the budgetary restraints of a single position. These restraints could mean sharing of facilities or technology in cases where this would be feasible and when space and budget limitations make it necessary.

3. In assigning student advisees and forming departmental and college committees, expectations for two persons sharing one position should not exceed those for one person holding the same position. Additional assignments may be made, however, at the request of the individuals. Department chairs should take particular care to limit college expectations in non-teaching as well as teaching assignments so as not to exceed the proportion of full-time work assigned to each individual.

4. Each appointee to the shared position is considered a voting member of the department and the college, but must observe the college's policy on employment of relatives, Section 6.7.

    If an additional opening is declared in the department in which two individuals currently share a single position, the usual procedures for the conduct of a national search will be followed. Individuals holding reduced-load appointments may apply for such an opening, but they will receive no special preference over others. . . .

Source: http://www.calvin.edu/admin/provost/fac_hb/chap_3/3_3.htm (retrieved June 30, 2006).

drops off significantly after the age of thirty-five. Many women wait to have children until after they have completed the doctorate, but then they realize that the biological clock cannot wait until they achieve tenure before they have children. For this reason, many women earn a Ph.D. and, shortly thereafter, decide to work full- or part-time, off the tenure track, or they leave the workplace altogether for a few years in order to focus on family responsibilities. Others work on the tenure track for a few years and then leave the workplace altogether for a few years. They do not want to manage the high demands of young children and those of a tenure-track position simultaneously. Certainly, there are other significant personal responsibilities that can also trigger the need for a career break, for men as well as women.

William Kirwan, chancellor of the University System of Maryland, explains:

> When you think about a faculty career, it is 40 years long. The idea that for good and legitimate reasons a faculty member might need to step back for a couple of years, for family reasons or whatever, then come back into a faculty position—for most of us this just wouldn't have been possible. But it makes all the sense in the world to allow for this kind of flexibility [cited in Wilson, 2005c].

In the context of this chapter, career breaks are necessary for those with significant personal responsibilities. But they are appropriate for professional reasons as well, and so they are discussed again with these purposes in mind in Chapter Twelve, which addresses professional growth. For now, we offer the following recommendation:

Recommendation 21

Establish policies that allow faculty members to leave the workplace completely for an extended period of time, or to delay initial entry into a faculty position while focusing on family responsibilities.

Individuals who stop work altogether immediately after they have completed a terminal degree or a postdoctoral fellowship need opportunities for entry to academic careers. Option for delayed entry into a career can allow individuals to enter a faculty position even though they have not followed the traditional path of taking a faculty position right after graduate school or postdoctoral fellowship.

Delayed-Entry Opportunities

Institutions, by rethinking their view of career gaps, can broaden promising academics' access to tenure-track positions. Rather than dismissing as applicants people with breaks in service, institutions need to rethink whom they consider for positions. They should assume that breaks in service can be for completely legitimate reasons, and that applicants with breaks in service still have the potential to be productive and valuable members of the faculty (American Council on Education, 2005).

One approach to broadening access to tenure-track positions is to recruit potential faculty members who have career gaps and hire them into postdoctoral fellowships for a few years so they can update and expand their teaching and research skills before moving onto the tenure track (American Council on Education, 2005; Mason and Goulden, 2002). A postdoctoral fellowship can be a valuable tool for attracting individuals in high-demand fields, as well as women who chose to focus on family responsibilities after earning the doctorate, so institutions might even consider creating some fellowships using centralized funds.

Alternatively, institutions might decide to hire delayed-entry individuals directly into faculty positions, and to include in their hiring packages a clear structure of guidance and supervision to be provided by senior colleagues (American Council on Education, 2005). This support structure would allow individuals to refresh their skills after being away from the academy for some time. Extension of the probationary period, discussed in Chapter Nine, is ideally suited to this situation.

At times an institution may also be aware that a highly desirable individual is about to graduate or to complete a postdoctoral fellowship but plans to take a career break rather than pursue a faculty position immediately. The institution could consider offering this person a faculty position, with the understanding that he or she would not assume the position's duties until a specified future date. This approach would open up unique opportunities to hire junior faculty members who have particular talents or skills that the institution is seeking but who need to delay their arrival to their first positions while they devote their full attention to family responsibilities for a period of time. Indeed, some institutions already use this approach to hire "superstars," agreeing on the terms of employment a year or more before the individual actually joins the institution.

REENTRY OPPORTUNITIES

The concept of career breaks also encompasses individuals who work for a few years as faculty members before leaving the workplace to care for family members. Rather than permanently losing the talents and skills of these individuals, institutions can design policies that allow them to take extended but time-defined breaks from their current positions.

Other individuals will have left their faculty positions to care for family members, without the option of returning to their positions. A few years later, such an individual may present himself or herself as an applicant for a faculty position, with a curriculum vitae that includes a substantial career break. Institutions need to rethink their current hiring policies and screening procedures so that such an individual is not inadvertently screened out because of the career break. Clearly, rethinking screening criteria would help institutions identify many well-qualified applicants for tenure-track positions. It would also offer equitable consideration to the many talented individuals who have the potential to make significant contributions to their fields even after having taken a career break to care for family members or for other reasons.

THE CHALLENGES OF IMPLEMENTING NEW POLICIES AND PRACTICES

A concluding caveat is needed here with regard to the work-life policies that have been described. Institutional policies cannot solve all of a faculty member's conflicting demands between work and personal responsibilities. But with this chapter's recommended policies in place, it is possible to find creative solutions that take into account personal as well as professional constraints. For example, a probationary faculty member who chooses to pursue a faculty career in the sciences at a research university would know at the outset that, given her research commitments, an extended career break would not be possible for her. Instead, when she gave birth or adopted a child, she and her colleagues could work to make the labs safe enough for an infant to spend extended time there. And this woman, rather than taking an extended leave, could choose a reduced workload while her children were young. Personal and professional compromises might still be required in this scenario, but a workable option could be found, and the primary goal of flexible work-life policies would have been achieved. The faculty member would not have to abandon her academic career altogether simply because of her need to focus more intensely on family responsibilities for a relatively short period, and the institution would benefit by retaining a satisfied and productive faculty member.

Resources for Managing Personal Responsibilities

Opening up options to faculty members through new and revised policies that provide increased work-life flexibility is a crucial step if institutions are to address adequately the needs of today's faculty. Institutions can also provide valuable assistance to faculty in managing their personal responsibilities on a day-to-day basis by offering services as well as referrals to various local-area programs. A central location for referral services, such as a campus-run Web site, can be very helpful to faculty members, particularly those who are new to the campus. With these considerations in mind, we offer the following recommendation:

Recommendation 22

Help faculty members manage their personal responsibilities for basic household needs, child care, or elder care either by offering such services or by offering referrals to local providers.

Employer-Sponsored Child Care and/or Referrals

Many large institutions, for good reason, choose to provide child care services on campus. A 2003 survey of professors in the University of California system found that campus-based child care was the most important "family-friendly resource" that the university could provide (Wilson, 2005b). When on-campus child care is available, parents are able to check in on their children at different times during the day—a particularly important benefit, given the long workweeks that are typical for faculty. These centers are especially helpful if they offer a variety of part-time options that fit faculty members' varied schedules as well as extended evening and weekend hours. Summer programs for school-age children are also valuable to many parents. The Massachusetts Institute of Technology, George Washington University, and Bowdoin College are examples of institutions that have recently opened on-campus child care facilities (Wilson, 2005b).

The costs associated with on-campus child care are often prohibitive to an institution, however. At a cost of far fewer resources, institutional leaders can coordinate backup child care to provide a safety net for parents when their usual caregivers are unavailable or their children are ill. In addition, all colleges and universities can provide a valuable service for faculty with young children by supplying references to local child care programs and in-home day care providers. Coordinating a system that allows parents to easily share child care information with each other through a Web page, an e-mail listserv, or an electronic newsletter is another approach that requires minimal resources. Easy access to reliable information can go a long way toward easing the stress of finding a child care provider or a summer camp program that meets a family's needs. The following four examples illustrate the range of institutional approaches to supporting faculty members as they seek high-quality care for their children, ranging from on-site child care to referral services:

1. Cornell University is one of many large universities that offers on-campus child care. The university provides two nursery school facilities for children between the ages of three and five and an infant center for full-time care of infants. In addition, Cornell provides references to other local programs and private providers of day care (see www.ohr.cornell.edu/benefits/lifeEvents/childcare.html, retrieved June 29, 2006).
2. Wellesley College, in Massachusetts, also has an on-site day care facility. This facility is sustainable because it is a joint effort

shared by Wellesley, nearby Babson College, and a community children's center. The private children's center operates the facility, and one-third of the openings are reserved for children of Wellesley faculty and staff (see http://wccc.wellesley.edu/philo.html, retrieved June 29, 2006).

3. Stanford University's WorkLife Office provides very helpful emergency and backup child care services through FamilyCare, Inc. If a regular caregiver is unavailable or a child is mildly ill, staff and faculty members can contact FamilyCare for a referral to an in-home agency or child care center. The university will reimburse the cost of emergency care up to 80 percent of the total, to a maximum of $10 per hour for sixteen hours. If the maximum subsidy has been reached, the referral service can still be utilized, but the employee must pay the full cost of child care (see http://worklife.stanford.edu/emergency_child care.html, retrieved July 20, 2006).

4. The University of California–Berkeley offers Parents Network, which is run by a group of volunteer parents. They produce an advice newsletter for the community of parents at the institution, and the network's Web site provides reviews and recommendations of services and products used by other families. Topics include everything from pediatricians, obstetricians/gynecologists, and home-repair services to entertainment activities. The Web site also offers links for parents of infants, toddlers, and teenagers (see http://parents.berkeley.edu, retrieved June 29, 2006).

ELDER CARE INFORMATION

As Americans live longer, the issue of elder care is increasing in importance. Institutions can help faculty who care for aging relatives by providing information on options for elder care that are available in the community. Information dissemination can be handled by a campus office that provides general support services to employees, or through coordination with a Web site that pools the knowledge and experiences of faculty and staff members who have responsibility for elder care.

The University of California–Berkeley offers an extensive number of elder care services. The program, which is a segment of

University Health Services, provides workshops, lectures, and support groups. A licensed social worker who specializes in elder care services is also available to answer questions and help faculty and staff members locate Berkeley-area services related to caregiving (see www.uhs.berkeley.edu/Facstaff/CARE/eldercare, retrieved June 29, 2006).

WEB-BASED INFORMATION FOR MANAGING OTHER PERSONAL RESPONSIBILITIES

The power of the Internet can be extended beyond its ability to offer assistance with finding child and elder care providers. The Internet can also help faculty manage other personal responsibilities. For example, the University of Texas Health Sciences Center offers a link from its work-life program's Web site through which employees can connect to a company offering a concierge service for $20 per hour. The service will perform miscellaneous tasks, such as shopping, transporting children, and picking up dry cleaning. A comprehensive Web site at the Massachusetts Institute of Technology provides links related to career development, community life, family life, financial matters, health, housing, and transportation (see http://web.mit.edu/lifesites/, retrieved June 29, 2006). Exhibit 11.10 shows a sample of the information about local schools that is available to MIT community members from that Web site.

CONVENIENT, ONE-STOP SERVICES ON OR NEAR CAMPUS

Colleges and universities seeking to help faculty members use their time as efficiently as possible could consider providing an easily accessible location, on or near the campus, where essential services could be offered to campus employees. This one-stop center would situate local businesses that perform basic household and personal services in a conveniently close location. Such services are already offered in the community, but the idea here is to put them together in a one-stop location adjacent to the campus—ideally, next to child care facilities. Services to be provided could include banking, dry cleaning and laundry, car servicing, haircuts, mailing and shipping, filling of prescriptions and other pharmaceutical services,

Exhibit 11.10. The MIT Center for Work, Family, and Personal Life: Schools

Answers to Common Questions About Schools	An introduction to the "basics" of public and private education in the Boston area, including differences among private, public, and parochial schools, choosing a school, school visits, the enrollment process, and more.
Web Sites	Links for information on private, public, and parochial schools, special needs, after-school care, and more.
Sample Private School Tuition	Tuition fees charged by a selection of private and parochial schools in the area. Download as a PDF or request from the Center.
Kindergarten Age Requirements	Age that your child must be to enter kindergarten in selected area cities and towns. Download as a PDF or request from the Center.
Tutoring Programs	Local non-profit and for-profit organizations that provide tutoring services for elementary and secondary school students. Download as a pdf or request from the Center.

Source: http://hrweb.mit.edu/worklife/schools.html.

and grocery shopping. Ample parking, and drive-through convenience where that was appropriate, would make all these essential services readily available to faculty members who must take care of household errands as part of a long work day.

Institutions might also want to offer take-out dinners for sale through their auxiliary food services. This practice has met with success at some corporations that maintain on-site cafeterias. Google is one example of a corporation that offers a generous array of services, including several that are on site, to employees who work at the home office in California (see Exhibit 11.11).

EXHIBIT 11.11. SAMPLE OF SERVICES OFFERED
BY GOOGLE TO EMPLOYEES IN THE HOME OFFICE

Food

Hungry? Check out our free lunch and dinner—our gourmet chefs create a wide variety of healthy and delicious meals every day. Got the munchies? Google also offers snacks to help satisfy you in between meals.

On-Site Doctor

At Google headquarters in Mountain View, California, you have the convenience of seeing a doctor on site.

Shuttle Service

Google is pleased to provide its Mountain View employees with free shuttles to several San Francisco, East Bay, and South Bay locations.

Financial Planning Classes

Google provides objective and conflict-free financial education classes. The courses are comprehensive and cover a variety of financial topics.

Other On-Site Services

At Google headquarters in Mountain View, there's on-site oil change, car wash, dry cleaning, massage therapy, gym, hair stylist, fitness classes, and bike repair.

Source: http://www.google.com/support/jobs/bin/static.py?page=benefits.html&benefits=us (retrieved June 30, 2006).

IMPLEMENTATION OF FLEXIBLE WORK-LIFE POLICIES AND PROGRAMS

Faculty members are often fearful of utilizing work-life policies. To do so could hurt junior faculty members' chances for tenure because, on many campuses, using these policies is simply not perceived as something that a committed faculty member does. Therefore, not only do campus leaders have a responsibility to establish policies that acknowledge the changing needs of today's workers, they also must work to create a campus culture where programs and policies that support flexibility are viewed as a strategic and appropriate investment in human resources.

Formalized Work-Life Policies

Earlier chapters discuss the discriminatory, disparate impacts that exist when formal policies are lacking, particularly where women faculty members are concerned. Establishing such policies and procedures that provide necessary flexibility in an academic career is an essential component of ensuring equitable treatment for all faculty members. It also allows institutions to monitor use of the policies and procedures, and the outcomes that result. This information is essential to evaluating how successful the policies and practices have been.

The first step in creating a more flexible workplace is to formalize policies so that they are accessible to all faculty members rather than available only on a case-by-case basis. Formalizing policies also raises their visibility so that faculty members and administrators alike understand them more completely, and so that administrators can apply them more easily and more uniformly (Sullivan, Hollenshead, and Smith, 2004). Clear procedures for implementing new policies should convey crucial information about how and when they are to be used, and to whom one should apply for their use.

Once they are formally established, any new policies or policy enhancements must be promulgated with strong administrative support and plenty of guidance in their implementation. Presidents and provosts need to announce the new policies with their full support and explain what the policies are intended to address, who has participated in their development, how they will be implemented, and who can answer faculty members' questions. Faculty members who have participated in the policies' development at the college or university level must support the policies' implementation in their departments and ensure that information about the policies is incorporated into faculty manuals and widely disseminated.

Financial Support for Implementing Work-Life Policies from Central Administration Resources

Some of these policies will require additional resources before they can be fully implemented. To ensure that the flexibility they offer is truly available to each faculty member, these policies need to be funded through the central administration rather than through departmental resources. Requiring departments to fund the policies with their own scarce resources will lead to differential and thus inequitable use of the policies across the campus, reflecting the various departments' ability and willingness to pay. Therefore, we offer the following recommendation:

Recommendation 23

Provide funding for work-life policies from centrally administered institutional resources, to ensure that the policies are equally available across the campus and not dependent on an individual unit's resources.

One major university learned through experience about the value of centralized funding for work-life policies. At this institution, leave policies were interpreted, leaves were negotiated, and approvals were signed by department heads and deans. What evolved was an inequitable system. Resource-rich departments granted longer leaves with more generous terms than did resource-poor departments. Leave conditions had more to do with a department's budgetary ability to maintain the required teaching and research loads than with a fair interpretation of policy. After eighty-nine faculty members signed a petition requesting the central administration's oversight, the university created a centralized fund to reimburse all departments for faculty leaves, and it centralized approval for all extended faculty leaves as well. Departments still have some flexibility in determining how to meet individual needs, but that is now balanced with review by the central administration to ensure equity across schools and departments (see http://directives.ucdavis.edu/2003/03-006.cfm, retrieved June 29, 2006).

SHARED RESPONSIBILITY FOR THE SUCCESS OF NEW POLICIES

Establishing policies for career breaks, job sharing, parental leave, and modified duties for new parents would make the academic workplace far more responsive to the needs of today's faculty and thus more attractive to potential faculty members. But creating new policies or revising those that already exist will not necessarily ensure change in institutional practices. As has been pointed out in earlier chapters, faculty members and administrators share responsibility for creating a culture that actually supports utilization of such policies. Faculty and administrators also share responsibility for working through the logistical challenges inherent in implementing new work-life polices.

Faculty members using these policies must recognize the impact on their departments and their colleagues. For example, a faculty member planning to take a leave or change his or her time base needs to provide the department chair with as much notice as possible. He or she must be willing to relinquish his or her office space if taking a full-time leave, and anyone teaching at the graduate level will probably need to continue advising doctoral students during the leave. Faculty also must understand that the ability to accommodate the recommendations offered in this book is based in part on the type of institution and on the characteristics of the particular discipline. For example, those whose work consists primarily of teaching and service may find it easier to take an extended leave of absence than will those who conduct a significant amount of laboratory-based research.

All faculty members in a unit must support each other if work-life policies are to be implemented successfully. For example, they can demonstrate their commitment to their colleagues through their verbal support of someone who reduces his or her total work effort. They may also need to take on extra advisees for a faculty member on leave, or teach courses they do not typically teach, or temporarily manage more committee work for an absent colleague. If members of a department establish a genuine community of scholars, the faculty member who utilizes a work-life policy will not be made to feel guilty for doing so. Moreover, the other faculty members will recognize that they, too, can use the same policy if the need should arise for them to give increased attention to family responsibilities.

Faculty senates, as campuswide organizations, can also communicate their involvement in policy development, their support for the policies, and their encouragement of faculty members' use of the policies.

Communication on the part of administrators is essential if work-life policies are to become an established feature of campus culture. Administrators must be enthusiastic proponents of the policies, and they should express their support widely through written and verbal communications that publicize work-life policies, discussing them in a positive light and encouraging people to utilize them. When chairs and deans clearly explain to tenure and promotion committees that faculty must not be penalized for having used work-life policies, "attitudes about the academic value of colleagues with family responsibilities begin to change" (Sullivan, Hollenshead, and Smith, 2004, p. 24).

Administrators, in their decisions about who will have access to the new work-life policies, also have significant responsibility for ensuring that the new policies, which enhance flexibility, become an acceptable feature of the campus culture. A study of work-life policies across institutional types found that noninstructional research faculty were eligible for such policies only about half as often as their tenure-track and tenured colleagues (Hollenshead et al., 2005). This approach seems very shortsighted. If a faculty member is performing well, it is far less expensive for an institution to retain the individual and allow him or her to use leave policies than it is to lose the employee and then recruit, hire, and train a replacement, who may then also request a leave.

PROMOTING CAMPUSWIDE USE OF NEW WORK-LIFE POLICIES

The initial launching of work-life policies can play an important part in stimulating campuswide interest in and discussion of them. Presidents and provosts can use the occasion of announcing the new policies as an important opportunity to express their strong support.

Educating Faculty and Administrators About New Policies

Many eligible faculty members underuse work-life programs and policies to avoid the risks that taking advantage of them might entail. Research shows that faculty members underuse these programs because they do not know about them, or because there is confusion about eligibility (Mason and Goulden, 2004).

Disseminating work-life policy information to new faculty members at orientation sessions, and to new department heads and deans at training sessions, is an important first step in promoting the policies' appropriate use. This step will help faculty and administrators to view the policies as legitimate and treat them as routine (Quinn, Lange, and Olswang, 2004). But faculty members may not need information about work-life policies until they have been at the institution for a few years, and so it also important to provide this information in faculty handbooks, in work-life brochures, on the institution's Web site, and in existing faculty and administrative forums (Mason and Goulden, 2004; Sullivan, Hollenshead, and Smith, 2004).

Trial Periods for New Policies

For some institutions, these policies are a significant departure from the status quo. Implementation will not be without challenges and real costs. For this reason, institutions may find it helpful to try the new policies out for a period of time. Implementation of the policies for perhaps three years, coupled with monitoring of the results, will provide the information necessary for evaluating the strengths and weaknesses of the policies and determining any adjustments that may be needed to enhance their usefulness and viability.

Monitoring the Success of Policies That Provide Flexibility

To enhance institutionwide commitment to work-life policies, the success of these policies must be evaluated, as the previous paragraph implies. Questions such as these are useful for institutional monitoring of policy use:

What proportion of faculty members took a leave after giving birth, or adopting a child?

What proportion of faculty members took a leave to care for themselves or a family member in cases of family illness or other emergencies?

What proportion of new faculty members taking leaves requested an extension of their probationary period if it was not automatically granted?

What proportion of these requests were granted?

How well have policy users made the transition back to their regular duties?

Does stopping the tenure clock indeed improve faculty members' tenure achievement?

Have rates of retention for faculty members changed as a result of the new policies?

Administrative accountability is essential to the achievement of consistency in use of the new policies across academic departments. Deans and department chairs must take responsibility for policy use by regularly evaluating how they are implementing work-life policies in their units, and use of the policies in their academic units should be a component of their periodic evaluations.

A periodic campuswide climate survey is one means of evaluating whether work-life policies are meeting their intended purposes. Results of such a survey need to be shared on a campuswide basis to foster ongoing discussion about the policies and their use. Routine monitoring of cohorts of new faculty is another good way to determine how the policies are being used and whether there are discrepancies in their use across departments or schools. Exit interviews for all departing faculty members who have chosen to leave the institution offer yet another effective way to gather information because these faculty members will be able to speak freely about use and integration of the policies. For non-tenured faculty members, the exit interview may be the only forum where they feel they can be truly candid about the problems they encountered while working for the institution. When exit interviews take place, data collected should include a faculty member's demographic information, faculty rank, departmental affiliation, and his or her reasons for leaving (Quinn, Lange, and Olswang, 2004). Such data, of course, must be maintained in confidence. These data are fairly easy to collect, but surprisingly few institutions actually collect them (Sullivan, Hollenshead, and Smith, 2004).

CONCLUSIONS

This chapter has made recommendations intended to help institutions envision and implement the kind of flexible work environment needed by an increasing number of today's faculty members. These suggestions are not intended as definitive solutions. Each institution will need to establish a type and degree of flexibility that will work in its unique context. Nevertheless, many of the ideas presented in this chapter do represent the latest thinking from researchers in the field and from leading higher education associations, such as the American Council on Education.

Of the five essential elements, flexibility is perhaps the one that requires the most institutional commitment to achieve. More than the other elements, flexibility requires the institution's commitment of some of its financial resources, particularly if the institution chooses to offer paid leaves. Moreover, without some years of experience in the use of policies that enhance flexibility, the institutional costs are difficult to anticipate completely.

Flexibility also requires serious commitment at the individual level. Establishing a culture that embraces flexibility requires faculty members to expand their perceptions of what constitutes an effective and successful faculty member. It requires individuals to become more comfortable with the legitimacy of policies allowing parental leave, career breaks, and less than full-time work. Further, at times it requires the individual seeking increased flexibility to take the initiative in pursuing with the institution what may need to be quite a creative solution to fit his or her unique circumstances.

Clearly, institutions that adopt these recommendations will be at the cutting edge of current practice because to do so involves redefining the cultural norms that surround how one defines commitment to work as well as the variety of ways in which faculty can construct work to achieve significant outcomes. But this effort is worth the trouble. A large proportion of faculty members today do not fit the traditional work patterns originally defined for the ideal worker of the twentieth century, but these traditional patterns continue to characterize institutional policies regarding time commitment and flexibility. To recruit and retain excellent and diverse faculty members, an expanded view of flexibility is essential.

CHAPTER TWELVE

PROFESSIONAL GROWTH

New knowledge, new students, new technology, and new expectations require faculty members to learn continuously even as they facilitate the learning of their students. Whether a faculty member is starting his or her career or is at the midlevel or senior stage, whether he or she has a full-time tenure-track appointment, a contract-renewable appointment, or a fixed-term appointment, participation in professional growth activities can contribute to the vitality of the individual faculty member and his or her university or college (Rice and Austin, 1988; Sorcinelli, Austin, Eddy, and Beach, 2006; Svinicki, 2002). Professional growth opportunities that enable faculty members to broaden and deepen their knowledge, abilities, and skills, to address challenges, concerns, and needs, and to find deeper satisfaction in their work are more important than ever with the changing and expanding responsibilities that faculty members must handle.

Professional development opportunities for faculty have expanded over the past half century. In the 1950s and 1960s, faculty development primarily meant sabbaticals to enable tenured faculty to renew or deepen their research activities. From the mid-1960s on, many universities and colleges focused faculty development on improving teaching. Then, during the 1980s, some institutions began to recognize faculty needs at different career stages, particularly those of new faculty members. In the last decade, some institutions have organized their professional development support to address more broadly the full array of faculty responsibilities, including service, engagement, and leadership duties (Sorcinelli et al., 2006).

Although professional growth opportunities have increased in number and expanded in focus in recent years, all faculty members' needs and preferences are not yet met. For example, time constraints preclude some faculty from taking advantage of programs that currently require attendance on campus but would be of interest if available online. Other faculty members need support for new responsibilities—teaching online, assuming new leadership responsibilities, or engaging in a new relationship with a community group—that have not traditionally been addressed by institutions' faculty development programs. A recent survey of faculty developers from the United States and Canada identified top issues for faculty development to address today. They include how to encourage student learning, teach underprepared students, assess student learning outcomes, and integrate technology into teaching and learning environments (Sorcinelli et al., 2006).

This chapter urges universities and colleges to provide professional growth opportunities for all faculty members, including those in contract-renewable and fixed-term appointments. Opportunities for continuous development help faculty stay vibrant, creative, adaptive, and responsive. Many institutions offer time-tested formal programs that are successful in meeting the needs of some faculty. But, given the increasing demands on faculty time and faculty members' diverse work roles, innovative ways of integrating professional growth opportunities into faculty members' ongoing work will help many more faculty develop the skills they need now and in the future. All told, faculty development deserves thoughtful institutional attention because it is "a key lever for ensuring institutional quality, responsiveness, creativity, and excellence" (Sorcinelli et al., 2006, p. 169).

The "new workplace" literature concerning current and anticipated changes across a range of workplaces offers helpful perspectives pertaining to creative and effective professional development. As discussed in depth in Chapter Two, employees in many organizations are shifting from a focus on the "organizational career" to what scholars studying workplaces are calling the "protean career" (Hall, 1996). This new perspective on careers acknowledges that individuals are likely to have a number of different work experiences during their lives. For such employees, "the career of the future is a continuous learning process" (Hall and

Moss, 1998, p. 36). The organization's responsibility is to contribute to the "employability" of the employee by providing resources and opportunities that develop and enhance skills and abilities (Waterman, Waterman, and Collard, 1994). The "new workplace" scholars suggest that adaptability—the ability to respond to changes in the environment (Hall and Moss, 1998)—is highly important for employees in order for them to keep pace in a changing workplace and to help them enhance their employability. Adaptability makes sense for all faculty members today, because all faculty members must deal with the many changes occurring in the academic workplace.

In academe as well, as the "new workplace" scholars suggest, the availability of professional development deserves attention from both administrators and faculty. Administrators need to be sure that professional growth opportunities ensure a vibrant, productive faculty. Faculty need to make time in their schedules to take advantage of the opportunities that benefit not only their own growth but also the well-being of their institutions. Overall, effective faculty development requires the involvement and efforts of an array of people—deans and department chairs, faculty development professionals, and faculty members themselves.

In sum, then, why should universities and colleges invest in faculty development? Professional growth opportunities contribute to faculty productivity, morale, and creativity. Vibrant faculty members who are engaged in continuous learning and exploration of new ideas also serve as models of intellectual engagement for students (Svinicki, 2002). Individuals who are involved in frequent or ongoing professional growth continuously improve their adaptability and expand their sense of professional identity. Furthermore, faculty members are more invested and committed to their institutions when they feel that their institutions have invested in them (Bland and Schmitz, 1988).

Finally, as Gaff (1975) pointed out more than thirty years ago, universities and colleges invest in their faculty when they hire them; given this original investment, institutional attention to professional growth and development makes a great deal of sense as a strategy to ensure the continuing viability of that original investment. The hiring of a tenure-track faculty member today can lead to an institutional investment that well exceeds several million dollars over the course of a typical faculty career (Svinicki, 2002). Therefore, finding ways to help faculty stay current, engaged, and flexible, merits the investment of institutional resources. Faculty development is an institutional responsibility that deserves to be included in comprehensive institutional planning and resouce allocation (Sorcinelli et al., 2006).

This chapter highlights specific recommendations for professional growth for faculty members in all appointment types. First, the chapter discusses five different ways to provide professional development: information and resources, work-related assignments, flexible unit planning, collegial interactions, and individualized professional growth plans. Then it addresses specific professional growth strategies that are relevant to institutions' missions, and to faculty members in fixed-term appointments. The chapter then suggests strategies for professional growth for each faculty career stage: early, middle, and late. Some, but by no means all, of the examples used to illustrate various concepts were purposefully chosen from institutions that have received TIAA-CREF Hesburgh Awards, bestowed in recognition of excellence in institutional approaches to faculty development.

PROFESSIONAL GROWTH THROUGH INFORMATION AND RESOURCES

A key way in which universities and colleges can support the continuous learning of their faculty is to provide easily accessible information about a variety of topics that affect them. It is critical that faculty know about the professional development opportunities and resources available on campus. Thus, we offer the following recommendation:

Recommendation 24

Ensure that all faculty members have ready access to information needed to perform their jobs, and to information about the professional development resources available to them on campus.

Faculty members are busy. Web sites are a useful way for universities and colleges to provide faculty with information and links to resources on such topics as teaching, grant writing, and curriculum planning. Faculty members are more likely to use Web resources if they can easily find them on institutional Web sites, if links are provided to related units and resources, and if the information is directly relevant to issues important to them.

The Professional and Organizational Development (POD) Network, which is the professional association for faculty developers, has a particularly useful Web site that includes links to centers and programs for professional growth at many universities and colleges. Exhibit 12.1 illustrates the variety of available print and online resources concerning faculty development, including the POD Web site.

Many universities and colleges have faculty development centers that provide an array of services to help faculty with teaching and other aspects of their careers. At some institutions, a teaching center helps faculty improve as instructors, whereas support for other professional development needs—for example, procuring external funding for research—is provided elsewhere. When several different units have responsibility for supporting various aspects of the faculty career, coordination is critical to be sure that faculty can easily find the information they seek.

EXHIBIT 12.1. RESOURCES ON FACULTY DEVELOPMENT

A number of resources are available that describe faculty development structures and programs and are useful to interested readers seeking guidance or inspiration about specific programmatic ideas:

- Materials of the Professional and Organizational Development (POD) Network (http://www.podnetwork.org).
- Articles in *To Improve the Academy* (the journal sponsored by the POD Network).
- Published materials on faculty development (see, for example, Berquist and Phillips, 1975; Bland and Berquist, 1997; Gillespie, Hilsen, and Wadsworth, 2002; Lewis and Lunde, 2001; Menges and Mathis, 1988; Schuster, Wheeler, and Associates, 1990; Sorcinelli et al., 2006; Wadsworth, 1988).

Professional Growth Through Work-Related Assignments

Embedding faculty development in the daily work of faculty members is another way to foster professional growth. This strategy helps busy faculty members because it does not involve additional time commitments beyond usual work responsibilities but instead takes advantage of commitments already in place. Because of the benefits that can accrue to faculty when professional development is part of institutional work, we offer the following recommendation:

Recommendation 25

Assign faculty members—including, when appropriate and possible, contract-renewable and fixed-term faculty—to institutional committees, task forces, and responsibilities where they can simultaneously foster their professional growth and fulfill their work responsibilities.

A growing literature on "job-embedded professional development" focuses on learning opportunities that emerge during typical work activities (Galloway, n.d.; Sparks, 1994; West, 2002). Deans and department chairs can take the lead in helping faculty find ways to use their ongoing responsibilities as opportunities for professional growth. Assignments to committees can be made strategically to help faculty members explore areas where they wish to enhance their knowledge. For example, someone considering develoment of a study abroad course could be assigned to a school-wide committee charged with internationalizing the curriculum in order to meet colleagues with similar interests and expand his or her knowledge of international education.

We especially encourage department chairs and deans to look for opportunities, as appropriate, to use faculty with contract-renewable or fixed-term appointments in the work of committees and task forces or in special assignments related to their professional goals and to provide occasions for strengthening these faculty members' bonds with their institutions. The participation of fixed-term faculty can offer insights valuable to departmental curriculum committees, for example, or to committees assigned to assess graduates' success in the workforce. A fixed-term faculty member with experience and interest in online learning might serve on a college task force to develop an online master's degree, or a finance or business faculty member employed in the local community, but teaching occasionally for a college, could be an invaluable addition to a variety of college-level committees. In order not to take undue advantage of fixed-term faculty members, such assignments should be made only when a faculty member shows interest, or when the assignment can be part of his or her workload or appropriately compensated.

PROFESSIONAL GROWTH THROUGH FLEXIBLE UNIT PLANNING

Academic departments are at the heart of faculty life. When department members engage in flexible thinking and unit-level planning that focuses on a three- to five-year period, they can foster an environment in which faculty members' work and their professional growth can occur simultaneously. Because unit-level decisions can affect and enhance the opportunities that individual faculty members have to grow professionally, we offer the following recommendation:

Recommendation 26

Encourage departmental leaders and faculty to think in new and flexible ways about the relationship between units' responsibilities and individuals' interests, aspirations, and professional goals.

Typically, faculty work is organized and assigned on an individual basis. Each faculty member in a department usually is expected to teach a specific number of courses per academic year, unless he or she is "bought out" by a research grant. However, if members of departmental and program units conceptualize the work of the unit in a more collective way, the specific work of each faculty member can be arranged more flexibly. If a program must teach thirty courses a year, for example, a flexible approach could enable the program chair and the faculty to agree that some faculty members would teach more than a typical load during a given semester in order to free other faculty members to engage in professional growth activities while the unit as a whole met its obligation to teach the necessary courses. Similar adjustments could be made in departmental service responsibilities. In such a system, over time, all faculty members would have opportunities to vary their responsibilities and pursue new interests.

Some institutions use time-banking programs, in which extra teaching and/or service commitments in one semester are exchanged for a reduced load in another. Time banking programs, "open" semesters, or "internal sabbaticals," all open up opportunities for professional growth that can benefit the department and institution as well as the individual faculty member interested in pursuing new areas of interest or other professional goals.

Professional Growth Through Collegial Interaction

Learning through collegial interaction and collaboration is another vehicle for professional growth. Faculty developers have long understood the value of providing opportunities for faculty members to interact through programs that bring diverse colleagues together, either on a one-time basis or on a periodic basis over an extended time. When faculty members interact with colleagues who differ from them in background or discipline, they have the opportunity to encounter perspectives different from their own, which can foster professional growth. Given that faculty often learn as they interact with colleagues, we offer the following recommendation:

Recommendation 27

Encourage and arrange long- and short-term, formal and informal, collegial interactions among faculty members that provide opportunities for professional growth.

Collaboration in Teaching and Research

Collaborative relationships can easily be encouraged in the context of faculty members' regular work. For example, faculty members can engage in team teaching. Such arrangements might bring together an experienced faculty member with a newcomer, or they can pair a person on the tenure track with a part-time faculty member. These interactions are likely to enrich both partners. A new faculty member just out of graduate school may have advanced technological skills to bring to course planning, and these could contribute to the professional growth of a seasoned professor who has little or no experience with using technology in teaching; in return, the experienced faculty member could help the novice reflect on the pedagogical challenges that arise in teaching a particular course. When colleagues with varying types of expertise within a department, or faculty members across disciplines within a university, teach courses together, they learn about other scholarly perspectives, observe alternative approaches to teaching, and, ideally, become closer as colleagues. Similarly, cross-disciplinary research teams can enlarge the perspectives of all team members.

Mentoring Relationships

Other collaborations for fostering professional growth require more formal arrangements and more time from the schedules of faculty members. Mentoring, although it can be organized in various ways, is one professional growth arrangement that requires some structure and time. However, mentoring arrangements can be fruitful for faculty at all career stages and in all appointment types, and many who participate find that the time was well-spent.

Early-career faculty members, in particular, are often interested in participating in mentoring relationships to guide them as they get established at the institution. They often prefer a mentoring team rather than a single mentor so that they have access to people who can address a variety of issues related to teaching, disciplinary networking, research skills, and the institution in general. The disciplinary home of a mentor is an important consideration as well. Mentors in the same department with a new faculty member understand the specific field, but the new faculty member may not want to reveal concerns or weaknesses to a senior person who may ultimately evaluate the promotion dossier.

Some early-career faculty members prefer to find their own mentors, whereas others appreciate the assistance of a professional development center or of a department chair who can identify colleagues with similar interests. Some universities have organized programs that emphasize mentoring opportunities specifically for early-career women faculty. For example, a number of universities participating in the National Science Foundation–sponsored ADVANCE Program have organized mentoring programs for faculty who are women or members of ethnic and racial minority groups, and who teach primarily in the fields of science, technology, engineering, and mathematics. One ADVANCE Program, the Women in Science & Engineering Leadership Institute, describes the central role of mentoring in its programs (see Exhibit 12.2).

Both senior faculty and their newer colleagues benefit from mentoring. Senior faculty experience the satisfaction of helping new colleagues take the initial steps toward success, and they themselves may gain fresh perspectives or knowledge from their junior colleagues. The newer faculty members benefit from the institutional knowledge, friendly support, and collegial interest of their mentors. Institutional recognition and reward for the contributions of senior faculty who serve as mentors encourage more faculty members to participate in promoting the professional growth of their junior colleagues.

Long-term mentoring relationships, when the participants are dedicated to nurturing them, can be very satisfying for both parties, but short-term interactions between early-career and established faculty can also be useful. One dean at a large university

EXHIBIT 12.2. WOMEN IN SCIENCE & ENGINEERING
LEADERSHIP INSTITUTE, UNIVERSITY OF WISCONSIN

The Women in Science & Engineering Leadership Institute (WISELI) is a centralized, visible administrative structure with a mission to address a number of impediments to women's academic advancement. The center structure of WISELI allows the institute to bring the issues of women scientists and engineers from obscurity to visibility. It will provide an effective and legitimate means of networking women faculty across departments, decreasing isolation, advocating for and mentoring women faculty, and linking women postdoctoral fellows in predominantly male environments with a variety of women faculty.

Source: http://wiseli.engr.wisc.edu (retrieved July 1, 2006).

encourages each new faculty member to host three lunches (at the dean's expense), each with a different established colleague whom the newcomer would like to know. Faculty development centers at other institutions provide lunch and dinner coupons for mentoring pairs or short-term colleague pairs. Such mentoring meals provide opportunities for the new colleague and the experienced faculty member to develop a professional connection.

Most mentoring programs link early-career faculty with senior colleagues, but some programs help faculty at any career stage learn from others. Opportunities to get 360-degree feedback—that is, feedback from everyone with whom one interacts—can provide a model for lateral mentoring. Peer or lateral mentoring involves faculty members interacting regularly with colleagues for the purpose of discussing each others' personal and professional challenges, successes, and plans for growth. The support, guidance, and information exchanges that characterize traditional mentoring relationships continue as an integral part of lateral mentoring.

PROFESSIONAL GROWTH THROUGH INDIVIDUALIZED GROWTH PLANS

The various strategies mentioned—information and resources, work-related assignments, flexible unit planning, and collegial interactions—each can help faculty members learn and grow in ways that enhance the intellectual capital and enrich the professional and personal satisfaction of the individual. Individualized professional growth plans help faculty members recognize their options and make strategic choices that will enhance their careers. Individual faculty professional growth plans can also help department chairs and deans

- Assess the interests, strengths, and needs of their faculty members
- Help faculty members locate resources and fit professional development opportunities into their responsibilities
- Ensure that the institution's needs are also being met

Recognizing these benefits of individualized professional growth plans for faculty, we offer the following recommendation:

Recommendation 28

Ensure that campus faculty development professionals, as well as department chairs, are knowledgeable about the benefits of individualized faculty professional growth plans and how to help faculty members prepare them.

Some department chairs work with their faculty members to develop five-year professional development plans that include faculty members' goals, plans for achieving those goals, and ways in which the institution can support the achievement of those goals (Austin, Rice, Splete, with Associates, 1991). Faculty development centers also can offer faculty members guidance for preparing ongoing professional development plans and maintaining records of their professional development experiences.

Self-reflection and analysis is an important part of developing an individualized professional development plan. Taking time for self-reflection has long been recognized as a strategy that helps faculty members make good use of feedback about teaching (McKeachie, 2006), and it can be equally useful as faculty members review other domains of their work. The use of teaching portfolios facilitates self-reflection; faculty members who develop teaching portfolios often chronicle their teaching goals, successes, concerns, plans, and strategies for improvement. This use of portfolios could be expanded to include other aspects of faculty work in addition to teaching. Combined with opportunities to discuss one's professional program and goals with an interested colleague, department chair, or professional developer, portfolios can serve as the basis for developing individualized growth plans.

PROFESSIONAL DEVELOPMENT THAT ADDRESSES INSTITUTIONAL MISSIONS

Although faculty development historically has focused most heavily on supporting the teaching mission, a strategic approach to encouraging faculty growth calls for a comprehensive institutional program that addresses each aspect of faculty work, including teaching, research, and outreach. Thus, in this section, we discuss strategies for meeting the following recommendation:

Recommendation 29

Provide support for professional growth pertaining to all aspects of the institution's mission.

PROGRAMS THAT SUPPORT THE RESEARCH MISSION

Seed grant money is one form of support that helps faculty fulfill the research mission. At Western Michigan University, an early-career faculty member can be nominated by his or her college dean and selected by the vice president to receive a research development award of several thousand dollars to support research and efforts to find grant funds. Each recipient participates in campus workshops, interacts with a mentor at another institution, and visits funding agencies to discuss research ideas. In return, he or she is expected to submit two research proposals for external funding. At other institutions, first-year tenure-track faculty members are eligible to apply for research grants to cover travel, equipment, computers, and other expenses. Other types of institutional support for research include seminars on grant writing, Web resources about grant writing, and the availability of colleagues who will read and provide feedback on proposal drafts.

PROGRAMS THAT SUPPORT THE OUTREACH MISSION

Some institutions are offering programs to help faculty develop the knowledge and skills that support their outreach efforts. At Portland State University, the Community-University Partnership Program has won acclaim for involving faculty members and students with people in the community in various collaborative projects (see Exhibit 12.3).

At Michigan State University, faculty members are invited to participate in Meet Michigan bus tours to learn more about the university's 150-year-old land-grant tradition, to visit specific examples of research and outreach activities led by faculty members in various locations throughout the state, and to interact with and develop collegial connections with colleagues from other parts of campus. In the spring, a three-day trip, often organized around a

EXHIBIT 12.3. COMMUNITY-UNIVERSITY
PARTNERSHIPS PROGRAM, PORTLAND STATE UNIVERSITY

Faculty Resources

PSU's motto of "Let Knowledge Serve the City" could never be realized without the support of faculty dedicated to making a difference in both the lives of students and all of the citizens of Portland.

In order to ensure that PSU faculty are supported in their efforts, the Center for Academic Excellence offers a variety of services, including community-based learning, curriculum development, assistance in publishing scholarly works, and access to the latest community-based learning and civic engagement research.

In addition to one-on-one faculty support, the Center for Academic Excellence offers support in the following areas:

Capstone Resources—A clearinghouse for information regarding the Senior Capstone course offered through the University Studies department.

Civic Engagement—Resources for faculty who desire a deeper understanding of civic engagement and the various forms in which it may manifest.

Instructional Resources—Information on designing community-based learning courses, such as syllabus design, the community-based learning course designation process, and effective reflection strategies.

Publication Outlets—Our continually updated database of publications that consistently accept scholarly work related to community-based learning and civic engagement.

Published Research—A listing of published works relating to various branches of community-based learning, such as theory, pedagogy, and reflective strategies.

International CBL—Expanding community-based learning beyond our geographic borders through PSU President Dan Bernstine's Internationalization Initiative.

Promotion and Tenure—PSU's complete set of guidelines for all issues relating to faculty promotion and tenure.

Source: http://www.pdx.edu/cae/faculty_resources.html (retrieved July 1, 2006).

disciplinary theme, takes about thirty faculty members to visit project sites throughout the state; one-day trips are offered at other times in the year (see Exhibit 12.4).

PROGRAMS THAT SUPPORT THE TEACHING MISSION

Historically, many faculty development opportunities have helped faculty enhance their abilities and skills as teachers. Workshops and seminars for faculty who are interested in teaching topics or seek to improve their teaching practice are typically considered the backbone of the professional growth opportunities offered by institutional faculty development and teaching centers. Many colleges and universities offer faculty the opportunity for peer review of their teaching or video taping of a class session, followed by debriefing and discussion with a faculty development professional or a colleague trained for this work. Some institutions offer midterm assessment of courses, in which an experienced colleague or faculty development specialist, by invitation of the faculty member, meets with the members of a class to discuss strengths of the course and ways it could be improved to enhance the students' learning. Subsequently, the facilitator of the class discussion meets with the faculty member to discuss the findings of the meeting and to help the faculty member brainstorm next steps for improving the course.

Nationally, the Carnegie Foundation has been at the forefront of a movement to encourage faculty to study, reflect on, and improve their teaching through scholarly work. Some faculty members participate in its Academy for the Scholarship of Teaching and Learning, sponsored by the Carnegie Foundation for the Advancement of Teaching, which provides a national opportunity to support faculty members' teaching. Participants in the Carnegie program meet with others on their campuses and across the nation in communities that encourage and support scholarship on issues in teaching and learning.

PROFESSIONAL GROWTH FOCUSED ON FIXED-TERM FACULTY

Professional growth opportunities aimed specifically at fixed-term faculty are essential to meet the needs of an increasingly

EXHIBIT 12.4. MEET MICHIGAN PROGRAM, MICHIGAN STATE UNIVERSITY

The Meet Michigan program is a very successful "traveling seminar" that provides members of the MSU community with an opportunity to learn more about MSU's extensive research, outreach, and cooperative efforts throughout the state.

The Meet Michigan program offers a one-day interdisciplinary trip each fall semester and a three-day broadly defined disciplinary trip each spring semester.

Goals of the Meet Michigan Program

To increase awareness of:

- Opportunities for outreach, service and research to meet the needs of Michigan's diverse communities and citizens.
- MSU collaborations throughout Michigan in research, teaching and outreach/service.
- Resources at MSU to assist in developing collaborations.
- Funding sources to support these collaborations.

To promote collegiality and community among MSU faculty, administrators, and graduate students across the disciplines.

To clarify the faculty role in outreach to:

- Increase the involvement of MSU faculty in collaborations.
- Increase the interest and involvement of graduate students in pursuing community collaborations during their careers.

To increase MSU collaborations through:

- New relationships with potential community partners across the state of Michigan.
- New relationships with academic and professional peers within one's local community and across the University.
- Increased grant activity.

Source: http://www1.provost.msu.edu/facdev/meetmich/about.asp (retrieved July 1, 2006).

large proportion of faculty members. Thus, we offer the following recommendation:

Recommendation 30

Welcome the participation of fixed-term faculty in faculty professional development activities, and design resources and events tailored to meet their needs.

Professional development opportunities that do not require additional time on campus (for example, resources available via the World Wide Web) may be especially attractive to fixed-term faculty, who typically spend limited time on campus. Encouraging fixed-term faculty to use the resources of a campus faculty development center can contribute to their performance and can serve as a clear message of their importance to the college or university. This may require, however, that these centers expand their working hours so that part-timers who teach in the evening or on weekends can also participate.

Those faculty in fixed-term appointments who are teaching for the first time should receive immediate assistance with teaching strategies and classroom management. They also should receive an orientation to the campus and all its resources. One example of how to do this is shown in Exhibit 9.8 (Chapter Nine).

New fixed-term faculty also need orientation to their departments, to departmental resources for helping them, and to the specific programs in which they will teach so that they understand how their courses are related to other courses. They should have an explicit introduction to the resources that their institutions provide to support student learning, including libraries, technologies, and services to help students with academic or personal concerns.

Institutions are increasingly developing formal faculty development programs for fixed-term faculty (Krupar, 2004; Lyons, 2003). Some departments assign specific faculty committees to meet with and mentor fixed-term faculty (Rice, Sorcinelli, and Austin, 2000). The College of the Canyons, for example, has a professional development program for temporary faculty that includes a microteaching workshop, where participants get feedback on their own teaching and provide feedback to others; a three-day advanced teaching workshop that goes into greater depth on such issues as classroom assessment techniques, technology, and active learning; and an opportunity for the individual participant to plan lessons with the assistance of a faculty mentor, get feedback from the mentor, and then write a reflective paper about the experience (see http://www.canyons.edu/offices/asso_prog/, retrieved August 6, 2006). Other components that would benefit the professional development of fixed-term faculty include departmental mentoring and grants to support teaching development. These opportunities, when designed to help fixed-term faculty develop skills directly related to their teaching, help them become informed colleagues able to contribute to high-quality teaching, advising, curriculum development, and student experiences.

PROFESSIONAL GROWTH FOCUSED ON CAREER-STAGE NEEDS

Considerable research over the past four decades has illuminated the professional development needs of faculty at various career stages, with particular attention to the early stage (usually defined as pretenure, for those in tenure-track positions), the middle stage (usually defined as starting immediately after the tenure decision, for those in tenure-track positions), and the senior stage (often defined as the period within ten years of retirement). We urge institutions to ensure that all faculty members with continuing commitments to their colleges or universities—those in tenure-track and contract-renewable appointments—have opportunities for professional growth appropriate to their career stages.

PROFESSIONAL GROWTH SUPPORT FOR EARLY-CAREER FACULTY

As novices in their roles, early-career faculty have special needs, particularly since many graduate programs do not provide future faculty with extensive preparation for all the roles they must fulfill. Everyone benefits when new faculty have the support they need to succeed. Thus, we offer the following recommendation:

Recommendation 31

Ensure that professional growth programs and resources are in place to support faculty members during the early years of their careers.

The research on early-career faculty and the challenges they experience at this career stage is very consistent (Austin, 1992b, 1992c; Sorcinelli and Austin, 1992; Rice, Sorcinelli, and Austin, 2000; Tierney and Bensimon, 1996), as discussed in depth in Chapter Four. New faculty members report concerns about specific aspects of their work experience:

- The expectations they face and whether they can meet them
- Lack of regular and systematic feedback
- The standards and processes of tenure (for those on the tenure-track)
- The sense of isolation they often feel
- The question of whether they can find a sense of balance that will work in their life situations

Many universities and colleges have invested considerable effort and resources in helping early-career faculty make the transition to successful faculty careers and welcoming them into a collegial environment. Here, we look at programs aimed at early-career faculty needs: orientation programs, information fairs, programs that encourage collegial interactions, and preparation for the tenure process.

Orientation Programs

Some institutions have taken creative approaches to the orientation of new faculty, recognizing that the initial period of adjustment can create an important base for future success. For example, Brigham Young University provides a year-long orientation program for new faculty in which they participate in regular luncheons during the first year as well as in ongoing meetings with faculty mentors. After the first two semesters, new faculty members participate in a two-week learning experience to solidify their integration into the institution. At Georgia Institute of Technology, cohorts of new faculty participate in weekly meetings about teaching, interact with mentors, and receive feedback from staff in the Center for the Enhancement of Teaching and Learning.

Information Fairs for New Faculty

When new faculty discuss their first days at a new institution, they often comment that they feel overwhelmed by receiving too much information at initial orientations. Nevertheless, when faculty members first join a college or university, they have many questions and concerns that should be addressed. Issues such as housing, spousal or partner employment, child care, and schools will be the first order of business for some. In addition to placing resources related to these topics on their Web sites, universities and colleges can use other strategies to highlight information new faculty members need. Information fairs connected with faculty orientation sessions can provide easy opportunities for newcomers to pick up materials on a variety of topics, such as resources in the community, policies related to dependents, leisure-time options, teaching support, and key resource people available to assist them.

Information fairs are usually organized to be in-person events, but many institutions have developed extensive online resources, offering Web sites with links to teaching- and research-related resources on campus, resources at other institutions, and information that can be found in electronic formats. These resources can be useful to faculty seeking easy access to information at any time, but they are critical for newcomers. Some institutions or regional consortia, such as the Bay Area Consortium in California, also offer relocation specialists to help those who are moving make arrangements for housing, dependent support, and spousal or partner employment.

Programs to Build Collegial Connections

A number of institutions support early-career faculty by offering ways to connect with other colleagues and build collegial relationships. A simple, informal way is for a department chair to assign an established faculty member to greet and mentor a new faculty member upon the latter's arrival, and during the initial days and weeks. The experienced faculty member may not continue as a long-term mentor, but he or she can do much to help the new colleague through the demands of relocating and starting work by being available to answer the innumerable questions that arise.

Some colleges and universities invite first-year faculty members to regularly scheduled lunches that occur periodically through the fall term or the entire academic year. During each fall semester since 1988, for example, the University of Oklahoma has been holding its New Faculty Seminar for all first-year faculty members (both junior and senior) to meet colleagues, become acquainted with the university's culture, and learn about institutional resources (see Exhibit 12.5).

EXHIBIT 12.5. NEW FACULTY SEMINAR, UNIVERSITY OF OKLAHOMA

Each fall, IDP [the Instructional Development Program] offers this seminar for faculty members, junior and senior, who are new to the University of Oklahoma. It begins [in] the 2nd week of classes and then meets weekly until the 15th week of the semester.

This seminar, commonly known as the "New Faculty Seminar," has been operating since 1988 and has received strong positive comments from the participants. The participants meet once a week for 14 weeks. Each meeting consists of (a) a half-hour lunch followed by (b) a 75-minute program. Each week's program has 2–3 sessions that address different aspects of the following five areas:

1. RESEARCH: Resources on this campus to support your research program.

2. TEACHING: Ideas on and support services for your teaching activities.

3. THIS UNIVERSITY: Information on offices, policies, organization, etc., of this particular institution of higher education.

4. YOUR OWN PROFESSIONAL DEVELOPMENT: Ideas that may be helpful to managing your professional work, e.g., time management, "being a new faculty member," etc.

5. NORMAN & OKLAHOMA: Information to allow you to enjoy the resources of this great city and state.

Source: http://www.ou.edu/idp/faculty/newfaculty.htm (retrieved July 1, 2006).

Teaching Fellows programs, originally sponsored by the Lilly Endowment, are available at many universities (for example, Miami University of Ohio, Michigan State University, the University of Massachusetts at Amherst, and the University of Georgia). These programs involve year-long fellowships for selected early-career faculty who meet with others on their campuses to learn more about teaching and learning, work on individual projects that enhance their teaching, interact with institutional leaders, expand their knowledge of university resources, and develop collegial bonds with other participants. The programs are time-intensive for participants, but research has shown that they help participants develop effective teaching abilities, enhance participants' confidence as new scholars, provide participants with useful information about the university, and help participants develop long-lasting collegial networks (Austin, 1992b, 1992c).

Support for the Tenure Process

The tenure process looms as one of the major issues on the minds of early-career faculty members on the tenure track, as discussed in Chapter Four. They wonder about the expectations that faculty face, the steps of the process, and the timeline they must follow (Austin and Rice, 1998). Many universities and colleges are finding creative ways to provide support so that faculty members experience this process both as an opportunity for professional growth and as an occasion for evaluation. Some institutions offer workshops or provide Web resources that explain the procedural aspects of the tenure and promotion process (dates, forms, expectations) as well as the informal aspects (how to keep track of material, to whom to go for advice, how to organize a dossier). Resources might include excerpts from successful tenure dossiers (with names redacted) to give faculty members examples of the statements that successful tenure applicants have written about their career focuses and trajectories.

Explicit annual feedback from department chairs is critical to helping early-career faculty members stay on track during the tenure process. Without clear feedback about their progress in light of departmental, college, and institutional expectations, early-career faculty can easily feel a great deal of stress and worry. Not every aspect of the tenure expectations can be spelled out, but early-career faculty should not be left to wonder how the process works or about the overall expectations against which they will be evaluated.

PROFESSIONAL GROWTH SUPPORT
FOR MID- AND LATE-CAREER FACULTY

Just as higher education institutions should be attentive to the particular concerns often experienced by early-career faculty, they should also support faculty in midcareer. Recognizing the challenges facing faculty as they move throughout their careers, we offer the following recommendation:

Recommendation 32

Ensure that programs and resources are in place to support the continuing professional development of faculty members during the middle and late stages of their careers.

Mid-career faculty may be concerned about a number of issues such as: staying current in their fields, succeeding in their applications for promotion, exploring alternative career options, handling stress, and resisting burnout (American Council on Education, 2005). These concerns may lead to some mid-career faculty exploring other opportunities. In fact, according to the 1999 National Survey of Postsecondary Faculty, more than 12 percent of professors at the associate rank indicated that leaving academe within the coming three years for a full-time position outside higher education was somewhat or very likely (U.S. Department of Education, National Center for Education Statistics, 1999). Addressing the concerns of mid-career faculty can help them stay vibrant and engaged in their work, and may help their institutions retain those who are considering leaving.

Senior faculty may worry about staying current in their fields and enthusiastic about their profession after many years on the job. Faculty at the later stages of their careers may need support as the context for teaching changes, as they seek fulfilling projects to conclude their careers, and as they plan the transition to retirement.

A variety of strategies can be used to support faculty as they move through the middle and advanced stages of their careers:

- Opportunities to explore new interests through seed grants awarded on the basis of competitive proposals for exploration of new areas of research or teaching
- Workshops focused on professional renewal, reflection, and planning for the next stages in their careers
- Opportunities to try new ways of working—for example, by using more flexible multiyear work plans that may involve replacing research responsibilities with teaching for some period of time, or vice versa

Professional leaves or sabbaticals for a semester or year of work or study at another institution or for overseas assignments, such as through the Fulbright Program, also provide exciting opportunities for established faculty. However, some faculty members have personal responsibilities that preclude their spending time at another location. Thus, we urge colleges and universities to ensure that faculty can be awarded sabbaticals to pursue projects that do not require travel away from campus.

Established faculty members occasionally are interested in leadership opportunities as a way to grow professionally or change career emphasis. Faculty in their late career years are likely to be particularly interested in phased retirement options.

Leadership Development Opportunities

Leadership development can help individuals expand their skills, and institutions gain more proficient and effective administrators. Leadership development focuses on the skills and abilities relevant to particular roles, such as department chair or dean. Midcareer faculty leading research or curriculum centers or programs, or chairing important committees can also benefit from leadership development programs that focus on topics such as strategic planning, conflict resolution, human resources, budget management, and organizational change. Leadership development programs can offer faculty expanded career options and a broader understanding of their institutions, and give the university or college more informed faculty on whom to call for a variety of leadership roles.

Many colleges and universities, recognizing the critical roles of department chairs, are allocating resources to support new and continuing chairs' professional growth (see Chapter Eight). The University of Massachusetts at Amherst, for example, holds an annual retreat for chairs and deans to discuss important institutional issues, including faculty concerns, roles, and reward structures. We think that some leadership development opportunities available to department chairs could also include midcareer or senior faculty members who have been chosen to lead new campus programmatic initiatives or to chair campuswide task forces.

Phased-Retirement Plans

Phased-retirement plans, relatively common in recent years, address the concerns of many senior faculty members who want to adjust the level of their involvement in work while continuing some level of professional affiliation. In addition to continuing their teaching and research at reduced levels, faculty members in phased-retirement plans, or those who have already retired, can make significant contributions to their institutions. They can serve as mentors for early-career faculty, work in fund raising, or lead special task forces that address key institutional issues. For example, in Chapter Ten we suggested that such faculty would be valuable resources for educating campus communities about academic freedom. Once faculty members have retired, providing them some office space and including them in intellectual and social events will send a strong message that they are valued and thus will encourage them to continue contributing to the well-being of their departments, colleges, and universities.

Concluding Thoughts

All faculty members need opportunities for professional growth that strengthen the knowledge and abilities they bring to their immediate work and that contribute to their preparation for future assignments. Effective institutional strategies that support professional growth recognize and address the particular needs associated with each faculty appointment type, with aspects of the institutional missions, and with faculty members' career stages. Career development opportunities also help faculty members explore their professional identity in the context of the institution's mission, as well as expand their adaptability—both important attributes in handling a continuously changing context.

Thus, professional development not only enriches the individual faculty member but also optimizes the institution's considerable investment in its faculty members by enhancing their intellectual vitality and expanding their repertoire of skills and abilities.

CHAPTER THIRTEEN

COLLEGIALITY

Faculty members commonly refer to each other as colleagues. Indeed, the concept of being part of a "collegium of scholars," all working together in service to knowledge and truth, is historically embedded in the academic career (Pelikan, 1992). Collegiality is more than a nostalgic or historical notion, however; it is a key element of the kind of academic workplaces that faculty members seek and value (Boice, 1992; Rice, Sorcinelli, and Austin, 2000; Sorcinelli, 1988; Tierney and Bensimon, 1996; Whitt, 1991). In fact, graduate students aspiring to faculty careers and early-career faculty are quite articulate about their hopes to participate in communities characterized by collegial interactions. For example, one graduate student who participated in a recent study of early-career and aspiring faculty members' perceptions about academic careers explained, "What I want most in a faculty career is a profession that makes me feel connected to my students, to my colleagues, to the larger community, and to myself" (Rice, Sorcinelli, and Austin, 2000, p. 16).

Collegiality refers to opportunities for faculty members to feel that they belong to a mutually respectful community of scholars who value each faculty member's contributions to the institution and feel concern for their colleagues' well-being. When people feel that they are included in this community in explicit, implicit, and symbolic ways, they feel that they are respected, that they belong, and that they have sufficient status. As colleagues find opportunities to interact with each other, they typically deepen their understanding of what each can offer and develop scholarly connections. A sense of belonging is likely to enhance both satisfaction with work and the feeling of overall morale (Rice and Austin, 1988).

Furthermore, faculty members who feel connected with their institutions are more likely to want to stay (Barnes, Agago, and Coombs, 1998). Thus a collegial environment enhances the satisfaction of faculty members who experience it, and it strengthens the quality of the institution overall.

Collegiality is not simply a matter of being sociable. Auburn University is noteworthy for its comprehensive statement about collegiality in its faculty handbook (see Exhibit 13.1). This statement recognizes the distinction between sociability and collegiality as a professional criterion, and it provides explicit guidance to peer-review committees.

Because collegiality is a key element of the academic workplace, this chapter discusses institutional strategies for enriching the sense

---

EXHIBIT 13.1. STATEMENT ON COLLEGIALITY, AUBURN UNIVERSITY

In appraising a candidate's collegiality, department members should keep in mind that the successful candidate for tenure will assume what may be an appointment of 30 years or more in the department. Collegiality should not be confused with sociability or likeability. Collegiality is a professional, not personal, criterion relating to the performance of a faculty member's duties within a department. The requirement that a candidate demonstrate collegiality does not license tenured faculty to expect conformity to their views. Concerns relevant to collegiality include the following: Are the candidate's professional abilities and relationships with colleagues compatible with the departmental mission and with its long-term goals? Has the candidate exhibited an ability and willingness to engage in shared academic and administrative tasks that a departmental group must often perform and to participate with some measure of reason and knowledge in discussions germane to departmental policies and programs? Does the candidate maintain high standards of professional integrity?

Collegiality can best be evaluated at the departmental level. Concerns respecting collegiality should be shared with the candidate as soon as they arise; they should certainly be addressed in the yearly review and third-year review. Faculty members should recognize that their judgment of a candidate's collegiality will carry weight with the Promotion and Tenure Committee.

Source: http://www.auburn.edu/academic/provost/handbook/policies. html#introduction (retrieved July 2, 2006).

of collegiality experienced by faculty members in all types of faculty appointments, with particular emphasis on those who have not always felt that they were fully valued members. While recognizing challenges to achieving collegiality, the chapter encourages individual faculty members to assume personal responsibility for nurturing a sense of collegiality. It also discusses institutional strategies for fostering connections across campuses.

CHALLENGES TO ACHIEVING COLLEGIALITY

Changes occurring in universities and colleges are making it more challenging for some faculty to experience fully the sense of collegiality that would enrich their work lives. Time pressures related to the hectic pace of work, and the need to balance personal and professional responsibilities, can interfere with opportunities for collegial interaction. Faculty who are in fixed-term appointments may find opportunities to interact with others difficult if their schedules vary, or may feel inhibited by the contrasting nature of their responsibilities. Differences among faculty in gender, race, ethnicity, or age also can thwart collegial interaction. In some departments, an age gap exists between long-standing faculty members and those newly hired; early-career faculty may find senior colleagues unfamiliar with their subspecialties, and senior faculty may feel that their personal life situations are considerably different from those of their younger peers (Rice, Sorcinelli, and Austin, 2000). As faculty demographics and appointment types become more diverse, collegiality becomes more important than ever to cultivate—but perhaps more challenging than ever to achieve.

It is also difficult to maintain collegiality when a university or college, like any other organization, is confronted with the occasional employee who has personal problems that interfere significantly with his or her ability to perform responsibly or appropriately. And, occasionally, financial constraints require departments to release some faculty members. These are examples of situations in which collegiality may be difficult to maintain.

Another challenge involves the role of collegiality in tenure decisions. When collegiality is used as a criterion for tenure, it can become a mask for other factors, including discrimination, in tenure decisions. Also, efforts to enhance collegiality can end up pushing individual faculty members to conform more than they wish in their personal characteristics, work habits, or intellectual contributions. Concerns such as these have fueled discussion and advice about the place of collegiality in tenure decisions. The American Association of University Professors' 1999 Statement "On Collegiality as a Criterion for Faculty Evaluation" (http://www.aaup.org/statements/Redbook/collegia.htm, retrieved July 4, 2006) takes the position that collegiality plays an important role in faculty performance, but that it should not constitute a fourth criterion for positive tenure decisions. In various legal cases, courts have ruled that collegiality can be taken into account in decisions pertaining to faculty employment because it relates to fulfillment of the institution's mission of teaching, research, and service (Connell and Savage, 2001). However, the courts have also recognized that while cooperation is a necessary feature of faculty work, they also "agree with critics that collegiality may not be used to engage in covert discrimination or to punish the exercise of academic freedom" (Connell and Savage, 2001, p. 40). The question of whether a faculty member's perceived collegiality should play a part in peer-review decisions will undoubtedly continue to be debated by various interested parties, including faculty members themselves.

The challenge, of course, is to create a collegial environment in which all faculty members are valued for the unique ways in which they contribute, and in which all faculty members, regardless of tenure or appointment status or departmental cultures, see themselves as members of a collegial community. Particularities in disciplinary cultures mean that faculty members in different departments often experience the university in varying ways (Austin, 1992a, 1994, 1996; Becher and Trowler, 2001; Clark, 1997). Tierney (1993) has drawn attention to the need to encourage and build multicultural campus communities characterized by mutual respect and caring. A sense of collegiality and connection in an institutional community enhances the overall intellectual vitality of the institution and contributes to the kind of environment that *all* faculty say they value (Austin, 1992b, 1992c; Austin, Rice, and Splete, 1991; Rice and Austin, 1988; Rice, Sorcinelli, and Austin, 2000).

FACULTY RESPONSIBILITY FOR COLLEGIALITY

The quality of the community, like the nature of collegiality as it is experienced at a college or university, depends to a great extent on faculty members themselves. Faculty members should expect mutual civility, respect, and responsibility.

We believe that faculty members should hold each other accountable for professional standards of behavior (see also Chapter Nine). This may mean speaking tactfully but directly to a colleague who fails to attend meetings of committees of which he or she is a member. It may also mean insisting that a disagreement about a decision never constitutes grounds for disrespect or incivility. Universities and colleges are sites for vigorous exchanges about ideas and perspectives, exchanges characterized by strongly held views and by equally strong commitments to respect and civility; these exchanges should be models of the democratic process in shared decision making.

With these thoughts about the nature of collegial environments in mind, we offer the following recommendation:

Recommendation 33

Encourage faculty members to take personal responsibility for the quality of their academic community and the professional behavior of their colleagues.

INCLUSION IN GOVERNANCE

Governance structures, departmental organization, and faculty commitment to professional and ethical behavior all play a role in sustaining a collegial environment. Institutions that welcome and value faculty who are diverse in their characteristics and appointment types must have avenues for those faculty members to make significant contributions to their campuses and their academic units. Primary responsibility for including faculty members in appropriate governance activities, regardless of their appointment types, belongs to the faculty.

Many institutions include tenure-track and contract-renewable faculty members in faculty governing bodies and in advisory groups for institutional matters, such as search committees for new institutional

leaders. Fixed-term faculty also should have the option of participating in decision-making roles commensurate with their positions
and experience. For example, tenure-track and contract-renewable
faculty are usually the appropriate decision makers for the curricula
that departments offer, but fixed-term faculty often have good ideas
and suggestions regarding course content and teaching strategies.
Fixed-term faculty frequently are employed as professionals outside
the academy, and thus they may be on the cutting edge of their professions. They often have a great deal to offer their departments with
regard to what students need to know to prepare for their future careers. Therefore, we offer the following recommendation:

Recommendation 34

Ensure that faculty governance policies, structures, and practices offer opportunities for all faculty members to participate in roles appropriate to their experience and types of their appointments.

Inclusion in Campus Activities and Organizations

Some faculty members may feel marginalized because of gender,
race, age, or other characteristic, or because of appointment type
or assignment. Finding ways to ensure an inclusive campus environment for all faculty members enriches the campus climate for
everyone. Thus, we offer the following recommendation:

Recommendation 35

Find ways to include all faculty members in explicit and welcoming ways in
the institution's community.

Campus leaders, offices, organizations, and associations can play
leadership roles in ensuring that a sense of community, collegiality,
and connection is a reality for every faculty member. These leaders
and their organizations can initiate or monitor campuswide policies to ensure that the environment offers respect and inclusion to
all its members. For example, Purdue University's vice president for
human relations is responsible for promulgation of and adherence
to the university's antiharassment policy (see Exhibit 13.2).

EXHIBIT 13.2. ANTIHARASSMENT POLICY, PURDUE UNIVERSITY

Preamble

The major goal of this policy is to prevent harassment within the Purdue University community. The University believes that harassment is repugnant and inimical to our most basic values. . . .

. . . Purdue University demonstrate[s] its intellectual and ethical leadership by reaffirming its strong position against harassment in all forms. All members of the University community must be able to pursue their goals, educational needs, and working lives without intimidation or injury generated by intolerance and harassment. . . .

This policy addresses harassment in all forms, covering those (harassed) . . . for reasons of race, gender, religion, . . . as well as those harassed for other reasons such as sexual orientation.

Policy

. . . Purdue University (seeks) to maintain the campus as a place of work and study for faculty, staff, and students free from all forms of harassment. In providing an educational and work climate that is positive and harassment-free, faculty, staff, and students should be aware that harassment in the workplace or the educational environment is unacceptable conduct and will not be tolerated.

Definitons

Harassment is conduct toward another person or identifiable group of persons that has the purpose or effect of:

1. creating an intimidating or hostile educational (or work) environment. . . .

2. unreasonably interfering with a person's educational (or work) environment. . . .

3. unreasonably affecting a person's educational or work opportunities . . . . [specific definitions of racial and sexual harassment and amorous relationships are included in the policy]

Financial Liability

Faculty and staff who are determined to have violated this policy may be held personally liable for any damages, settlement costs, or expenses, including attorney fees incurred by the University.

Source: http://www.purdue.edu/univregs/pages/state_equal/antiharassment. html (retrieved July 27, 2006).

Some institutions have resource centers for women, to ensure that their commitment to including and supporting women is met, and to provide practical support in the form of information, seminars, and resources specifically relevant to the needs of women faculty and staff. Universities and colleges may also have faculty women's organizations that provide opportunities for networking and social interaction and that serve as advocates for policies and issues pertaining to the institutional climate for women faculty.

Similarly, organizations such as the Hispanic Faculty and Staff Association at the University of Texas–Austin offer networking opportunities, promote communication among Hispanic professionals, and highlight the Hispanic cultural presence on campus (see http://www.utexas.edu/staff/hfsa, retrieved July 2, 2006). At Johns Hopkins University, the Black Faculty and Staff Association supports the professional and personal development of African American faculty, staff, and students as well as members of the greater community (see Exhibit 13.3).

Retired faculty are another group that can benefit from special institutional support. Because retired faculty may feel that their relationships with their campuses have weakened over time, some universities and colleges have established associations for emeriti faculty to encourage these individuals' ongoing connections and to offer them opportunities to give back to their institutions by sharing their knowledge and expertise. In 2003, for example, Yale established the Henry Koerner Center for Emeritus Faculty (see Exhibit 13.4).

Faculty members in fixed-term and contract-renewable appointments may also sometimes feel marginalized in the academic community. Universities and colleges can take practical but important steps to ensure that they feel welcome and included. All new faculty members should be invited to participate in orientations, and in various faculty development programs and activities. All faculty members should have office space, parking privileges, library cards, and access to campus health and recreational facilities. Collegial connections are also forged when fixed-term and contract-renewable faculty are invited to participate in campus events, to be speakers in campus seminars, and to participate actively in departmental meetings and social events.

EXHIBIT 13.3. BLACK FACULTY AND STAFF ASSOCIATION, JOHNS HOPKINS UNIVERSITY

The mission of the Johns Hopkins Black Faculty and Staff Association is to be a visible and viable agency dedicated to promoting and enhancing identity, sense of community, [and] professional welfare and development among Black faculty, staff, and students of the Johns Hopkins University.

BFSA Goals

1. Exert influence and participation of the Black community at JHU, both in terms of Black concerns and the total structure of the university

2. Advocate for the employment of a more representative number of Black faculty and staff (in particular at the senior staff level) at the Johns Hopkins University

3. Promote professional excellence, scholarship, and cooperative research among Black faculty, staff, and students

4. Urge the JHU to provide equal educational and career opportunities for professional growth and upward mobility for all members of the Black community

5. Provide JHU with a comprehensive and representative Black perspective on institutional, societal, and programmatic development at the JHU and in the community

6. Serve as a resource bureau for JHU and the Black community

7. Provide both leadership and supportive service on the administrative and academic levels to facilitate the delivery of efficient and effective service to all elements of the JHU

8. Stimulate a sense of social responsibility and cultural sensitivity to improve communication among Black faculty, staff, and students

Source: http://www.jhu.edu/bfsa/about_bfsa.htm (retrieved July 2, 2006).

EXHIBIT 13.4. HENRY KOERNER CENTER FOR EMERITUS FACULTY, YALE UNIVERSITY

The principal aims of the Center are:

To provide a focal point for the activities of the Emeritus Faculty and further to integrate them into the life of the University.

To encourage and facilitate their involvement with the students and active faculty.

To develop a variety of formats for teaching by Emeriti, including participation in established courses as guest lecturer[s] or discussant[s], and the offering of seminars reflecting individual interests and expertise.

To assist with the arrangement of teaching assignments for those interested in teaching (compensation for teaching will be at the customary rates set by the Provost and prorated based on the percentage of a course taught).

To support Emeriti in the continuation of research and scholarly writing, and to provide small grants to promote such activities.

To provide technical and instructional assistance with computer problems. There will be a part-time computer assistant at the Center.

To provide assistance in interactions with the administrative departments of the University.

Source: http://www.yale.edu/emeritus/index.html (retrieved July 2, 2006).

STRATEGIES THAT FOSTER COLLEGIALITY

Collegiality is seeded and nurtured when faculty interact and get to know each other. Physical locations that attract faculty and enable them to mingle help foster connections, as do structured programs and other similar opportunities for interaction that simultaneously encourage collegiality and nurture the professional growth of participants.

PHYSICAL LOCATIONS THAT BRING PEOPLE TOGETHER

On many campuses, faculty members are separated by physical distance and may find that the only colleagues they see with any regularity are the colleagues in their own buildings. Faculty clubs, in past decades, were popular sites for informal interaction at many institutions but they are decreasing in number. Today, some universities and colleges are developing other attractive options for informal faculty gatherings. Coffee shops in easily accessible academic buildings, or bookstores with specific areas for faculty to meet, support the serendipitous connections that occur when people frequent the same locations. Easily accessible meeting rooms provided in central locations around campus also help colleagues from different parts of campus interact and work together. We offer the following recommendation for bringing faculty together:

Recommendation 36

Provide gathering spaces and meeting rooms at a variety of campus locations to bring faculty members together outside their academic departments for informal interactions.

STRUCTURED OPPORTUNITIES FOR MAKING CONNECTIONS

While faculty members value collegial interaction for the intellectual stimulation it can provide, many of them report that they do not have regular opportunities to get to know their colleagues in other fields or to talk with them. Occasions for gathering and discussing ideas or learning about particular aspects of the institutional mission enhance collegial interaction and professional growth. When colleagues exchange ideas in informal settings their bonds to their institutions are deepened, they learn about possibilities for cross-disciplinary collaboration, and they expand their understanding of the many facets of higher education. Therefore, we offer the following recommendation:

Recommendation 37

Provide structured opportunities for faculty members to interact with colleagues around topics of intellectual interest.

An example of an inexpensive, informal, structured opportunity to enhance collegiality and foster community is offered by one of this book's coauthors. Several years ago, she worked with her colleagues to organize a semester-long biweekly faculty lunchtime seminar titled "The Academic Life." Each week, a specific facet of academic life, such as teaching or institutional citizenship, served as the focus for discussion. Faculty members read several essays in preparation for each session, and then they participated in a facilitated discussion of the topic over lunch. An open invitation, extended to all campus faculty, was received with so much enthusiasm that it resulted in the seminar's being held across several semesters.

Groups Focused on Teaching

Some universities and colleges have organized collegial groups around the teaching mission (Austin, 1992b, 1992c). For example, Miami University of Ohio is one of many institutions that offer programs in which early-career faculty members are awarded year-long fellowships that enable them to participate in seminars on teaching and learning, to conduct teaching projects, to interact with mentors, and to attend regional and national conferences on teaching issues. For years, Miami has hosted a national Lilly Conference on teaching in higher education (see Exhibit 13.5); similar regionally based Lilly Conferences are now available across the country and bring faculty members together from an array of colleges and universities who are all very committed to developing as excellent teachers.

Learning Communities

Learning communities are another structured approach to facilitating collegiality among faculty and fostering professional growth. Again, Miami University of Ohio has shown its leadership with a project, sponsored by the Fund for the Improvement of Postsecondary Education (FIPSE). In this project, groups of faculty interact for sustained periods around issues of mutual interest. Faculty learning communities are either cohort-based (including, for example, department chairs, alumni teaching scholars, and senior faculty) or topic-based. Recent topical faculty learning communities have addressed such issues as using diversity and difference to enhance learning, using technology to improve teaching and learning, and ethics across the curriculum (see http://www.units.muohio.edu/celt/flcs/index.php, retrieved July 2, 2006).

EXHIBIT 13.5. ALUMNI TEACHING SCHOLARS PROGRAM, MIAMI UNIVERSITY OF OHIO

Miami University established the Alumni Teaching Scholars Program in 1978 with the support of a three-year grant from the Lilly Endowment. Since 1982, the Miami Alumni, through the Miami University Fund, have generously supported the Program. The Program won the 1994 Hesburgh Award, given to the best faculty development program that enhances undergraduate education in the United States.

The community assists selected early-career faculty in developing their teaching abilities and interests by enabling them to participate in a two-semester series of special activities and to pursue individual projects related to teaching. The Teaching Scholars receive financial assistance for their projects and reduced teaching assignments during one semester. They select and work with experienced faculty who agree to be mentors and with students who are involved as consultants.

Each Teaching Scholar selects an experienced faculty member to partner as his or her mentor. The mentor can be from the same department or from another department. The structure of the Teaching Scholar–mentor relationship is flexible. For example, mentors and protégés may attend one another's classes, discuss teaching philosophies, and explore University issues together.

Each participant selects one or two student associates who provide student perspectives on the topics and practices covered in the Program.

Source: http://www.units.muohio.edu/celt/flcs/miami/flc-atsearly.php (retrieved July 2, 2006).

The Washington Center for Improving the Quality of Undergraduate Education, at Evergreen State College, also is a national leader in developing and modeling the use of faculty learning communities as a vehicle for fostering collegiality while addressing curriculum reform, assessment, and faculty development. These efforts are embedded in the center's mission to support "collaborative, low-cost, highly effective approaches to educational reform" (see http://www.evergreen.edu/washcenter/about1.asp, retrieved July 2, 2006).

Some institutions' learning communities help faculty members learn more about the institution or the academic profession while also helping them develop more collegial connections. In a program originally supported by FIPSE, the University of Wisconsin offers faculty and graduate students the opportunity to participate in expeditionary learning groups, in which participants visit different parts of campus in order to learn more about each other's work and about the university (see Exhibit 13.6).

From 1989 to 1996, approximately eighty-five faculty members at Emory University participated in the Luce Seminars, semester-long seminars to build collegiality among faculty across disciplinary boundaries (see Exhibit 13.7). Most were awarded release time to support their involvement in this project. A case study written about the program highlighted its benefits:

> As a unique program of faculty learning that traversed disciplinary perspectives in a structured way, the Luce Seminars encouraged a deep level of intellectual community across disciplines and sent a signal of the university's support for intellectual growth among its faculty [Frost and Jean, 1999].

EXHIBIT 13.6. EXPEDITIONS IN LEARNING, UNIVERSITY OF WISCONSIN

The program is designed to foster a community of peers that will work together in groups of 7–9 in weekly meetings for one semester. Every other week, participants will head out on campus on an "expedition" to experience a learning activity or environment that will help to stretch their understanding of diverse approaches to learning and teaching. In the weeks between the expeditions, the small groups will come together to engage in a facilitated discussion of what they experienced the previous week, what they learned, and the implications it may have for their teaching. Occasionally, the discussions will be supplemented by a short reading.

In addition to the weekly meetings, participants will be invited to monthly Roundtable dinners with all other groups from other Delta teaching and learning programs, courses, and opportunities. These dinners will bring people together to build community, further explore common and provocative topics in teaching, learning, and research in a different venue, and spark new ideas and questions for deeper discussion in their small groups.

Source: http://www.delta.wisc.edu/Programs/EL/explrn.html (retrieved July 2, 2006).

EXHIBIT 13.7. LUCE SEMINARS, EMORY UNIVERSITY

The Luce Seminars program was designed to support structured intellectual conversation among faculty members across disciplines over an eight-year period (1988–1996). The program was funded in part by a grant from the Henry Luce Foundation. As Henry Luce Professor, theologian James Gustafson led discussions centered on semester-long themes such as "nature" and "responsibility." The leader carefully designed the syllabus, readings, and format to reflect both participant input and a mix [of] disciplinary perspectives appropriate to the sequence of materials and discussions.

Source: Frost and Jean, 1999.

Social Opportunities

Opportunities to make connections often occur around shared interest in an intellectual topic or a particular area of faculty responsibility such as teaching, but other occasions to connect faculty members with each other are simply social. Early-career faculty members often enjoy social events that enable them to meet and mingle. Occasional social gatherings that bring together colleagues in a department or college enhance morale and help faculty members feel connected and valued. Once each semester, for example, faculty members at one college sponsor a poetry reading for faculty and students. Faculty picnics to start or end an academic year can be used to celebrate the beginning of a new academic season or the successful accomplishment of a year of work while also bringing faculty members together to enjoy each other's company and deepen their collegial connections. Inviting faculty members' families to participate in social activities also makes participation easier for those with personal commitments and signals that the culture is supportive of faculty members' personal lives.

CONCLUDING THOUGHTS

Faculty members have a right to expect collegiality and a responsibility to demonstrate it. When colleges and universities foster inclusion and collegial communication, and when they provide opportunities for faculty members to make connections with each other, the benefits accrue both for the institution and the individual faculty member. Faculty members' engagement with their colleagues produces new ideas, thus enriching the intellectual climate of the entire community.

Collegiality stands as one of the five essential elements of an academic workplace, and, like each of the elements, it stimulates activity on behalf of all the others. For example, by fostering good communication and positive interactions, collegiality certainly encourages a climate where academic freedom flourishes. Collegial interactions also lead to cross-campus initiatives on behalf of excellent teaching and interdisciplinary research ventures. Thus, a college or university's efforts to achieve a collegial community is a crucial and lasting investment in its most precious resource: its faculty members and the intellectual capital they bring to their campus and their work.

CHAPTER FOURTEEN

WHY RETHINK FACULTY WORK AND WORKPLACES?
A Call to Action

In baseball, successful managers recognize the importance of each player, from the star shortstop to the intimidating closer to the second-string infielder. They, in turn, get players to perform at their best by helping them understand and respect their roles as well as their importance to the team. Likewise, if they are to form a winning team, players need to value their teammates' unique roles. The pitcher, for example, cannot defend the entire playing field; he needs help from his teammates when a ball is put into play.

Players must also put effort into maintaining good working relationships with their teammates. Outfielders, for example, must know how to communicate effectively with each other when a fly ball is threatening to drop between them. And although individual players must be able to function autonomously in their roles, they must also work as team players with a common vision of a winning season. They must be ready to assist someone who is playing with an injury or step in to fill the shoes of someone who must miss a game.

This analogy, although simple, shares many similarities with the importance of supporting and valuing all of an institution's faculty members. Dramatic changes are occurring in higher education and in the environments where colleges and universities operate. Institutions are trying to educate a more diverse student body, produce more research, and engage more meaningfully with the public while simultaneously facing dramatic fiscal constraints. External demands for increased accountability are strong, and technology, despite its powerful advantages, demands ever-increasing fiscal resources while changing the traditional ways in which faculty work.

As institutions seek to manage these changes, the faculty, their key asset, has also changed. Tenured and tenure-track faculty are no longer the majority in many institutions; they are increasingly replaced with faculty in renewable-contract or fixed-term appointments, and today's new faculty are also more diverse in their backgrounds and work-life situations.

These changes, taken as a whole, translate into a workplace and a workforce of a very different kind from what was common a few decades ago. Nevertheless, colleges and universities have been slow to adapt their policies and practices to reflect this new reality. Important faculty traditions, such as protection of academic freedom and collegial communities of scholars, often do not encompass those who are off the tenure track. In addition, cultural norms and practices underlying faculty employment still largely reflect the outdated concept of an ideal worker who is fully committed to his or her career and who has few other responsibilities.

For some faculty members, particularly those who are already tenured, the essential elements presented in this book are already in place, and job satisfaction is high. For others—for example, those who do not have tenure-track appointments, or those who are on the tenure track and also have significant caregiving responsibilities—a faculty career is often less attractive and satisfying, in large part because these faculty do not always experience fully the essential elements of equity, academic freedom and autonomy, flexibility, professional growth, and collegiality.

Our purpose in writing this book has been twofold: to rethink faculty work and workplaces, and to propose a framework that can embrace the rich diversity of faculty members and appointment types while also retaining the key features of traditional academic appointments that have made America's faculty the envy of the world. We have sought, by rethinking the essential elements of faculty workplaces, to articulate the outlines of a framework that can preserve and enhance the talents that every faculty member brings to his or her college or university. From our perspective, the way to do this is to maximize the presence of these elements as key components of the faculty workplace. In this, the final chapter, we briefly revisit our key themes to emphasize why change is needed now.

WHY IS RETHINKING ACADEMIC WORK AND WORKPLACES A STRATEGIC IMPERATIVE?

Colleges and universities must rethink academic work and workplaces for several strategic reasons. Institutions make enormous investments in the intellectual capital that faculty represent because faculty are the means through which institutions achieve their missions. Naturally, colleges and universities want to benefit fully from the array of talents that faculty have to offer. In fact, demands on the higher education sector are so great today that institutions must have top-notch faculty in order to achieve their outcomes. Therefore, attention to effective ways of enhancing the intellectual capital represented in the faculty is critical.

Establishing effective ways to support faculty is a challenging task, however, because so much has changed. Faculty members today are different from who they used to be. What attracted ideal workers to the academic career in the past is different from what attracts individuals to the academic career today. Faculty appointments have also changed, as have general societal understandings and expectations of work. Any efforts to support faculty must acknowledge and respond to these changes if all faculty members are to contribute at the highest possible level to the work of their institutions. Today's diversity of faculty members and appointment types demands that colleges and universities have a variety of policies and practices in place that enable people to do the work they are capable of doing.

In sum, we must rethink academic work and workplaces because of the enormous investment in intellectual capital that faculty represent, and because the needs of today's faculty are more diverse than were those of previous generations of faculty. We must also rethink academic work and workplaces because the desirability of a faculty career may be diminishing. Historically, a faculty career has been considered a very desirable profession. This perception has allowed the academy to consistently attract outstanding people, despite competition from other employers. We must ensure that an academic career remains an attractive choice because colleges and universities, as well as society at large, need talented and committed individuals to serve as faculty members. To accomplish this aim, we must find ways to keep academic work meaningful and satisfying for all faculty members and potential recruits, regardless of their diverse characteristics or appointment types.

But what if colleges and universities choose to do nothing in response to this rapidly changing environment? Institutional leaders must understand that doing nothing is in fact a choice, and that the negative consequences of this choice may be substantial. It is shortsighted to believe that these dramatic changes in the academic workplace and workforce will permit business as usual:

- When an institution offers inequitable pay to faculty members who work in fixed-term appointments, and when it provides them with minimal support services and treats them with little respect, it can hardly expect that these faculty members will feel highly committed to the institution and its mission. The institution has not demonstrated a high commitment to them.
- When faculty members off the tenure track believe that because their academic freedom is not protected, they cannot speak freely as they teach their courses, some of their enthusiasm in the classroom may be stifled.
- When institutions do not offer professional development opportunities to faculty members in all types of appointments, non-tenure-eligible faculty do not acquire the insights and new information that could strengthen their teaching and research. Similarly, when departmental colleagues do not include these faculty members in work groups and roundtable discussions, the departmental synergy is lost that could have resulted from bringing together varied perspectives, and these faculty members are likely to feel alienated from the work of their units.
- When a faculty member has a tenure-track position and two preschoolers at home, she may find that there is not adequate time to manage either role well. The absence of flexible policies may keep her from being able to reconfigure her work responsibilities for a few years in order to more effectively take care of household and child care responsibilities. This

situation may ultimately cause her to leave the institution and the academic career to which she has much to contribute.

- When an African American faculty member carries a heavier advising load and sits on more committees than most of his peers, when he feels that his research is not understood by his colleagues, or when he is seldom invited to join informal conversations with his departmental colleagues, he probably will not feel valued as a scholar in his department. As a result, concerns about tenure reviews, frustration with colleagues, and intellectual isolation may lead him to question the decision to work at that institution. He may begin looking for a position at an institution where he believes he will be more respected and more readily accepted.

These scenarios can and do arise when an institutional culture continues to project the message that only those on the tenure track truly matter, and that only those who dedicate their entire lives to academic work are sufficiently committed to their careers to be able to make valuable contributions to their fields. Also, this mismatch between long-standing norms and the realities of today's diverse workforce can lead to suboptimal environments where not all faculty members are supported in ways that let them do their best work.

How Do Institutions Create Academic Workplaces That Attract Excellent Faculty?

Step 1: Recognizing Opportunities

The first step in creating an attractive academic workplace is to view the changes highlighted throughout this book not just as tremendous challenges for colleges and universities but also as opportunities. Institutions must rethink the question of how to support academic work if they are to strategically benefit from the opportunities that all faculty members bring with them.

For example, hiring two faculty members into one shared position, or into two positions at less than full time, could mean an institution is securing two sets of expertise rather than one. Likewise, creating a research team from a mix of contract-renewable, fixed term, and tenure-track faculty could allow an institution to pull together a particularly strong group because the individuals would bring different professional backgrounds and interests to solving a particular problem.

The diverse characteristics of today's faculty members present tremendous opportunities for colleges and universities. Women faculty, and faculty who are members of ethnic and racial minorities, arrive with experiences and backgrounds different from those of their white male colleagues. They approach the courses they teach with unique perspectives and styles. The lines of research that they pursue, or their interpretations of the implications of research results, can add a richness to knowledge production that would not be achievable with a more homogeneous faculty. Moreover, increased diversity among future and early-career faculty gives colleges and universities opportunities to hire faculties that reflect the diversity that already exists in their student bodies.

Investing in every member of the faculty is a critically important strategic decision aimed at making the most of a time of new opportunities. We challenge institutions to take advantage of the broad range of skills, talents, and experiences that nontraditional faculty members have to offer, and to support them so that they can make their fullest possible contributions to the work of their institutions.

STEP 2: CREATING A CULTURE OF RESPECT

The second step in creating an attractive academic workplace is to establish a culture where every faculty member is valued and respected. The faculty is no longer made up of a core—tenure-track faculty, who do the real work—supplemented by expendable add-ons in the form of faculty in fixed-term or renewable contract appointments, who support the work of the core. Rather, the goals of the institution can be accomplished only when the contributions of every faculty member are viewed as important and when all faculty members are valued contributors to the institution's vision. If this fundamental step is accomplished, changes in many other facets of an institution's culture will follow naturally.

Respecting every faculty member means, for example, that fixed-term faculty are viewed not just as "corks" to plug holes in the curriculum. A part-time faculty member who cares for a dying parent on a full-time basis, and who teaches only a few courses each year, may offer students, in addition to thoughtful teaching about the subject at hand, an invaluable perspective on life and death and the process of establishing personal priorities. A full-time employee of a financial firm who teaches an investments course at night may provide unique insights into succeeding in a financial career that no member of the department's full-time faculty could offer.

Likewise, full-time faculty members working under renewable-contracts add value to faculty resources. An engineering research professor may have spent fifteen years working in industry before accepting a position at the institution. Because of her experience working on teams and in a for-profit environment, she may offer important insights to her tenure-track colleagues as they conduct interdisciplinary research and develop grant proposals together.

STEP 3: RESHAPING THE INSTITUTION'S CULTURE

The third important step in creating an academic workplace that attracts and retains excellent faculty involves taking concrete steps to reshape the institutional culture. Faculty and administrators together need to examine and update policies and practices to reflect the characteristics of today's workers. In practical terms, creating an attractive workplace means including faculty members in fixed-term and renewable-contract appointments among the nominees for teaching, research, and service awards and opening up professional development opportunities to them as well. It means considering the needs of all faculty members when administrative support services are assigned in a department. It means moving away from traditional norms and toward a culture that values the heterogeneity of today's faculty and faculty appointments. It means creating desirable opportunities for less than full-time work and holding colleagues to be respectful to each other and accountable for their behavior. In sum, when everyone is treated equitably, has academic freedom, and is welcomed into a collegial community, the academic workplace becomes one where everyone's talents and skills are supported and respected.

HOW MUCH WILL THIS COST?

We would be remiss if we did not acknowledge that some of the recommendations we have made regarding the essential elements require additional resources from institutions that are already experiencing significant financial challenges. Paid leaves, more equity in faculty salaries, some benefits for fixed-term faculty, and the allocation of additional assigned time for faculty development or shared governance are examples of recommendations that require reallocation of or additional financial resources.

Institutions will clearly have to prioritize the changes they want to make in their workplaces, given their financial constraints, and creatively consider how to fund the initiatives they initially choose to pursue. One institution may determine that providing more equitable salaries for those in contract-renewable appointments must be its priority, whereas another may decide that it will offer more paid leaves. Still another may begin by focusing on changes that require little in the way of an initial financial investment, such as revisions in professional development program emphases or the opening up of campus awards to faculty members in new appointment types. Similarly, some academic departments may decide to reconfigure their workload policies to allow release time on a rotating basis for professional growth, and others may revise their traditional orientation programs to include new faculty outside the tenure system. The essential elements comprise a large agenda, with many options for where to start and how to proceed. The point is to get started and keep going.

Leaders will also need to consider whether new policies and practices will be funded centrally or by individual departments. As discussed in Chapter Eleven, experience shows that central funding is essential to ensure equity in the matter of who benefits from institutional policies and practices. Centralized funding also ensures that new programs and policies are equally available campuswide, and it discourages resource-rich departments from offering more generous work-life policies than those units with fewer resources. It also keeps departments that have a high percentage of women faculty members from needing to come up with unusually large amounts of the necessary funds to support leaves for caregiving purposes, thus depleting resources for other important activities.

That said, most of our recommendations do not in fact require substantial resources. Creating opportunities for faculty to develop a collegial environment in a department, extending the protections of academic freedom to all faculty members, formalizing policies related to extension of the tenure clock, permitting career breaks, and developing a culture of respect for all faculty members all require little or no funds but can have a substantial impact on the academic workplace. Most of our recommendations require, more than anything else, goodwill, creative thinking, and a commitment to reshaping the culture.

One final point must be made regarding costs. Most of the costs just described are easily measurable, but very real costs are also associated with doing nothing. The costs of doing nothing are not generally viewed as expenses against scarce institutional resources, however, nor are they as easily defined. For example, it is expensive to replace a faculty member who has left because she was not able to take a leave or because he did not feel respected or equitably treated. To hire a replacement requires time for conducting a search and interviews, and time is money. Departmental faculty will spend hours reviewing credentials, discussing applicants, and narrowing the search to finalists, and this is time that could be spent on other work. The expense of bringing the finalists to the campus add to the overall costs, as does the faculty and staff time expended in the interview process. Once a person is chosen, a competitive salary offer will most likely match closely or exceed the salary of the previous incumbent and will also include relocation expenses and a start-up package. In addition, there are costs associated with a possible decline in morale resulting from a faculty member's departure, although these are difficult to measure. Many institutions that examine their turnover data may come to the conclusion that incorporating policies and practices in keeping with the suggestions made throughout this book is a better use of scarce resources than continuing to spend large amounts of money replacing dissatisfied faculty who have departed.

Moreover, turnover is not the only cost of doing nothing. Institutions must also realize that it is expensive to employ faculty members who eventually decide to do the bare minimum in their work because they feel that their institutions are unwilling to invest in their futures. Costs, in terms of decreased productivity or increased health care expenditures, can be substantial for faculty members who are under enormous stress because they are not able to adjust their work responsibilities to address family needs or make midcareer changes in work priorities to pursue new interests. Costs can also be significant for faculty members who feel isolated and stagnant in their work because they do not benefit from close relationships with their colleagues. These very real costs should be considered when resources are allocated. Institutions need to see their financial investments in faculty as investments in excellence and institutional health.

WHO IS RESPONSIBLE FOR MAKING THE CHANGES?

Every member of an institution must take responsibility for making the changes that we have argued for in this book. Each person, within his or her own domain of influence, needs to be a responsible team member and respond proactively to the changing workforce and workplace. For example, presidents champion changes in policies, practices, and programs by speaking or writing about them for institutional and external audiences. Presidents also have numerous opportunities to convey respect and admiration for the multifaceted accomplishments of all faculty members. Provosts and deans play key roles by insisting on adherence to new policy initiatives in their respective domains, by allocating funds in support of new policies and programs, and by formally recognizing the accomplishments of faculty across appointment types. Department chairs determine the culture of the departments to a large degree. They also ensure equity in the treatment of faculty members by providing each person with adequate office space and administrative support, and by supervising peer-review processes. Faculty members collectively and individually play key roles in making change happen through their leadership in shared governance at all levels and in all academic units of their campuses, and through their actions to foster communities where collegiality and respect flourish.

In sum, it will take the committed efforts of individuals across the campus to replace "ideal worker" and "ideal appointment" norms with norms reflecting the belief that every member of the faculty represents important intellectual capital for the institution. Administrators alone cannot mandate widespread respect for each faculty member, nor can the institution truly extend academic freedom to every faculty member if, for example, tenure peer-review committees are unwilling to support those who pursue a nontraditional research agenda, no matter how excellent their work. Likewise, a department chair cannot recruit new faculty members with young children by promising a flexible work environment and family-friendly policies if the central administration is unwilling to allocate financial support that enables faculty to utilize these policies.

In addition, when everyone works together to reshape the environment, the institution is more likely to realize the interactive effects of the essential elements. The result of all the elements together is much greater than their individual contributions because each element supports the realization of other elements. For example, when more opportunities for professional development are available, collegiality is likely to be enhanced simply because faculty members often spend time together as they learn. Likewise, when flexible policies are established and promoted, a more equitable workplace is likely to result because all faculty members will now be in a better position to do their best work.

WHY WORRY NOW? WHAT'S THE HURRY?

Colleges and universities are not likely to return to an employment system built on the concept that one size fits all. We do not know what the characteristics of higher education will be in twenty or thirty years, but the environment doubtless will continue to be volatile. It may be that much of the teaching will be performed by for-profit institutions and that a majority of students will learn through distance education. Perhaps many private and some public institutions will have closed their doors because they were unable to maintain financial viability, and this situation will have led to a very different infrastructure of higher education in this country.

What we do know is that the pace of societal change is unlikely to be slow enough to allow institutions more time than they have now to make decisions or adjust to new demands. It is also unlikely that the financial picture for higher education will improve greatly, at least in the near future. It is unlikely as well that faculty will be anything but more diverse in terms of who they are and the positions they fill.

We also know that the work that colleges and universities traditionally have done will continue to be critical to society. In the future, America will need an educated citizenry more than ever, and the demand for new knowledge will probably only increase. Therefore, colleges and universities must strategically pursue a course of recognizing and understanding the significance of the changes taking place instead of simply letting the environment control them or operating as if the environment were not changing. They must create supportive work environments that utilize the talents of all faculty members as fully as possible, and they must do so in a timely manner, something that is often difficult for colleges and universities.

Our recommendations for incorporating the essential elements into faculty work and workplaces build on the traditional values underlying the academic career, including academic freedom, sufficient permanence to engage in thoughtful long-term work, continuous professional development, and collegiality in a scholarly community. If institutions are to continue attracting and retaining excellent faculty, they must now extend these traditional concepts to more diverse faculty members working in a variety of appointment types. They must also incorporate heightened attention to equitable treatment and flexibility in order to fully reflect the structural and cultural changes that have taken place in the academy. The essential elements proposed in this book can guide decision making and prepare colleges and universities for the many uncertainties that they will surely face in the future.

Nevertheless, the essential elements represent only the beginning of the resourcefulness needed to establish attractive workplaces for today's faculty. If institutions are to continue attracting and retaining excellent faculty from diverse backgrounds, and if they are to more strategically utilize the intellectual capital that all faculty members represent, they must squarely and creatively address the challenges today's higher education environment presents. We hope that these essential elements will be helpful tools in that endeavor.

References

Aguirre, A. (2000). *Women and minority faculty in the academic workplace: Recruitment, retention and academic culture.* ASHE-ERIC Higher Education Report, Volume 27, No. 6. San Francisco: Jossey-Bass.

Alderfer, C. P. (1972). *Existence, relatedness and growth: Human needs in organizational settings.* New York: Free Press.

Altbach, P. G. (1999). Harsh realities: The professoriate faces a new century. In P. G. Altbach, R. O. Berdahl, & P. J. Gumport (Eds.), *American higher education in the twenty-first century: Social, political, and economic challenges.* Baltimore: The Johns Hopkins University Press.

Alter, J. (1991). Retaining women CPAs [Electronic version]. *Journal of Accountancy, 171*(5), 50–55.

American Association of University Professors. (2001a). Statement on collective bargaining. In *AAUP Policy Documents and Reports* (9th ed.). Washington, DC: American Association of University Professors.

American Association of University Professors. (2001b). Statement on government of colleges and universities (1966). In *AAUP Policy Documents and Reports* (9th ed.). Washington, DC: American Association of University Professors.

American Association of University Professors. (2001c). Statement on principles of academic freedom and tenure (1940). In *AAUP Policy Documents and Reports* (9th ed.). Washington, DC: American Association of University Professors.

American Association of University Professors. (2001d). Statement on professional ethics (1987). In *AAUP Policy Documents and Reports* (9th ed.). Washington, DC: American Association of University Professors.

American Association of University Professors. (2003). *AAUP policy statement: Contingent appointments and the academic profession.* Retrieved August 18, 2005, from http://www.aaup.org/statements/SpchState/Statements/contingent.htm

American Council on Education. (2005). *An agenda for excellence: Creating flexibility in tenure-track faculty careers.* Washington, DC: Author.

American Federation of Teachers and the National Education Association. (2005). *The truth about unions and shared governance* [brochure]. Washington, DC: Author.

Armenti, C. (2004). May babies and posttenure babies: Maternal decisions of women professors. *The Review of Higher Education, 27*(2), 211–231.

Armour, S. (2004). Some moms quit as offices scrap family-friendliness. *USA Today.* Retrieved May 5, 2004 from http://www.usatoday.com/money/workplace/2004-05-03-working-moms.htm.

Arnolds, C. A., & Boshoff, C. (2000). Does higher remuneration equal higher job performance? An empirical assessment of the need-progression proposition in selected need theories. *South African Journal of Business Management, 31*(2), 53–64.

Association of American Colleges and Universities. (2005). *Academic freedom and educational responsibility* (AAC&U Board of Directors' Statement). Retrieved April 2, 2006, from http://www.aacu.org/press_room/press_releases/2006/AacdFreedom.cfm

Astin, H. S., & Milem, J. F. (1997). The status of academic couples in U.S. institutions. In M. A. Ferber & J. W. Loeb (Eds.), *Academic couples: Problems and promises* (pp. 128–155). Urbana: University of Illinois.

Austin, A. E. (1991). Faculty values, faculty cultures. In W. Tierney (Ed.), *Assessing academic climates and cultures.* New Directions for Institutional Research Series, No. 68. San Francisco: Jossey-Bass.

Austin, A. E. (1992a). Faculty cultures. In B. R. Clark & G. Neave (Series Eds.) & A. I. Morey (Vol. Ed.), *The encyclopedia of higher education: Vol. 4.* New York: Pergamon Press.

Austin, A. E. (1992b). Supporting junior faculty through a teaching fellows program. In M. D. Sorcinelli & A. E. Austin (Eds.), *Developing new and junior faculty.* New Directions for Teaching and Learning Series, No. 50. San Francisco: Jossey-Bass.

Austin, A. E. (1992c). Supporting the professor as teacher: The Lilly teaching fellows program. *The Review of Higher Education, 16*(1), 85–106.

Austin, A. E. (1994). Understanding and assessing faculty cultures and climates. In M. K. Kinnick (Ed.), *Providing useful information for deans and department chairs.* New Directions for Institutional Research Series, No. 84. San Francisco: Jossey-Bass.

Austin, A. E. (1996). Institutional and departmental cultures and the relationship between teaching and research. In J. Braxton. (Ed.), *Faculty teaching and research: Is there a conflict?* New Directions for Institutional Research Series, No. 90. San Francisco: Jossey-Bass.

Austin, A. E. (2002). Preparing the next generation of faculty; graduate education as socialization to the academic career. *The Journal of Higher Education, 73*(2), 94–122.

Austin, A. E. (2003). Creating a bridge to the future: Preparing new faculty to face changing expectations in a shifting content. *Review of Higher Education, 26*(2), 119–144.

Austin, A. E., & Rice, R. E. (1998). Making tenure viable: Listening to early career faculty. *American Behavioral Scientist, 41*(5), 736–754.

Austin, A. E., Rice, R. E., & Splete, A. P., with Associates. (1991). *A good place to work: Sourcebook for the academic workplace.* Washington, DC: The Council of Independent Colleges.

Bailyn, L. (1993). *Breaking the mold: Women, men, and time in the new corporate world.* New York: The Free Press.

Bailyn, L., Drago, R., & Kochan, T. A. (2001). *Integrating work and family life: A holistic approach.* Retrieved September 19, 2002, from http://mitsloan.mit.edu/iwer/WorkFamily.pdf

Bailyn, L., & Fletcher, J. K. (1997). Unexpected connections: Considering employees' personal lives can revitalize your business [Electronic version]. *Sloan Management Review, 38*(4), 11–19.

Baldwin, R. G., & Chronister, J. L. (2001). *Teaching without tenure: Policies and practices for a new era.* Baltimore: Johns Hopkins University Press.

Bankert, E. C., & Googins, B. K. (1996). Family-friendly—says who? *Across the Board, 33*(7), 45–49.

Barnes, L.L.B., Agago, M. O., & Coombs, W. T. (1998). Effects of job-related stress on faculty intention to leave academia. *Research in Higher Education, 39*(4), 457–469.

Barrett, J. T. (2004). *A history of alternative dispute resolution.* San Francisco: Jossey-Bass.

Becher, T. (1984). The cultural view. In B. R. Clark (Ed.), *Perspectives on higher education: Eight disciplinary and comparative views.* Los Angeles: University of California Press.

Becher, T. (1987). Disciplinary shaping of the profession. In B. R. Clark (Ed.), *The academic profession: National, disciplinary, and institutional settings.* Berkeley: University of California Press.

Becher, T., & Trowler, P. R. (2001). *Academic tribes and territories: Intellectual enquiry and the culture of disciplines* (2nd ed.). Buckingham, United Kingdom: The Society for Research into Higher Education & Open University Press.

Benjamin, E. (1998a). Declining faculty availability to students is the problem—but tenure is not the explanation. *American Behavioral Scientist, 41*(5), 716–735.

Benjamin, E. (1998b). Variations in the characteristics of part time faculty by general fields of instruction and research. In D. W. Leslie (Ed.), *The growing use of part-time faculty: Understanding causes and effects.* New Directions for Higher Education, No. 104. San Francisco: Jossey-Bass.

Benjamin, E. (2003). Reappraisal and implications for policy and research. In E. Benjamin (Ed.), *Exploring the role of contingent instructional staff in undergraduate learning.* New Directions for Higher Education, No. 123. San Francisco: Jossey-Bass.

Berger, A., Kirshstein, R., & Rowe, E. (2001). *Institutional policies and practices: Results from the 1999 national study of postsecondary faculty* (NSOPF: 99), Institution survey. *Statistical analysis report* (Report No. NCES-2001–201). Washington, DC: National Center for Education Statistics. Retrieved April 13, 2004, from http://nces.ed.gov/pubs2001/2001201.pdf

Berger, A., Kirshstein, R., Zhang, Y., & Carter, K. (2002). *A profile of part-time faculty: Fall 1998* (NCES Publication No. 2002–08). Washington, DC: U.S. Department of Education, National Center for Education Statistics.

Berquist, W. H., & Phillips, S. R. (1975). Components of an effective faculty development program. *Journal of Higher Education, 46*(2), 177–215.

Black, M. M., & Holden, E. W. (1998). The impact of gender on productivity and satisfaction among medical school psychologists. *Journal of Clinical Psychology in Medical Settings, 5*(1), 117–131.

Blackburn, J. L. (1969). *Perceived purposes of student personnel programs by chief student personnel officers as a function of academic preparation and experience.* Unpublished doctoral dissertation, Florida State University.

Blackburn, R. T., & Lawrence, J. H. (1995). *Faculty at work: Motivation, expectation, satisfaction.* Baltimore: Johns Hopkins University Press.

Bland, C. J., & Berquist, W. H. (1997). *The vitality of senior faculty: Snow on the roof—fire in the furnace.* ASHE-ERIC Higher Education Report, Volume 25, No. 7. Washington, DC: The George Washington University, Graduate School of Education and Human Development.

Bland, C. J., Center, B. A., Finstad, D. A., Risbey, K. R., & Staples, J. (2006). The impact of appointment type on the productivity and commitment of full-time faculty in research and doctoral institutions. *Journal of Higher Education 77*(1), 89–124.

Bland, C. J., & Schmitz, C. C. (1988). Faculty vitality on review: Retrospect and prospect. *Journal of Higher Education, 59*(2), 190–224.

Bluedorn, A. C., & Dernhardt, R. B. (1988). Time and organizations. *Journal of Management, 14,* 299–320.

Boice, R. (1992). *The new faculty member: Supporting and fostering professional development.* San Francisco: Jossey-Bass.

Bolman, L. G., & Deal, T. E. (1997). *Reframing organizations: Artistry, choice and leadership* (2nd ed.). San Francisco: Jossey-Bass.

Bond, J. T., Galinsky, E., & Hill, J. E. (2004). *When work works: Summary of Family and Work Institute research findings.* Retrieved March 29, 2006, from http://familiesandwork.org/3w/research/downloads/3wes.pdf

Bond, J. T., Galinsky, E., & Swanberg, J. (1998). *The 1997 national study of the changing workforce.* New York: Families and Work Institute.

Bond, J. T., Thompson, C., Galinsky, E., & Prottas, D. (2002). *Highlights of the national study of the changing workforce.* New York: Families and Work Institute.

Bonner, F. A. (2004, June 11). Black professors: On the track but out of the loop. *Chronicle of Higher Education,* p. B11.

Borges, W. (2001). Guidelines or physicians' judgment? *Texas Medicine, 97*(7), 35–39.

Bowen, H. R., & Schuster, J. H. (1986). *American professors: A national resource imperiled.* New York: Oxford University Press.

Boyd, D. (2005, June). *State fiscal outlook from 2005 to 2013: Implications for higher education.* Boulder, CO: National Center for Higher Education Management Systems, 2005. Retrieved March 6, 2005, from www.higheredinfo.org/analyses/

Boyer, E. (1990). *Scholarship reconsidered: Priorities of the professoriate.* Princeton, NJ: The Carnegie Foundation for the Advancement of Teaching.

Breneman, D. W. (1997). Alternatives to tenure for the next generation of academics. *New Pathways Working Paper Series #14.* Washington, DC: American Association for Higher Education.

Breneman, D. W., Finney, J. E., & Roherty, B. M. (1997, April). *Shaping the future: Higher education finance in the 1990s.* San Jose, CA: California Higher Education Policy Center.

Brown, J. S. (2002, March/April). Growing up digital: How the web changes work, education, and the way we learn. *Change,* pp. 11–20.

Bryne, J. P. (1997). Academic freedom without tenure? *New Pathways Working Paper Series no. 5.* Washington, DC: American Association for Higher Education.

Bryne, J. P. (2001). Academic freedom of part-time faculty. *The Journal of College and University Law, 27*(3), 583–593.

Catalyst. (1998). *Advancing women in business—the Catalyst guide: Best practices from the corporate leaders.* San Francisco: Jossey-Bass.

California State University. (2002, July). *A plan to increase the percentage of tenured and tenure-track faculty in the California State University.* Retrieved January 2, 2006, from www.calstate.edu/AcadSen/Records/Reports/ACR73_07222002.pdf

Campbell, A., & Koblenz, M. (1997). *The work and life pyramid of needs.* Deerfield, IL: Baxter Healthcare Corporation & MK Consultants.

Chait, R. P. (1994, January). Creating incentives for faculty to forsake tenure. *Association of Governing Boards of Universities and Colleges,* pp. 28–34.

Chait, R. P. (1995, spring). The future of academic tenure. *AGB Priorities 3,* 1–11.

Chait, R. P. (1998). Ideas in incubation: Three possible modifications to traditional tenure policies. *New Pathways Working Paper Series no. 9.* Washington, DC: American Association for Higher Education.

Chait, R. P. (Ed.). (2002). *The question of tenure.* Cambridge, MA: Harvard University Press.

Chait, R. P., & Ford, A. T. (1982). *Beyond traditional tenure.* San Francisco: Jossey-Bass.

Chait, R. P., & Trower, C. A. (1997). Where tenure does not reign. *New Pathways Working Paper Series, No. 3.* Washington, DC: American Association for Higher Education.

Chait, R. P., & Trower, C.A. (1998). Build it and who will come? *Change, 30*(5) 20–29.

Christensen, K. E., & Gomory, R. E. (1999). *New economy: Three jobs, two people.* San Francisco: The Congress for the New Urbanism. Retrieved October 12, 2003, from http://www.cnu.org/pdf/Christensen.pdf

Chronister, J. L., & Baldwin, R. G. (1999). Marginal or mainstream? Full-time faculty off the tenure track. *Liberal Education, 85*(4), 16–23.

Cintrón, L. (1999). *Professional pathways: Examining work, family and community in the biotechnology industry: An executive summary.* Retrieved July 5, 2006, from http://www.radcliffe.edu/research/pubpol/Professional Pathways.pdf

Clark, B. R. (1987). *The academic life: Small worlds, different worlds.* Princeton, NJ: The Carnegie Foundation for the Advancement of Teaching.

Clark, B. R. (1997). Small worlds, different worlds: The uniquenesses and troubles of American academic professionals. *Daedalus, 126*(4), 21–42.

Clotfelter, C. T. (2002). Can faculty be induced to relinquish tenure? In R. P. Chait (Ed.), *The questions of tenure.* Cambridge, MA: Harvard University Press.

Cohen, A. M. (1998). *The shaping of American higher education: Emergence and growth of the contemporary system.* San Francisco: Jossey-Bass.

Cohen, A. R., & Gadon, H. (1978). *Alternative work schedules: Integrating individual and organizational needs.* Reading, MA: Addison-Wesley.

Colbeck, C. L., Weaver, L. D., & Burkum, K. R. (2004, November). *How female and male faculty with families manage work and personal roles.* Paper presented at the annual meeting of the Association for the Study of Higher Education, Kansas City, MO.

College of the Canyons. (2006). *The associate program: A program of professional development exclusively for adjunct faculty.* Retrieved April 2, 2006, from http://www.canyons.edu/offices/asso_prog

Committee on Non-Tenure Track Faculty, University of North Carolina. (2002, March 6). *Report and recommendations: Presented to the Personnel Committee of the University of North Carolina Board of Governors Report.* Retrieved March 28, 2006, from http://www.northcarolina.edu/content.php/aa/reports/ntt_faculty/BOG_NTT_Faculty_Report.pdf

Conlin, M. (2000, September 18). The new debate over working moms. *Business Week,* pp. 102–104.

Connell, M. A., & Savage, F. G. (2001). Does collegiality count? *Academe, 87*(6), 37–40.

Cooper, J. E., & Stevens, D. D. (Eds.). (2002). *Tenure in the sacred grove: Issues and strategies for women and minority faculty.* Albany: State University of New York Press.

Cooper, M. (2000). Being the "go-to guy": Fatherhood, masculinity, and the organization of work in Silicon Valley [Electronic version]. *Qualitative Sociology, 23*(4), 379–405.

Costello, M. A. (1997). Women in the legal profession: You've come a long way—or have you? [Electronic version]. Detroit College of Law at Michigan State University *Law Review, 3,* 909–915.

Crittenden, A. (2001). *The price of motherhood.* New York: Henry Holt.

Cunningham, K. (2001). Father time: Flexible work arrangements and the law firm's failure of the family [Electronic version]. *Stanford Law Review, 53,* 967–1008.

Curry, A. (2003, February 24/March 3). Why we work. *U.S. News and World Report,* pp. 49–56.

Damrosch, D. (1995). *We scholars: Changing the culture of the university.* Cambridge, MA: Harvard University Press.

Department of Defense Directive. (1988). Number 1400.33. [on-line]. Retrieved August, 2, 2002, from http://usmilitary.about.com/library/milinfo/dodreg1400–33.htm

Didion, C. J. (1996). Dual-careers and shared positions: Adjusting university policy to accommodate academic couples. *Journal of College Science Teaching, 26*(2), 123–124.

Dimitrova, D. (1994). Work, commitment and alienation. *International Social Science Journal, 46*(2), 201–211.

Donohue, J. D. (1986). Faculty perceptions of organizational climate and expressed job satisfaction in selected baccalaureate schools of nursing. *Journal of Professional Nursing, 2*(6), 373–379.

Downey, D., March, T., Berkman, A., & Steinauer, J. M. (2001). The keys to retention [Electronic version]. *Incentive, 175*(10), 117–118.

Drago, R., & Colbeck, C. (2003). *Final report from the mapping project: Exploring the terrain of U.S. colleges and universities for faculty and families.* Retrieved July 29, 2006, from http://lsir.la.psu.edu/workfam/MAPexecsummary.doc

Drago, R., & Williams, J. (2000). A half-time tenure track proposal. *Change, 32*(6), 47–51.

Duderstadt, J. J. (2000). *A university for the 21st century.* Ann Arbor: University of Michigan Press.

Eckel, P. D., Couturier, L., & Luu, D. T. (2005). *Peering around the bend: The leadership challenges of privatization, accountability, and market-based state policy.* Washington, DC: American Council on Education.

Elias, M. (2004). The family-first generation. *USA Today.* Retrieved May 25, 2005, from http://www.usatoday.com/life/lifestyle/2004-12-12-generation-usat_x.htm?POE=click-refer

Euben, D. R. (2002). Academic freedom: Whose right? Reprinted in K. F. Brevitz, B. A. Snow, & W. E. Thro, Eds. (2003). *The 2003 NACUA handbook for lawyers new to higher education.* Washington DC: The National Association of College and University Attorneys.

Euben, D. R. (2004, February). *Academic freedom and professorial speech.* Paper presented at the annual conference on Law and Higher Education, Stetson University, College of Law. Retrieved May 16, 2005, from http://www.aaup.org/Legal/info%20outlines/AF&profspeech.htm retrieved 5/16/05.

Faculty hiring in recent years has focused on part-timers at for-profit colleges, report suggests. (2005, May 20). *Chronicle of Higher Education.*

Finkel, S. K., & Olswang, S. G. (1996). Child rearing as a career impediment to women assistant professors. *The Review of Higher Education, 19*(2), 123–139.

Finkelstein, M. J. (1984). *The American academic profession.* Columbus: The Ohio State University Press.

Finkelstein, M. J. (2003). The morphing of the American academic profession. *Liberal Education, 89*(4), 6–15.

Finkelstein, M. J., Liu, M., & Schuster, J. H. (2003, November). *The career trajectories of current part-time and full-time faculty: Mobility across employment and appointment statuses.* Paper presented at the annual meeting of the Association for the Study of Higher Education, Portland, OR.

Finkelstein, M. J., & Schuster, J. H. (2001). Assessing the silent revolution: How changing demographics are reshaping the academic profession. *AAHE Bulletin, 54*(2), 3–7.

Fisher, R., & Ury, W. (1981). *Getting to yes: Negotiating agreement without giving in.* Boston: Houghton Mifflin.

Fortney, S. S. (2000). Soul for sale: An empirical study of associate satisfaction, law firm culture, and the effects of billable hour requirements [Electronic version]. *University of Missouri at Kansas City Law Review, 69,* 239–309.

Fried, Y., & Ferris, G. R. (1987). The validity of the job characteristics model: A review and meta-analysis. *Personnel Psychology, 40,* 287–322.

Friedman, D. E. (n.d.). *Workplace flexibility: A guide for companies.* Retrieved March 31, 2006, from http://www.whenworkworks.org

Froom, J. D., & Bickel, J. (1996). Medical school policies for part-time faculty committed to full professional effort. *Academic Medicine, 71*(1), 92–96.

Frost, S. H., & Jean, P. M. (1999, August). *Intellectual community across disciplines: Structural support for faculty culture.* Paper presented at the conference of the European Association for Institutional Research, Lund, Sweden. Retrieved April 2, 2006, from http://www.emory.edu/PROVOST/IPR/faculty/EAIR99final.htm

Fulton, R. D. (2000, May/June). The plight of part-timers in higher education: Some ruminations and suggestions. *Change Magazine, 32*(3), 39–43.

Gaff, J. G. (1975). *Toward faculty renewal: Advances in faculty, instructional, and organizational development.* San Francisco: Jossey-Bass.

Galinsky, E., Bond, J. T., Kim, S. S., Backon, L., Brownfield, E., and Sakai, K. (2005). *Overwork in America: When the way we work becomes too much. Executive summary.* Families and Work Institute (2005). Retrieved July 24, 2006, from http://www.familiesandwork.org/summary/overwork2005.pdf

Galloway, H. (n.d.). *Job-embedded professional development.* Retrieved August 1, 2006, from http:www.txstate.edu/edphd/PDF/jpbpd.pdf

Gappa, J. M. (1996). Off the tenure track: Six models for full-time nontenurable appointments. *New Pathways Working Paper Series no. 10.* Washington, DC: American Association for Higher Education.

Gappa, J. M. (2002). Academic careers for the 21st century: More options for new faculty. In J. C. Smart (Ed.), *Higher education: Handbook of theory and research: Vol. 17* (pp. 425–475). New York: Agathon Press.

Gappa, J. M., & Leslie, D. W. (1993). *The invisible faculty: Improving the status of part-timers in higher education.* San Francisco: Jossey-Bass.

Gappa, J. M., & Leslie, E. W. (1997). Two faculties or one: The conundrum of part-timers in a bifurcated work force. *New Pathways Working Paper Series no. 6.* Washington, DC: American Association for Higher Education.

Gappa, J. M., & MacDermid, S. M. (1997). Work, family, and the faculty career. *New Pathways Working Paper Series no. 8.* Washington, DC: American Association for Higher Education.

Geiger, R. (1999). The ten generations of American higher education. In P. G. Altbach, R. O. Berdahl, & P. J. Gumport (Eds.), *American higher education in the twenty-first century: Social, political, and economic challenge* (pp. 38–69). Baltimore: Johns Hopkins University Press.

Geller, A. (2003, October 25). Employers looking for places to cut trim back worker flexibility programs. *Naples Daily News.* Retrieved October 28, 2003, from http://www.naplesnews.com

Gerstel, N., & Clawson, D. (2000). Introduction to the special issue on work and families [Electronic version]. *Qualitative Sociology, 23*(4), 375–378.

Gillespie, K. H., Hilsen, L. R., & Wadsworth, E. C. (Eds.). (2002). *A guide to faculty development: Practical advice, examples, and resources.* Bolton, MA: Anker.

Glass, J., & Estes, S. (1997). Family responsive workplace [Electronic version]. *Annual Review of Sociology, 23,* 289–313.

Glass, J. L., & Finley, A. (2002). Coverage and effectiveness of family-responsive workplace policies. *Human Resource Management Review, 12,* 313–337.

Gmelch, W. H. (1996, September/October). It's about time. *Academe,* pp. 22–26.

Gmelch, W. H. (1998, February). *Conflict management: Mending the cracks in the ivory tower.* Paper presented at the meeting of the American Council for Education, San Diego, CA.

Gmelch, W. H., & Miskin, V. D. (2004). *Chairing an academic department.* Madison, WI: Atwood.

Goodman, E. (2003, August 7). America's incredible shrinking vacation. *Boston Globe.* Retrieved August 11, 2003, from http://www.boston.com

Gross, J. (2005, November 24). Forget the career: My parents need me at home. *New York Times,* p. A1.

Gumport, P. J., & Chun, M. (2005). Technology and higher education: Opportunities and challenges for the new era. In P. G. Altbach, R. O. Berdahl, & P. J. Gumport (Eds.), *American higher education in the twenty-first century: Social, political, and economic challenge* (2nd ed., pp. 393–424). Baltimore: Johns Hopkins University Press.

Hackman, J. R., & Oldham, G. R. (1976). Motivation through the design of work: Test of a theory. *Organizational Behavior and Human Performance, 16,* 250–279.

Hagedorn, L. S. (1996). Wage equity and female faculty job satisfaction: The role of wage differentials in a job satisfaction causal model. *Research in Higher Education, 37*(5), 569–598.

Hagedorn, L. S. (2001). *Gender differences in faculty productivity, satisfaction, and salary: What really separates us?* ERIC Document 464 548.

Hall, D. T. (1996). Protean careers of the 21st century. *Academy of Management Executive, 10*(4), 8–16.

Hall, D. T., & Moss, J. E. (1998). The new protean career contract: Helping organizations and employees adapt. *Organizational Dynamics, 26*(3), 22–37.

Hammonds, K. H. (1996, September 16). Balancing work and family. *Business Week,* pp. 74–80.

Handy, C. (1994). *The age of unreason.* Boston: Harvard Business School Press.

Healy, C. (n.d.). *A business perspective on workplace flexibility: When work works, an employer strategy for the 21st century.* Retrieved April 2, 2006, from the When Works Project of the Families and Work Institute Web site http://familiesandwork.org/3w/about/index.html

Hearn, J. C., & Anderson, M. S. (2001). Clinical faculty in schools of education. In W. G. Tierney (Ed.), *Faculty work in schools of education.* Albany: State University of New York Press.

Hecht, I.W.D., Higgerson, M. L., Gmelch, W. H., & Tucker, A. (1999). *The department chair as academic leader.* Phoenix, AZ: ACE Oryx Press.

Hendel, D. D., & Horn, A. S. (2005, November). *Changes between 1989–90 and 2001–02 in the relationship between academic life conditions and perceived sources of faculty stress.* Paper presented at the annual meeting of the Association for the Study of Higher Education, Philadelphia, PA.

Herzberg, F. (1966). *Work and the nature of man.* Cleveland, OH: World.

Hewlett, S. A. (2002). *Executive women and the myth of having it all.* Cambridge, MA: Harvard Business School.

Hoffer, T. B., Welch, V., Jr., Williams, K., Hess, M., Webber, K., Lisek, B., Lowew, D. et al. (2005). *Doctorate recipients from United States universities: Summary report 2004.* Chicago: National Opinion Research Center. Retrieved December 6, 2005, from http://www.norc.uchicago.edu/issues/docdata.htm

Hogan, P. C. (1998). The ethics of tenure decisions. *Higher Education Review, 30*(3), 23–41.

Hollenshead, C., Waltman, J., August, L., Bailey, J., Miller, J., Smith, G., & Sullivan, B. (2005). *Family-friendly policies in higher education: Where do we stand?* Retrieved April 2, 2006, from http://www.umich.edu/~cew/PDFs/pubs/wherestand.pdf

Honan, J. P., & Rule, C. S. (Ed.). (2002). *Casebook 1: Faculty employment policies.* San Francisco: Jossey-Bass.

Hughes, R. (2005, November). *African American women in the academy: Stressors, struggles, and successes.* Paper presented at the annual meeting of the Association for the Study of Higher Education, Philadelphia, PA.

Hull, K. E., & Nelson, R. L. (2000). Assimilation, choice, or constraint? Testing theories of gender differences in the careers of lawyers. *Social Forces, 79*(1), 229–264.

Hult, C., Callister, R., & Sullivan, K. (2005, Summer/Fall). Is there a global warming toward women in academia? *Liberal Education,* Retrieved May 12, 2006, from http://www.aacu-edu.org/liberaleducation/le-sufa05/le-sufa05perspective.cfm

Hunnicutt, B. K. (1988). The New Deal: The salvation of work and the end of the shorter-hour movement. In G. Cross (Ed.), *Worktime and industrialization: An international history.* Philadelphia: Temple University Press.

Hunnicutt, B. K. (1992). Kellogg's six-hour day: A capitalist vision of liberation through managed work reduction. *Business History Review, 66,* 475–522.

Hussar, W. J. (2005). *Projections of education statistics to 2014* (NCES 2005–074). U.S. Department of Education, National Center for Education Statistics. Washington, DC: U.S. Government Printing Office.

Hustoles, T. P. (2000). Auditing a tenure policy from the perspective of the university administration. 2000 NACUA Annual Conference Outline. Reprinted in Brevitz, K. F., Snow, B. A., and Thro, W. E. (2003). *The NACUA handbook for lawyers new to higher education.* Washington, DC: National Association of College and University Attorneys.

It's not too much to ask, says a part-time instructor, that she be treated as if she belonged on campus. (2005, May 12). *Chronicle of Higher Education.*

Iiacqua, J. A., Schumacher, P., & Li, H. C. (1995). Factors contributing to job satisfaction in higher education. *Education, 116*(1), 51–61.

Jiang, J. J., & Klein, G. (1999–2000). Supervisor support and career anchor impact on the career satisfaction of the entry-level information systems professional. *Journal of Management Information Systems, 16,* 219–240.

Johnsrud, L. K., & Des Jarlais, C. D. (1994). Barriers to tenure for women and minorities. *The Review of Higher Education, 17*(4), 335–353.

Johnsrud, L. K., & Rosser, V. J. (2002). Faculty members' morale and their intentions to leave: A multilevel explanation. *The Journal of Higher Education, 71*(1), 34–59.

Jones, E. (2002–2003, Winter). Beyond supply and demand: Assessing the Ph.D. job market. *Occupational Outlook Quarterly,* pp. 22–33.

Jones, R. F., & Gold, J. S. (2001). The present and future of appointment, tenure, and compensation policies for medical school clinical faculty. *Academic Medicine, 76*(10), 993–1004.

Judy, R. W., & D'Amico, C. (1997). *Workforce 2020: Work and workers in the 21st century.* Indianapolis, IN: Hudson Institute.

Keller, G. (2001, Spring). The new demographics of higher education. *Review of Higher Education, 24*(3), 219–235.

Kelly, J. R., & McGrath, J. E. (1980). Effects of time limits and task types on task performance and interaction of four-person groups. *Journal of Personality and Social Psychology, 49,* 395–407.

Kerber, L. K. (2005, March 18). We must make the academic workplace more humane and equitable. *Chronicle of Higher Education*, pp. B6–B9.

Knapp, L. G., Kelly-Reid, J. E., Whitmore, R. W., Huh, S., Zhao, L., Levine, B. et al. (2005). *Staff in postsecondary institutions, fall 2003 and salaries of full-time instructional faculty, 2003-04*. NCES Report No. 2005-155. Washington, DC: U.S. Department of Education, National Center for Education Statistics. Retrieved December 8, 2005, from http://www.nces.ed.gov.libary.unl.edu/pubs2005/

Kossek, E. E., Barber, A. E., & Winters, D. (1999). Using flexible schedules in the managerial world: The power of peers. *Human Resources Management, 38*(1), 33–46.

Kruper, K. (2004). Making adjunct faculty part of the academic community. In C. M. Wehlburg & S. Chadwick-Blossey (Eds.), *To improve the academy: Vol. 22. Resources for faculty, instructional, and organizational development* (pp. 305–319). Bolton, MA: Anker.

Leslie, D. W. (1998a, May). Part-time, adjunct, and temporary faculty: The new majority? *Report of the Sloan Conference on Part-time and Adjunct Faculty*. Williamsburg, VA: The College of William and Mary.

Leslie, D. W. (Ed.). (1998b). *The growing use of part-time faculty: Understanding causes and effects*. New Directions for Higher Education, No. 104. San Francisco: Jossey-Bass.

Leslie, D. W. (2002). Resolving the dispute: Teaching is academe's core value. *Journal of Higher Education, 73*(1), 49–73.

Leslie, D. (2005, November). *Faculty careers and flexible employment*. Paper presented at the annual meeting of the Association for the Study of Higher Education, Philadelphia, PA.

Leslie, D. W., & Janson, N. (2005). Phasing away: How phased retirement works for *college faculty and their institutions*. Report for the Alfred P. Sloan Foundation.

Levine, A. (2000). *Higher education at a crossroads*. Earl Pullias Lecture in Higher Education. Los Angeles: Center for Higher Education Policy Analysis, Rossier School of Education, University of Southern California.

Lewis, K. G., & Lunde, J. P. (2001). *Face to face: A sourcebook of individual consultation techniques for faculty/instructional developers* (2nd ed.). Stillwater, OK: New Forums Press.

Lindholm, J. A. (2003). Perceived organizational fit: Nurturing the minds, hearts and personal ambitions of university faculty. *Review of Higher Education, 27*(1), 125–149.

Lindholm, J. A., Astin, A. W., Sax, L. J., & Korn, W. S. (2002). *The American college teacher: National norms for the 2001–02 HERI faculty survey*. Los Angeles: Higher Education Research Institute, UCLA.

Lindholm, J. A., Szelenyi, K., Hurtado, S., & Korn, W. S. (2005). *The American college teacher: National norms for the 2004–2005 HERI faculty survey.* Los Angeles: Higher Education Research Institute, UCLA.

Locke, E. A. (1976). The nature and causes of job satisfaction. In M. D. Dunnette (Ed.), *Handbook of industrial and organizational psychology* (pp. 1297–1349). New York: Wiley.

Lucas, A. F. (1994). *Strengthening departmental leadership: A team-building guide for chairs in colleges and universities.* San Francisco: Jossey-Bass.

Lyons, R. E. (2003). *Success strategies for adjunct faculty.* Boston: Allyn & Bacon.

MacDermid, S. M., Lee, M. D., & Smith, S. (2001). Forward into yesterday: Families and work in the 21st century. *Minding the Time in Family Experience, 3,* 59–81.

Maslow, A. H. (1970). *Motivation and personality* (2nd ed.). New York: HarperCollins.

Mason, M. A., & Goulden, M. (2002, November/December) Do babies matter? The effect of family formation on the lifelong careers of academic men and women. *Academe, 88*(6), 21–27.

Mason, M. A., & Goulden, M. (2004, November/December). Do babies matter (Part II)? Closing the baby gap. *Academe, 90*(6), 10–15.

McClelland, D. C. (1975). *Power: The inner experience.* New York: Irvington Press.

McKeachie, W. (2006). *McKeachie's teaching tips: Strategies, research, and theory for college and university teachers* (12th ed.). Boston: Houghton Mifflin.

McKinlay, J. B., & Marceau, L. D. (2002). The end of the golden age of doctoring. *International Journal of Health Services, 32*(2), 379–416.

Medcof, J. W., & Hausdorf, P. A. (1995). Instruments to measure opportunities to satisfy needs, and degree of satisfaction of needs, in the workplace. *Journal of Occupational and Organizational Psychology, 68,* 193–208.

Menges, R. J., & Mathis, B. C. (1988). *Key resources on teaching, learning, curriculum, and faculty development: A guide to the higher education literature.* San Francisco: Jossey-Bass.

MetLife. (1997, June). *The MetLife study of employer costs for working caregivers.* Westport, CT: Metropolitan Life Insurance Company. Retrieved March 29, 2006, from http://www.caregiving.org/pubs/data.htm

MetLife Mature Market Institute and National Alliance for Caregiving. (2006). *The MetLife Caregiving Cost Study: Productivity Losses to U.S. Business,* 2006. Retrieved August 1, 2006, from http://www.caregiving.org/data/MetlifeEmployerCostStudy2006.pdf

Meyer, H. D., & Kaloyeros, A. E. (2005, June 10). What campuses can do to pick up the pace of decision making. *Chronicle of Higher Education,* p. B16.

Michaelson, M. (2001). Should untenured as well as tenured faculty be guaranteed academic freedom? A few observations. *Journal of College and University Law, 27*(3), 565–573.

Moore, E. (2000). One road to turnover: An examination of work exhaustion in technology professionals [Electronic version]. *MIS Quarterly, 24,* 141–168.

Mullins, L. J. (1996). *Management and organizational behavior.* London: Pitman.

Murphy, M. (2002, March 29). Adjuncts should not just be visitors in the academic promised land. *Chronicle of Higher Education,* pp. B14–B15.

National Center for Education Statistics. (1997, August). *Statistical analysis report: Instructional Faculty and Staff in Higher Education Institutions—Fall 1987 and Fall 1992.* Washington, DC: U.S. Department of Education. Retrieved October 12, 2001, from nces.ed.gov/pubs97/ 97470

National Center for Education Statistics. (2000). *Digest of Education Statistics, 1999.* Washington, DC: U.S. Department of Education. Retrieved October 12, 2001, from nces.ed.gov/pubs2001/digest/ch3

National Center for Education Statistics. (2002). *Digest of Education Statistics, 2001.* Washington, DC: U.S. Department of Education. Retrieved October 16, 2002, from http://www.nces.ed.gov/pubs2002/ digest2001/tables/dt226.asp

National Center for Educational Statistics. (2003). Table 332. *Current-fund revenue of public degree-granting institutions by source of funds: Selected Years, 1980–81 to 2000–1.* Retrieved March 6, 2006, from http:// www.nces.ed.gov

National Center for Educational Statistics. (2004). *FT Faculty in Each Racial Group.* Retrieved February 1, 2006, from http://www.nces. ed.gov

NEA Higher Education Research Center. (1996, September). Full-time non-tenure track faculty. *NEA Update, 2*(5). Washington, D.C.: National Education Association.

NEA Higher Education Research Center. (2001, December). Faculty retirement: Loss or opportunity? *NEA Update, 7*(5). Washington, DC: National Education Association.

NEA Higher Education Research Center. (2004, December). Faculty salaries. *NEA Update. 10*(5). Washington, DC: National Education Association.

Nesteruk, J. (2005, July 8). Midlife in academe. *The Chronicle of Higher Education,* p. B5.

Newman, F., Couturier, L., & Scurry, J. (2004). *The future of higher education: Rhetoric, reality, and the risks of the market.* San Francisco: Jossey-Bass.

Nieves-Squires, S. (1992). Hispanic women in the U.S. academic context. In L. Welch (Ed.), *Perspectives on Minority Women in Higher Education* (pp. 71–92). New York: Praeger.

Norrell, J. E., & Norrell, T. H. (1996). Faculty and family policies in higher education. *Journal of Family Issues, 17*(2), 204–226.

Nutting, M. M. (2003). Part-time faculty: Why should we care? In E. Benjamin (Ed.), *Exploring the role of contingent instructional staff in undergraduate learning.* New Directions for Higher Education, No. 123. San Francisco: Jossey-Bass.

Olsen, D. (1993). Work satisfaction and stress in the first and third year of academic appointment. *Journal of Higher Education, 64*(4), 453–471.

Olsen, D., Maple, D., & Stage, F. K. (1995). Women and minority faculty job satisfaction: Professional role interests, professional satisfactions, and institutional fit. *Journal of Higher Education, 66*(3), 267–293.

Olsen, D., & Near, J. P. (1994). Role conflict and faculty life satisfaction. *Review of Higher Education, 17*(2), 179–195.

Olswang, S. G. (2001). College and university faculty: Academic freedom and tenure. *The NACUA handbook for lawyers new to higher education* (pp. 583–607). Washington, DC: National Association of College and University Attorneys.

O'Neil, R. M., & White, L. (2002). Understanding tenure: History, purpose and relationship to academic freedom. *NACUA continuing legal education outline.* Washington, DC: National Association of College and University Attorneys.

Pelikan, J. (1992). *The idea of the university: A reexamination.* New Haven, CT: Yale University Press.

Perkins, H. W., & DeMeis, D. K. (1996). Gender and family effects on the "second-shift" domestic activity of college-educated young adults [Electronic version]. *Gender & Society, 10*(1), 78–93.

Quinn, K., Lange, S. E., & Olswang, S. G. (2004, November/December). Family-friendly policies and the research university. *Academe, 90*(6), 32–34.

Radcliffe Public Policy Institute. (1999). *Professional pathways: Examining work, family, and community in the Biotechnology Industry: An executive summary.* Cambridge, MA: Author. Retrieved April 27, 2004, from http://www.radcliffe.edu/research/pubpol/publications.php

Rhoades, G. (1998). *Managed professionals: Unionized faculty and restructuring academic labor.* Albany: State University of New York Press.

Rhode, D. L. (2002). Balanced lives for lawyers [Electronic version]. *Fordham Law Review, 70,* 2207–2220.

Rice, R. E. (1986). The academic profession in transition: Toward a new social friction. *Teaching Sociology, 41,* 12–23.

Rice, R. E. (1996a). *The forum on faculty roles and rewards: project.* Washington, DC: U.S. Dept. of Education, Office of Educational Research and Improvement, Educational Resources Information Center.

Rice, R. E. (1996b). Making a place for the new American scholar. *New Pathways Working Paper Series no. 1.* Washington, DC: American Association for Higher Education.

Rice, R. E. (2004). The future of the American faculty: An interview with Martin J. Finkelstein and Jack H. Schuster. *Change, 36*(2), 26–35.

Rice, R. E., & Austin, A. E. (1988, March/April). High faculty morale: What exemplary colleges do right. *Change, 20*(2), 51–58.

Rice, R. E., Sorcinelli, M. D., & Austin, A. E. (2000). *Heeding new voices: Academic careers for a new generation.* New Pathways Working Paper Series, No. 7. Washington, DC: American Association for Higher Education.

Riggio, R. E. (1990). *Introduction to industrial organizational psychology.* Glenview, IL: Scott Foresman/Little, Brown Higher Education.

Roediger, D., & Foner, P. (1989). *Our own time: A history of American labor and the working day.* New York: Verso Books.

Ronen, S. (1984). *Alternative work schedules: Selecting, implementing, and evaluating.* Homewood, IL: Dow Jones-Irwin.

Rosser, V. J. (2004). Faculty members' intentions to leave: A national study on their worklife and satisfaction. *Research in Higher Education, 45*(3), 285–309.

Rubin, B. M. (2002, October). Think outside the [cereal] box. *Working Mother,* pp. 61–62.

Rudolph, F. (1990). *The American college and university: A history.* Athens, GA: University of Georgia Press.

Rule, C. S. (2002). Georgia State University: Tackling salary inequity, posttenure review, and part-time employment. In J. P. Honan, & C. S. Rule (Eds.), *Using cases in higher education: Casebook 1: Faculty employment policies.* San Francisco: Jossey-Bass.

Schiltz, P. J. (1999). Symposium: Attorney well-being in large firms: Choices for young lawyers: On being a happy, healthy and ethical member of an unhappy, unhealthy, and unethical profession [Electronic version]. *Vanderbilt Law Review, 57.*

Schmidt, P. (2006, March 17). In the states. *Chronicle of Higher Education,* p. A34.

Schuster, J. H., & Finkelstein, M. J. (2006). *The American faculty: The restructuring of academic work and careers.* Baltimore: Johns Hopkins University Press.

Schuster, J. H., Wheeler, D. W., & Associates. (1990). *Enhancing faculty careers: Strategies for development and renewal.* San Francisco: Jossey-Bass.

Shafer, W. E., Lowe, D. J., & Fogarty, T. J. (2002). The effects of corporate ownership on public accountants' professionalism and ethics [Electronic version]. *Accounting Horizons, 16,* 109–124.

Shavers, F. L. (2000). Academic ranks and titles of full-time nontenure-track faculty. In C. A. Trower (Ed.), *Policies on faculty appointments: Standard practices and unusual arrangements.* Bolton, MA: Anker.

Slaughter, S. (1993). Retrenchment in the 1980s: The politics of prestige and gender. *Journal of Higher Education, 64,* 250–282.

Slaughter, S., & Leslie, L. L. (1999). *Academic capitalism: Politics, policies, and the entrepreneurial university.* Baltimore, MD: Johns Hopkins University Press.

Slaughter, S., & Rhoades, G. (2004). *Academic capitalism and the new economy: Markets, state, and higher education.* Baltimore: Johns Hopkins University Press.

Smallwood, S. (2003, August 15). Where the bucks are. *Chronicle of Higher Education,* p. A12.

Snyder, T. D., & Tan, A. G. (2005). *Digest of education statistics, 2004* (NCES 2006005). U.S. Department of Education, National Center for Education Statistics. Washington, DC: U.S. Government Printing Office.

Sorcinelli, M. D. (1988). Satisfactions and concerns of new university teachers. *To Improve the Academy, 7,* 121–133.

Sorcinelli, M. D., & Austin, A. E. (Eds.). (1992). *Developing new and junior faculty.* New Directions for Teaching and Learning, No. 50. San Francisco: Jossey-Bass.

Sorcinelli, M. D., Austin, A. E., Eddy, P. L., & Beach, A. L. (2006). *Creating the future of faculty development: Learning from the past, understanding the present.* Bolton, MA: Anker.

Sparks, D. (1994). A paradigm shift in staff development. *Journal of Staff Development, 15*(4), 26–29.

Stanford University. (2006). *Emergency and back-up child care.* Retrieved April 2, 2006, from www.stanford.edu/dept/ocr/worklife/emergency backup.html

Stanford University. (2002a). *Faculty handbook: The university and the faculty* (chap. 1). Retrieved April 2, 2006, from http://facultyhandbook. stanford.edu/ch1.html#theacademiccouncil

Stanford University. (2002b). *Faculty handbook: Appointments and promotions* (chap. 2). Retrieved April 2, 2006, from http://facultyhandbook. stanford.edu/ch2.html

Stein, S., DiTullio, A., Forsman, T., & Miller, A. (2002, October). 100 best companies for working mothers. *Working Mother,* pp. 42–146.

Sullivan, B., Hollenshead, C., & Smith, G. (2004, November/December). Developing and implementing work-family policies for faculty. *Academe, 90*(6), 24–27.

Svinicki, M. (2002). Faculty development: An investment for the future. In R. M. Diamond & B. Adam (Eds.), *Field guide to academic leadership.* San Francisco: Jossey-Bass.

Syverson, P. (October, 1996). The new American graduate student: Challenge or opportunity? *CGS Communicator, 29*(8), 7–11.

Tack, M. W., & Patitu, C. J. (1992). *Faculty job satisfaction: Women and minorities in peril.* ASHE-ERIC Higher Education Volume 4. Washington, DC: The George Washington University Clearinghouse on Higher Education.

Tierney, W. G. (1993). *Building communities of difference: Higher education in the twenty-first century.* Westport, CT: Bergin & Garvey.

Tierney, W. G., & Bensimon, E. M. (1996). *Promotion and tenure: Community and socialization in academe.* Albany: State University of New York Press.

Townsend, R. B. (2003). Changing relationships, changing values in the American classroom. In E. Benjamin (Ed.), *Exploring the role of contingent instructional staff in undergraduate learning.* New Directions for Higher Education, No. 123. San Francisco: Jossey Bass.

Trower, C. A. (1998). Employment practices in the professions: Fresh ideas from inside and outside the academy. *New Pathways Working Paper Series, No. 13.* Washington, DC: American Association for Higher Education.

Trower, C. A. (Ed.). (2000). *Policies on faculty appointment: Standard practices and unusual arrangements.* Bolton, MA: Anker.

Trower, C. A. (2002). Can colleges competitively recruit faculty without the prospect of tenure? In R. P. Chait (Ed.), *The questions of tenure.* Cambridge, MA: Harvard University Press.

Trower, C. A., & Bleak, J. L. (2004a). Study of new scholars. *Gender: Statistical report* [Universities]. Cambridge, MA: Harvard Graduate School of Education. Retrieved May 12, 2006, from, http://www.gse.harvard.edu/news/features/trower04122004.pdf

Trower, C. A., & Bleak, J. L. (2004b). Study of new scholars. *Race: Statistical report* [Universities]. Cambridge, MA: Harvard Graduate School of Education. Retrieved May 12, 2006, from http://www.gse.harvard.edu/~newscholars/newscholars/downloads/racereport.pdf

Trower, C. A., & Chait, R. P. (2002, March/April). Faculty diversity: Too little for too long. *Harvard Magazine, 104*(4) 33–37. Retrieved May 17, 2006, from http://www.harvardmagazine.com/on-line/030218.html

Trower, C. A., & Honan, J. P. (2002). How might data be used? In R. P. Chait (Ed.), *The questions of tenure.* Cambridge, MA: The Harvard University Press.

Twigg, C. (2002). The impact of the changing economy on four-year institutions of higher education: The importance of the Internet. In C. Twigg (Ed.), *The knowledge economy and postsecondary education: Report of a workshop*. Washington, DC: National Academy Press.

Ulrich, D. (1998, Winter). Intellectual capital = competence X commitment. *Sloan Management Review, 39*(2), 15–26.

University of California, Berkeley. (2006a). *Berkeley parents network*. Retrieved April 2, 2006, from http://parents.berkeley.edu

University of California, Berkeley. (2006b). *Elder care program*. Retrieved April 2, 2006, from www.uhs.berkeley.edu/Facstaff/CARE/eldercare/

University of California, Davis. (2003). *UCD directives: Work/life balance initiative*. Retrieved April 2, 2006, from http://directives.ucdavis.edu/2003/03–006.cfm

University of Texas, Austin. (2006). *Hispanic faculty and staff association*. Retrieved April 2, 2006, from http://www.utexas.edu/staff/hfsa

U.S. Bureau of Labor Statistics. (2005). *Employment Projections Home Page*. Retrieved May 12, 2006, from http://www.stats.bls.gov/emp/home.htm#tables

U.S. Census Bureau. (2000). Labor force, employment, and earnings [Table 644]. *Statistical abstract of the United States*. Washington, DC: Author. Retrieved April 2, 2006, from http://www.census.gov/prod/2001pubs/statab/sec13.pdf

U.S. Department of Education. (2001). *Digest of educational statistics, 2000* (NCES Publication No. 2001–034). Washington, DC: Author.

U.S. Department of Education. (2002). *Digest of educational statistics, 2001* (NCES Publication No. 2002–130). Washington, DC: Author.

U.S. Department of Education. (2004). *Digest of educational statistics, 2004* (NCES Publication No. 2004–331). Washington, DC: Author.

U.S. Department of Education, National Center for Education Statistics. (1988). *National study of postsecondary faculty* (NSOPF: 88). Washington, DC: Author. Retrieved April 2, 2006, from http://nces.ed.gov/das

U.S. Department of Education, National Center for Education Statistics. (1993). *National study of postsecondary faculty* (NSOPF: 93). Washington, DC: Author. Retrieved April 2, 2006, from http://nces.ed.gov/das

U.S. Department of Education, National Center for Education Statistics. (1999). *National study of postsecondary faculty* (NSOPF: 99). Washington, DC: Author. Retrieved April 2, 2006, from http://nces.ed.gov/das

U.S. Department of Education, National Center for Education Statistics. (2004). *National study of postsecondary faculty* (NSOPF:04). Washington, DC: Author. Retrieved April 2, 2006, from http://nces.ed.gov/das

U.S. Department of Health and Human Services, Health Resources and Services Administration, Maternal and Child Health Bureau. (2004). *Child health USA 2004*. Rockville, Maryland: U.S. Department of Health and Human Services. Retrieved May 17, 2006, from http://www.mchb.hrsa.gov/mchirc/chusa_04/pages/0310wm.htm

Wadsworth, E. C. (1988). *A handbook for new practitioners.* Stillwater, OK: New Forums Press.

Ward, K., & Wolf-Wendel, L. (2004). Academic motherhood: Managing complex roles in research universities. *Review of Higher Education, 27*(2), 233–257.

Waterman, R. H., Waterman, J. A., & Collard, B. A. (1994). Toward a career-resilient workforce. *Harvard Business Review, 72*(4), 87–95.

Wellesley College. (2006). *Wellesley community children's center.* Retrieved April 2, 2006, http://wccc.wellesley.edu/philo.html

Wergin, J. F. (2003). *Departments that work: Building and sustaining cultures of excellence in academic programs.* Boston: Anker.

West, P. R. (2002). 21st Century professional development: The job-embedded, continual learning model. *American Secondary Education, 30*(2), 72–86.

Whitt, E. (1991). Hit the ground running: Experiences of new faculty in a school of education. *The Review of Higher Education, 14*(2), 177–197.

Whyte, W. H. Jr. (1956). *The organization man.* New York: Simon & Schuster.

Williams, J. (1996). Restructuring work and family entitlements around family values. *Harvard Journal of Law and Public Policy,* 1996, *19*(3), 753–757.

Williams, J. (1999). *Unbending Gender: Why family and work conflict and what to do about it.* New York: Oxford Press.

Williams, J. (2000, December 15). What stymies women's academic careers? It's personal. *Chronicle of Higher Education,* p. B10.

Williams, J. (2002, November 11). Your money or your time. *Chronicle of Higher Education.* Retrieved March 29, 2006, from http://chronicle.com/jobs/2002/11/2002111101c.htm

Williams, J. (2005, February 7). Are your parental-leave policies legal? *Chronicle of Higher Education.* Retrieved April 27, 2005, from http://chronicle.com/jobs/2005/02/2005020701c.htm

Williams, J., & Calvert, C. T. (2002). Balanced hours: Effective part-time policies for Washington law firms: The project for attorney retention; Final report third edition, April 2002 [Electronic version]. *Women and the Law, 8,* 357–441. Retrieved from http://www.pardc.org/Publications/BalancedHours2nd.pdf

Wilson, R. (1995, November 17). Colleges help professors balance work and family. *Chronicle of Higher Education,* p. A24.

Wilson, R. (1999, October 22). How a university created 95 faculty slots and scaled back its use of part-timers. *Chronicle of Higher Education,* pp. A18–A20.

Wilson, R. (2002, January 25). Working half time on the tenure track. *Chronicle of Higher Education,* pp. A10–A11.

Wilson, R. (2004a, April 9). This academic life. *Chronicle of Higher Education*, p. A11.

Wilson, R. (2004b, October 23). Whose professor is it anyway? *Chronicle of Higher Education*, p. A12.

Wilson, R. (2005a, February 11). Tenure system should be made less rigid to reflect modern lifestyles, report by college leaders says. *Chronicle of Higher Education*. Retrieved February 11, 2005, from http://chronicle.com/daily/2005/02/2005021105n.htm

Wilson, R. (2005b, February 25). Keeping kids close: Campuses provide child-care centers to help professors cope. *Chronicle of Higher Education*, p. A10.

Wilson, R. (2005c, July 22). Family science. *Chronicle of Higher Education*, p. A6.

Wimsatt, L. A., & Trice, A. G. (2006). *A profile of grant administration burden among faculty within the federal demonstration partnership: A report of the faculty advisory committee of the Federal Demonstration Partnership.* Washington, DC: The National Academy of Sciences.

Witt, L. A., & Nye, L. G. (1992). Gender and the relationship between perceived fairness of pay or promotion and job satisfaction. *Journal of Applied Psychology, 77*(6), 910–917.

Wolfinger, N., Mason, M., & Goulden, M. (2004). *Problems in the pipeline: Gender, marriage and fertility in the Ivory Tower.* Paper presented at the annual meeting of the American Sociological Association, San Francisco, CA.

Wolf-Wendel, L. E., Twombly, S. B., & Rice, S. (2003). *The two-body problem: Dual-career-couple hiring policies in higher education.* Baltimore: Johns Hopkins University Press.

Wulff, D. H., & Austin, A. E., Eds. (2004). *Paths to the professoriate.* San Francisco: Jossey-Bass.

Wulff, D. H., Austin, A. E., Nyquist, J. D., & Sprague, J. (2004). The development of graduate students as teaching scholars: A four-year longitudinal study. In D. H. Wulff & A. E. Austin (eds.), *Paths to the professoriate.* San Francisco: Jossey-Bass.

Working Mother Magazine. (2002, October). *100 best companies for working mothers.* New York: Working Mother Media.

Yager, J. (2005, July 8). Getting back on track. *Chronicle of Higher Education*, p. C2.

Young, J. (2005, April 12). Knowing when to log off: Wired campuses may be causing "information overload." *Chronicle of Higher Education*.

Zusman, A. (2005). Challenges facing higher education in the twenty-first century. In P. G. Altbach, R. O. Berdahl, & P. J. Gumport (Eds.), *American higher education in the twenty-first century: Social, political, and economic challenge* (2nd ed., pp.115–160). Baltimore: Johns Hopkins University Press.

Name Index

A

Agago, M. O., 79, 102, 115, 116, 123, 306
Aguirre, A., 80
Alderfer, C. P., 119, 122, 124, 139, 146
Altbach, P.G., 53
Alter, J., 35
Anderson, M. S., 84
Armenti, C., 68, 73
Armour, S., 39
Arnolds, C. A., 119
Astin, A. W., 111, 116, 243
Astin, H. S., 77
August, L., 240, 246, 247
Austin, A. E., 18, 20, 68, 69, 70, 71, 72, 77, 78, 135, 280, 281, 283, 284, 291, 296, 298, 301, 305, 307, 308, 316

B

Backon, L., 33
Bailey, J., 240, 246, 247
Bailyn, L., 25, 28, 29, 36, 43, 69, 240–241, 243–244, 256
Baldwin, R. G., 82, 84, 86, 87, 88, 89, 90, 195, 209, 218, 219, 227
Banker, E. C., 29, 43
Barber, A. E., 43
Barnes, L.L.B., 79, 102, 115, 116, 123, 306
Barrett, J. T., 168
Beach, A. L., 280, 281, 283, 284
Becher, T., 135, 308
Benjamin, E., 93, 96
Bensimon, E. M., 20, 68, 71, 77, 78, 79, 80, 298, 305

Berger, A., 54, 93, 96, 97, 98, 111
Berkman, A., 5, 30
Berquist, W. H., 284
Bickel, J., 91
Black, M. M., 115, 123
Blackburn, R. T., 133
Bland, C. J., 83, 91, 282, 284
Bleak, J. L., 103, 106, 107
Bluedorn, A. C., 254
Boice, R., 20, 305
Bolman, L. G., 148–149
Bond, J. T., 28, 29, 33, 45, 47, 242, 244
Bonner, F. A., 81
Borges, W., 31
Boshoff, C., 119
Bowen, H. R., 53, 105
Boyd, D., 8
Boyer, E., 15
Breneman, D. W., 8, 209, 213
Brown, J. S., 21
Brownfield, E., 33
Bryne, J. P., 231, 234, 235, 236
Burkum, K. R., 74

C

Callister, R., 109, 115, 116, 123
Calvert, C. T., 35, 40, 43, 45
Campbell, A., 139, 146
Carter, K., 93, 96, 97
Center, B. A., 83, 91
Chait, R. P., 53–54, 70, 81, 110, 193, 207, 214, 217
Christensen, K. E., 28
Chronister, J. L., 82, 84, 86, 87, 88, 89, 90, 195, 209, 218, 219, 227
Chun, M., 13, 14

Cintrón, 5, 31
Clark, B. R., 53, 56–57, 135, 308
Clawson, D., 26
Clotfelter, C. T., 214
Cohen, A. M., 52
Cohen, A. R., 256
Colbeck, C., 74, 253
Collard, B. A., 46, 47, 130
Conlin, M., 34, 35
Connell, M. A., 308
Coombs, W. T., 79, 102, 115, 116, 123, 306
Cooper, J. E., 68, 80
Cooper, M., 44
Costello, M. A., 35
Couturier, L., 8, 9
Cunningham, K., 43, 44
Curry, A., 32, 37, 38, 44–45, 47

D
D'Amico, C., 5, 30
Damrosch, D., 51
Deal, T. E., 148–149
DeMeis, D. K., 29
Dernhardt, R. B., 254
Des Jarlais, C. D., 79
Didion, C. J., 77, 241
Dimitrova, D., 30, 118
DiTullio, A., 35, 38, 39, 40
Donohue, J. D., 115, 123
Downey, D., 5, 30
Drago, R., 28, 29, 43, 199, 253, 261
Duderstadt, J. J., 3, 9, 12

E
Eckel, P. D., 8
Eddy, P. L., 280, 281, 283, 284
Elias, M., 28, 34
Estes, S., 38–39, 43
Euben, D. R., 226, 232, 234

F
Ferris, G. R., 121
Finkel, S. K., 72
Finkelstein, M. J., 15, 20, 53, 59, 105, 114

Finley, A., 43, 44
Finney, J. E., 8
Finstad, D. A., 83, 91
Fisher, R., 168
Fletcher, J. K., 43
Fogarty, T. J., 32
Foner, P., 37
Ford, A. T., 53–54
Forsman, T., 35, 38, 39, 40
Fortney, S. S., 32, 45
Fried, Y., 121
Froom, J. D., 91
Frost, S. H., 319
Fulton, R. D., 93

G
Gadon, H., 256
Gaff, J. G., 282
Galinsky, E., 28, 29, 33, 45, 47, 242, 244
Galloway, H., 285
Gappa, J. M., 71, 77, 83, 84, 85, 86, 87, 88, 89, 90, 91, 94–95, 96, 97, 98, 99, 103, 147, 195, 208, 213, 219
Geiger, R., 51, 52
Geller, A., 44
Gerstel, N., 26
Gillespie, K. H., 284
Glass, J., 38–39, 43
Glass, J. L., 43, 44
Gmelch, W. H., 170
Gold, J. S., 84, 91, 214
Gomory, R. E., 28
Goodman, E., 33
Googins, B. K., 29, 43
Goulden, M., 36, 75, 76, 110, 196, 242, 265, 276, 277
Gross, J., 29
Gumport, P. J., 13, 14

H
Hackman, J. R., 121, 122, 124
Hagedorn, L. S., 102, 109, 115
Hall, D. T., 46, 47, 281–282
Hammonds, K. H., 39

Handy, C., 15
Hausdorf, P. A., 120
Healy, C., 240
Hearn, J. C., 84
Hecht, I.W.D., 170
Hendel, D. D., 108, 109
Herzberg, F., 120, 122, 124, 139, 146
Hess, M., 61, 62, 64, 262
Hewlett, S. A., 27, 29, 32–33, 34, 45, 46, 47
Higgerson, M. L., 170
Hill, J. E., 242, 244
Hilsen, L. R., 284
Hoffer, T. B., 61, 62, 64, 262
Hogan, P. C., 71–72
Holden, E. W., 115, 123
Hollenshead, C., 240, 246, 247, 248, 253, 273, 276, 277, 278
Honan, J. P., 175, 185
Horn, A. S., 108, 109
Hughes, R., 81
Huh, S., 66
Hull, K. E., 35
Hult, C., 109, 115, 116, 123
Hunnicutt, B. K., 37
Hurtado, S., 5, 106, 108, 110, 111
Hussar, W. J., 11
Hustoles, T. P., 205

I

Iiacqua, J. A., 115

J

Janson, N., 75, 111, 196
Jean, P. M., 319
Jiang, J. J., 45
Johnsrud, L. K., 79, 116, 123
Jones, E., 110, 113
Jones, R. F., 84, 91, 214
Judy, R. W., 5, 30

K

Kaloyeros, A. E., 162
Keller, G., 11
Kelly, J. R., 254
Kelly-Reid, J. E., 66

Kim, S. S., 33
Kirshstein, R., 54, 93, 96, 97, 98, 111
Klein, G., 45
Knapp, L. G., 66
Koblenz, M., 139, 146
Kochan, T. A., 28, 29, 43
Korn, W. S., 5, 106, 108, 110, 111, 116, 243
Kossek, E. E., 43
Kruper, K., 296

L

Lange, S. E., 277, 278
Lawrence, J. H., 133
Lee, M. D., 34
Leslie, D. W., 73, 75, 90, 94–95, 95, 96, 97, 99, 105, 111, 147, 195, 196, 208, 219, 241
Leslie, L. L., 8
Levine, A., 11
Levine, B., 66
Lewis, K. G., 284
Li, H. C., 115
Lindholm, J. A., 5, 105, 106, 108, 110, 111, 116, 243
Lisek, B., 61, 62, 64, 262
Liu, M., 114
Locke, E. A., 115, 118, 121–122
Lowe, D. J., 32
Lowew, D., 61, 62, 64, 262
Lunde, J. P., 284
Luu, D. T., 8
Lyons, R. E., 94, 296

M

MacDermid, S. M., 34, 77
Maple, D., 115, 123
Marceau, L. D., 31
March, T., 5, 30
Maslow, A. H., 119, 122, 124, 139, 146
Mason, M., 76, 110, 242
Mason, M. A., 36, 75, 196, 265, 276, 277
Mathis, B. C., 284
McClelland, D. C., 120, 122, 124

McGrath, J. E., 254
McKeachie, W., 291
McKinlay, J. B., 31
Medcof, J. W., 120
Menges, R. J., 284
Meyer, H. D., 162
Michaelson, M., 193, 235
Milem, J. F., 77
Miller, A., 35, 38, 39, 40
Miller, J., 240, 246, 247
Moore, E., 33, 45
Moss, J. E., 46, 47, 281–282
Mullins, L. J., 118, 121

N

Near, J. P., 68
Nelson, R. L., 35
Nesteruk, J., xi
Newman, F., 8, 9
Nieves-Squires, S., 80
Norrell, J. E., 77
Norrell, T. H., 77
Nutting, M. M., 95, 96, 97, 99
Nye, L. G., 117

O

Oldham, G. R., 121, 122, 124
Olsen, D., 68, 69, 115, 123
Olswang, S. G., 72, 231, 277, 278
O'Neil, R. M., 51, 52

P

Patitu, C. J., 74
Pelikan, J., 305
Perkins, H. W., 29
Phillips, S. R., 284
Prottas, D., 28, 33

Q

Quinn, K., 277, 278

R

Rhoades, G., 8, 16, 34, 96, 128
Rhode, D. L., 35
Rice, R. E., 15, 18, 20, 22, 51, 52,
     67, 68, 69, 70, 71, 72, 77, 78, 280,
     291, 296, 298, 301, 305, 307, 308

Rice, S., 68, 72, 75
Riggio, R. E., 120, 121
Risbey, K. R., 83, 91
Roediger, D., 37
Roherty, B. M., 8
Rosser, V. J., 102, 107, 116, 123
Rowe, E., 54, 98, 111
Rubin, B. M., 39
Rudolph, F., 52
Rule, C. S., 175

S

Sakai, K., 33
Savage, F. G., 308
Sax, L. J., 111, 116, 243
Schiltz, P. J., 32, 45
Schmidt, P., 10
Schmitz, C. C., 282
Schumacher, P., 115
Schuster, J. H., 15, 53, 59, 77, 105,
     108, 114, 284
Scurry, J., 8, 9
Shafer W. E., 32
Shavers, F. L., 89
Slaughter, S., 8, 16
Smallwood, S., 223, 224
Smith, G., 240, 246, 247, 248, 273,
     276, 277, 278
Smith, S., 34
Snyder, T. D., 11
Sorcinelli, M. D., 18, 20, 68, 69, 70,
     71, 72, 77, 78, 280, 281, 283, 284,
     296, 298, 305, 307, 308
Sparks, D., 285
Splete, A. P., 291, 308
Stage, F. K., 115, 123
Staples, J., 83, 91
Stein, S., 35, 38, 39, 40
Steinauer, J. M., 5, 30
Stevens, D. D., 68, 80
Sullivan, B., 240, 246, 247, 248, 273,
     276, 277, 278
Sullivan, K., 109, 115, 116, 123
Svinicki, M., 280, 282, 283
Swanberg, J., 29, 45, 47
Syverson, P., 11
Szelenyi, K., 5, 106, 108, 110, 111

T

Tack, M. W., 74
Tan, A. G., 11
Thompson, C., 28, 33
Tierney, W. G., 20, 68, 71, 77, 78, 79, 80, 298, 305, 308
Townsend, R. B., 97
Trice, A. G., 5, 113
Trower, C. A., 40, 81, 83, 84, 87, 103, 106, 107, 110, 116, 185, 207, 217
Trowler, P. R., 308
Tucker, A., 170
Twigg, C., 13
Twombly, S. B., 68, 72, 75

U

Ulrich, D., 4, 5
Ury, W., 168

W

Wadsworth, E. C., 284
Waltman, J., 240, 246, 247
Ward, K., 68, 72, 75
Waterman, J. A., 46, 47, 130
Waterman, R. H., 46, 47, 130
Weaver, L. D., 74
Webber, K., 61, 62, 64, 262

Welch, V., Jr., 61, 62, 64, 262
Wergin, J. F., 170
West, P. R., 285
Wheeler, D. W., 284
White, L., 51, 52
Whitmore, R. W., 66
Whitt, E., 20, 305
Witt, L. A., 117
Whyte, W. H. Jr., 24, 25, 44
Williams, J., 24, 25, 34, 35, 40, 43, 44, 45, 199, 241, 244, 246, 248, 249, 256, 261
Williams, K., 61, 62, 64, 262
Wilson, R., 77, 175, 225, 264, 268
Wimsatt, L. A., 5, 113
Winters, D., 43
Wolfinger, N., 76, 110, 242
Wolf-Wendel, L. E., 68, 72, 75, 262

Y

Yager, J., xi
Young, J., 18

Z

Zhang, Y., 93, 96, 97
Zhao, L., 66
Zusman, A., 10

SUBJECT INDEX

A

AAC&U. *See* Association of American Colleges and Universities (AAC&U)

AAUP. *See* American Association of University Professors (AAUP)

ABN AMRO North America, 39–40

Academic appointments. *See* Faculty appointments

Academic freedom, 51–52; definition of, 140–141, 231–232; educating faculty about, 229–234; and inclusive institutional policy statements, 228–229, 230*e*; and organizational values, 152; overview, 226–228; protection of, 234–237; rights and duties of, 231–232; and technological advances, 232. *See also* Autonomy

Academic Freedom and Educational Responsibility (AAC&U), 233

The Academic Life: Small Worlds, Different Worlds (Clark), 56–57

Academic Revolution, 52

Academic units, 136

Access, to workers, 32–33

Accountability, calls for: for collegiality, 309; data collection in, 187; effects of, 10, 18–19; overview of, 9–10; response to, 10

Accounting professionals, 31–32, 35, 40

Achievement needs, 120

Adaptability, 282

Administrators: communication of, 175–176; flexibility policy support from, 273–274, 275–276;

higher education change responsibilities of, 330; importance of, 4; and job satisfaction, 117; and organizational values, 152; and response to accountability calls, 10; role of, 157–158, 160; traditional view of, 158; and work-life policy evaluations, 278. *See also specific types*

ADVANCE Program, 289

Affiliation needs, 120

African Americans: in diversified workplace, 27; doctorates earned by, 62; in faculty positions, 62, 63*t*; job satisfaction of, 104*t*

Age, of faculty, 111, 307

Agriculture, 92

Alternative academic appointments, 54–57, 208. *See also specific appointments*

Alternative-career model, 85–86

American Association of Retired Persons, 308

American Association of University Professors (AAUP), 51, 52, 129, 131, 141, 155, 159, 160, 164, 165, 194, 196, 219, 226, 227, 236

American Council on Education, 159, 196, 244, 265

American Federation of Teachers, 160

American workplace. *See* National workplace

Amherst College, 257, 259*e*

Annual Conference on Law and Higher Education, 237

Antiharassment policies, 310–312

Appointments, faculty. *See* Faculty appointments

Arcadia University, 223–224

Arizona Board of Regents, 205

Artists, 213

Asians: in diversified workplace, 27; doctorates earned by, 62; in faculty positions, 62, 63*t*; job satisfaction of, 104*t*

Associate academic vice presidents, 177–178

Associate deans, 182

Association of American Colleges and Universities (AAC&U), 232–233

Auburn University, 306

Autonomy: decline of, 16–17, 31–32; definition of, 140–141, 227; need for, 105; as reason for job satisfaction, 105, 106, 115–116, 121. *See also* Academic freedom

B

Babson College, 269

Baruch College, 221, 222*e*, 223*e*

Baxter Healthcare Corporation, 146

Bay Area Consortium, 299

Behavior, faculty, 152, 164–168

Benchmarking, 187

Black Faculty and Staff Association, 312, 313*e*

Bonuses, 215

Bookstores, 315

Boston University, 214

Bottom fishing, 96

Bowdoin College, 268

Brigham Young University, 298

Burden of proof, in academic freedom violation, 236

Burnout, 243, 302

Business managers, 183–184

Business schools, 84

C

California State University, 112

Calvin College, 257, 258*e*, 262, 263*e*

Campus activities, 310–314

Campus planning committees, 162–163

Campus-based child care, 267–269

Career advancement, 34–35, 52

Career associates, 40

Career break, 45, 262–265

Career changes, 30–31, 47

Career counseling, 46, 47

Carleton College, 171, 172*e*, 173*e*, 257, 260*e*

Carnegie Foundation for the Advancement of Teaching, 103, 294

Cedar Valley Community College, 160

Center for Academic Excellence, 293*e*

Centralized services, 181–184, 274

Child care: corporate responses to, 38–42; employer-sponsored, 267–269; and ideal worker norm, 25, 26, 36; link of stress to, 108; of nation's workforce, 28–29; personal leaves for, 245–254; and rationale for workplace flexibility, 241–242; and tenure-track demands, 72–75

Citigroup, 39

City University of New York, 221

Climate survey, 278

Clinical positions, 84, 85

Coffee shops, 315

Cohort-based learning communities, 316

Collaboration: professional development for, 21–22, 287–290, 299–301; as source of job satisfaction, 117

Collective bargaining, 159, 160, 168–169

College of the Canyons, 296–297

Collegiality: benefits of, 320; and campus activity inclusion, 310–314; challenges to achieving, 307–308; definition of, 142; faculty responsibility for, 309–310; overview of, 305–307; strategies that foster, 314–319. *See also* Community, sense of

Commitment, to work, 243

Committees: faculty's role on, 162, 163; for job-embedded professional development, 285–286; in tenure process, 201, 203

Common law, 226

Communication: of administrators, 175–176; of collected data, 184–188; for fixed-term employment equity, 221, 222*e*; and flexibility policy implementation, 275–276; and respect, 154, 155; in tenure process, 201

Community colleges, 93

Community, sense of: benefits of, 305–306; current state of, 19–20; of early tenure-track faculty, 78–82; importance of, 20; as reason for job satisfaction, 105–106, 115, 117; and respect, 154–156. *See also* Collegiality

Community-University Partnership Program, 292, 293*e*

Competition, 7–9, 113

Consumption, 37

Content theories, 118, 119, 121

Contingent contracts. *See* Contract-renewable appointments; Fixed-term appointments

Contract negotiations, 168–169

Contract-renewable appointments: attractive features of, 217–218; benefits of, 83; definition of, 67; employment equity in, 208–218; employment models of, 82–87; and faculty-institution relations, 130; overview of, 82–84; and policy statements regarding academic freedom, 236; recommendations for, 90–92; status differentials in, 88–90; versus tenure-track faculty, 91; types of

work in, 91. *See also* Full-time faculty

Control, of faculty, 16–17

Cornell University, 51, 268

Corporate management, 5, 34

Corporations, 38–44

Creativity, 12–13, 17

Credentials, 88, 95

Cultural taxation, 80

Culture: audit of, 147, 148–151; and corporate responses to workplace challenges, 43–44; cultivating respect in, 147–156; in diversified workplace, 27; enhancing, 325–327; and extension of tenure clock for personal leave, 253–254; and ideal worker norm, 26; importance of department chair to, 169; and part-time faculty's job satisfaction, 99–100; as reason for job satisfaction, 115, 123; shared responsibility for, 136–137; and use of data, 188; varieties of, 135; and work-life policy success, 277–278

Curriculum, control of, 16–17

Curry College, 216–217

D

Data collection, 184–188

Daughter track, 29

Deans: and faculty staffing plans, 178; monitoring of tenure process by, 205; role of, 174–175

Decentralization, 10

Decision making: about faculty staffing plans, 178–179; centralized services for, 181–184; data collection for, 184–188; faculty's role in, 161–164

Delayed-entry opportunities, 265–266

Department chairs: best use of time for, 182; centralized services for, 181–184; challenges of, 169–174, 180; and faculty staffing plans,

178; monitoring of tenure process by, 205; responsibilities of, 163–164, 169–170, 180–181; in tenure process, 70, 201

Department heads, 169

Devotion, to work, 33–34

Disability leave, 246, 247

Disciplines: and effects of Information Age, 12, 13; history of, 51; and institutional characteristics, 136

Discrepancy theories, 118–119, 121–122

Discrimination: and campus activity inclusion, 310–312; of women, 75–76, 79

Distance education, 93–94

Distinguished lecturers, 85

Diversity, of faculty. See Faculty diversity

Diversity, of students, 11–12, 20

Diversity, of workforce, 27–28

Doctoral degrees: earned by ethnic minorities, 62, 64; earned by women, 61; in history of tenure-track positions, 51; and increased competition for recruitment, 113; and rationale for part-time faculty appointments, 95; tenure-review changes for, 207; women's age of attainment of, 262

Downsizing, 30, 94

Dual-career couples, 33, 36, 77

Due process, 168

Duke University, 201, 203e

E

Early-career faculty. See Junior faculty

Eddie Bauer, 39

E-mail, 18, 32–33

Emory University, 318, 319e

Employability, 46–47, 282

Employment benefits: for fixed-term appointment equity, 219–220; flexibility as, 146; part-time faculty policies regarding, 97, 98;

part-time faculty's satisfaction with, 100; and work hours, 27. See also specific types

Employment equity, 117, 118; in contract-renewable appointments, 208–218; definition of, 140, 195–196; in fixed-term appointments, 218–224; in tenure process, 196–208

Enrollment: after GI Bill, 52; and increased demand for faculty, 110–111; overview of, 11; and part-time faculty job security, 98–99; response to, 11–12; students' purpose for, 11

Entitlements, 146–147

Entrepreneurialism, 8, 9, 21

Ernst and Young LLP, 39

Escrow accounts, 214

Essential elements, framework of. See Framework of essential elements

Ethics, 32, 164–165

European scholarship, 51

Evaluations: for contract-renewable appointment equity, 217; for fixed-term appointment equity, 219; in integrated model, 86; senior faculty's role in, 164; in tenure process, 70, 199–200; of work-life policies, 277–278

Evergreen State College, 317

Exempt employees, 26–27

Exit interviews, 187, 278

Experts, 94, 95

Exports, 232

F

Factory workers, 30

Faculty: assumptions about, 52–53; behavior of, 152, 164–168; changes affecting, 14–22; characteristics of, 133–135; effects of Information Age on, 13, 14; in governance hierarchy, 159–160; growth in, 57–59, 66; and higher education challenges, 4, 14–22; as ideal workers, 25–26; importance of, 4; increasing demand for, 110–114; institutions' reciprocal relationship with, 130–131, 136, 137*f;* needs of, 48; number of, 66; ranks of, 51; resignation of, 5; role of, 159, 160, 161–169; staffing plans, 178–179; traditional view of, 158. *See also specific types*

Faculty appointments: changes affecting, 15–16; diversification in, 50–57; innovative approaches to, 224–225; new terminology for, 67–68; overview of, 49–50; tripartite system of, 15; types of, 66. *See also specific types*

Faculty clubs, 314–315

Faculty control, 16–17

Faculty development centers, 283–284, 291, 296

Faculty development leave track, 215, 216*e*

Faculty diversity: by ethnicity, 62–65; by gender, 59–62; increase in, 58; and tenure process, 196–208

Faculty handbooks: administrators' responsibilities regarding, 176, 177; for fixed-term employment equity, 221, 222*e*; and orientations, 201

"Faculty Hiring in Recent Years," xi

Faculty recruitment. *See* Recruitment, faculty

Faculty retention, 112–113

Faculty senates, 275

Faculty support: conveying respect through, 155; for fixed-term appointment equity, 220, 223–224; importance of, 6; need for, 4–5; part-time faculty policies regarding, 97; as reason for job satisfaction, 116, 117; strategies for, 6

Faculty work: appeal of, xii, 323–324; challenges of, 127–128;

differentiation in, 16–17, 19; enhancing, 325–327; key questions about, xi–xii; rationale for rethinking, 321–325; traditional foundations of, 129–131

Fair Labor Standards Act (1938), 26–27

Fairness. *See* Employment equity

Family and Medical Leave Act (FMLA), 247

Family demands: corporate responses to, 38–41; and ideal worker norm, 25, 34–36; in nation's workforce, 28–29; of tenure-track faculty, 72–76

Family leave policies, 39, 247–252

FamilyCare, Inc., 269

Fannie Mae, 39

Federal funding, 8, 52, 71

Feedback, on performance: early-career faculty's concerns with, 70; as job satisfaction factor, 121; for junior faculty regarding tenure process, 301; from mentors, 290; and tenure criteria, 203

Fertility, 262, 263

Finance committees, 162–163

Financial aid, 52

Fine arts, 92, 95

First Amendment (U.S. Constitution), 226, 234

Fiscal constraints, 7–9, 16

Five College Consortium, 225

Fixed-term appointments: data collected about, 187; definition of, 67; employment equity in, 218–224; employment policies for, 95–99; and governing collegiality, 310; inclusion of, in campus activities, 312; increased use of, 93–94; job satisfaction of faculty in, 99–101; overview of, 92–93; and policy statements regarding academic freedom, 236; professional growth for faculty in, 294–297; rationale for,

94–95; work-related professional development for, 285–286. *See also* Part-time faculty

Flexibility: career breaks for, 262–265; changing workplace norms regarding, 243–245; definition of, 141, 240–241; as employee benefit, 146; employees' needs for, 45–46; and gender diversity, 62; importance of, 196; institutional and individual commitment for, 279; overview of, 239–240; policy implementations regarding, 272–278; rationale for, 241–243; resources for, 267–272; in tenure-track appointments, 197–199; through leaves, 245–254; in time bases of appointments, 254–262; in unit planning, 286–287

Flextime, 40, 44–46

Florida Gulf Coast University, 215

FMLA. *See* Family and Medical Leave Act (FMLA)

Framework of essential elements: illustration of, 134*f*; importance of respect in, 137–139; interaction of essential elements in, 139–140, 142; outcomes of, 134*f*, 142–143; overview of, 131–133; rationale for, 127–129, 144. *See also specific essential elements*

Freedom. *See* Academic freedom

Freelancers, 95

Fulbright Program, 302

Full professor ranking, 208

Full-time faculty: age of, 111; decrease in, 54–56; effects of increased enrollment on, 110–111; job satisfaction of, 105–106; number of, 66; transition of part-time faculty to, 113–114; work hours of, 76–78. *See also* Contract-renewable appointments; Tenure-track faculty

Fund for the Improvement of Postsecondary Education, 316

G

General Mills, 39

Geographical location, of job, 116

George Washington University, 268

Georgia Institute of Technology, 298

Georgia State University, 175

"Getting Back on Track" (Yager), xi

GI Bill (1944), 52

Global economy, 15

Goals, 244

Google, 271, 272*e*

Governing boards: and collegiality, 309–310; faculty's role in, 160; responsibilities of, 159

Graduate students, 20, 305

Grants, faculty: as response to fiscal constraints, 9; to support research mission, 292; and tenure process, 71

Grants, student, 8

Great Depression, 30, 37

Greene v. Howard University, 226

Greensboro College, 215–216, 217*e*

Grievance procedures, 176, 187; for academic freedom violations, 236–237; and challenges to collegiality, 307; and due process, 168; for fixed-term appointment equity, 220

Grinnell College, 250–251

H

Half-time tenure policies, 261–262

Harvard University, 208, 211, 213, 248, 250*e*

Health care, 31

Health sciences, 95

Heeding New Voices project, 71, 77, 78, 79

Henry Koerner Center for Emeritus Faculty, 312, 314*e*

HERI. *See* Higher Education Research Institute (HERI)

Hidden workload, 80
Hierarchical structure of governance, 159–160
Higher education changes: cost of, 328–330; effects of, 14–22; overview of, 6–7, 321–322; responsible parties of, 330–331; shared responsibility for, 136–137; timing of, 331–332; types of, 6–14
Higher education institution: challenges of, 3–4; characteristics of, 134*f*, 135–136; faculty's reciprocal relationship with, 130–131, 136, 137*f*; growth in, 57–59; history of, 50–51; role of, 3
Higher Education Research Institute (HERI), xvii, 5, 106, 109, 116
Hispanic Faculty and Staff Association, 312
Hispanics: in diversified workplace, 27; doctorates earned by, 62; in faculty positions, 62, 63*t*; inclusion in college activities, 312; job satisfaction of, 104*t*
Household responsibilities: and characteristics of today's workforce, 28–29; and corporate policies, 41–42; leaves for, 245–254; link between stress and, 108, 109; and rationale for workplace flexibility, 241–242
Human resources staff, 181–182
Humanities, 93, 95, 113
Hygienes, 120, 121

I

Ideal worker norm, 25–27, 34–36, 41
Individualized growth plans, 290–291
Industrial Revolution, 37
Information Age, 12–14
Information dissemination: and decision making, 184–188; at information fairs, 298–299; and policy implementation, 276–277;

for professional growth, 283–284, 298–299
Institutional assets, 4
Instructional platforms, 21
Integrated model, 86
Intellectual capital, 4, 5, 132
Interdisciplinary work, 21–22
Interest-based bargaining, 168
International students, 64
International Traffic in Arms Regulations, 232
Internet resources, 270, 284

J

Job market, 52
Job satisfaction, 47; current trends in, 103–104; definition of, 115; factors working against, 107–108; of full-time faculty, 105–106; of minority faculty, 107; of part-time faculty, 99–101, 103; personal needs related to, 119–120; reasons for, 105–106, 114–123; subpopulation differences in, 106–107; of tenure-track faculty, 69; of women, 104*t*, 106–107
Job security: and characteristics of today's workforce, 30–31; corporate policies regarding, 43; employees' needs regarding, 46–47; and ideal worker, 25; as incentive for contract-renewable appointments, 216–217; part-time faculty policies regarding, 98–99; as source of job satisfaction, 116, 117
Job sharing: corporate responses regarding, 39–40; and productivity, 256; and tenure time clock, 262, 263*e*
Job vacancies, 96
Job-characteristics model, 121
Job-embedded professional development, 285–286
Johns Hopkins University, 312, 313*e*
Joint leadership, 157–160

Journal reviews, 71
Junior faculty, 213; administrators' responsibilities regarding, 163–164; challenges of, 298; professional growth for, 297–301

K

Kent State University, 148
Knowledge pursuit, 105

L

Land-grant colleges, 51
Law faculty, 84
Layoffs, 30
Leadership development opportunities, 303
Learning: collegiality strategies related to, 316–319; effects of technology on, 13, 14
Leaves, 245–254, 266. *See also specific types*
Lecturers, 87, 213
Legal field, 32, 35, 40, 43
Lehigh University, 87
Leisure time: and access to workers, 32–33; decrease in, 33; employees' need for, 45, 47; link of stress to, 108; past view of, 37
Letter of appointment, 201
Lilly Conference, 316
Loans, 8
Loyalty, 31
Luce Seminars, 318, 319*e*
Luncheons, 299, 315–316

M

Managed health care, 31
Managers, corporate, 5, 34
Mandatory retirement, 83
Marginalized model, 87
Marriage, 35–36, 75
Massachusetts Institute of Technology, 268, 270, 271*e*
Maternity leave, 25, 39, 246–247
Medical field, 31
Medical insurance, 98

Medical schools, 84; contract-renewable appointments at, 209–211, 214; contract-renewable faculty in, 91–92
Meet Michigan Program, 295*e*
Meeting rooms, 315
Men, 61–62, 76–77
Mentoring, 288–290
MetLife Mature Market Institute, 242
Miami University of Ohio, 300, 316, 317*e*
Michigan State University, 201, 204*e*, 292, 294, 295*e*, 300
Middle class, 26
Minority faculty: benefits of, in workplace, 326; and challenges to collegiality, 307; in collegiate community, 79–82; and inclusion in campus activities, 310–314; increase in, 62–65; increased stress of, 108; job satisfaction of, 107; nonacademic career considerations of, 110; workload of, 80. *See also specific ethnic groups*
Minority students, 11
Mission, institutional, 291–294
Mom work, 79
Mommy track, 29, 34
Morrill Land Grant Act, 51
Mothers. *See* Women
Motivation, 118–121, 146
Mount Holyoke College, 225
Multiyear appointments, 215, 219
Musicians, 213

N

National Alliance for Caregiving, 242
National Association for College and University Attorneys, 237
National Association of Law Placement, 43
National Center for Education Statistics (NCES), xvii, 11, 64, 66, 75, 82, 92, 95, 97, 98, 100, 103, 106, 107, 116, 193, 241, 256

National Education Association, 160
National Opinion Research Center (NORC), xvii
National Science Foundation, 289
National Study of Postsecondary Faculty (NSOPF), xvii, 73, 91, 95, 98, 100, 103, 107, 112
National workplace: changing flexibility norms in, 243–245; characteristics of, 30–34; corporate responses to, 38–44; current challenges of, 34–38; employees' needs in, 44–47; ideal worker in, 25–27; responsibilities of workers in, 28–29; workers' characteristics in, 27–28
NCES. See National Center for Education Statistics (NCES)
NEA Higher Education Research Center, 87, 108, 112
Needs, personal, 119–120, 122
New workplace, 282
New York University, 164, 165e
Nondegree programs, 11
NORC. See National Opinion Research Center (NORC)
NSOPF. See National Study of Postsecondary Faculty (NSOPF)

O

Older students, 11
Ombudspersons, 178
Online teaching, 21
Organizational culture. See Culture
Organizational values, 151–153
Orientation programs: and faculty characteristics, 135; for fixed-term appointment equity, 220; for fixed-term faculty growth, 296; for junior-faculty professional growth, 298; for new tenure-track faculty, 200–201
Outreach mission, 292–294
Outsourcing, 94
Overseas assignments, 302–303
Overtime wages, 26–27

P

Pace, of work, 17–19
Parental leave, 247–252, 255e
Parents, care of: and characteristics of today's workforce, 28, 29; resources for, 269–270; as source of stress, 108
Parkinson's Law, 254, 256
Part-time faculty: data collected about, 187; employment policies for, 95–99; increase in, 53, 93–94; job satisfaction of, 99–101, 103, 104t; in marginalized model, 87; number of, 54–56, 66; overview of, 92–93; protection of academic freedom for, 234–237; rationale for using, 94–95; recruitment of, 96–97; titles of, 219; transition of, to full-time position, 113–114. See also Fixed-term appointments
Part-time hours, 39–40, 44, 45
Paternity leave, 25, 39
Peer review: employment equity in, 201–205; and protection of academic freedom, 234–235; senior faculty's role in, 164
Performance evaluations. See Evaluations
Perry v. Sindermann, 226
Personal discrimination, 79
Personal leaves, 246–254
Personal needs, 119–120, 122
Personal services, 270–271, 272e
Phased-retirement plans, 303–304
Physicians, 31
Policy statements: for flexibility, 272–278; inclusiveness in, for academic freedom, 228–229; for protection of academic freedom, 235–237
Political environment, 149–150
Portfolios, 213, 291
Portland State University, 292, 293e
Postdoctoral fellowships, 265
Power: distribution of, 149–150; need for, 120

Pregnancy: demands of, 72–73; and job sharing, 263; and maternity leave, 246–247

Pregnancy Discrimination Act, 246

President's Academic Leadership Institute, 171–172

Presidents, role of, 175–178

Prestige, 52, 61, 88–90

Pricewaterhouse Coopers LLP, 35, 40

Private colleges, 107–108

Pro rata positions, 256–257

Probationary periods: changing tenure-review system in, 207–208; flexibility in, 197–199; job satisfaction in, 106; monitoring tenure process during, 205–207; and organizational values, 152; tenure process during, 70–82; and tenure review, 203

Process theories, 118–119, 121–122

Productivity: of contract-renewable faculty, 91; current state of, 18; greater calls for, 37–38; past view of, 37; relationship of time to, 254, 256; and time-productivity relationship, 256

Professional and Organizational Development Network, 284

Professional growth: to address career-stage needs, 297–304; areas of, 20–22; benefits of, 280, 281–282; definition of, 141–142; for employability, 46–47; for fixed-term faculty, 294–297; importance of, 20; and institutional missions, 291–291; institutional differences in, 138; and job satisfaction, 117, 121; and organizational values, 152; overview of, 280–281; to prepare department chairs, 171–172; rationale for, 282–283; shortcomings of, 281; through collaboration, 287–290; through flexible unit planning, 286–287; through individualized growth plans, 290–291; through

information and resources, 283–284; through work-related assignments, 285–286

Professional schools: contract-renewable appointments at, 83–84, 209–213; fixed-term appointments at, 93

Professorial titles, 211, 213, 219

Professors of practice, 84, 85, 211, 213

Project on Faculty Appointments, 89, 185

Protean careers, 281–282

Provosts, 175–178, 184

Public accountability. See Accountability, calls for

Public institutions, 7–8, 108

Purdue University, 183–184, 310, 311e

R

Racial Battle Fatigue (RBF), 81

Racism, 80, 81

Radcliffe Public Policy Institute, 31

Ratcheting, 17, 19

Recognition, 115, 146, 220

Recruitment, faculty: centralized of services for, 181–182; and competition for faculty, 113–114; cost of, 329; and delayed-entry opportunities, 265–266; and fixed-term appointment equity, 220–221; importance of, 101; incentives for, 88; of international students, 64; of part-time faculty, 96–97; and rationale for professional growth, 282–283; reentry opportunities, 266

Reentry opportunities, 266

Relocation resources, 299

Reporting requirements, 18–19, 188

Research: and academic freedom rights and duties, 231; assumptions about, 53; collaboration in, 287–288; historical increase in, 52; meaning of autonomy regard-

ing, 227; mission of, 292; of tenure-track faculty with family demands, 73–74
Research universities, 108
Respect: and appeal of faculty work, 326–327; cultivating culture of, 147–156; definition of, 139; and employment equity, 195; for fixed-term appointment equity, 219, 220; importance of, 137–139, 145–147; overview of, 145
Responsibility-centered budgeting, 10
Retention, 112–113
Rethinking, 190
Retired faculty, 312
Retirement plans, 46; part-time faculty policies regarding, 95, 98; senior faculty professional growth regarding, 303–304
Retiring faculty, 111, 135
Reward systems, 162, 213–215
Richland College, 151–152, 153e
Rightsizing, 30

S

Sabbatical leaves, 86, 97, 302
Saint Louis University, 83–84
Salary: in alternative-career model, 86; for contract-renewable appointment equity, 213–214, 217e; for fixed-term appointment equity, 219–220, 223; historical trends in, 53; in integrated model, 86; of medical school faculty, 84; of men versus women, 61; parental and family leaves, 251–252, 255e; part-time faculty policies regarding, 97–98; part-time faculty's satisfaction with, 100; at public versus private institutions, 107–108; as source of job dissatisfaction, 107–108, 115, 118
San Francisco State University, 201, 202e
Satisfaction, job. See Job satisfaction

Sciences, 93
Seed grant money, 292
Self-reflection, 291
Senior faculty: and academic freedom abuses, 233–234; in collegiate community, 78–79; as mentors, 288–290; professional growth support for, 301–304; professorial titles for, 213; responsibilities of, 163–166; status of, 88, 89; and women's job satisfaction, 107
Severance pay, 216
Sexual harassment, 79
Shared governance, 136–137; benefits of, 190; and collegiality, 309–310; data collection and *dissemination* for, 184–188; for faculty staffing plans, 178–179; faculty's role in, 161–169; for flexibility policy implementation, 274–276; overview of, 157–158; traditions of, 158–160
Sick leave, 246, 247
Skill variety, 121
Smile work, 79
Smith College, 223, 225
Social events, 319
Social sciences, 113
Society for Human Resource Management, 38, 44
Split appointments, 80
Spousal employment, 28
Standardized reporting, 188
Stanford University, 177, 211, 269
"Statement on Government of Colleges and Universities" (AAUP), 159
Statement on Professional Ethics (AAUP), 164–165
Stereotyping, 79
Stetson University, 237
Stress: and current state of workload, 18; and rationale for workplace flexibility, 242–243; and senior faculty professional growth

support, 302; as source of job dis-
satisfaction, 108–109; of women
as ideal workers, 36
Structural discrimination, 79
Student diversity. *See* Diversity, of
students
Students, understanding of, 20
Subcontracting, 94
Support services. *See* Faculty support
Survey of Earned Doctorates, xvii

T

Take-out dinners, 271, 272*e*
Task identity, 121
Task significance, 121
Teacher certification, 84
Teaching: and academic freedom
rights and duties, 231; assumptions about, 53; collaboration in,
287–288; collegiality strategies
related to, 316; effects of technology on, 13; mission of, 294
Teaching centers, 283–284
Teaching Fellows programs, 300–301
Technological advances: and academic freedom, 232; and access
to workers, 32–33; centralized
services for, 183; and declining
autonomy, 16–17; effects of, 13,
18; to manage personal responsibilities, 269–270; overview of, 13;
professional development for, 21;
response to, 14
Telecommuting, 39
Tenure: and challenges to collegiality, 307–308; definition of, 129;
denial of, 205; and employment
equity, 196–208; flexibility in time
clock for, 254–262; importance of
data to, 184–185; junior faculty
professional growth for, 301;
monitoring process of, 205–207;
and personal leave, 252–254; purpose of, 226; senior faculty's role
in, 164, 165*e*; status of, 193; traditional system of, 193–194

Tenure-track faculty: challenges
for female, 36; changes affecting,
15–16; collegiate community of,
78–82; versus contract-renewable
faculty, 91; decrease in, 54; early
expectations of, 69; family demands of, 72–76; and governing
collegiality, 310; growth in, 58,
59; history of, 50–54; job satisfaction of, 69, 103, 104*t*; number of
appointments to, 49, 66, 193;
overview of, 68–69; part-timers'
aspirations to, 95; priorities of,
69; redefinition of, 193–194; time
constraints of, 76–78; traditional
foundation of, 129–131. *See also*
Full-time faculty
Tenure-track process, 68–72
Terminology, 188
TIAA-CREF Hesburgh Awards, 283
Tiered partnership, 40
Tokenism, 79
Topic-based learning communities,
316
Towers Perrin, 37, 44–45
Trend data, 186–187
Trust, of public, 9–10
Tuition grants, 98
Turnover, faculty, 112, 329

U

Unionism, 53–54, 160, 248
University of California, 267–268,
269, 270
University of Georgia, 300
University of Massachusetts, 225,
300, 303
University of Mississippi, 228–229
University of Missouri system,
171–172
University of New Mexico, 229, 230*e*
University of North Carolina,
112–113, 220
University of Oklahoma, 299, 300*e*
University of Phoenix, 94
University of Rhode Island, 248, 249*e*

University of Rochester, 166
University of Texas at Austin, 312
University of Texas Health Sciences
    Center, 270
University of Virginia, 205, 209,
    210*f*, 212*e*
University of Wisconsin, 51, 318
U.S. Bureau of Labor Statistics, 27,
    110, 112, 113
U.S. Census Bureau, 28
U.S. Department of Commerce, 232
U.S. Department of Education, 49,
    61, 62, 64, 75, 77, 82, 92, 93, 95,
    97, 98, 100, 103, 106, 107, 116,
    193, 241, 256
U.S. Department of Health and
    Human Services, 27, 28
Utah State University, 166–168

V

Vacation leave, 246
Vacation time, 33, 39
Values, organizational, 151–153
Vancouver Community College, 223
Vanderbilt University, 254, 255*e*
Virginia, 10
Voting rights, 89

W

Washington Center for Improving
    the Quality of Undergraduate
    Education, 317
Webster University, 215, 216*e*
Wellesley College, 268–269
Western Michigan University, 292
Women: age of doctoral degree
    attainment by, 262; benefits of,
    in workplace, 326; and collegiate
    community, 79; discrimination
    against, 75–76, 79; in diversified
    workplace, 27–28; doctoral
    degrees earned by, 61; in faculty
    positions, 59–62; household
    responsibilities of, 29; and ideal
    worker norm, 34–36; inclusion

of, in campus activities, 312;
    increased stress of, 108, 109; job
    satisfaction of, 104*t*, 106–107;
    in legal field, 35; mentoring for,
    289–290; nonacademic career
    considerations of, 110; and ratio-
    nale for workplace flexibility,
    241–242; status of, 89; and
    tenure-track demands, 72–76,
    81–82
Women in Science & Engineering
    Leadership Institute, 289–290
Work ethic, 38
Work hours: average number of,
    33; of contract-renewable and
    fixed-term appointments, 67;
    corporate response to, 39,
    41–42; and flexibility in tenure
    process, 254–262; of full-time
    faculty, 76–78; of ideal worker,
    26–27; increase in, 77; past
    view of, 37; as reflection of
    commitment to work, 243–244;
    as source of job dissatisfaction,
    108; of tenure-track faculty
    with family demands, 73–74;
    of women, 28
Work-life policies, 272–278
Workload: in alternative-career
    model, 85; current state of, 17–
    19; employees' needs regarding,
    44–45; and ideal worker norm,
    25–26; in integrated model, 86;
    in marginalized model, 87; of
    minority faculty, 80; of part-time
    faculty, 96; as reflection of com-
    mitment to work, 243–244; short-
    comings of corporate response
    to, 42–43; as source of job dissat-
    isfaction, 107–108; workers' feel-
    ings about, 37
Workplace, national. *See* National
    workplace

Y

Yale University, 312, 314*e*